NCERT MCQs

Indian Polity and Governance

Class 6-12 (Old+New)

NCERT MCQs

Indian Polity and Governance

Class 6-12 (Old+New)

Authors
Sundram Thakur
Shoaib Khan

Series Editor
Surya Singh

arihant
SUCCESS AND NOTHING LESS

arihant
SUCCESS AND NOTHING LESS

ARIHANT PUBLICATIONS (INDIA) LIMITED

卐 **Administrative & Production Offices**

Regd. Office
'Ramchhaya' 4577/15, Agarwal Road, Darya Ganj, New Delhi -110002
Tele: 011- 47630600, 43518550

Head Office
Kalindi, TP Nagar, Meerut (UP) - 250002
Tel: 0121-7156203, 7156204

卐 **Sales & Support Offices**
Agra, Ahmedabad, Bengaluru, Bareilly, Chennai, Delhi, Guwahati, Hyderabad, Jaipur, Jhansi, Kolkata, Lucknow, Nagpur & Pune.

卐 **PRICE** ₹165.00

卐 **PO No :** TXT-59-T065965-07-25

Published by Arihant Publications (India) Ltd.

For further information about the books published by Arihant, log on to www.arihantbooks.com or e-mail at info@arihantbooks.com

Follow us on

Few Words

NCERTs are the Foundation in the Journey of IAS...

Civil Service Examinations are the most prestigious, tough and challenging examinations in India.

Being the toughest exam, it automatically consists of a vast and a detailed syllabus. Aspirants often find it difficult to cover the entire syllabus and lack a right direction for a proper and a systematic study for the exam.

The most important aspect of this preparation journey are the NCERT books. Every year approximately **35-40 questions** directly or indirectly asked from NCERT books.

NCERT books also play a key role in understanding the Basic Concepts; so that aspirants can easily form the basic foundation of the entire syllabus. But due to the demand for many NCERT books which are required for study, it becomes exhausting to cover each and every NCERT book.

NCERT MCQs series presented by Arihant Publications covers MCQs from Class 6th to 12th NCERT books (both Old & New) in a comprehensive manner.

Features of Revised Edition

- Each and Every Question is designed as per Latest Pattern of UPSC and State PCS.
- The chapter-wise questions given in the sequential form in the series along with the source of the questions.
- 100% Error free and detailed explanations will make the preparation easy and convenient.
- Additional coverage of Tamil Nadu Board and NIOS Books.
- 3 Practice Sets also provided for overall practice related to subject.

The book is adorned with questions prepared by a team of experts along with a vital role played by the Project Management team with members: Mona Yadav (Project Manager), Manshi Gupta (Project Coordinator), Seema Saini (Proof Reading TL), Pradeep Chaudhary (DTP TL), Bilal and Ankit Tyagi (Cover and Inner designer).

We hope this book will help the aspirants to achieve their goals of clearing UPSC as well as State PCS exams. Your valuable suggestions have always inspired us to strive for useful, authentic and more trustworthy publications.
Your inputs and suggestions are welcomed for subsequent editions.

We wish you all the very best for your preparation and journey!!

Authors

CONTENTS

NCERT MCQS

Chapter 01

Constitutional Development

Constitutional Development

Constitutional Development Under East India Company

Regulating Act, 1773
- Passed by the British Parliament to control the affairs of East-India Company
- Governor of Bengal Warren Hastings was nominated as Governor; General for all three presidencies of Bengal, Madras and Bombay under Bengal control

Act of Settlement, 1781
- Removed the shortcomings of Regulating Act, 1773
- Also known as Declaratory Act, 1781

Pitts India Act of, 1784
- Established the Board of Control over the Court of Directors to guide and supervise the affairs of Company

Amending Act of 1786
- Provided the power of both Governor-General and Commander in Chief to Lord Cornwallis become the first effective ruler of British India

Charter Act, 1793
- Trade monopoly of company extended for another 20 years
- Board of control and their staff paid out of Indian revenue

Charter Act, 1813
- Abolished trade monopoly of East India Company with China for 20 years

Charter Act, 1833
- Final steps towards centralisation in British India
- Made Governor-General of Bengal as Governor-General of India with all civil and military powers
- Lord William Bentinck was the first Governor-General of India

Charter Act, 1853
- Established Indian Central Legislative Council; Introduced local representation in the Central Legislative Council

Constitutional Development Under Crown Rule

Government of India Act, 1858
- Transferred the Government, territories and revenues on India from Company to British Crown

Indian Council Act, 1861
- Enlarged Imperial Legislative Council
- Initiated the process of decentralisation by restoring the legislative powers to Bombay and Madras presidencies

Indian Council Act, 1892
- Function of Legislative Council was increased and was conferred power to discuss budget and to ask question
- Non-official member of the Imperial Legislative Council to be nominated by Bengal Chamber of Commerce and Provincial Legislative Council

Indian Councils Act,1909
- Also known as Morley-Minto Reforms
- Satyendra Prasad Sinha became in 1919 the first Indian to join the **Viceroy's Executive Council**
- This act system of communal representation for Muslim, separate electorate

August Declaration, 1917
- Proposed increased participation of Indians in administration and development of self-governing institutions in India

Government of India Act, 1919
- Also known as Montague-Chelmsford Reform
- Dyarchy system introduced in province in which subjects were divided into 2 parts-transferred and reserved

Government of India Act, 1935
- Established All India Federation consisting of provinces and Princely States
- Divided the power between Center and States into-federal, provincial concurrent list

Cripps Mission, 1942
- Proposed dominion status after World War
- Cripps Mission Rejected by All Indian Parties and Section in India (Indian National Congress)

Cabinet Mission, 1946
- Constitutional Assembly consisting of 389 members to be established
- Union of India to be consisted of Indian states and British provinces

India Independence Act, 1947
- British rule in India came to an end and India was partitioned
- Provided for boundary commission to demarcate the boundaries between India and Pakistan
- It was based on the famous Mountbatten plan

SOURCE *Old NCERT Class XI* (Important Turning Points of Constitutional Development)

1 With reference to Regulating Act of 1773, consider the following statements. *(Chap 1, Class-XI, Old NCERT)*

1. This was the first Act by British Government to regulate the affairs of East India Company.
2. The government of the presidencies of Calcutta and Madras were subordinated to the government in Bombay.
3. This Act provides for a Governor-General and a council of four members who exercised their authority jointly.

Which of the statements given above is/are incorrect?

(a) 1 and 2 (b) 2 and 3 (c) Only 2 (d) 1, 2 and 3

Ans. *(c)*

Exp. Only statement (2) is incorrect with reference to Regulating Act of 1773 because this Act subordinated the Governor of Bombay and Madras to the Governor of Calcutta (Bengal).

The Regulating Act of 1773 was laid to control and regulate the affairs of East India Company because the political power of the company was expanding.

2 Assertion (A) The Regulating Act of 1773 played a pivotal role in reshaping the governance structure of British India. *(Chap 1, Class-XI, Old NCERT)*

Reason (R) Through the elevation of Warren Hastings to Governor-General, consolidation of presidencies and the establishment of the Supreme Court in Calcutta, the Act laid the foundation for a centralised administration and functions within the East India Company.

Codes

(a) Both A and R are true and R is the correct explanation of A.
(b) Both A and R are true, but R is not the correct explanation of A.
(c) A is true, but R is false.
(d) Both A and R are false.

Ans. *(a)*

Exp. Both Assertion (A) and Reason (R) are true and Reason (R) is the correct explanation of Assertion (A).

The Regulating Act of 1773 indeed played a pivotal role in reshaping the structure of British India's governance. The elevation of Warren Hastings, consolidation of presidencies and the establishment of the Supreme Court in Calcutta collectively laid the foundation for centralised administration.

3 Assertion (A) Lord Cornwallis, through the Amending Act of 1786, sought to expand the powers of the Governor-General, enabling him to act independently of the majority council decisions.

Reason (R) The Act aimed to establish Cornwallis as the first effective ruler of British India, operating under the authority of the Board of Control and the Court of Directors. *(Chap 1, Class-XI, Old NCERT)*

Codes

(a) Both A and R are true and R is the correct explanation of A.
(b) Both A and R are true, but R is not the correct explanation of A.
(c) A is true, but R is false.
(d) Both A and R are false.

Ans. *(a)*

Exp. Both Assertion (A) and Reason (R) are true and Reason (R) is the correct explanation of Assertion (A).

Lord Cornwallis, under the Act of 1786, indeed sought enhanced powers for the Governor-General, allowing independent action. This move aimed to establish Cornwallis as the first effective ruler of British India, functioning under the authority of the Board of Control and the Court of Directors. This Act reflected a deliberate effort to streamline decision-making and empower the Governor-General, marking a significant shift in the governance dynamics during that period.

4 Consider the following statements about the Governor-General in Council with respect to the Charter Act of 1833. *(Chap 1, Class-XI, Old NCERT)*

1. The Council's functions were divided into three categories.
2. A law member was added to the Council.

Which of the statements given above is/are correct?

(a) Only 1 (b) Only 2 (c) Both 1 and 2 (d) Neither 1 nor 2

Ans. *(b)*

Exp. Only statement (2) is correct about the Governor-General in Council with respect to the Charter Act of 1833.

The Council consists of four members, of whom one was to be a law member who could attend the council meetings when it was to perform legislative functions.

Statement (1) is incorrect because the Council's functions were divided into two categories which are as follows :

(i) When it performed executive functions, it consisted of the Governor-General and three members only.
(ii) When it performed legislative functions, it consisted of Governor-General and four members.

5 By which one of the following Acts was the Governor-General of Bengal designated as the Governor-General of India? *(Chap 1, Class-XI, Old NCERT) (IAS Pre 2023)*

(a) The Regulating Act (b) The Pitt's India Act
(c) The Charter Act of 1793 (d) The Charter Act of 1833

Ans. *(d)*

Exp. The Charter Act of 1833 made the Governor- General of Bengal designated as the Governor-General of India. William Bentinck was the first Governor-General of India.

The Charter Act of 1833 was a significant constitutional instrument defining the scope and authority of the East India Company. The liberal and utilitarian philosophy of Bentham was made popular by the provisions of this Act. The Governor-General of Fort William was hereafter called 'the Governor-General of India'.

6 **Consider the following Assertion (A) and Reason (R) and choose the correct code.**

(Chap 1, Class-XI, Old NCERT)

Assertion (A) The Charter Act of 1853 further extended the machinery of legislation.

Reason (R) The strength of the Legislative Council became nine under this Act.

Codes

(a) Both A and R are true and R is the correct explanation of A.
(b) Both A and R are true, but R is not the correct explanation of A.
(c) A is true, but R is false.
(d) A is false, but R is true.

Ans. *(c)*

Exp. Assertion (A) is true, but Reason (R) is false.

In order to strengthen the legislative machinery, the Charter Act of 1853 was enacted. Under the new Act, the Governor-General's Council, when acting in its legislative power, was enlarged by the addition of six new members. Out of these six members, one was to be an official representative from each of the four provinces (viz, Madras, Bombay, Bengal and North-West Provinces), the Chief Justice and puisne judge of Supreme Court and a Commander-in-Chief. Thus, the strength of Legislative Council became twelve.

7 **Consider the following statements with respect to the Charter Act of 1858.** *(Chap 1, Class-XI, Old NCERT)*

1. It abolished the Board of Directors and the Board of Control and vested their powers in one of his/her Majesty's Secretary.
2. The Governor-General and Governors of the Presidencies were to be appointed by the Secretary of state.
3. Appointments to the Covenanted Civil Services were not to be made through open competition.

Which of the statements given above is/are incorrect?

(a) 2 and 3
(b) Only 1
(c) 1 and 2
(d) 1, 2 and 3

Ans. *(a)*

Exp. Statements (2) and (3) are incorrect with respect to the Charter Act of 1858.

In 1858, the British Crown took over the rights of the Company's government in India to its own hands. Therefore, this Act brought substantial changes in the Constitutional set-up.

Under this Act, the Governor-General and Governors of the Presidencies were to be appointed by the Crown. However, the members of the Governor-General's Councils were to be appointed by Secretary-in-State.

Under this Act, the Covenanted Civil Services were to be made through open competitive examinations with the assistance of Civil Service Commission.

8 **Which of the following statements is correct regarding Indian Councils Act of 1861?** *(Chap 1, Class-XI, Old NCERT)*

(a) The term of the members of Governor- General's Council nominated, were for three years.
(b) Every Act passed by the legislature in India was subject to approval of her Majesty acting through Secretary of State-in-Council.
(c) The Governor-General was not authorised to issue ordinance and exercise veto even in an emergency.
(d) The strength of the Governor-General's Council was raised to six by addition of two more members for executive purposes.

Ans. *(b)*

Exp. Statement (b) is correct regarding Indian Councils Act of 1861 as every Act passed by the legislature in India was subject to approval of her Majesty acting through Secretary of State-in-Council.

Statements (a), (c) and (d) are incorrect because under the Indian Councils Act of 1861, the term of nominated members of Governor- General's Council (by adding 6-12 new members) was for two years.

Under this Act, Governor-General was authorised to exercise a veto and issue ordinances in an emergency.

The strength of the Governor-General's Council for executive purposes was raised to five by addition of one more member.

9 **Match the following lists correctly and choose the correct code.** *(Chap 1, Class-XI, Old NCERT)*

List I (Acts)	List II (Provisions)
A. The Charter Act of 1853	1. Office of the Secretary of State
B. The Act of 1858	2. Membership to Puisne Judge of Supreme Court
C. The Indian Councils Act of 1861	3. Addition of Law Member
D. The Charter Act of 1833	4. Ordinance Power

Codes

	A	B	C	D		A	B	C	D
(a)	2	3	1	4	(b)	2	1	4	3
(c)	3	1	4	2	(d)	1	3	4	2

Ans. *(b)*

Exp. The correct matching is A-2, B-1, C-4, D-3.

The Charter Act of 1853 It talked about Chief Justice and a Puisne Judge of Supreme Court, among the six members, added in Governor-General's Council.

The Act of 1858 It created the office of Secretary of State who was to be assisted by a Council of India.

The Indian Councils Act of 1861 It authorised Governor-General to exercise a veto and issue ordinances in case of an emergency.

The Charter Act of 1833 It made the Council which consist of four members, of whom one was to be a law member.

10 **Which of the following statements regarding the Indian Councils Act of 1892 is not correct?**
(Chap 1, Class-XI, Old NCERT)

(a) The Act increased the number of additional members in the Central Council.
(b) Non-official members of the Imperial Legislative Council were nominated by British authorities.
(c) The Act empowered Provincial Legislative Councils to nominate non-official members through local bodies.
(d) Legislative Councils gained the authority to discuss the budget and address questions to the executive under the Act.

Ans. (*b*)

Exp. Statement (b) is not correct regarding Council Act of 1892.

The Indian Councils Act of 1892 shifted the nomination of non-official members in the Imperial Legislative Council from British authorities to entities like the Bengal Chamber of Commerce and Provincial Legislative Councils. This move aimed to involve local bodies, such as universities, district boards and Municipalities, in the nomination process. The Act aimed to decentralise authority and enhance the representation of non-official members in Legislative Councils, contributing to a more diversified and inclusive decision-making process.

11 **Consider the following statements regarding the Indian Councils Act of 1892.** ***(Chap 1, Class-XI, Old NCERT)***

1. The strength of the Central and Provincial Legislative Councils was expanded by adding 8-20 new members.
2. Three-fifth of additional members in these councils were to be non-officials.

Which of the statements given above is/are correct?

(a) Only 1 (b) Only 2
(c) Both 1 and 2 (d) Neither 1 nor 2

Ans. (*a*)

Exp. Only statement (1) is correct regarding the Indian Councils Act of 1892.

Indian Councils Act of 1892 was passed to further expand and strengthen the Legislative Councils. Under this Act, the strength of Central and Provincial Legislative Councils was expanded by adding 8-20 new members.

Statement (2) is incorrect because two-fifth of these new additional members were to be non-officials.

12 **Consider the following statements regarding Indian Councils Act of 1909.** ***(Chap 1, Class-XI, Old NCERT)***

1. There were ex-officio members, nominated officials, nominated non- officials and elected members in Central Legislative Council.
2. This Act empowered the members of Legislative Councils to discuss the budget and move resolutions.
3. The resolutions moved by the members of Legislative Councils were binding on the government.

Which of the statements given above are correct?

(a) 1 and 2 (b) 2 and 3 (c) 1 and 3 (d) 1, 2 and 3

Ans. (*a*)

Exp. Statements (1) and (2) are correct regarding the Indian Councils Act of 1909.

There were ex-offico members, nominated officials, nominated non-officials and elected members in Central Legislative Council. Act empowered the members of the Legislative Council to discuss the budget and move resolution before it was finally approved.

Statement (3) is incorrect because the resolutions adopted by the house were not binding on the government.

13 **Which of the following statements is incorrect with respect to Government of India Act, 1919?**
(Chap 1, Class-XI, Old NCERT)

(a) The Governor-General had the last word on any bill passed by the Central Legislature.
(b) The budget was divided into two categories, i.e., votable and non-votable, in Central Legislature.
(c) The Executive Council of Governor-General was responsible to the Central Legislature.
(d) The control of the Secretary of State for India over the Central and Provincial administration was reduced through this Act.

Ans. (*c*)

Exp. Statement (c) is incorrect with respect to the Government of India Act, 1919. Under the Government of India Act, 1919, the Governor-General's Executive Council was not responsible to the Central Legislature but to the Secretary of State. Under this Act, the maximum limit imposed on the membership of the Governor-General's Executive Council was also removed.

14 **In the Government of India Act 1919, the functions of Provincial Government were divided into 'Reserved' and 'Transferred' subjects. Which of the following were treated as 'Reserved' subjects?**
(Chap 1, Class-XI, Old NCERT) (IAS Pre 2022)

1. Administration of justice
2. Local self-government
3. Land revenue
4. Police

Select the correct answer using the codes given below.

(a) 1, 2 and 3 (b) 2, 3 and 4 (c) 1, 3 and 4 (d) 1, 2 and 4

Ans. (*c*)

Exp. The correct codes are (1), (3) and (4).

Reserved subjects were administration of justice, the police, land revenue, irrigation, law and order. Transferred subjects under the control of Indian ministers are Local self-government, education, public health, public works, agriculture, forests and fisheries.

However, local self-government was transferred to the state or provinces.

15 Which of the following is/are the principal feature(s) of the Government of India Act, 1919?

(Chap 1, Class-XI, Old NCERT) (IAS Pre 2012)

1. The introduction of dyarchy in the executive Government of the provinces.
2. The introduction of separate communal electorates for muslims.
3. Devolution of legislative authority by the centre to provinces.

Select the correct answer using the codes given below.

(a) Only 1
(b) 2 and 3
(c) 1 and 3
(d) 1, 2 and 3

Ans. (c)

Exp. Statements (1) and (3) are the principal features of the Government of India Act, 1919. The Act introduced dyarchy in the provinces. Under this, provincial subjects were divided into transferred and reserved.

It provided for devolution of legislative authority by the centre to the provinces. Under this act, there was provision for central as well as provincial subjects. Provincial legislature were empowered to legislate on provincial subjects.

Statement (2) is not the principal feature of the Act because the introduction of separate Muslims electorate was done by Government of India Act, 1909 and not by Government of India Act, 1919. However, it was continued under this Act.

16 Consider the following statements regarding the Government of India Act, 1935.

(Chap 1, Class-XI, Old NCERT)
(Unit-1, Class-XI, Tamil Nadu Board)

1. The Act provided for the establishment of the Federal Court of India.
2. Provincial autonomy was introduced, discontinuing dyarchy in 1937.
3. Communal representation exclusively extended to privileged classes.

Which of the statements given above is/are correct?

(a) Only 1 (b) 2 and 3
(c) 1 and 2 (d) Only 3

Ans. (c)

Exp. Statements (1) and (2) are correct regarding the Government of India Act, 1935. This Act led to the establishment of a Federal Court in India in 1937. The Act introduced provincial autonomy, putting an end to the dyarchy system in 1937 and it marked as a significant change in governance at the provincial level.

Statement (3) is not correct because communal representation under the Government of India Act, 1935 was not exclusively extended to privileged classes. It included representation for marginalised groups such as depressed classes, women and labour.

17 Consider the following statements about the Council of States with respect to the Government of India Act, 1935. *(Chap 1, Class-XI, Old NCERT)*

1. The Council must consist of 260 members, of whom 156 were to represent the provinces and 104 were to represent the native states.
2. The seats fixed for Hindus, Muslims and Sikhs were to be filled by indirect elections and the seats reserved for Europeans, Anglo-Indian Community and Indian Christians were to be filled by a direct method.
3. One-third of its members were to retire every third year.

Which of the statements given above is/are correct?

(a) Only 1 (b) 1 and 2 (c) 1 and 3 (d) Only 3

Ans. (c)

Exp. Statements (1) and (3) are correct about the Council of States with respect to the Government of India Act, 1935. The Upper House consists of 260 members of whom 156 were to be represent the provinces and 104 to represent the native states.

As per the act, the proposed federal polity of India was to have a bicameral legislature at the centre. The Council of States was to be a permanent house and one-third of its members were to retire every third year.

Statement (2) is incorrect because the seats fixed for Hindus, Muslims and Sikhs were to be filled by direct elections and the seats reserved for Europeans, Anglo-Indian Community and Indian Christians were to be filled by indirect method.

18 Consider the following statements with reference to Government of India Act, 1935.

(Chap 1, Class-XI, Old NCERT)
(Unit-1, Class-XI, Tamil Nadu Board)

1. This Act introduced dyarchy at the provincial level.
2. Ecclesiastical affairs, defence, external affairs and tribal areas were under transferred subjects.

Which of the statements given above is/are correct?

(a) Only 1 (b) Only 2
(c) Both 1 and 2 (d) Neither 1 nor 2

Ans. (d)

Exp. Neither statement (1) nor (2) is correct with reference to Government of India Act, 1935.

Government of India Act, 1935 introduced dyarchy at the federal level and not at provincial level.

The federal subjects were divided into two categories – the reserved and transferred. Ecclesiastical affairs, (external affairs of other monasteries, mandir and religious institutions) defence, external affairs and Tribal areas were under reserved subjects and not in transferred subjects. In the matters of reserved subjects, the Governor-General possessed the discretionary power and was not even required to consult with the Council of Ministers (COM).

19 Consider the following statements with respect to Government of India Act, 1935.

(Chap 1, Class-XI, Old NCERT)

1. This Act enumerated the discretionary power of the Governor.
2. This Act provided for unicameral legislatures in six provinces and bicameral in five provinces.

Which of the statements given above is/are correct?

(a) Only 1
(b) Only 2
(c) Both 1 and 2
(d) Neither 1 nor 2

Ans. *(d)*

Exp. Neither statement (1) nor (2) is correct with respect to Government of India Act, 1935.

The Government of India Act, 1935 introduced the dyarchy by the Government of India Act, 1919 and Governor-General were required to act accordingly on the advice of Council of Ministers. However, in exceptional cases, Governor-General were given some discretionary powers or powers of individual judgement but this Act did not enumerate discretionary powers of the Governor.

This Act provided for bicameral legislatures in six provinces and unicameral in five provinces. The Upper House was to be called as Legislative Council and Lower House was to be called as Legislative Assembly.

20 Consider the following statements regarding the Cripps Mission, 1942. *(Chap 1, Class-XI, Old NCERT)*

1. Dominion status was promised to India after the conclusion of the Second World War.
2. The Cripps Mission proposed the immediate establishment of an elected body in India to frame its Constitution.
3. Indian states were excluded from participating in the Constitution making process as per the Cripps Mission's recommendations.
4. The proposals presented by the Cripps Mission were widely accepted and embraced by various political parties and sections in India.

Which of the statements given above are correct?

(a) 1 and 2 (b) 2 and 3
(c) 1, 2 and 4 (d) 3 and 4

Ans. *(a)*

Exp. Statements (1) and (2) are correct regarding Cripps Mission, 1942. The Cripps Mission proposed the promise of dominion status for India after the Second World War and it also propose the establishment of an elected body in India for framing its Constitution after the war.

Statements (3) and (4) are not correct because the Cripps Mission included the participation of Indian states in Constitution making process and the proposals were widely rejected by almost all parties and sections in India.

21 With reference to the proposals of Cripps Mission, consider the following statements.

(Chap 1, Class-XI, Old NCERT) (IAS Pre 2022)

1. The Constituent Assembly would have members nominated by the Provincial Assemblies as well as the princely states.
2. Any Province, which is not prepared to accept the new Constitution would have the right to sign a separate agreement with Britain regarding its future status.

Which of the statements given above is/are correct?

(a) Only 1 (b) Only 2 (c) Both 1 and 2 (d) Neither 1 nor 2

Ans. *(b)*

Exp. Statement (2) is correct about the proposals of Cripps Mission. Any province not willing to join the union would be eligible to sign an agreement with British regarding its future status.

Statement (1) is not correct because a Constituent Assembly members were to be partly elected by the Provincial Assemblies and partly nominated by the princely states.

22 Consider the following Assertion (A) and Reason (R) and choose the correct code. *(Chap 1, Class-XI, Old NCERT)*

Assertion (A) The Cabinet Mission Plan envisaged the setting up an Interim Government.

Reason (R) In the Interim Government, all the portfolios were to be held by Indians.

Codes

(a) Both A and R are true and R is the correct explanation of A.
(b) Both A and R are true, but R is not the correct explanation of A.
(c) A is true, but R is false.
(d) A is false, but R is true.

Ans. *(b)*

Exp. Both Assertion (A) and Reason (R) are true, but Reason (R) is not the correct explanation of Assertion (A). The Cabinet Mission envisaged the immediate setting up of an Interim Government in order to carry on the administration while Constitution making was in progress. In the Interim Government, all the portfolios were to be held by Indians and the British Government was to give full co-operation in the accomplishment of the tasks that confronted the Interim government.

23 Consider the following statements.

(Chap 1, Class-XI, Old NCERT)

1. On 14th August, 1946, an Interim Government was formed under the leadership of Jawaharlal Nehru.
2. This Interim Government remained in office till 28th October, 1946.

Which of the statements given above is/are incorrect?

(a) Only 1 (b) Only 2
(c) Both 1 and 2 (d) Neither 1 nor 2

Ans. (b)

Exp. Only statement (2) is incorrect as the Interim Government remained in office till the partition of India in August, 1947.

The Interim Government of India, also known as the Provisional Government of India had the task of assisting the transition of British India to Independence.

24 **Consider the following statements in respect of the Constitution Day.** *(Chap 3, Class-IX, New NCERT)* *(IAS Pre 2023)*

Statement-I The Constitution Day is celebrated on 26th November every year to promote constitutional values among citizens.

Statement-II On 26th November, 1949, the Constituent Assembly of India set up a Drafting Committee under the Chairmanship of Dr. BR Ambedkar to prepare a Draft Constitution of India.

Which one of the following is correct in respect of the above statements?

(a) Both Statement-I and Statement-II are correct and Statement-II is the correct explanation for Statement-I.
(b) Both Statement-I and Statement-II are correct and Statement-II is not the correct explanation for Statement-I.
(c) Statement-I is correct but Statement-II is incorrect.
(d) Statement-I is correct but Statement-II is incorrect.

Ans. (c)

Exp. Statement-I is correct but Statement-II is incorrect.

The Constitution Day is celebrated on 26th November every year to promote constitutional values among citizens. Constitution Day, also known as Samvidhan Diwas.

It commemorates the adoption of the Constitution of India on 26th November, 1949. The Constituent Assembly of India, under the leadership of Dr. BR Ambedkar, worked tirelessly for almost three years to draft the Constitution. On 26th November, 1949, the final draft of the Constitution was adopted, marking a significant milestone in India's journey towards becoming a sovereign, socialist, secular and democratic republic. The Constitution of India is the supreme law of the country, providing a framework for governance and protecting the rights freedoms of its citizens.

25 **Which of the following provisions was/were not under the Indian Independence Act, 1947?** *(Chap 1, Class-XI, Old NCERT)*

1. The Act provided for the creation of two independent dominions, *viz* India and Pakistan.
2. It provided for the partition of Punjab and Bengal.
3. The Princely States were free to join India or Pakistan or remain independent.
4. The British Government was to exercise authority over the tribal areas.

Select the correct answer using the codes given below.

(a) 1 and 2 (b) Only 4 (c) 2 and 3 (d) 3 and 4

Ans. (b)

Exp. Only statement (4) was not under the provisions of Indian Independence Act, 1947.

Under the Indian Independence Act, 1947, the British Government was not to exercise any authority in future over the tribal areas. Any treaty or agreement in force, at the time of passing of this Act, between British Government and any tribal authority also lapsed.

26 **Consider the following statements regarding Indian Independence Act of 1947.** *(Chap 1, Class-XI, Old NCERT)*

1. It was based on the famous Mountbatten Plan (3rd June, 1947).
2. The Act relieved the assent of the crown on 18th July, 1947.
3. It provided for the partition of Punjab and Bengal with separate Boundaries Commission.

Which of the statements given above is/are not correct?

(a) Only 1
(b) 2 and 3
(c) Only 2
(d) None of the above

Ans. (d)

Exp. None of the given statements are incorrect because the Indian Independence Act of 1947 was based on the famous Mountbatten Plan. It also relived the assent of the crown on 18th July, 1947 and become effective on 15th August, 1947. It also provided for the Partition of Punjab and Bengal with separate Boundaries Commission to demarcate the boundaries between them.

Chapter 02

Making of the Indian Constitution

Making of the Indian Constitution

Constitution

Introduction

- The Constitution is the Supreme Law that guides all the future laws and determines the relationship between the people and government

Need of the Constitution

- Defines national ideals and aspirations
- Protects Fundamental Rights and minorities
- Specifies the political system and roles of government organs
- Check misuse of governmental authority
- Fosters trust and coordination in diverse societies
- Also provides a set of rules that allow for smooth coordination between diverse members of society
- Generates a degree of trust and coordination that is necessary for different kinds of people to live together
- Constitution also protects us from ourselves as often we might take certain decisions which are harmful to us as well as to others

Historical Background

- Prior to independence, India's Fundamental Laws were governed by British statutes
- The British Cabinet Mission was sent to facilitate discussions on India's independence and the framework for a Constitution
- The demand for an Indian Constituent Assembly was raised by leaders like Motilal Nehru and the Indian National Congress

Development of the Indian Constitution

- The Constituent Assembly was indirectly elected by method of proportional representation by means of single transferable vote
- The Constituent Assembly came into force in 1946
- The seats in each province were distributed among the three main communities, Muslims, Sikhs and General, in proportion to their respective populations
- The Constituent Assembly met for the first time in December 1946 and by November 1949 the draft Constitution was approved
- It included prominent leaders like Nehru, Prasad and Patel
- Assembly consisted of 389 members representing provinces (292), states (93), the Chief Commissioner Provinces (4) that include Delhi, Ajmer-Merwara, Coorg and British Baluchistan

Framing and Important Facts

Framing of the New Constitution

- The Constituent Assembly set up 22 committees for framing the Constitution
- The drafting Constitution was published in January 1948
- Committees were formed to draft the Constitution, with extensive debates and discussions
- Dr. BR Ambedkar chaired the Drafting Committee
- The Constitution was adopted on 26th November, 1949, and came into effect on 26th January, 1950

Objective Resolution

- Introduced by Jawaharlal Nehru, it outlined the aspirations and principles guiding the Constitution.
- The principles outlined in the resolution are reflected in the Preamble of the Constitution

Important Terms Related to Constitution

- Duration of making Constitution : 2 Years 11 Months 18 Days
- 284 members signed : Constitution

Important Committees of the Constituent Assembly and their Chairmen

Committee	Chairman
Committee on the Rules of Procedure	Rajendra Prasad
Steering Committee	Rajendra Prasad
Finance and Staff Committee	Rajendra Prasad
Credential Committee	Alladi Krishnaswami Ayyar
House Committee	B Pattabhi Sitaramayya
Order of Business Committee	KM Munsi
Ad-Hoc Committee on the National Flag	Rajendra Prasad

SOURCE *Old NCERT Class VII* (*How we Made our Constitution?*), ***New NCERT Class IX*** (*Making of the Constitution*), ***New NCERT Class XI*** (*Constitution: Why and How?*)

1 **Given below are two statements, one labelled as Assertion (A) and the other labelled as Reason (R). Select the correct answer from the codes given below.** *(Chap 2, Class-IX, New NCERT)*

Assertion (A) The Constitution of a country plays a crucial role in defining the nature of its political system and establishing the relationship between citizens and the Government.

Reason (R) By laying out specific ideals and rules, the Constitution reflects the collective aspirations of the people and prevents the misuse of authority by different branches of the Government.

Codes

(a) Both A and R are true and R is the correct explanation of A.
(b) Both A and R are true, but R is not the correct explanation of A.
(c) A is true, but R is false.
(d) A is false, but R is true.

Ans. *(b)*

Exp. Both Assertion (A) and Reason (R) are true, but Reason (R) is not the correct explanation of Assertion (A).

The role of the Constitution is to define a country's political system and citizen-government relations.

It emphasises the Constitution's role in reflecting people's aspirations and preventing misuse of authority, which are additional functions but not a direct explanation for the nature of the political system or citizen-government relationship.

2 **Consider the following statements.** *(Chap 1, Class-XI, New NCERT)*

1. India's Constitution does make ethnic identity a criterion for citizenship.
2. Different nations embody different conceptions of national identity in their Constitution.

Which of the statements given above is/are incorrect?

(a) Only 1 (b) Only 2
(c) Both 1 and 2 (d) Neither 1 nor 2

Ans. *(a)*

Exp. Statement (1) is incorrect because the Indian Constitution does not make ethnic identity a criterion for citizenship. But there are many countries e.g., Germany in the world who made ethnicity as their national identity.

3 **Consider the following Assertion (A) and Reason (R) and choose the correct code.** *(Chap 2, Class-IX, New NCERT)*

Assertion (A) The experience gained by Indians in the working of the legislative institutions created by British proved to be very useful for the country in setting up its own institutions.

Reason (R) The Indian Constitution adopted many institutional details and procedures from colonial laws like the Government of India Act, 1935.

Codes

(a) Both A and R are true and R is the correct explanation of A.
(b) Both A and R are true, but R is not the correct explanation of A.
(c) A is true, but R is false.
(d) A is false, but R is true.

Ans. *(a)*

Exp. Both Assertion (A) and Reason (R) are true and Reason (R) is the correct explanation of Assertion (A).

The experience gained by Indians in the working of the legislative institutions created by British proved to be very useful for the country in setting up its own institutions.

The familiarity with political institutions of colonial rule helped Indians to develop an agreement over the institutional design.

The Indian Constitution adopted many institutional details and procedures from colonial laws like the Government of India Act, 1935. Our leaders gained confidence to learn from other countries, but on our own terms. At each step, they were questioning whether these things suited our country or not.

4 **Consider the following statements regarding the historical background of Indian Constitution.** *(Chap 2, Class-IX, New NCERT)*

1. In 1928, Motilal Nehru and other Congress leaders drafted a Constitution for India.
2. In 1929, at the Karachi Session of the Indian National Congress (INC), it was decided that the rights of minorities will be included in the Constitution of Independent India.
3. In 1934, Indian National Congress presented the demand for the creation of an Indian Constituent Assembly in front of the British Indian Government.

Which of the statements given above is/are correct?

(a) Only 1
(b) Only 2
(c) 1 and 2
(d) 1 and 3

Ans. *(d)*

Exp. Statements (1) and (3) are correct regarding the historical background of the Indian Constitution. The Constituent Assembly convened in 1948 to draft the Indian Constitution. The Fundamental Law of India was mostly enshrined in statues enacted by the British Parliament.

Statement (2) is not correct because in 1931, Karachi Session of the Indian National Congress (INC) was decided that Universal Adult Franchise, the Right to Freedom and Equality and protecting the Rights of Minorities will be included in the Constitution of Independent of India.

5 Consider the following statements.
(Chap 2, Class-IX, New NCERT)

1. The drafting of the document called the Constitution was done by an assembly called the Drafting Assembly.
2. Elections to the Constituent Assembly were held in July, 1946.
3. The first meeting of the Constituent Assembly was held in September, 1946.
4. There was same Constituent Assembly for India and Pakistan.

Which of the statements given above is/are incorrect?

(a) 1, 2 and 3 (b) 1, 3 and 4
(c) 2, 3 and 4 (d) 1, 2, 3 and 4

Ans. *(b)*

Exp. Statements (1), (3) and (4) are incorrect.
The drafting of the document called the Constitution was done by an assembly of elected representatives called the Constituent Assembly and not the Drafting Assembly.
The first meeting of the Constituent Assembly in December, 1946.
After the partition of India, the Constituent Assembly was also divided into India and Pakistan.

6 With reference to important committees of the Constituent Assembly and their chairman.
(Chap 2, Class-IX, New NCERT)

	Committee		Chairman
1.	Credential Committee	–	Alladi Krishnaswami Ayyar
2.	Minorities Sub Committee	–	HC Mukherjee
3.	Union Powers Committee	–	Jawaharlal Nehru
4.	House Committee	–	KM Munshi

How many of the above pairs is/are not correctly matched?

(a) Only one (b) Only two
(c) Only three (d) All four

Ans. *(a)*

Exp. Only one pair i.e., (4) is not correctly matched because the Chairman of the House Committee was B. Pattabhi Sitaramayya not KM Munshi. The committees were appointed by the Constituent Assembly to draft a new Constitution for Independent India. They were divided into 8 major committees and 14 minor committees. The Provincial Assembly elected the Constitution Committee and the committee members of the Constituent Assembly functioned as the nation's first Parliament.

7 Which of the following statements are correct regarding Indian Constituent Assembly?
(Chap 2, Class-IX, New NCERT) (RAS Pre 2018)

1. It was not based on adult franchise.
2. It resulted from direct election.
3. It was not a multi-party body.
4. It worked through several committees.

Select the correct answer using the codes given below.

(a) 1 and 4 (b) 1 and 2
(c) 2 and 3 (d) 1, 2, 3 and 4

Ans. *(a)*

Exp. Statements (1) and (4) are correct regarding Indian Constituent Assembly.
The Constituent Assembly met for the first time on 9th December, 1946. There was not any adult suffrage during that time, so the Constituent Assembly could not have been chosen directly by the people of India.
The Constituent Assembly formed a number of committees to deal with different tasks of Constitution-making.
Statements (2) and (3) are incorrect because they were indirectly elected by the members of the Provincial Assembly, who themselves were elected on a limited franchise. It was a multi-party body as the Congress, the Muslim League and some other political parties also got representation.

8 Consider the following Assertion (A) and Reason (R) and choose the correct code. *(Chap 1, Class-XI, New NCERT)*
(Unit 1, Class-XI, Tamil Nadu Board)

Assertion (A) Some countries have subjected their Constitution to a full-fledged referendum.

Reason (R) The Indian Constitution was never subjected to such a referendum.

Codes

(a) Both A and R are true and R is the correct explanation of A.
(b) Both A and R are true, but R is not the correct explanation of A.
(c) A is true, but R is false.
(d) A is false, but R is true.

Ans. *(b)*

Exp. Both Assertion (A) and Reason (R) are true, but Reason (R) is not the correct explanation of Assertion (A).
Some countries have subjected their Constitution to a full-fledged referendum, where all the people vote on the desirability of a Constitution.
The Indian Constitution was never subjected to such referendum. Although, the Constitution itself was not subjected to such a referendum, but nevertheless carried enormous public authority. It is because it had the consensus and backing of leaders who were themselves popular.

9 Consider the following statements with respect to the composition of Constituent Assembly.
(Chap 1, Class-XI, New NCERT)

1. Constituent Assembly consisted of 389 members, 296 representing the provinces and 93 representing the princely states.
2. Each province was to be allotted a number of seats proportional to its population.

Which of the statements given above is/are correct?

(a) Only 1 (b) Only 2 (c) Both 1 and 2 (d) Neither 1 nor 2

Ans. *(c)*

Exp. Both the statements are correct with respect to the composition of Constituent Assembly. According to the scheme recommended by the Cabinet Mission, the arrangement was–292 members were elected through the Provincial Legislative Assemblies; 93 members represented the Indian princely states; 4 members represented the provinces. Thus, the total membership of the Assembly was to be 389.

Each province and princely state or group of states were allotted seats proportional to their respective population roughly in the ratio of 1:10,00,000.

10 Consider the following statements with regard to drafting of the Constitution. *(Chap 2, Class-IX, New NCERT)*

1. The Drafting Committee was chaired by Dr. Rajendra Prasad.
2. More than two thousand amendments were considered on the draft Constitution.
3. The members deliberated for 90 days over three years on the draft Constitution.

Which of the statements given above is/are correct?

(a) 1 and 2 (b) Only 2 (c) 1 and 3 (d) 1, 2 and 3

Ans. (b)

Exp. Only statement (2) is correct regarding the drafting of the Constitution. It is because more than two thousand amendments were considered while drafting the Constitution, after several rounds of thorough discussion, clause by clause.

Statements (1) and (3) are incorrect because the Drafting Committee was chaired by Dr. BR Ambedkar and not by Dr. Rajendra Prasad.

The members deliberated over 114 days spread over three years on the draft Constitution.

11 With reference to procedure adopted in the Constituent Assembly consider the following statememts. *(Chap 1, Class-XI, New NCERT)* *(Unit 1, Class-XI, Tamil Nadu Board)*

1. The Constituent Assembly worked in a systematic, open and consensual manner.
2. A Drafting Committee prepared a draft Constitution for discussion.
3. The assembly met for one hundred and ninety-seven days.
4. It spread over two years, nine months and twelve days.

Which of the statements given above is/are correct?

(a) Only 1 (b) 2 and 3
(c) 1 and 2 (d) 3 and 4

Ans. (c)

Exp. Statements (1) and (2) are correct with reference to the procedure adopted by the Constituent Assembly. The Constituent Assembly worked in a systematic, open and consensual manner. Some basic principles were decided and agreed, then a Drafting Committee prepared a draft Constitution.

Statements (3) and (4) are not correct because the assembly met for one hundred and sixty-six days and it spread over two years, eleven months and eighteen days. Its session were opened to the press and the public.

12 Consider the following Assertion (A) and Reason (R) and choose the correct code. *(Chap 1, Class-XI, New NCERT) (UPPSC Pre 2015)*

Assertion (A) The Constitution of India has become the longest one.

Reason (R) The chapter on Fundamental Rights has been borrowed from the model of American Constitution.

Codes

(a) Both A and R are true and R is the correct explanation of A.
(b) Both A and R are true, but R is not the correct explanation of A.
(c) A is true, but R is false.
(d) A is false, but R is true.

Ans. (b)

Exp. Both Assertion (A) and Reason (R) are true, but Reason (R) is not the correct explanation of Assertion (A). The Constitution of India has become the longest written Constitution of the world.

Several provisions of Indian Constitution have been adopted from the constitutional model of various countries.

The provisions of Fundamental Rights in our Constitution have been based on Bill of Rights in the American Constitutional model.

13 Consider the following Assertion (A) and Reason (R) and choose the correct code. *(Chap 1, Class-XI, New NCERT)*

Assertion (A) The members of the Constituent Assembly placed a great emphasis on discussion and reasoned argument.

Reason (R) They did not simply advance their own interests, but gave principled reasons to other members for their positions.

Codes

(a) Both A and R are true and R is the correct explanation of A.
(b) Both A and R are true, but R is not the correct explanation of A.
(c) A is true, but R is false.
(d) A is false, but R is true.

Ans. (a)

Exp. Both Assertion (A) and Reason (R) are true and Reason (R) is the correct explanation of Assertion (A).

The members of the Constituent Assembly were eloquent in expressing their divergent points of views and laid great emphasis on discussion and reasoned argument.

They did not simply advance their own interests, but gave principled reasons to other members for their positions.

The Constitution drew its authority from the fact that members of the Constituent Assembly engaged in what one might call public reason.

14 Consider the following statements with respect to the committees of Constituent Assembly. *(Chap 1, Class-XI, New NCERT)*

1. The Constituent Assembly had ten major committees on different subjects.
2. Usually Nehru, Rajendra Prasad or BR Ambedkar chaired these committees.

Which of the statements given above is/are correct?
(a) Only 1
(b) Only 2
(c) Both 1 and 2
(d) Neither 1 nor 2

Ans. *(d)*

Exp. Both the statement is incorrect with respect to the committees of Constituent Assembly.

Statement 2 is incorrect because Rajendra Prasad, Jawaharlal Nehru, Sardar Patel and BR Ambedkar chaired some of the important committees of Constituent Assembly.

They all worked together in order to reach consensus so that provisions agreed to by all would not be detrimental to any particular interests.

Statement (1) is incorrect because the Constituent Assembly had eight major committees on different subjects. Some of them were Drafting Committee, Union Power Committee, etc.

15 Consider the following statements. *(Chap 2, Class-IX, New NCERT)*

1. HC Mukherjee was the member of the Drafting Committee.
2. Jaipal Singh was the member of Constituent Assembly.

Which of the statements given above is/are correct?
(a) Only 1
(b) Only 2
(c) Both 1 and 2
(d) Neither 1 nor 2

Ans. *(b)*

Exp. Only statement (2) is correct as Jaipal Singh was the member of Constituent Assembly. He was a sportsperson as well as an educationist. He was also the Founder President of Adivasi Maha Sabha.

Statement (1) is incorrect because HC Mukherjee was the Vice-Chairman of the Constituent Assembly. He was also the member of All India Christian Council and Bengal Legislative Assembly. Later, he became the Governor of West Bengal.

16 Match the following lists and choose the correct code. *(Chap 1, Class-XI, New NCERT)*

List I (Minister in First Interim Government)	List II (Portfolio)
A. Vallabhbhai Patel	1. Finance Minister
B. C. Rajagopalachari	2. Defence Minister
C. John Mathai	3. Information and Broadcasting Minister
D. Baldev Singh	4. Education Minister

Codes

	A	B	C	D
(a)	3	1	2	4
(b)	3	4	1	2
(c)	3	1	4	2
(d)	3	2	1	4

Ans. *(b)*

Exp. The correct matching is A-3, B-4, C-1, D-2.

Sardar Vallabhbhai Patel He was India's first minister for Home, Information and Broadcasting in the Interim Government. Later, he became the Deputy Prime Minister of India. He played a decisive role in the integration of the Indian princely states.

C. Rajagopalachari He was the Education Minister in the first Union Cabinet. He was a Congress leader.

John Mathai He was the Finance Minister in the Interim Government.

Baldev Singh He was the first Defence Minister in the Union Cabinet of India. He was a successful entrepreneur and leader of the Panthic Akali Party in Punjab.

17 Consider the following pairs with reference to important personalities of Constituent Assembly. *(Chap 1, Class-VII, Old NCERT)*

	Personalities		Description
1.	BR Ambedkar	–	Born in Uttar Pradesh, Chairman of the Drafting Committee.
2.	Rajendra Prasad	–	Born in Bihar, President of the Constituent Assembly.
3.	Durgabai Deshmukh	–	Born in Andhra Pradesh, member of the Constituent Assembly.
4.	HC Mukherjee	–	Born in Hyderabad, represented the tribal people in Constituent Assembly.

How many of the above pairs is/are correctly matched?
(a) Only one
(b) Only two
(c) Only three
(d) All four

Ans. *(b)*

Exp. Only two pairs i.e., (2) and (3) are correctly matched. Rajendra Prasad was born in Bihar and he was the President of the Constituent Assembly and Durgabai Deshmukh was born in Andhra Pradesh and she was a member of the Constituent Assembly and the Planning Commission of India.

Pairs (1) and (4) are not correctly matched because BR Ambedkar was born in Madhya Pradesh and he was the Chairman of the Drafting Committee. He was also a social revolutionary thinker.

HC Mukherjee was born in Bengal and he was the Vice-Chairman of the Constituent Assembly.

18 Consider the following statements regarding the Objective Resolution. *(Chap 1, Class-XI, New NCERT)*

1. Based on this resolution, our Constitution gave institutional expression to equality, liberty, democracy, sovereignty and cosmopolitan identity.
2. As per this resolution, the minorities, backward and tribal areas, depressed classes and Other Backward Classes shall be provided adequate safeguards.
3. According to this resolution, territories forming the Union shall be unitary units.

Which of the statements given above is/are incorrect?

(a) 1 and 2 (b) 2 and 3 (c) 1 and 3 (d) Only 3

Ans. (d)

Exp. Only statement (3) is incorrect regarding Objective Resolution because as per the Objective Resolution moved by Nehru in 1946, India shall be a Union of erstwhile British Indian territories. But the territories forming the Union shall be autonomous units and exercise all powers and functions of the government and administration, except those assigned or vested in the Union. It also provides that all powers and authority of sovereign and independent India shall flow from the people.

19 Consider the following Assertion (A) and Reason (R) and choose the correct code. *(Chap 1, Class-XI, New NCERT)*

Assertion (A) The Constituent Assembly adopted for the Parliamentary form of government.

Reason (R) The Constituent Assembly spent a lot of time on evolving the right balance among the various institutions like the Executive, the Legislature and the Judiciary.

Codes

(a) Both A and R are true and R is the correct explanation of A.

(b) Both A and R are true, but R is not the correct explanation of A.

(c) A is true, but R is false.

(d) A is false, but R is true.

Ans. (a)

Exp. Both Assertion (A) and Reason (R) are true and Reason (R) is the correct explanation of Assertion (A). The Constituent Assembly spent a lot of time on evolving the right balance of powers among different institutions like Executive, Legislature and Judiciary. This led to the adoption of parliamentary form of government. It adopted federal arrangement that distributed governmental powers between Legislature and the Executive as well as among Centre and the States.

Chapter 03

Salient Features of Indian Constitution and Preamble

Indian Constitution : Preamble and Its Features

Preamble of the Indian Constitution

Introduction

- The Preamble serves as an introductory statement outlining the aims and objectives of the Constitution
- It was based on 'the Objectives Resolution' drafted by Jawaharlal Nehru and was adopted by the Constituent Assembly
- The Preamble has been amended once by the 42nd Constitutional Amendment in 1976
- Through the amendment words socialist, secular and integrity were added
- It is not enforceable in a court of law but serves as a guiding principle
- The components of the Preamble include the date of adoption, objectives, justification of the nature of the Indian state and the acknowledgement of the people of India as the ultimate source of authority
- In the Berubari Union Case, SC stated that Preamble cannot be considered part of the Constitution
- In the LIC of India case, SC held that Preamble is an integral part of the Constitution

Importance and Utility of the Preamble

- It does not grant any power but it gives direction and purpose to the Constitution
- It also enshrines the grand objectives and socio-economic goals, which are to be achieved through constitutional processes
- The Court stated that 'Preamble is the key to open the mind of the makers' but it cannot be considered as part of the Constitution

Components of Preamble

- The Preamble shows that the people of India are the source of authority
- It comprises the date of its adoption, which is 26th November, 1949.
- It states that the objectives of the Constitution of India, are to secure justice, liberty, equality to all citizens and promote fraternity to maintain the integrity and unity of the nation

Features of the Indian Constitution

Introduction

- The Indian Constitution is the world's longest written Constitution, containing 448 Articles, 25 Parts and 12 Schedules
- It establishes a parliamentary democracy with a separation of powers between the Executive, Legislature and Judiciary
- Fundamental Rights are guaranteed to citizens which include
  - Right to Equality
  - Right to Freedom
  - Right Against Exploitation
  - Right to Freedom of Religion
  - Cultural and Educational Rights
  - Right to Constitutional Remedies
- The Constitution is drawn from various sources and includes features borrowed from different countries
- The Constitution includes Fundamental Duties, Directive Principles of State Policy
- The Constitution also includes provision for a federal system with a strong centralising tendency
- It provides for an independent and integrated judicial system
- It ensures balance between parliamentary sovereignty and judicial supremacy
- The Constitution is amendable through different processes and it also contains provisions for emergency situations
- It establishes a Three tier Government Structure
- It provides for independent bodies like the Election Commission and Comptroller and Auditor-General (CAG)
- While India is federal in structure, it also has unitary features, making it a quasi-federal system

These features collectively reflect the complex and comprehensive nature of the Indian Constitution, which provides the framework for governance and protects the rights and liberties of its citizens

SOURCE ***Old NCERT Class VII*** *(What our Ideals Are : The Preamble),* ***New NCERT Class VII*** *(Chief Features of Our Constitution),* ***New NCERT Class VIII*** *(Indian Constitution),* ***Old NCERT Class IX & X*** *(The Constitution of India and its Salient Features),* ***New NCERT Class XI*** *(Constitution : Why and How?),* ***Old NCERT Class XI*** *(Preamble, its Main Features and Indian Union)*

Preamble

1 Arrange the following words in the correct sequence as they are mentioned in the Preamble and choose the correct code. *(Chap 4, Class-IX & X, Old NCERT)* *(Chap 5, Module-2, NIOS)*

1. Socialist
2. Democratic
3. Sovereign
4. Secular

Codes

(a) 3, 1, 4 and 2 (b) 3, 4, 1 and 2
(c) 3, 4, 2 and 1 (d) 4, 1, 3 and 2

Ans. (a)

Exp. The correct sequence of words as mentioned in the Preamble is 3, 1, 4, 2. i.e., Sovereign, Socialist, Secular, Democratic and Republic.

The Preamble aims at a social order wherein the people would be sovereign, the government would be elected by people, the powers of the government shall be restricted by the rights of the people and people would have ample opportunity to develop their talents.

2 Which of the following words have been added to the Preamble by the 42nd Amendment? *(Chap 3, Class-XI, Old NCERT) (JPSC Pre 2016)*

1. Socialist
2. Gram Swarajya
3. Secular
4. Sovereign

Codes

(a) 1, 2 and 3 (b) 1 and 3
(c) 1, 2 and 4 (d) 2, 3 and 4

Ans. (b)

Exp. The words 'Socialist' and 'Secular' have been added to the Preamble by the 42nd Amendment, 1976. The word 'Integrity' was also added through this amendment. It provides for common brotherhood which leads to the unity and integrity of the nation.

The term 'socialist' indicates the incorporation of the philosophy of Socialism in the Constitution.

The term 'Secular' means that the state shall not discriminate between different religions and all religions shall be treated equally.

3 Consider the following statements about the Preamble. *(Chap 3, Class-XI, Old NCERT)*

1. It is enforceable through courts of law.
2. It keeps liberty of thought, expression, belief, faith and worship as its ideals.
3. It is based on the objective resolution which was drafted in the Constitution Assembly by Pt. Jawaharlal Nehru.
4. It contains ideas that the Constitution seeks to achieve. It does not grant any power but it gives direction to the Constitution.

Which of the statements given above is/are correct?

(a) Only 1 (b) 2, 3 and 4 (c) 1 and 3 (d) 1 and 2

Ans. (b)

Exp. Statements (2), (3) and (4) are correct about the Preamble. The ideals set forth in the Preamble for the Indian state are liberty of thought, expression, belief, faith and worship. It is based on the objective resolution, which was drafted in the Constituent Assembly by Pt. Jawaharlal Nehru on 13th December, 1946 and adopted on 22nd January, 1947. The Preamble of the Constitution contains ideas that the Constitution seeks to achieve. It does not grant any power but gives direction and purpose to the Constitution.

Statement (1) is not correct because the Preamble is not enforceable by courts but is a part of the Constitution. The Preamble is non-justiciable. This means that courts cannot pass orders against the Government of India to implement the ideas in the Preamble. The courts can take recourse to the Preamble in order to explain and clarify other provisions of the Constitution.

4 Consider the following Assertion (A) and Reason (R) and choose the correct code. *(Chap 4, Class-IX & X, Old NCERT)*

Assertion (A) The common brotherhood, to be developed in India, would be based on the dignity of the individual without any consideration of his status in society.

Reason (R) The Preamble aims at developing fraternity assuring the dignity of individuals and the unity and integrity of the nation.

Codes

(a) Both A and R are true and R is the correct explanation of A.
(b) Both A and R are true, but R is not the correct explanation of A.
(c) A is true, but R is false.
(d) A is false, but R is true.

Ans. (a)

Exp. Both the Assertion (A) and Reason (R) are true and Reason (R) is the correct explanation of Assertion (A). The term 'Fraternity' in the Preamble means a feeling of brotherhood and an emotional attachment with the country and all the people. Fraternity helps to promote dignity and unity in the nation. Without fraternity, liberty and equality could not become a natural course of things.

5 The Preamble to the Constitution of India is *(Chap 3, Class-XI, Old NCERT)* *(IAS Pre 2020)*

(a) a part of the Constitution but has no legal effects.
(b) not a part of the Constitution and has no legal effect.
(c) part of the Constitution and has same legal effect as any other part.
(d) a part of the Constitution but has no legal effect independently of other parts.

Ans. (d)

Exp. The Preamble to the Constitution of India is a part of the Constitution but has no legal effect independently of other parts.

It means it is not technically enforceable through courts of law, though it is useful in interpreting various provisions of the Constitution. It also acts as a beacon in conflicting situations.

6 Consider the following statements regarding the Preamble of Constitution.

(Chap 3, Class-XI, Old NCERT) (Chap 5, Module-2, NIOS)

1. The Objectives Resolution by Jawaharlal Nehru finally became Preamble.
2. It is non-justiciable.
3. It can't be amended.
4. Preamble cannot override the specific provisions of the Constitution.

Which of the statements given above are correct?

(a) 1 and 2
(b) 1, 2 and 4
(c) 1, 2 and 3
(d) 2, 3 and 4

Ans. *(b)*

Exp. Statements (1), (2) and (4) are correct regarding the Preamble of Constitution. The Objectives Resolution moved by Jawaharlal Nehru on 13th December, 1946 became the foundation of the Preamble.

In Kesavananda Bharati Case (1973), the Supreme Court held that the Preamble is a part of the Constitution. It also held that it can be used to explain the ambiguous areas of the Constitution.

However, it is non-justiciable as it cannot be enforced in the court of law. It cannot override the specific provisions of the Constitution. In case of any conflict between the two the latter shall prevail.

Statement (3) is incorrect because Preamble can be amended. It was amended in 1976 by 42nd Amendment.

7 Which one of the following statements best reflects the chief purpose of the 'Constitution' of a country?

(Chap 1, Class-XI, New NCERT) (IAS Pre 2023)

(a) It determines the objective for the making of necessary laws.
(b) It enables the creation of political offices and a government.
(c) It defines and limits the power of government.
(d) It secures social justice, social equality and social security.

Ans. *(c)*

Exp. Statement (c) best reflects the chief purpose of the Constitution of the country as the Constitution defines and limits the powers of government.

One of the functions of a Constitution is to provide a set of basic rules that allow for minimal coordination amongst members of society and it also specifies who has the power to make decisions in a society.

8 Consider the following statements and select the correct code. *(Chap 3, Class-XI, Old NCERT)*

Statement-I The Preamble of the Indian Constitution declares the people as the source of authority.

Statement-II This is evident through the citizen's power to elect representatives and criticise them, reflecting their integral role in shaping the nation's governance.

Codes

(a) Both Statement-I and Statement-II are correct and Statement-II is the correct explanation for Statement-I.
(b) Both Statement-I and Statement-II are correct and Statement-II is not the correct explanation for Statement-I.
(c) Statement-I is correct but Statement-II is incorrect.
(d) Statement-I is incorrect but Statement-II is correct.

Ans. *(a)*

Exp. Both Statement-I and Statement-II are correct and Statement-II is the correct explanation for Statement-I. The Preamble shows that the people of India are the source of authority. It means that the power lies with the citizens to elect their representatives and they also have the right to criticise their representatives. It also justifies the nature of the Indian state, which is sovereign, socialist, secular, democratic and republic.

9 Consider the following statements.

(Chap 4, Class-IX & X, Old NCERT)

1. The date of adoption of the Constitution of India as mentioned in the Preamble is 26th January, 1949.
2. Preamble was enacted after the enactment of the entire Constitution of India.

Which of the statements given above is/are incorrect?

(a) Only 1 (b) Only 2
(c) Both 1 and 2 (d) Neither 1 nor 2

Ans. *(a)*

Exp. Statement (1) is incorrect because on 26th November, 1949, the Constituent Assembly of India formally adopted the Constitution of India. However, it came into force on 26th January, 1950.

Statement (2) is correct as the Preamble was enacted after the enactment of the Constitution of India.

Salient Features of Indian Constitution

10 Consider the following statements.

(Chap 4, Class-IX & X, Old NCERT)

1. A Constitution is considered as the source of power and authority of the government.
2. It provides for three branches of government i.e. Executive, Legislature and Judiciary.
3. Judiciary controls all the organs of government.

Which of the statements given above is/are incorrect?

(a) Only 1 (b) 1 and 2 (c) Only 3 (d) 1, 2 and 3

Ans. *(c)*

Exp. Statement (3) is incorrect because each branch is separate and independent from the other. However, these branches are designed to hold checks and balances over one another. Hence, Judiciary does not control all the organs of government.

11 Consider the following statements. *(Chap 3, Class-XI, Old NCERT)*

1. The membership of the Commonwealth of Nations limits the sovereignty of India.
2. Commonwealth of Nations is a voluntary association of independent sovereign states.

Which of the statements given above is/are correct?

(a) Only 1 (b) Only 2 (c) Both 1 and 2 (d) Neither 1 nor 2

Ans. (b)

Exp. Only statement (2) is correct as the Commonwealth of Nations is purely a voluntary association of independent sovereign states.

Statement (1) is incorrect because sovereignty does not mean limitation rather it implies that people of India are not subordinate to any other external agency.

12 Which of the following are the unique features of the Indian Constitution? *(Chap 3, Class-XI, Old NCERT)*

1. Framed by representatives of the people of India
2. Derived from the various sources
3. Republican polity
4. Sovereignty of the people

Codes

(a) 1, 2 and 3 (b) 2, 3 and 4 (c) 1, 2, 3 and 4 (d) 1, 3 and 4

Ans. (c)

Exp. All the given options are the unique features of the Indian Constitution. Some of the other unique features of the Indian Constitution are as follows

- Derived from the various sources i.e., US Constitution, UK Constitution, German Constitution, etc.
- Secular polity
- Fundamental Rights and Fundamental Duties
- Directive Principles of State Policy
- Universal Adult Franchise
- Judicial review
- Unique blend of rigidity and flexibility
- Recognition of Hindi as an official language
- Sovereign
- Socialist

13 Match the following lists and choose the correct code. *(Chap 1, Class-XI, New NCERT) (IAS Pre 2003)*

List I (Items of Indian Constitution)	List II (Country from which it was derived)
A. Directive Principles of State Policy	1. Australia
B. Fundamental Rights	2. Canada
C. Concurrent list for Union-State relations	3. Ireland
D. India as a Union of states with greater powers to the Union	4. United Kingdom
	5. United States of America

Codes

	A	B	C	D		A	B	C	D
(a)	5	4	1	2	(b)	3	5	2	1
(c)	5	4	2	1	(d)	3	5	1	2

Ans. (d)

Exp. The correct matching is A- 3, B-5, C-1, D-2.

Directive Principles of State Policy These have been borrowed from Ireland.

Fundamental Rights These have been borrowed from United States of America.

Concurrent list for Union-State relations It has been borrowed from Australia.

India as a Union of states with greater powers to the Union It has been borrowed from Canada.

Besides these Provisional line First Past The Post System, Parliamentary form of government, the idea of rule of law, etc have been borrowed from the British Constitution.

14 Consider the following statements. *(Chap 1, Class -VIII, New NCERT)*

1. The Constitution of India guarantees Universal Adult Suffrage for all citizens.
2. Under this system, every Indian citizen who has completed the age of 18 years has the right to vote and participate in choosing the governments at different levels.
3. The Constitution of India is federal and it provides for single citizenship for the whole of India.

Which of the statements given above is/are incorrect?

(a) Only 1 (b) Only 2
(c) Only 3 (d) None of these

Ans. (d)

Exp. None of the given statements are incorrect. The Constitution of India guarantees Universal Adult Suffrage for all citizens. Under this system, every Indian citizen who has completed the age of 18 years has the right to vote and participate in choosing the governments at different levels, regardless of income, property, religion, race, social status, political status etc. are restriction, only subjected to minor expectations.

Though the Constitution of India is federal, it provides for dual polity, i.e, centre and state governments, it also provides for single citizenship for the whole of India.

15 Consider the following statements. *(Chap 1, Class -VIII, New NCERT)*

1. The Indian Constitution recognises every person as equal.
2. As per Constitution, every person is equal before the law.
3. The basic features of the Constitution have been openly defined by the Judiciary.

How many statements given above is/are correct?

(a) Only one (b) Only two
(c) All three (d) None of these

Ans. (b)

Exp. Only two statements i.e., (1) and (2) are correct.

The Indian Constitution recognises every person as equal. This means that every individual in the country, including male and female persons from all castes, religions, tribes, educational and economic backgrounds are recognised as equal.

As per the Constitution, every person is equal before the law. It means that every person will be treated equally in similar circumstances.

Statement (3) is not correct because the basic features of the Constitution have not been openly defined by the Judiciary. Atleast, 20 features described as 'basic' or 'essential' by the Judiciary in numerous cases, have been incorporated in the basic structure.

16 Which of the following statement is not correct regarding the Indian Parliamentary System? *(Chap 4, Class-IX & X, Old NCERT)*

(a) In this system, the Parliament is supreme and represents the people.

(b) The administration is actually carried on by the Council of Ministers which is responsible to the legislature.

(c) The Central as well as State Legislatures are bicameral.

(d) The government is carried on in the name of the President at the centre and the Governor in the states.

Ans. (c)

Exp. Statement (c) is not correct regarding the Indian Parliamentary System because only 6 states of India those have bicameral legislature– Andhra Pradesh, Bihar, Karnataka, Maharashtra, Telangana and Uttar Pradesh. Bicameral Legislature is a system of Government in which the Legislature consists of two Houses. Rest of the states in India have unicameral legislature.

17 Consider the following statements. *(Chap 4, Class-XI & X, Old NCERT)*

1. Fundamental Rights have been often referred as the 'Conscience of the Indian Constitution.'
2. Universal Adult Franchise in our Constitution has been taken from Government of India Act, 1935.
3. The Constitution provides for a single integrated Judicial system common for the union and the states.
4. The Constitution (42nd Amendment), Act, 1976 introduced a code of ten 'Fundamental Duties' for citizens.

How many statements given above is/are correct?

(a) Only one (b) Only two (c) Only three (d) All of these

Ans. (c)

Exp. Only three statements i.e., (1), (3) and (4) are correct. Fundamental Rights have been often referred as the 'Conscience of the Indian Constitution'. The Constitution provides for a single integrated Judicial system common for both the union and the states. Ten Fundamental Duties were introduced by the Constitutional 42nd Amendment Act, 1976.

Statement (2) is not correct because Universal Adult Franchise has not been taken from the Government of India Act, 1935. This Act provided for restricted Franchise. Universal Adult Franchise was largely adopted after the Independence of India to conduct free and fair elections.

18 Which of the following are the features of the Constitution of India? *(Chap 3, Class-VII, Old NCERT)*

1. Dual Citizenship
2. Secularism
3. Democracy
4. Independent Judiciary
5. Lengthiest Constitution

Codes

(a) 2, 3, 4 and 5 (b) 1 and 3

(c) 1, 3 and 4 (d) All of these

Ans. (a)

Exp. Options (2), (3), (4) and (5) are correct. The Indian Constitution provides for single citizenship, secularism, democracy, independent Judiciary, etc. It is also the lengthiest written Constitution of the world. Originally, Constitution of India contained 395 Articles, 22 Parts and Eight Schedules.

Presently, the Constitution of India consists of 448 Articles, 25 Parts and 12 Schedules. However, unlike federal countries like the USA and Switzerland which have dual citizenship, the Indian constitution provides single citizenship to its citizens.

19 Consider the following statements and select the correct code. *(Chap 3, Class-XI, Old NCERT)*

Statement-I The Constitution declares the Parliament of India to be the supreme authority.

Statement-II Prior to it, the supreme authority laid with the British Parliament.

Codes

(a) Both Statement-I and Statement-II are correct and Statement-II is the correct explanation for Statement-I.

(b) Both Statement-I and Statement-II are correct and Statement-II is not the correct explanation for Statement-I.

(c) Statement-I is correct but statement-II is incorrect.

(d) Statement-I is incorrect but statement-II is correct.

Ans. (d)

Exp. Statement-I is incorrect, but Statement-II is correct. The Constitution declares the people of India to be the supreme authority i.e., they are sovereign. It means that the people of India are not subordinate to any other external agency.

Prior to the present Constitution, the supreme authority laid with the British Parliament. The Indian Independence Act, 1947 recognised the supremacy of the British Parliament.

20 **With reference to borrowed features of Indian Constitution.** *(Chap 4, Class-IX & X, Old NCERT)* *(Unit 1, Class-XI, Tamil Nadu Board)*

	Countries		Borrowed Features
1.	Australia	–	Concurrent list, Freedom of trade, commerce and intercourse
2.	Ireland	–	Directive Principles of State Policy, method of election of the President.
3.	Japan	–	Fundamental Duties, ideals of justice (social, economic and political)
4.	US	–	Suspension of Fundamental Rights during emergency.

How many pairs given above is/are correctly matched?

(a) Only one (b) Only two
(c) Only three (d) All of these

Ans. (b)

Exp. Only two pairs i.e., (1) and (2) are correctly matched. Concurrent list, freedom of trade, commerce and intercourse and joint sitting of the two Houses of Parliament are borrowed from Australia.

Directive Principles of State Policy, nomination of members to Rajya Sabha and method of election of the President are taken from Ireland.

Pairs (3) and (4) are not correctly matched because Fundamental Duties and ideals of justice are borrowed from Soviet Union (USSR).

Suspension of Fundamental Rights during emergency has been borrowed by Germany.

Procedure established by law has been borrowed from Japan.

Fundamental Rights, Independence of Judiciary etc., have been borrowed from US.

21 **Consider the following statements and select the correct code.** *(Chap 3, Class-XI, Old NCERT)*

Statement-I The procedure for an amendment to Indian Constitution is a unique blend of rigidity and flexibility.

Statement-II Some provisions of the Constitution can be amended by simple majority, others require absolute majority of the total strength of the two Houses of Parliament and two-thirds majority of the members present and voting.

Codes

(a) Both Statement-I and Statement-II are correct and Statement-II is the correct explanation for Statement-I.
(b) Both Statement-I and Statement-II are correct and Statement-II is not the correct explanation for Statement I.
(c) Statement-I is correct but Statement-II is incorrect.
(d) Statement-I is incorrect but Statement-II is correct.

Ans. (a)

Exp. Both Statement-I and Statement-II are correct and Statement-II is the correct explanation for Statement-I. The procedure for an amendment to Indian Constitution is a unique blend of rigidity and flexibility.

Some provisions of the Constitution can be amended by simple majority, other require absolute majority of the total strength of the two Houses of Parliament and two-third majority of the members present and voting. Article 368 of the Constitution mention two types of amendments in the Constitution. By special majority of Parliament and by the special majority of the Parliament with the ratification by half of the total states.

22 **Which of the following pairs is/are correctly matched?** *(Chap 1, Class-XI, New NCERT)* *(Unit 1, Class-XI, Tamil Nadu Board)*

	Features		Sources
1.	Parliamentary form of government	–	British Constitution
2.	Directive Principles of State Policy	–	Japanese Constitution
3.	Independence of Judiciary	–	Constitution of United States

Codes

(a) Only 1 (b) 2 and 3 (c) 1 and 3 (d) 1, 2 and 3

Ans. (c)

Exp. Pairs (1) and (3) are correctly matched.

The Parliamentary form of government was adopted from the British Constitution and the Independence of Judiciary has been adopted from the United States Constitution.

Pair (2) is incorrectly matched because Directive Principles of State Policy (DPSP) have been adopted from the Irish Constitution.

23 **With reference to Constitutional bodies, consider the following statements.** *(Chap 4, Class-IX & X, Old NCERT)*

1. The Election Commission of India is an autonomous constitutional authority responsible for election process in India.
2. Comptroller and Auditor-General (CAG) is a Constitutional functionary. The CAG is responsible for actions of various organs of the Government like the Executive and Legislature.
3. The Constitution of India had made UPSC (Union Public Service Commission) and SPSC (State Public Service Commission) to provide advice on the subject sent to it by President or by the Governors.

How many of the given statements about the independent bodies is/are not correct?

(a) Only one (b) Only two
(c) All three (d) None of these

Ans. (a)

Exp. Only one statement i.e., (2) is not correct because the CAG is responsible for audit of accounts of Ministries and departments of Government of India and the State Governments. The Comptroller and Auditor-General (CAG) is a constitutional functionary, independent of Parliament/Legislature and Executives.

Chapter 04

Union and Its Territories

Indian Federation and Re-organisation of States

Federalism

Introduction

- Federalism divides power between a central authority and constituent units
- India's federalism combines features of a federation and a union

Nature of Indian Federalism

- India's federalism is a quasi-federal, with a blend of flexibility and rigidity
- The appointment of governors by the Central Government indicates a bias toward central authority
- The Union List grants more powers to the Central Government
- The representation of the states in the upper house is based on the state's population
- All India Services such as the Indian Administrative Services (IAS), Indian Police Services (IPS), etc., the centre interferes in the Executive Powers of the states.
- These services also offer uniformity in administration throughout the nation

Conflicts in Indian Federal System

- **Regional Assertion vs Central Dominance** Indian federalism has a bias for the Central Government
- **Absence of Fiscal Federalism** Asymmetrical sharing of revenue and resource crunch at the periphery results in uneven development across the country
- **Creation of Linguistic States** Union government has the authority to make, unmake and remake state boundaries
- **Centralised Planning** Economic and social planning is found in the Concurrent List of the Seventh Schedule to the Constitution

Post-Independence Consolidation of India

- British India had two types of territories Provinces, governed directly by British officials
- Princely States under the control of local hereditary rulers having British Government as the sovereign but enjoying autonomy based on the treaty
- When India gained independence on 15th August, 1947, the British Government dissolved their treaty relations

State Re-organisation

State Re-organisation

State Re-organisation
- Need for Re-organisation
- Linguistic Line → Formation of Committees
  - Dhar Commission
  - JVP Committee
  - Fazl Ali Commission
    - States Re-organisation Act of 1956
    - Creation of New States and Union Territories

Creation of Constitutional Units

India divided into
- Part-A → Former British Provinces → Specific Administrative Structure
- Part-B → Former Princely States
- Part-C → Former Princely States and Provinces Administered by Chief Commissoner
- Part-D → Union Territories Created → Areas not Fully Incorporated

Creation of New States

- **Article 2** Parliament may by law admit into the Union or establish, new states on such terms and conditions as it thinks fit
- **Article 3** Parliament may by law provide for formation of new states and alteration of areas, boundaries or names of existing states

Formation of Union Territories

- After States Re-organisation Act; Part-C and Part-D states merged into Union Territories
- Delhi, Puducherry and Chandigarh granted partial statehood

SOURCE *Old NCERT Class IX & X (Our Government in States),* ***New NCERT Class X*** *(Federalism),* ***New NCERT Class XI*** *(Federalism),* ***New NCERT Class XII*** *(Regional Aspirations),* ***New NCERT Class XII*** *(Challenges of National Building),* ***Old NCERT Class XII*** *(Regional Imbalances : Regionalism, Linguism and Separatism)*

Indian Federation and Re-organisation of States

1 Consider the following statements.
(Chap 2, Class IX & X, Old NCERT) (Chap 8, Module-2, NIOS)

1. The Constitution of India avoids using the term 'federal state'.
2. The Constitution declares India to be a 'Union of States'.
3. The Constitution declares India as a 'Center of States'.

How many of the statements given above is/are incorrect?

(a) Only one (b) Only two
(c) All three (d) None of these

Ans. (a)

Exp. Only one statement i.e., (3) is incorrect because the Constitution declared India as a Union of States. The Indian Union is based on the principles of federalism. Federalism is a system of government in which the power is divided between a central authority and various constituent units of the country.

2 Consider the following statements.
(Chap 2, Class-X, New NCERT)

1. Union Territories are areas which are too small to become an independent state but which could not be merged with any of the existing states.
2. The adjoining State Government has special powers in the administration of these areas.

Which of the statements given above is/are correct?

(a) Only 1 (b) Only 2 (c) Both 1 and 2 (d) Neither 1 nor 2

Ans. (a)

Exp. Statement (1) is correct. Union territories are units of the Indian Union which enjoy very little power and are too small to become an independent state. However, they could not be merged with any of the existing states.

Statement (2) is not correct because the adjoining State Government has no power to administer these areas. These areas are administered by the Central Government.

3 With reference to creation of states, consider the following pairs.
(Chap 1, Class-XII, New NCERT) (Unit 7, Class-XII, Tamil Nadu Board)

Creation of State		Year
1. Arunachal Pradesh	–	1987
2. Nagaland	–	1962
3 Uttarakhand	–	2000

How many of the pairs given above is/are correctly matched?

(a) Only one (b) Only two
(c) All three (d) None of these

Ans. (b)

Exp. Only two pairs i.e., (1) and (3) are correctly matched as the major reorganisation of states took place in the North-East in 1971. The state of Arunachal Pradesh came into being in 1987 and the state of Uttarakhand was formed in 2000.

Pair (2) is not correctly matched because the state of Nagaland came into existence in the year 1963.

4 Which one of the following is the correct chronological order for the formation of the following states in the Indian Union?
(Chap 8, Class-XII, New NCERT) (IAS Pre 2007)

(a) Sikkim-Arunachal Pradesh-Nagaland-Haryana
(b) Nagaland-Haryana-Sikkim-Arunachal Pradesh
(c) Sikkim-Haryana-Nagaland-Arunachal Pradesh
(d) Nagaland-Arunachal Pradesh-Sikkim-Haryana

Ans (b)

Exp The correct chronology is as follows Nagaland-Haryana-Sikkim-Arunachal Pradesh.

Nagaland became state in 1963. It was 16th state of India.

Haryana was carved out from Punjab along with Himachal Pradesh in 1966. Haryana was 17th state of India.

Sikkim become full-fledged state of India in 1975. It was 22nd state of India.

Arunachal Pradesh came into being as the 24th state of India in 1987.

5 Which of the following statements is incorrect regarding the incorporation of Sikkim to the Indian Union? *(Chap 8, Class-XII, New NCERT)*

(a) The first democratic elections to the Sikkim Assembly in 1974 were swept by the Sikkim Congress which stood for greater integration with India.
(b) The Sikkim Assembly first sought the status of 'associate state' and then in April 1975, passed a resolution asking for full integration with India.
(c) The Indian Parliament accepted their request immediately and Sikkim became the 23rd state of the Indian Union.
(d) None of the above

Ans. (c)

Exp. Statement (c) is incorrect because the Indian Parliament accepted their request immediately and Sikkim became the 22nd state of the Indian Union. This was followed by a hurriedly organised referendum that put a stamp of popular approval on the assembly's request.

6 Consider the following statements with respect to Goa. *(Chap 8, Class-XII, New NCERT)*

1 It was under the control of the Portuguese at the time of Independence.
2 In December 1961, the Government of India sent the army which liberated Goa and it became the 25th state of Indian Union.
3. In 1968, Goa was merged into the Republic of India.

How many of the statements given above is/are correct?

(a) Only one (b) Only two
(c) All three (d) None of these

Ans. (b)

Exp. Only two statements i.e., (1) and (2) are correct. Goa was under the control of the Portuguese at the time of independence. The Indian Government tried very patiently to persuade the Portuguese Government to withdraw.

In December 1961, the Government of India sent the army which liberated the territories after barely two days of action and on 30th May, 1987 Goa became the 25th state of Indian Union.

Only statement (3) is not correct because in 1961, Daman and Diu and Goa were merged into the Republic of India, after attaining independence from Portuguese rule.

7 With reference to integration of Manipur, consider the following statements. *(Chap 1, Class-XII, New NCERT)*

1. After Independence, the Maharaja of Manipur, Bodhachandra Singh signed the 'Instrument of Accession' with the Indian Government.
2. In June, 1948, Manipur became a constitutional monarchy.
3. Manipur was the first part of India to hold an election based on Universal Adult Franchise.
4. The Indian Government and the Maharaja signed the Merger agreement in September, 1949.

How many of the statements given above is/are incorrect?

(a) Only one (b) Only two (c) Only three (d) All of these

Ans. (a)

Exp. Only one statement i.e., (1) is incorrect with respect to integration of Manipur because the Maharaja of Manipur Bodhachandra Singh signed the 'Instrument of Accession' before the independence of India .

8 Consider the following statement with respect to Hyderabad. *(Chap 8, Class-XII, New NCERT)*

1. The Nawab of Hyderabad managed to assemble a fraction of traditional Muslims known as Ittehadul Muslimeen and a paramilitary force named Razakars.
2. The Nawab of Hyderabad faced a police action by the Government in 1948.
3. The Nawab agreed to accede Hyderabad to India after the action leading to the surrender on 17th September, 1948.

How many of the statements given above is/are correct?

(a) Only one (b) Only two
(c) All three (d) None of these

Ans. (c)

Exp. All of the given statements are correct.
The Nawab of Hyderabad succeeded in mobilising a group of orthodox Muslims called as Ittehadul Muslimeen and a paramilitary force named Razakars and they challenged the idea of India and after this incident finally a police action was taken by the Government of India in 1948 leading to the surrender of Hyderabad on 17th September of that year and lastly the Nawab agreed to accede Hyderabad to India.

9 Which of the following statement(s) is/are incorrect regarding Kargil Conflict? *(Chap 4, Class-XII, New NCERT)*

1. The Kargil Conflict was not only confined to Kargil as it was spreaded in other parts of the country.
2. After the conflict, the Government of Pakistan was taken over by the Pakistan Army led by the Army Chief, General Pervez Musharraf.

Codes

(a) Only 1 (b) Only 2 (c) Both 1 and 2 (d) Neither 1 nor 2

Ans. (a)

Exp. Statement (1) is incorrect regarding Kargil Conflict because the Kargil Conflict remained confined only to the Kargil region. The Kargil Conflict went from May to June 1999 when the Pakistani military infiltrated Kashmir. Operation Vijay was launched by the Indian Army to regain the possession of Kargil.

10 On the basis of their formation, arrange the following states in a chronological order. *(Chap 1, Class-XII, New NCERT)*

1. Mizoram 2. Jharkhand
3. Meghalaya 4. Goa

Codes

(a) 2, 1, 3, 4 (b) 3, 4, 1, 2
(c) 1, 2, 3, 4 (d) 2, 1, 4, 3

Ans. (b)

Exp. The correct chronological order is 3, 4, 1, 2 i.e. Meghalaya-Goa-Mizoram-Jharkhand.
Meghalaya was carved out of Assam in 1972.
Goa was conferred the statehood of India in 1987.
Mizoram became state of Indian Union in 1987.
Jharkhand was formed in 2000.

11 Consider the following statements. *(Chap 1, Class-XII, New NCERT)*

1. The States Reorganisation Commission in its report accepted that the boundaries of the state should reflect the boundaries of different languages.
2. On the basis of its report, the States Reorganisation Act was passed in 1956, which led to the creation of 15 states and 7 Union Territories.

Which of the statements given above is/are correct?

(a) Only 1 (b) Only 2
(c) Both 1 and 2 (d) Neither 1 nor 2

Ans. (a)

Exp. Statement (1) is correct as the establishment of Andhra Pradesh sparked a fight in other regions of the country to create states based on linguistic lines. The Central Government was forced to form the States

Reorganisation Commission in 1953 to examine into the issue of redrawing state boundaries as a result of these disputes. The Commission in its report accepted that the boundaries of the states should reflect the boundaries of different languages.

Statement (2) is incorrect because on the basis of its report, the States Reorganisation Act was passed in 1956. This led to the creation of 14 states and 6 Union Territories.

12 Match the lists with reference to creation of new states. *(Chap 1, Class-XII, New NCERT)*

List I	List II
A. Kerala	1. Punjab Reorganisation Act, 1966
B. Haryana	2. State Reorganisation Act, 1956
C. Chhattisgarh	3. 35th Constitutional Amendment Act, 1974
D. Sikkim	4. Constitutional Amendment Act, 2000

Codes

	A	B	C	D		A	B	C	D
(a)	3	4	1	2	(b)	1	2	3	4
(c)	2	1	4	3	(d)	4	3	1	2

***Ans.* (c)**

Exp. The correct matching is A-2, B-1, C-4, D-3.

Kerala was created by the State Reorganisation Act, 1956. It comprised Travancore and Cochin areas.

Haryana was carved out from the state of Punjab by the Punjab Reorganisation Act, 1966.

Chhattisgarh was formed by the Constitutional Amendment Act, 2000, by dividing Madhya Pradesh on 1st November, 2000.

Sikkim was first given the status of Associate State by the 35th Constitutional Amendment Act, 1974 while it was under the rule of Chogyal.

13 Consider the following statements and choose the correct code. *(Chap 7, Class-XI, New NCERT)*

Statement-I It is not easy to resolve the border disputes between states merely on the basis of linguistic majority.

Statement-II Though language is the basis of defining boundaries of the states, often border areas would have populations speaking more than one language.

Codes

(a) Both Statement-I and Statement-II are correct and Statement-II is the correct explanation for Statement-1.
(b) Both Statement-I and Statement-II are correct and Statement-II is not the correct explanation for Statements-I.
(c) Statement-I is correct but Statement-II is incorrect.
(d) Statement-I is incorrect but Statement-II is correct.

***Ans.* (a)**

Exp. Both Statement-I and Statement-II are correct and Statement-II is the correct explanation for Statement-I.

In border disputes, states have certain claims over territories belonging to neighbouring states. Though language is the basis of defining boundaries of the states, often border areas would have populations speaking more than one language.

So, it is not easy to resolve these disputes merely on the basis of linguistic majority.

14 Which of the following statements is incorrect regarding government's approach towards integration of Princely States? *(Chap 1, Class-XII, New NCERT)*

(a) The people of all the princely states want to become a part of the Indian union.
(b) The government was prepared to be flexible in giving autonomy to some regions.
(c) The integration and consolidation of the nation's territorial boundaries had taken paramount importance in the aftermath of partition, which brought the battle for territory demarcation into sharp focus.
(d) None of the above

***Ans.* (a)**

Exp. Statement (a) is incorrect regarding government's approach towards integration of Princely States. The people of most of the princely states wanted to become part of the Indian Union. There were some princely states which were refusing to join India in order to acquire independent statehood. While some were in tussle to choose between the two newly formed countries.

15 Consider the following statements about the integration of Hyderabad to India.

(Chap 1, Class-XII, New NCERT)
(Unit 7, Class-XII, Tamil Nadu Board)

1. The Nizam of Hyderabad wanted to join Pakistan.
2. He entered into the Standstill Agreement with Pakistan in November 1947.

Which of the statements given above is/are incorrect?

(a) Only 1 (b) Only 2
(c) Both 1 and 2 (d) Neither 1 nor 2

***Ans.* (c)**

Exp. Both the statements are incorrect as the integration of Hyderabad in India. Nizam wanted an independent status for Hyderabad.

He entered into the Standstill Agreement with India in November 1947, for a year, continuing all previous arrangements except for the stationing of Indian troops in the state. Claiming that it feared the establishment of a communist state in Hyderabad.

16 Consider the following statements about State's Reorganisation. *(Chap 14, Class-XII, Old NCERT)*

1. The States Reorganisation Commission was appointed to study the demand for organising states on the basis of language.
2. It recommended the principle of linguistic heterogeneity for reorganisation of states.

How many of the statements given above is/are correct?

(a) Only one (b) Only two
(c) All of the above (d) None of these

Ans. (a)

Exp. Only statement (1) is correct as the State Reorganisation Commission. It was constituted by the Government of India on 29th December, 1953. It was appointed to study the demands for organising states on language basis .

Statement (2) is incorrect because according to the Commission, linguistic minorities were denied an effective voice in the governance of their states. Commission, therefore, recommended the principle of linguistic homogeneity for reorganisation of states.

17 Consider the following statements regarding Fazl Ali Commission. *(Chap 1, Class XII, New NCERT)*

Statement-I The Fazl Ali Commission, appointed by Jawaharlal Nehru in 1953, proposed the reorganisation of the country into 16 states and three centrally administed areas.

Statement-II The government in response to the commissions recommendations enacted the States Reorganisation Act in 1956, dividing the country into 14 States and 6 Union Territories.

Which one of the following in respect of the above statements?

(a) Both Statement-I and Statement-II are correct and Statement-II is the correct explanation for Statement-I.
(b) Both Statement-I and Statement-II are correct and Statement-II is not the correct explanation for Statement-I.
(c) Statement-I is correct but Statement-II is incorrect.
(d) Statement-I is incorrect but Statement-II is correct.

Ans. (b)

Exp. Both the Statement-I and Statement-II are correct but Statement-II is not the correct explanation for Statement-I. The Fazl Ali Commission did propose the reorganisation of the country into 16 states and three centrally administered areas. However, the government, in response to the commission's recommendations, enacted the States Reorganisation Act in 1956, Union Territories, deviating from the commissions specific proposal.

18 Which of the following pairs is/are correctly matched? *(Chap 14, Class-XII, Old NCERT)*

New States		Parent States
1. Maharashtra	–	Bombay
2. Gujarat	–	Bombay
3. Punjab	–	Haryana

Codes

(a) Only 1
(b) 2 and 3
(c) 1 and 2
(d) 1, 2 and 3

Ans. (c)

Exp. Pairs (1) and (2) are correctly matched. The States Reorganisation Act created new boundaries for the state of Bombay, transferring some Kannada speaking areas to Mysore state and expanding the territories of Bombay to include Marathi-speaking Marathwada and Vidarbha, as well as Gujarati-speaking Saurashtra and Kutch.

Pair (3) is not correctly matched as Haryana was carved out of the former state of East Punjab on 1st November, 1966 on a linguistic basis.

19 With reference to creation of Constitutional Units, consider the following pairs. *(Chap 2, Class-X, New NCERT)*

1. Part - A States → West Bengal , Uttar Pradesh, Madhya Pradesh, Punjab and Bihar.
2. Part - B States → Mysore, Hyderabad, Jammu and Kashmir, Rajasthan and Saurashtra.
3. Part - C States → Patiala and East Punjab, Cochin, Indore and Gwalior.
4. Part - D States → Himachal Pradesh, Delhi, Kutch, Ajmer and Bilaspur.

How many of the pairs given above is/are not correctly matched?

(a) Only one (b) Only two (c) Only three (d) All of these

Ans. (b)

Exp. Only two pairs i.e., (3) and (4) are not correctly matched because Part-C States has a total of ten states including Himachal Pradesh, Delhi, Kutch, Ajmer, Bilaspur, Vindhya Pradesh, Bhopal, Tripura, Manipur and Coorg.

Part-D States has only one state. The extremely backward Andaman and the Nicobar Islands were constituted as a Part-D States.

20 Consider the following statements with reference to Kashmir issue. *(Unit 7, Class-XII, Tamil Nadu Board)*

Statement-I The 'Kashmir issue' is more than a border conflict between India and Pakistan. This problem involves both external and internal aspects.

Statement-II It involves the issue of Kashmiri identity known as Kashmiriyat .

Statement-III It concerns the people of Jammu and Kashmir's desire for political autonomy.

How many of the statements given above is/are correct?

(a) Only one (b) Only two
(c) All three (d) None of these

Ans. (c)

Exp. All the statements are correct regarding Kashmir issue. The 'Kashmir issue' has been regarded as a key point of contention between India and Pakistan. However, the state's political condition is multifacet. The 'Kashmir issue' is more than a border conflict between India and Pakistan. This problem involves both external and internal aspects. It involves the issue of Kashmiri identity known as Kashmiriyat. It concerns the people of Jammu and Kashmir's desire for political autonomy.

21 **Consider the following statements about the accession of Jammu and Kashmir.**
(Chap 8, Class-XII, New NCERT)

1. Maharaja Hari Singh of Kashmir wanted to join India.
2. In October 1947, Pakistan sent tribal infiltrators from its side to capture Kashmir.
3. Maharaja signed an 'Instrument of Accession' with the Government of India.
4. India agreed to grant it provisional autonomy under Article 371.

Which of the statements given above is/are incorrect?
(a) Only 1
(b) 1 and 3
(c) 1 and 4
(d) 1, 2 and 3

Ans. (c)

Exp. Statements (1) and (4) are incorrect about the accession of Jammu and Kashmir. Maharaja Hari Singh did not want to merge either with India or Pakistan but to have an independent status for his state.

When Sheikh Abdullah took over as the Prime Minister of the state in March 1948, India agreed to grant it provisional autonomy under the Article 370.

22 **Consider the following statements about North-East.**
(Chap 8, Class-XII, New NCERT)

1. Tripura, Manipur and Khasi Hills of Meghalaya were erstwhile Princely States which remained independent even after independence.
2. At the time of independence, the entire region except Mizoram comprised the state of Assam.

Which of the statements given above is/are correct?
(a) Only 1
(b) Only 2
(c) Both 1 and 2
(d) Neither 1 nor 2

Ans. (a)

Exp. Statement (1) is correct about North-East because Tripura, Manipur and Khasi Hills of Meghalaya were erstwhile Princely States which merged with India after independence in 1949.

Statement (2) is incorrect because at the time of independence, the entire region except Manipur and Tripura comprised the state of Assam.

23 **Which of the following statements is incorrect about Mizoram?** *(Chap 8, Class-XII, New NCERT)*

(a) After independence, the Mizo Hills area was made an autonomous district within Assam.
(b) The Mizos' anger led to the formation of the Mizo National Front (MNF) under the leadership of Laldenga.
(c) In 1966, the MNF started an armed campaign for independence.
(d) In 1985, a Peace Agreement was signed between Rajiv Gandhi and Laldenga which granted Mizoram full-fledged statehood.

Ans. (d)

Exp. Statement (d) is incorrect about Mizoram because in 1986 a Peace Agreement was signed between Rajiv Gandhi and Laldenga. As per this accord, Mizoram was granted full-fledged statehood with special powers and the MNF agreed to give up secessionist struggle. Laldenga took over as the Chief Minister. This accord proved a turning point in the history of Mizoram.

24 **Consider the following statements**
(Chap 1, Class-XII, New NCERT)

Statement-I The state of Nagaland was created by the State of Nagaland Act in 1952.

Statement-II It was carved out from the State of Sikkim.

Codes
(a) Both Statement-I and Statement-II are correct and Statement-II is the correct explanation for Statement-II.
(b) Both Statement-I and Statement-II are correct but Statement-II is not the correct explanation for Statement-I.
(c) Statement-I is correct but Statement-II is incorrect.
(d) Statement-I is incorrect but Statement-II is correct.

Ans. (c)

Exp. Statement-I is correct but Statement-II is incorrect. The state of Nagaland was created by the State of Nagaland Act in 1952. The state of Nagaland was carved out from the state of Assam not Sikkim. The Act provides the formation of the state of Nagaland as the 16th state in the Indian Union on 1st December, 1963. The bill passed by the Parliament received President's assent on the 4th September, 1962.

25 **Consider the following statements.**
(Chap 1, Class-XII, New NCERT)

Statement-I Chhattisgarh was formed by the Constitutional Amendment Act in 2000 by dividing Madhya Pradesh.

Statement-II Uttarakhand was also formed by the Constitutional Amendment Act in 2000 by dividing Uttar Pradesh.

Codes
(a) Both Statement-I and Statement-II are correct and Statement-II is the correct explanation for Statement-II.
(b) Both Statement-I and Statement-II are correct but Statement-II is not the correct explanation for Statements-I.
(c) Statement-I is correct but Statement-II is incorrect.
(d) Statement-I is incorrect but Statement-II is correct.

Ans. (a)

Exp. Both Statement-I and Statement-II are correct and Statement-II is the correct explanation for Statement-I. Chhattisgarh was formed by the Constitutional Amendment Act in 2000 by dividing Madhya Pradesh. Uttarakhand was indeed formed by the Constitutional Amendmend Act in 2000 by dividing Uttar Pradesh.

Chapter 05

Citizenship

Citizenship

Meaning and Provision

Meaning of Citizenship

- Widely accepted definition is full and equal membership in political community
- Definition given by Sociologist **TH Marshal**

Provisions for Citizenship

- Person Domiciled in India (Article-5)
- Person Migrated from Pakistan (Article-6)
- Person Migrated to Pakistan but Later Returned to India (Article-7)
- Person of Indian Origin Residing Outside India (Article-8)

Constitutional Provisions for Citizenship

- **Article-5** Citizenship was given to all residents and people born in India
- **Article-6** Grants citizenship to individuals Migrating from Pakistan to India or those who migrated before 19th July, 1948
- **Article-7** Certain migrants of Pakistan-migrated after 1st March, 1947
- **Article-8** Grants citizenship to certain persons of Indian origin residing outside India
- **Article-9** Person acquiring foreign citizenship voluntarily are not Indian citizens
- **Article-10** Addresses continuity of citizenship

Acquisition and Loss

Acquisition and Loss of Indian Citizenship

By Birth

- Every person born in India : on or after 26th January, 1950
- Born between 1st July and 2nd December, 2004
- Born on or after 3rd December, 2004

By Registration

- Must have lived in India for 7 years
- People of India origin residing outside undivided India are eligible

By Descent

- Citizen by descent if father was Indian citizen by birth
- Citizen if either parent was Indian citizen by birth

By Naturalisation

- Requires 12 years of ordinary residency in India

By Incorporation of Territory

- Allows Central Government to specify citizens; Persons connected to the territory to become citizens as per the specified date in order

Renunciation of Citizenship

- Declaration registered by prescribed authority

Termination

- If an Indian citizen voluntarily acquires the citizenship of another country

Deprivation

- If citizen shows disloyalty to Constitution of India
- Citizen has been ordinarily resident out of India for seven years continuously

NRI, PIO and OCI

Overseas Indians

Non-Resident Indian (NRI)

- If an Indian citizen does not reside in India for a specified period
- Non-residents, as per the Income Tax Act, are treated as NRIs for tax purposes

Person of Indian Origin (PIO)

- Foreign citizen with past Indian passport or Indian-born ancestry
- Excludes-Pakistan, Afghanistan, China, etc.
- Criteria: Held Indian passport, parents/grandparents not born in India

Overseas Citizen of India (OCI)

- Former Indian passport holder
- Parent, grandparent or great-grand parent born in and a permanent resident of India, without being a citizen of specified countries

National Population Register (NPR)

- NPR is a record of usual residents of the country
- prepared under provisions of the Citizenship Act, 1955 and the Citizenship (Registration of Citizens and Issue of National Identity Cards) Rules, 2003

National Register of Citizen (NRC)

- The register was first prepared and its updation process was put into action after the 1951 Census of India.
- The NRC is now being updated in Assam

SOURCE *Old NCERT Class VII* (Citizenship), *Old NCERT Class IX & X* (Society and Citizens), *Old NCERT Class XI* (Citizenship),

1 Consider the following statements.
(Chap 1, Class-IX & X, Old NCERT)

1. The idea of citizenship means that not only the government has some claims on the citizens but the citizens also have claims on the government.
2. It is closely related to the participation of people in government.
3. TH Marshall defined citizenship and social class in 1950.

How many of the statements given above is/are correct?

(a) Only one (b) Only two
(c) All three (d) None of these

Ans. *(c)*

Exp. All three statements i.e., (1), (2) and (3) are correct. The state has to make policies to ensure equality among citizens and meet the different needs and claims of people while making policies. The idea of citizenship means that not only the government has some claims on the citizens but the citizens also have claims on the government.

Also, citizenship is closely associated with participation of people in government and implies full and equal membership of a political community.

The definition of citizenship was given by the English Sociologist TH Marshall in his work 'citizenship and social class' written in the year 1950.

2 With respect to citizens of a country, consider the following statements. *(Chap1, Class-IX, Old NCERT)*

1. One essential condition for a democratic state is that citizens must participate in the governing process.
2. The quality of democracy improves if citizens participate in its activities.
3. Every inhabitant of the country become a citizen by default.
4. A citizen is one who is a member of the state and who participates in the process of government.

How many of the statements given above is/are incorrect?

(a) Only one (b) Only two
(c) Only three (d) None of these

Ans. *(a)*

Exp. Only one statement i.e., (3) is incorrect because citizens of a country participate in the governing process, in the process of government formation. The quality of democracy also gets better when citizens take part in different activities. The Constitution provides some criteria on the basis of which citizenship is granted, so every inhabitant of the country does not become a citizen by default.

3 With reference to components of citizenship, consider the following statements.
(Chap 6, Class-XI, New NCERT)

1. Civil citizenship is for individual freedoms and are institutionalised in the law courts.
2. Political citizenship guarantees the right to participate in the exercise of political power in the community, either by voting or by holding political office.
3. Social citizenship is the right to vote and right to equality.

How many of the statements given above is/are incorrect?

(a) Only one (b) Only two
(c) All three (d) None of these

Ans. *(a)*

Exp. Only one statement i.e., (3) is incorrect because social citizenship is the right to participate in an appropriate standard of living, this right is embodied in the welfare and educational system of modern societies.

4 Which one of the following is a feature of Indian citizenship? *(Chap 1, Class-IX & X, Old NCERT)*
(Unit 1, Class-X, Tamil Nadu Board) (UPPSC Pre 2015)

(a) Dual citizenship of the state and the union
(b) Single citizenship of a state
(c) Single citizenship of whole of India
(d) Dual citizenship of India and another country

Ans. *(c)*

Exp. Statement (c) is correct with reference to the feature of Indian citizenship. The provisions for citizenship is mentioned in Part II of Indian Constitution.

It provides for single citizenship of whole of India. It means a citizen of a particular state is also the citizen of whole of India.

5 Consider the following statements, with reference to constitutional provisions. *(Chap 6, Class-XI, New NCERT)*

Statement-I Article 6 provides citizenship to individuals who migrated form Pakistan before 19th July, 1948.

Statement-II This provision aims to adress the citizenship status of those who moved form Pakistan to India during a specific period.

Which one of the following is correct code in respect of the above statement?

(a) Both Statement-I and Statement-II are correct and Statement-II is the correct explanation for Statements-I.
(b) Both Statement-I and Statement-II are correct and Statement-II is not the correct explanation for Statements-I.
(c) Statement-I is correct but Statement-II is incorrect.
(d) Statement-I is incorrect but Statement-II is correct.

Ans. *(a)*

Exp. Both Statements-I and Statement-II are correct and Statement-II is the correct explanation for Statement-I. Article 6 provides citizenship to certain persons who have migrated to India from Pakistan or anyone who migrated to India before 19th July, 1948. Such persons also would automatically become and Indian citizen, if either of his parents or grandparent was born in India.

6 **With reference to constitutional provisions for citizenship, consider the following pairs.**
(Chap 11, Class-VII, Old NCERT)

	Articles	Statements
1.	Article 5 –	Citizenship was granted to all persons who were born and raised in India. Even people who were domiciled in India.
2.	Article 6 –	Includes migrants who returned to India after March, 1947 with resettlement permits.
3.	Article 7 –	Grants citizenship to migrants from Pakistan before 1948 with parents or grandparets born in India.
4.	Article 8 –	Allows persons of Indian origin residing abroad to register for citizenship.

How many of the pairs given above is/are correctly matched?
(a) Only one (b) Only two (c) All four (d) None of these

Ans. (b)

Exp. Only two pairs i.e., (1) and (4) are correctly matched. Article 5 provides citizenship at the commencement of the Constitution, based on domicile and birth in India or having one parent born in India. Article 8 allows persons of Indian origin residing abroad with Indian ancestry to register as citizen.
Pairs (2) and (3) are not correctly matched because Article 6 grants citizenship to those who migrated from Pakistan before 1948 with parents or grandparents born in India. Article 7 focuses on migrants who returned to India after March 1947 with resettlement permits.

7 **Which of the following are the methods for acquiring citizenship in India?**
(Chap 6, Class-XI, New NCERT)

1. Birth
2. Descent
3. Naturalisation
4. Registration

Select the correct answer from the codes given below.
(a) 1, 2 and 3 (b) 1, 2, 3 and 4 (c) 1 and 4 (d) 1, 2 and 4

Ans. (b)

Exp. All the given methods are correct for acquiring citizenship in India. The Indian Constitution adopted an essentially democratic and inclusive notion of citizenship. In India, citizenship can be acquired by birth, descent, registration, naturalisation or inclusion of territory.

8 **A citizen of India will lose his or her citizenship of he or she** *(Chap 1, Class-IX & X, Old NCERT) (UPPSC Mains 2017)*

1. renounces India citizenship.
2. voluntarily acquires the citizenship of another country.
3. marries a citizen of another country.
4. criticises the government.

Which of the statements given above is/are correct?
(a) 1, 2 and 3 (b) 2, 3 and 4 (c) 1 and 2 (d) 1 and 4

Ans. (c)

Exp. Statements (1) and (2) are correct with respect to the loss of citizenship of India. The Citizenship Act, 1955 lays the three modes by which an Indian citizen may his citizenship. These are
If he or she renounces Indian citizenship.
If he or she voluntarily acquires the citizenship of another country as Indian Constitution does not provide for dual citizenship.
If he or she acquires the citizenship by fraud, false representation, concealment of material fact.
Statement (3) and (4) are incorrect. Marrying a citizen of another country and criticising the government are not the grounds of losing citizenship in India.

9 **Consider the following statements.**
(Chap 6, Class-XI, New NCERT)

Statement-I Article 9 of the Constitution prohibits individual from being citizens of India if they voluntarily acquire the citizenship of a foreign state.

Statement-II This provision specifies that no person shall be a citizen of India by virtue of Article 5, or be deemed a citizen by virtue of Article 6 or Article 8 if they have voluntarily acquired the citizenship of any Foreign state.

Which one of the following is correct code in respect of the above statements?
(a) Both Statement-I and Statement-II are correct and Statement-II is the correct explanation for Statement-I.
(b) Both Statement-I and Statement-II are correct Statement-II is not the correct explanation for Statement-I.
(c) Statement-I is correct but Statement-II is incorrect.
(d) Statement-I is incorrect but Statement-II is correct.

Ans. (a)

Exp. Both Statement-I and Statement-II are correct and Statement-II is the correct explanation for Statement-I. Article 9 states that persons voluntarily acquiring citizenship of a foreign state will be citizens of India. No persons shall be a citizen of India by virtue of Article 5 or be a citizen of India by virtue of Article 6 or Article 8, if he has voluntarily acquired the citizenship of any Foreign state.

10 **Which of the following rights conferred by the Constitution of India is also available to non-citizens?** *(Chap 6, Class-XI, New NCERT)*
(Unit 1, Class-X, Tamil Nadu Board) (JPSC Pre 2011)

(a) Right to Constitutional Remedies
(b) Freedom of Speech
(c) Freedom to Move or Settle in Any Part of the Country
(d) Freedom to Acquire Property

Ans. (a)

Exp. The Right to Constitutional Remedies is a right conferred by the Constitution of India which is available to both citizens of India and non-citizens (foreigners). But the Right to Freedom of Speech, Freedom to Move or Settle in Any Part of the Country and Freedom to Acquire Property are available only to the citizens of India.

Chapter 06

Fundamental Rights

Fundamental Rights

Basics of Fundamental Rights

- **Fundamental Rights in Indian Constitution**
  - Part III
  - Borrowed from American Constitution
  - Aims to protect individual dignity
- **Importance of Fundamental Rights**
  - Essential for preserving human liberty
  - Developing human personality; Promoting an effective social and democratic life
- **Historical Background of Fundamental Rights**
  - First developed in Britain
  - French Constitution granted constitutional status to Fundamental Rights
  - In 1791, American Constitution incorporated bill of Rights
- **Historical Background of Fundamental Rights in India**
  - 1928 : All parties conference support Fundamental Rights
  - 1931 : At Karanchi sessions to individual Rights
  - 1944-45 : Sapru Committee
  - 1947 : Constituent Assembly forms Advisory Committee on Minorities and Fundamental Rights
- **Amendability of Fundamental Rights**
  - Article 13 (4) Empowers Parliament to amend part III of the Constitution
- **Salient Features of Fundamental Rights**
  - Integral Part of the Constitution
  - Lack of Social and Economic Rights
  - Fundamental Rights are Justiciable
  - Provision for the suspension of Rights

Classification of Fundamental Rights

- **Right to Equality** (Articles 14-18)
  - Equality before law (Article 14)
  - Prohibition of Discrimination on Certain Grounds (Article 15)
  - Equality of Opportunity in Matters of Public Employment (Article 16)
  - Abolition of Untouchability (Article 17)
  - Abolition of Titles (Article 18)
- **Right to Freedom** (Article 19-22)
  - Right to Freedom of Speech and Expression (Article 19)
  - Protection in Respect of Conviction for Offences (Article 20)
  - Protection of Life and Personal Liberty (Article 21)
  - Right to Education (Article 21 A)
  - Protection Against Arrest and Detention in Certain Cases (Article 22)
- **Rights Against Exploitation** (Article 23-24)
  - Prohibition of Traffic in Human Beings and Forced Labour (Article 23)
  - Prohibition of Employment of Children in Factories (Article 24)
- **Rights to Freedom of Religion** (Articles 25-28)
  - Freedom of Conscience and Free Profession, Practice and Propagation of Religion (Article 25)
  - Right to Manage Religious Affairs (Article 26)
  - Freedom from Payment of Taxes for Promotion of Any Particular Religion (Article 27)
  - Freedom from Attending Religious Instruction (Article 28)
- **Cultural and Educational Rights** (Article 29-30)
  - Protection of Interest of Minorities (Article 29)
  - Right of Minorities to Establish and Administer Educational Institutions (Article 30)
- **Right to Constitutional Remedies** (Article 32)
  - Writ of Habeas Corpus
  - Writ of Mandamus
  - Writ of Prohibition
  - Writ of Certiorari
  - Writ of Quo Warranto
- **Fundamental Rights : Citizen v/s Non-Citizen**
  - Fundamental Rights like Article 21, apply both citizens and foreigners
  - Article 19 are exclusive to Indian citizens
- **Other Important Aspects of Fundamental Rights**
  - Suspension of Fundamental Rights
  - Article 20 and 21 never suspended

SOURCE **Old NCERT Class VII** *(Our Fundamental Rights)*, **New NCERT Class IX** *(Constitutional Rights)*, **Old NCERT Class IX & X** *(Fundamental Rights and Directive Principles of State Policy)*, **New NCERT Class XI** *(Fundamental Rights, Rights in the Indian Constitution)*, **Old NCERT Class XI** *(Fundamental Rights, Fundamental Duties and Directive Principles of State Policy)*, **Old NCERT Class XII** *(Rights and Duties : Meaning and Relationship)*

1 With respect to the Fundamental Rights, consider the following statements. *(Chap 2, Class-XI, New NCERT)*

1. Right to Property was deleted from the list of Fundamental Rights by the 44th Amendment Act, 1978.
2. Right to Elementary Education is available to the citizens of India only.
3. Article 19 protects the citizen's right to move in and out of the country.

Which of the statements given above is/are incorrect?

(a) 1 and 2 (b) 2 and 3 (c) 1 and 3 (d) All of these

Ans. *(b)*

Exp. Statements (2) and (3) are incorrect with respect to Fundamental Rights because Right to Elementary Education is available to both citizens as well as foreigners. Article 19 protects the citizen's right to move inside the country whereas Article 21 protects the right to move out of the country and the right to come back to the country.

2 Consider the following statements with respect to Fundamental Rights. *(Chap 7, Class-XII, Old NCERT)* *(Chap 6, Module-2, NIOS)*

1. They are concessions granted by the society to enable human beings to realise their claims.
2. These are the media through which an individual can promote the good of society as his own good.

Which of the statements given above is/are incorrect?

(a) Only 1 (b) Only 2
(c) Both 1 and 2 (d) Neither 1 nor 2

Ans. *(d)*

Exp. Neither statement (1) nor (2) is incorrect.
Fundamental Rights are indeed entitlement or claims on the society to which we are entitled by virtue of being a citizen, an individual or simply a human being.
They are treated as concessions granted by the society to enable human beings to realise their claims. These Rights also give an opportunity to individuals for becoming the best version of themselves. They benefit the constituent members of the society which leads to the betterment of the whole society. In this way, by helping oneself, an individual helps society.

3 According to Dr. Ambedkar "the objective of Fundamental Rights is two-fold". Which of the following statements are correct regarding objectives of Fundamental Rights? *(Chap 4, Class-VII, Old NCERT)*

1. The primary goal is for every citizen to be able to assert his or her rights.
2. These rights must be enforceable by any authority with the capacity to create laws.

Codes

(a) Only 1 (b) Only 2
(c) Both 1 and 2 (d) Neither 1 nor 2

Ans. *(c)*

Exp. Both the statements (1) and (2) are correct regarding objective of Fundamental Rights. Dr Ambedkar has said about Fundamental Rights, that their object is two-fold. The first objective is that every citizen must be in a position to claim those rights. Secondly, these rights must be binding upon every authority that has got the power to make laws.

4 Consider the following differences between Ordinary Rights and Fundamental Rights. *(Chap 2, Class-XI, New NCERT)*

1. While ordinary legal rights are protected and enforced by ordinary law, Fundamental Rights are protected and guaranteed by the Constitution of the country.
2. Ordinary rights may be changed by the legislature by ordinary process of law-making, but a Fundamental Right may only be changed by amending the Constitution itself.

Which of the statements given above is/are correct?

(a) Only 1 (b) Only 2
(c) Both 1 and 2 (d) Neither 1 nor 2

Ans. *(c)*

Exp. Both the statements are correct regarding differences between Ordinary Rights and Fundamental Rights.
Ordinary legal rights are protected by the Constitutional courts. The remedy for the violation of ordinary legal rights can be sought in an ordinary court. They can be changed or molded by an ordinary legislative procedure. For example, the Right to Vote is not a Fundamental Right.
Fundamental Rights are mentioned in the Constitutional provisions and hence, the remedy for their infringement can be sought directly in the Supreme Court (Article 32) or High Court (Article 226). They can be amended (Article 368) without touching upon the basic structure of the Constitution.

5 Consider the following statements in respect of fundamental duties. *(Chap 7, Class-XII, Old NCERT)*

Statement-I Right of one involves a duty on the part of others to respect that right.

Statement-II Society in which people careless for their own duties and more for their rights sooner or later disintegrates.

Which of the statements given above is/are correct?

(a) Both Statement-I and Statement-II are correct and Statement-II is the correct explanation for Statement-I.
(b) Both Statement-I and Statement-II are correct and Statement-II is not the correct explanation for Statement-I.
(c) Statement-I is correct but Statement-II is incorrect.
(d) Statement-I is incorrect but Statement-II is correct.

Ans. *(a)*

Exp. Both Statement-I and Statement-II are correct and Statement-II is the correct explanation for Statement-I. Right and duties are closely related and cannot be separated from each other. With every right, there is a corresponding duty.
The state protects all the citizens of the country and citizens perform their duty with respect to their country. A society in which people are careless for their own duties and more for their rights, sooner or later disintegrates.

6 Consider the following statements with reference to rights and Fundamental Rights. *(Chap 4, Class-XI, Old NCERT)*

1. Rights have been described as those claims of an individual that are necessary for the development of his own self and recognised by society or state.
2. Fundamental Rights are those rights of an individual that are enforceable through courts of law.
3. Rights are only those claims which are recognised as such by society and enforced by the state.

Which of the statements given above is/are correct?
(a) Only 1 (b) Only 2
(c) 1, 2 and 3 (d) 2 and 3

Ans. (c)
Exp. All the given statements are correct.
The rights of individuals are necessary component of one's personality and are required for overall development of an individual.
Rights are always recognised by society for their operation. For example, the Right to Slave as a Property was once a recognised right but that is not the case now as it has been abolished and no longer is a right.
Fundamental Rights are mentioned in the Constitution of a country and thus are protected by courts having original jurisdiction for their enforcement.
Rights are called claims as they always emerge from others that is why it is necessary that they are recognised by society and enforced by the state to maintain parity among individuals.

7 Consider the following statements with reference to Bill of Rights in the South African Constitution. *(Chap 2, Class-XI, New NCERT)*

1. South African Constitution was drafted and promulgated at a time when South Africa was still on the verge of civil conflict following the breakdown of the apartheid administration.
2. The South African Constitution was inaugurated in December, 1998.
3. The South African Constitution says that its 'Bill of Rights' is a cornerstone of democracy in South Africa.
4. Right to healthy environment and right to protection of environment, right to dignity and right to privacy are some of the rights included in its Constitution.

How many of the statements given above is/are not correct?
(a) Only one (b) Only two (c) Only three (d) All of these

Ans. (a)
Exp. Only one statement i.e., (2) is not correct regarding Bill of Rights in South African Constitution because the South African Constitution was inaugurated in December, 1996.

8 With reference to Fundamental Rights, consider the following statements. *(Chap 2, Class-XI, New NCERT)*

1. Fundamental Right are absolute in nature.
2. Government can put reasonable restrictions on the exercise of our Fundamental Rights.
3. It aims at establishing a government of laws and not of men.

How many of the statements given above is/are correct?
(a) Only one (b) Only two
(c) All three (d) None of these

Ans. (b)
Exp. Only two statements i.e., (2) and (3) are correct. Government can put reasonable restrictions on the exercise of our Fundamental Rights. Reasonable restrictions are mentioned in the constitutional provisions like security of the state, friendly relations with the foreign states, public order, decency, morality, sovereignty and integrity of India. Also, courts decide from time to time about the power of reasonable restrictions put by the Executive or the Legislature and it means they prevent the establishment of an authoritarian and despotic rule in the country and a government of laws and not of men.
Statement (1) is incorrect because Fundamental Rights are not absolute but qualified. It implies that the state can curtail or put reasonable restrictions in case of emergency like war, external and internal emergency.

9 Which of the following statements is/are correct regarding Bill of Rights? *(Chap 2, Class-XI, New NCERT)*

1. The practice of listing the rights of the citizens in the Constitution is known as the Bill of Rights.
2. A Bill of Rights prohibits the government from thus acting against the rights of the individuals and ensures a remedy in case there is violation of these rights.

Codes
(a) Only 1 (b) Only 2
(c) Both 1 and 2 (d) Neither 1 nor 2

Ans. (c)
Exp. Both the statements (1) and (2) are correct regarding Bill of Rights.
Bill of Rights summarises the powers and duties of state and people creating a balance between the state and society. It also provides for remedies in case of violation of Fundamental Rights as provided under Article 32 of the Indian Constitution.

10 Article 13 states that any law that takes away or abridges any of the Fundamental Rights would be void. Which of the following Constitutional Amendment Act provided that restrictions imposed by Article 13 would not apply to the Constitution (Amendment) Act? *(Chap 4, Class-XI, Old NCERT)*

(a) 25th Amendment Act, 1971
(b) 24th Amendment Act, 1971
(c) 42nd Amendment Act, 1976
(d) None of the above

Ans. *(b)*

Exp. 24th Amendment Act, 1971 provided that restrict imposed by Article 13 would not apply to the Constitution (Amendment) Act.

It affirmed the power of Parliament to amend any part of the Constitution including Fundamental Rights by amending Articles 13 and 368. It also made it compulsory for the President to give his assent to a Constitutional Amendment Bill.

Under Keshvananda Bharati Act, Supreme Court proposed the doctrine of Basic Structure which curtails the powers given to Parliament by 24th Amendment Act.

11 Match the following lists correctly and choose the correct code. *(Chap 4, Class-XI, Old NCERT)*

List I (Article)	List II (Related to)
A. Article 34	1. Prohibition of Untouchability
B. Article 13	2. Martial Law
C. Article 17	3. Definition of Law
D. Article 12	4. Definition of State

Codes

	A	B	C	D
(a)	3	2	1	4
(b)	2	3	1	4
(c)	1	3	4	2
(d)	4	1	3	2

Ans. *(b)*

Exp. The correct matching is A-2, B-3, C-1, D-4.

Article 34 It provides for the restrictions on Fundamental Rights while martial law is in force in any area within the territory of India.

Article 13 It defines law as any ordinance, order, bye-law, rule, regulation, notification, custom, or usages having in the territory of India the force of law; laws in force includes laws passed or made by Legislature or other competent authority in the territory of India.

Article 17 It states abolition of untouchability and rendered its practice in any form is forbidden.

Article 12 It defines the term states which is mentioned in Fundamental Rights under Articles 13-32.

12 B R Ambedkar termed Article 32 of the Indian Constitution as the "Heart and Soul of the Indian Constitution". Which one of the following Fundamental Rights it contains? *(Chap 2, Class-XI, New NCERT) (IAS Pre 2002)*

(a) Right to Freedom
(b) Right to Constitutional Remedies
(c) Right to Elementary Education
(d) Right to Freedom of Religion

Ans. *(b)*

Exp. Article 32 contains Right to Constitutional Remedies. BR Ambedkar termed Article 32 of the Indian Constitution as the "Heart and Soul of the Indian Constitution". It is so because this right gives citizens the right to approach a High Court or the Supreme Court to get any of the Fundamental Rights restored in case of their violation. Supreme Court and High Courts can issue orders and give directives to the government for the enforcement of the rights.

13 Consider the following pairs. *(Chap 2, Class-XI, New NCERT)*

1. Article 19(4) - Sovereignty and Integrity
2. Article 19(3) - Public order
3. Article 19(6) - Protection of Scheduled Tribles
4. Article 19(5) - Public Interest

How many of the pairs given above is/are not correctly matched?

(a) Only one
(b) Only two
(c) All four
(d) Only three

Ans. *(b)*

Exp. Only two pairs i.e., (3) and (4) are incorrectly matched because Article 19(6) provides that the government may impose restrictions upon the freedom to practice any profession in the interest of the general public and Article 19(5) grants the government the power to impose reasonable restrictions upon the freedom to reside or settle in any part of the territory of India in the interest general public or for the protection of the interests of any Scheduled Tribe.

Pairs (1) and (2) are correctly matched. Article 19(4) states that the government may impose reasonable restrictions upon the freedom to form associations and unions in the interest of sovereignty and integrity of India, public order and morality.

14 Consider the following statements with reference to no one can be compelled to sing the National Anthem since *(Chap 2, Class-XI, New NCERT) (IAS Pre 1996)*

1. it will be violative of the right to freedom of speech and expression.
2. it will be violative of the right to freedom of conscience, practice and propagation of religion.
3. there is no legal provision obliging anyone to sing the National Anthem.

Select the correct answer by using the codes given below.
(a) 1 and 2 (b) 2 and 3 (c) 1, 2 and 3 (d) None of these

Ans. (c)

Exp. All the statements are correct.

In case of Bijoe Emmanvel v/s State of Kerala (1986), the Supreme Court hold that the act of not singing the National Anthem doesn't amount to a disrespect of the nation and is protected under the right to freedom of speech and expression.

Tharoor v/s Uo I (2018), the Supreme Court Meiterated that the right to not sing the National Anthem is protected under right to freedom of conscience.

The Supreme Court case Bijoe Emmanvel v/s State of Kerala (1986), stated that there is no enforceable duty on citizens to sing the National Anthem.

15 With reference to the following rights have not been conferred under Article 20 of Right to Freedom, consider the following statements.
(Chap 4, Class-XI, Old NCERT)

1. No person would be punished for the same offence more than once.
2. No one can be convicted for an act that was not an offence at the time of its commission.
3. No one can be forced to give witness against his own self.
4. No one can be punished except for violation of law.

Which of the statements given above is/are not correct?
(a) Only 1 (b) Only 2 (c) 1, 2 and 3 (d) Only 4

Ans. (d)

Exp. Statement (4) is not correct because no one can be punished except for the violation of law has not been conferred under Article 20 of Right to Freedom.

Statements (1), (2) and (3) are correct as Article 20 provides that no one can be convicted for an act that was not an offence at the time of its commission. It further provides that no one can be given punishment greater than what was provided in law prevalent at the time of its commission.

Article 20 further provides that no one can be prosecuted and punished for an offence more than once and no one can be forced to witness against oneself.

16 Right to Privacy is protected as an intrinsic part of Right to Life and Personal Liberty. Which of the following in the Constitution of India correctly and appropriately imply the above statement?
(Chap 2, Class-XI, New NCERT)

(a) Article 14 and the provisions under the 42nd Amendment to the Constitution.
(b) Article 17 and the Directive Principles of State Policy in Part IV.
(c) Article 21 and the freedoms guaranteed in Part III.
(d) Article 24 and the provisions under the 44th Amendment to the Constitution.

Ans. (c)

Exp. Right to Privacy is protected as an intrinsic part of Right to Life and Personal Liberty mentioned under Article 21 and the freedoms guaranteed in Part III of the Indian Constitution. In the case of Justice KS Puttaswamy (Retd) vs Union of India, Right to Privacy has been declared as Fundamental Right.

17 Which of the following Human Right/ Human Rights under 'Universal Declaration of Human Rights'? *(Chap 2, Class-XI, New NCERT) (IAS Pre 2011)*

1. Right to education
2. Right to equal access to public service
3. Right to food

Select the correct answer using the codes given below.
(a) Only 1 (b) 1 and 2 (c) Only 3 (d) 1, 2 and 3

Ans. (d)

Exp. All the given Human Rights are correct with reference to the Universal Declaration of Human Rights.

Article 26(1) says everyone has the right to education. Education shall be free, at least in the elementary and fundamental stages. Article 21(2) says everyone has the right of equal access to public service in his country.

Article 25 says everyone has the right to a standard of living adequate for the health and well-being of himself and of his family, including food, clothing, housing and medical care and necessary social services.

18 Consider the following statements.
(Chap 4, Class-XI, Old NCERT) (Unit 1, Class-XI, Tamil Nadu Board)

1. As per the Right to Education (RTE) Act, to be eligible for appointment as a teacher in a state, a person would be required to possess the minimum qualification laid down by the concerned State Council of Teacher Education.
2. As per the RTE Act, for teaching primary classes, a candidate is required to pass a Teacher Eligibility Test conducted in accordance with the National Council of Teacher Education guidelines.
3. In India, more than 90% of teacher's education institutions are directly under the State Government.

Which of the statements given above is/are correct?
(a) 1 and 2 (b) Only 2 (c) 1 and 3 (d) Only 3

Ans. (b)

Exp. Statement (2) is correct as per the RTE Act. It is mandatory that only those people may be appointed as teachers who are able to clear Teacher Eligibility Test. It provides for appointment of appropriately trained as teachers, i.e., teachers with the requisite entry and academic qualifications. It also provides prohibition of deployment of teachers for non-educational work.

Statements (1) and (3) is incorrect because in the Section 23 of the RTE Act (2009), the NCTE has laid down the minimum qualifications for a person to be eligible for appointment as a teacher.

More than 90% are private teacher education institutions not under the State Government.

19 As per the judgement of Supreme Court in Maneka Gandhi vs Union of India, which of the following rights also includes the right to live with human dignity, free from exploitation?

(Chap 2, Class-XI, New NCERT) (Chap 6, Module-2, NIOS)

(a) Right to Freedom of Religion
(b) Right to Life
(c) Right to Freedom of Expression
(d) Right against Exploitation

Ans. *(b)*

Exp. In Maneka Gandhi vs Union of India, the Supreme Court held that Right to Life (Article 21) also includes the right to live with human dignity. It is to the individual who can enjoy and nurture his life to the fullest possible extent.

20 As per Article 22, which of the following rights is not available to a person detained under punitive detention? *(Chap 4, Class-XI, Old NCERT)*

(a) He should be informed, as soon as may be, of the grounds for his arrest.
(b) He should be allowed to consult and to be defended by a legal practitioner of his choice.
(c) He can be retained ın detention beyond three months without the Advisory Board approves it.
(d) He should be produced before the nearest magistrate within a period of 24 hours of such an arrest.

Ans. *(c)*

Exp. As per Article 22, right mentioned in statement (c) is not available to a person detained under punitive detention. As per Article 22(4), a person under preventive detention cannot be detained beyond three months unless an Advisory Board consisting of persons who are qualified to be appointed as judges of a High Court has reported before the expiration of the said period of three months that there is in its opinion sufficient cause for such detention.

21 Consider the following statements.

(Chap 5, Class-IX, New NCERT)

1. Begar is a practice where the worker is forced to render service to the 'master' free of charge or at a nominal remuneration.
2. When this practice takes place on a life-long basis, it is called the practice of bonded labour.

Which of the statements given above is/are correct?

(a) Only 1 (b) Only 2
(c) Both 1 and 2 (d) Neither 1 nor 2

Ans. *(c)*

Exp. Both the statements (1) and (2) are correct as Begar (also known as Veth). It was a system of forced labour practiced in pre-independence India, in which members of populace were compelled to perform unpaid work for the government.

As part of 'Begar', the peasants and low-caste people were forced to supply water to the ruler's family; construct buildings, roads, and dams; and carry dead and wounded soldiers.

22 With child labour being made illegal and Right to Education becoming a Fundamental Right for children, this right against exploitation has become more meaningful. Which of the following pairs of Articles provide for Right to Education and Prohibition of Child Labour respectively?

(Chap 2, Class-XI, New NCERT) (UPPSC Mains 2009)

(a) Article 14 and 19 (b) Article 21(A) and 24
(c) Article 21(A) and 23 (d) Article 23 and 24

Ans. *(b)*

Exp. Article 21(A) and Article 24 provide for Right to Education and Prohibition of child labour respectively. The Constitution (Eighty-sixth Amendment) Act, 2002 inserted Article 21(A) in the Constitution of India to provide free and compulsory education of all children in the age group of six to fourteen years as a Fundamental Right in such a manner as the State may, by law, determine.

Article 24 of the Indian Constitution prohibit the employment of children below the age of fourteen years in factories, mines or any other hazardous employment. This Article is for the welfare of the children and ensures a safe and healthy life of children.

23 Which of the following pairs is/are incorrectly matched? *(Chap 4, Class-XI, Old NCERT) (UPPSC Mains 2015)*

	List I (Articles)		List II (Subject Matter)
(a)	Article 25	–	Freedom of conscience and free profession, practice, and propagation of religion.
(b)	Article 26	–	Freedom to manage religious affairs.
(c)	Article 27	–	Freedom as to payment of fees for promotion of any particular religion.
(d)	Article 28	–	Freedom to attend religious instruction or worship in certain educational institutions.

Ans. *(c)*

Exp. Pair (c) is incorrectly matched. Article 27 provides that no person shall be compelled to pay any taxes, the proceeds of which are specifically appropriated in payment of expenses for the promotion or maintenance of any particular religion or religious denomination.

24 Consider the following statements with respect to Article 25. *(Chap 4, Class-XI, Old NCERT) (Unit 1, Class-XII, Tamil Nadu Board)*

1. According to this Article, everyone is free to follow his own conscience and follow and practice any religion of his own choice.
2. The state can also impose restrictions on this right on grounds of public order, morality and health.
3. It guarantees freedom of conscience, freedom to profess, practice and propagate any religion.

Which of the statements given above is/are correct?

(a) Only 1 (b) Only 2
(c) 1, 2 and 3 (d) None of these

Ans. *(c)*

Exp. All the given statements (1), (2) and (3) are correct with respect to Article 25 because it guarantees the freedom of conscience, freedom to profess, practice and propagate religion to all citizens.

In other words, it provides that everyone is free to follow his own conscience and follow and practice any religion of his own choice. The state can also impose restrictions on this right on grounds of public order, morality and health.

It also guarantees freedom of conscience, freedom to profess, practice and propagate any religion. Reasonable restrictions to this freedom are religious liberties to public order, morality and health.

25 Which of the following statements is incorrect about the Right to Freedom of Religion?

(Chap 4, Class-XI, Old NCERT)

(a) 'The State' is empowered to throw open the Hindu religious institutions of public character to all classes and sections of Hindus.

(b) No religious instruction can be provided in any educational institution that is maintained wholly out of the 'State' funds.

(c) These rights aim at giving Indian polity a secular character.

(d) The State cannot regulate the economic, financial, political or other secular activity associated with religious practice.

Ans. *(d)*

Exp. Statement (d) is incorrect about the Right to Freedom of Religion.

State can regulate the economic, financial, political and other secular activity associated with religious practice when there is a violation of basic human rights or there is a threat to social harmony or of a criminal offence as enshrined in the Indian Constitution.

26 The Constitution of India recognises

(Chap 4, Class-XI, Old NCERT) (IAS Pre 1999)

(a) only religious minorities

(b) only linguistic minorities

(c) religious and linguistic minorities

(d) religious, linguistic and ethnic minorities

Ans. *(c)*

Exp. The Constitution of India recognises religious and linguistic minorities. Article 29 provides that any section of the citizens residing in any part of India having a distinct language, script or culture of its own, shall have the right to conserve the same.

27 Consider the following statements with reference to Article 29.

Statement-I Article 29 protects the interests of minorities.

Statement-II According to this Article, any minority having a distinct language, script or culture of its own has a right to conserve it. *(Chap 4, Class-XI, Old NCERT)*

Codes

(a) Both Statement-I and Statement-II are correct and Statement-II is the correct explanation for Statement-I.

(b) Both Statement-I and Statement-II are correct and Statement-II is not the correct explanation for Statement-I.

(c) Statement-I is correct but Statement-II is incorrect.

(d) Statement-I is incorrect but Statement-II is correct.

Ans. *(a)*

Exp. Both Statement-I and Statement-II are correct and Statement-II is the correct explanation for Statement-I.

Article 29 protects the interests of the minorities by making a provision that any citizen/section of citizens having distinct language, script or culture have the right to conserve the same. Article 29 mandates that no discrimination would be done by state on the grounds of religion, race, caste, language or any of them.

28 Consider the following statements.

(Chap 4, Class-XI, Old NCERT)

1. No person can be denied admission to any educational institutions maintained by the states or receiving aid 'out of state funds' on grounds of religion, race, caste, language or any of them.
2. The state can discriminate against any educational institution, owned or managed by a minority, while giving grants, simply because it is minority institution.

Which of the statements given above is/are correct?

(a) Only 1 (b) Only 2 (c) Both 1 and 2 (d) Neither 1 nor 2

Ans. *(a)*

Exp. Only statement (1) is correct as no citizen can be denied admission into any educational institution maintained by the state or receiving aid out of state funds on grounds of religion, race, caste, language or any of them, as per Article 29(2).

Statement (2) is not correct because the state shall not discriminate against any educational institution owned or managed by minority, while giving grants as per Article 30(2).

29 Which one of the following statements is/are correct? *(Chap 5, Class-IX, New NCERT) (IAS Pre 2017)*

(a) Rights are claims of the State against the citizens.

(b) Rights are privileges which are incorporated in the Constitution of a State.

(c) Rights are claims of the citizens against the State.

(d) Rights are privileges of a few citizens against the many.

Ans. *(c)*

Exp. Statement (c) is correct.

Rights are claims of the citizens against the State as State has to protect the citizens from oppression by society.

Statements (a), (b) and (d) are not correct.

The State cannot claim or demand against the citizens because it takes away the rights of individuals and restraint them.

The Constitution has no concept of special privileges because it will create inequality in the society.
As per Article 18, except for military and academic distinctions, no other citizens have titular privileges.

30 Consider the following statements.

(Chap 4, Class-XI, Old NCERT)

1. The enforcement of Fundamental Rights is guaranteed by Article 32 of the Indian Constitution.
2. BR Ambedkar described Right to Constitutional Remedies as 'The Heart and Soul of the Constitution'.

Which of the statements given above is/are correct?
(a) Only 1 (b) Only 2 (c) Both 1 and 2 (d) Neither 1 nor 2

Ans. *(c)*

Exp. Both the statements are correct.
Article 32 of the Indian Constitution provides guarantee in the forms of original writ jurisdiction to the Supreme Court for enforcement of Fundamental Rights.
According to BR Ambedkar, Article 32 of the Indian Constitution provides remedies to individuals whose Fundamental Rights have been violated. Thus, Article 32 is the protector of the rights of the citizens of India and is regarded as the 'Heart and Soul of the Constitution'.

31 Consider the following statements about the writ of Habeas Corpus. *(Chap 4, Class-XI, Old NCERT)*

1. It is an order issued by the court to the authority by which a person is alleged to be kept in confinement without legal justification to bring such a person before the court.
2. If there is no legal justification for the detention, the person is ordered to be released.
3. This writ can be filed by only government authorities.

Which of the statements given above is/are incorrect?
(a) Only 1 (b) Both 2 and 3 (c) Only 3 (d) None of these

Ans. *(c)*

Exp. Statement (3) is not correct because in the writ of Habeas Corpus, anyone can be filed this including the arrested person, his relatives, friends, etc. This petition will force the arresting authorities to produce the person bodily in the court.
It is a powerful safeguard against arbitrary acts not only on private individuals but also on the executive.

32 Consider the following pairs.

(Chap 4, Class-XI, Old NCERT) (CGPSC Pre 2016)

	Writ		Meaning
1.	Mandamus	–	Order to do legal duty
2.	Quo Warranto	–	To prevent courts from a case going beyond its jurisdiction
3.	Prohibition	–	Under what authority the person holds the office
4.	Certiorari	–	Transfer a matter pending before it to the higher authority or court

How many of the pairs given above is/ are correctly matched?
(a) Only one (b) Only two
(c) Only three (d) All four

Ans. *(b)*

Exp. Only two pairs i.e., (1) and (4) are correctly matched.
Mandamus is an order from a superior court to a lower court or tribunal or public authority to perform his duty.
Writ of Certiorari is issued by the Supreme Court to some inferior court or tribunal to transfer the matter to it or to some other superior authority for proper consideration.
While pairs (2) and (3) are matched incorrectly.
Quo Warranto is issued with a view to restrain a person from acting in a public office to which he is not entitled.
Prohibition Writ is issued by a superior court to lower court or a tribunal forbidding it to perform an act outside its jurisdiction.

33 With reference to the writs issued by the courts in India, consider the following statements.

(Chap 4, Class-XI, Old NCERT) (IAS Pre 2022)

1. Mandamus will not lie against a private organisation unless it is entrusted with a public duty.
2. Mandamus will not lie against a company even though it may be a government company.
3. Any public minded person can be a petitioner to move the court to obtain the writ of Quo Warranto.

Which of the statements given above is/are correct?
(a) 1 and 2 (b) 2 and 3 (c) 1 and 3 (d) 1, 2 and 3

Ans. *(c)*

Exp. Statements (1) and (3) are correct. A writ of Mandamus is issued by a court to compel a government, corporation or public authority to perform a specific act which is in the nature of a public duty.
A writ of Quo Warranto is used to challenge a person's right to hold a public or corporate office. Individual members of the public have standing as citizens and taxpayers when bringing a petition for a writ of Quo Warranto.
Statement (2) is incorrect because a writ of Mandamus can be issued against a government company, if it is obligated to perform a public duty. The write can also be issued to compel companies or corporations to carry out duties placed on them by statues.

34 Consider the following statements.

(Chap 4, Class-XI, Old NCERT)

1. Parliament has the power to determine the extent to which the Fundamental Rights are available to the personnel of the armed forces.
2. Some Fundamental Rights are available to citizens only while others are available to all persons, citizens as well as non-citizens.
3. Right to Property was omitted by the Forty-Fourth Constitutional Amendment Act, 1978.

Which of the statements given above is/are correct?
(a) 1 and 3
(b) 2 and 3
(c) 1, 2 and 3
(d) Only 2
Ans. (c)

Exp. All of the given statements are correct.
Article 33 empowers the Parliament to restrict or abrogate the Fundamental Rights of the 'Members of the Armed Forces', Paramilitary forces, police forces, intelligence agencies and analogous forces.
There are some Fundamental Rights available to citizens only while others are available to all persons, citizens as well as non-citizens. For instance, equality before the law or equal protection of the laws within the territory of India (Article 14) and protection of life or personal liberty (Article 21) are applicable to non-citizens as well.
Right to Property was removed from the Fundamental Rights by the 44th Amendment Act of 1978. The main motive of this removal was to reduce the boundaries of rich and poor.

35 **Consider the following statements.**
(Chap 5, Class-X, Old NCERT) (IAS Pre 2010)
The Supreme Court of India tenders advice to the President of India on matters of law or fact
1. on its own initiative (on any matter of larger public interest).
2. if he seeks such an advice.
3. only if the matters relate to the Fundamental Rights of the citizens.

Which of the statements given above is/are correct?
(a) Only 1
(b) Only 2
(c) Only 3
(d) 1 and 2
Ans. (b)

Exp. Statement (2) is correct as in Article 143 of the Indian Constitution, the President may seek the advice of the Supreme Court on any question of law or fact of public importance.
Statements (1) and (3) are incorrect because the Supreme Court of India tenders advice to the President of India on matters of law not on its own initiative.
The President of India may seek advice on any matters of law or any fact not only if the matters relate to the Fundamental Rights of the citizens.

36 **Consider the following statements with reference to constitutional doctrines related to Fundamental Rights.** *(Chap 2, Class-XI, New NCERT)*
1. Doctrine of Severability is a doctrine that protects the Fundamental Rights enshrined in the Constitution.
2. Doctrine of Eclipse states that any law that violates Fundamental Rights is not well or void but is only non-enforceable.
3. Doctrine of Waiver of a rights is based on the premise that a person is his best judge and he has the liberty to enjoyment of such rights.

How many of the statements given above is/are incorrect?
(a) Only one (b) Only two (c) All three (d) None of these
Ans. (d)

Exp. None of the given statements are incorrect. All are correct. Doctrine of Severability that protects the Fundamental Rights enshrined in the Constitution, also known as Doctrine of Severability. Doctrine of Eclipse implies that whenever that Fundamental Right is struck down, the law becomes active again.
In Doctrine of Waiver, the person must have the knowledge of his rights and that waive should be voluntary.

Chapter 07

Directive Principles of State Policy

Directive Principles of State Policy

Basics and Classification of DPSPs

Introduction
- Aims for a welfare state, prioritising social and economic democracy
- Guidelines to the Government in making and implementing law/policies

Constitutional Provisions for DPSP
- Articles 36 to 51 in Part IV
- Borrowed from Irish Constitution in 1937

Objective of DPSP
- Guidelines State in socio-economic development
- Illustrate 'welfare state' concept in the Constitution
- Guarantee Justice, Freedom and Equality for citizen
- DPSP covers social, economic and cultural rights

Nature of DPSPs
- Impose moral obligations on the state
- Implementation through executive action
- Avoiding contravention of any law
- State duty to apply DPSP while making law
- Non-Justiciable as Article 37
- Declared as Fundamental in the Governance of the country

Classification of DPSPs
- **Socio-economic Principles**
  - **Article 38** Promotes the welfare of the people
  - **Article 39** (A) Promote equal justice and free legal aid to the poor.
  - **Article 41** Provides protection in cases of unemployment, old age, sickness and disablement
  - **Article 42** Makes provision for just and humane conditions of work and maternity relief
- **Gandhian Principles**
  - **Article 40** Organise Village Panchayats
  - **Article 43** (B) Promote voluntary formation
  - **Article 46** Promote the educational and economic interests of SCs, STs
- **Liberal or Intellectual Principles**
  - **Article 45** Provide early childhood care and education
  - **Article 48** Organise agriculture and animal husbandry on modern and scientific lines
  - **Article 49** Protect monuments, places and objects of artistic or historic interest

Other Aspects of DPSPs

Amendments of DPSPs
- 42nd CAA, 1976 Added four Articles : 39, 39A, 43 A and 48 A
- 44th CAA, 1978 Added Article 38
- 86th CAA, 2002 modified Article 45
- 97th CAA, 2011 Article 43B

Conflict Between DPSP and Fundamental Rights
- Champakam Dorairajan v/s State of Madras, 1951
- Golaknath Case, 1967
- Minerva Mills Case, 1980
- Rajan Dwivedi v/s Union of India Case, 1983

Importance of DPSPs
- Though not legally enforceable, hold significance equal to Fundamental Rights in the Constitution
- Article 37 emphasises their non-enforceability but underscores their fundamental role in governance
- DPSP encompass social, economic, cultural and educational objectives, motivating peaceful political revolution
- KV Rao states DPSPs are the Constitution's Brain Centre, providing directions for its functioning

Implementation of DPSPs
- Implemented by both Centre and State Government
- Planning Commission established in 1950
- Minimum Wages Act, (1948)
- Child Labour Prohibition and Regulation Act (1986)
- Labour System Abolition Act, (1976)
- Passage of Legal Service Act, (1987)
- Wildlife Protection Act, (1972)
- Environment Protection Act, 1986
- Establishment of Panchayati Raj through 73rd Amendment Act

Difference between Fundamental Rights and Directive Principles

Fundamental Rights	Directive Principles
They have judicial protection	They do not have such protection
It provides individual freedom and liberty to the people	They are the guidelines for the state
Violation of Fundamental Rights is punishable	Violation of Directive Principles is not a punishable crime

SOURCE ***Old NCERT Class VII*** *(Directive Principles of State Policy),* ***Old NCERT Class IX & X*** *(Fundamental Rights and Directive Principles of State Policy),* ***New NCERT Class XI*** *(Rights in the Indian Constitution),* ***Old NCERT Class XI*** *(Fundamental Rights, Fundamental Duties and Directive Principles of State Policy)*

1 **Consider the following statements with respect to Directive Principles of State Policy (DPSP).**
(Chap 2, Class-XI, New NCERT) (Chap 7, Module-2, NIOS)

1. Part V of the Indian Constitution deals with the Directive Principles of State Policy.
2. They aim to establish social and economic democracy through a welfare state.
3. It also lists certain rights that individuals should enjoy apart from the Fundamental Rights.

Which of the statements given above is/are correct?
(a) Only 1 (b) Only 2 (c) 1, 2 and 3 (d) 2 and 3

Ans. *(d)*

Exp. Statements (2) and (3) are correct with respect to Directive Principles of State Policy. These principles aim at ensuring socio-economic justice to the people and establishing India as a welfare state.

DPSP imposes a duty upon the state not only to protect and acknowledge the Fundamental Right of the individual but also to achieve socio-economic goals.

Statement (1) is not correct because Part IV of the Constitution of India (Article 36–51) deals with the Directive Principles of State Policy (DPSP).

2 **The concept of Directive Principles of State Policy has been taken from the Constitution of which of the following countries?**
(Chap 4, Class-XI, Old NCERT) (JPSC Pre 2003)

(a) France (b) Spain
(c) Ireland (d) Germany

Ans. *(c)*

Exp. The concept of Directive Principles of State Policy has been taken from the Constitution of Ireland. Directive Principles of State Policy are the guidelines for the state which it must consider while formulating new laws.

3 **Which of the following statements with respect to distinction between Fundamental Rights and Directive Principles of State Policy is/are correct?**
(Chap 4, Class-XI, Old NCERT)

(a) While the Fundamental Rights are enforceable through court of law, the Directive Principles are not enforceable.
(b) The Fundamental Rights prohibit the State from doing certain things; the Directives are affirmative instructions to 'the State' to do certain things.
(c) There is dominance of civil and political rights in the Fundamental Rights, whereas economic and social rights are predominant in the Directive Principles.
(d) All of the above

Ans. *(d)*

Exp. All the given statements are correct with respect to distinction between Fundamental Rights and Directive Principles of State Policy.

Fundamental Rights are enforceable in the court of law on the other hand Directive Principles of State Policy (DPSP) is not enforceable in court of law. It means nobody can go in the court for the enforcement of DPSP.

Fundamental Rights are human rights conferred to the citizens of India. DPSP are ideals which are meant to be kept in mind by the State when it formulates policies and enacts laws. Fundamental Rights restrain the state from doing certain things on the other hand, DPSP directs the state to do certain things and hence DPSP has affirmative connotations.

Fundamental Rights deal with civil and political rights whereas DPSP deals with social and economic rights.

4 **Consider the following statements with respect to the non-enforceable nature of Directive Principles of State Policy.** *(Chap 4, Class-XI, Old NCERT)*

1. It has been criticised as 'pious expressions' or resolutions made on the New Year's Day.
2. They resemble the 'Instrument of Instructions'.

Which of the statements given above is/are correct?
(a) Only 1
(b) Only 2
(c) Both 1 and 2
(d) Neither 1 nor 2

Ans. *(c)*

Exp. Both the statements (1) and (2) are correct with respect to the non-enforceable nature of Directive Principles of State Policy.

Directive Principles have been described by some critics as 'pious expressions' or resolutions made on the New Year's day' as they are non-justiciable in nature.

For others they appear 'Instrument of Instructions' only and has no legal utility.

The Instrument of Instructions contained in the Government of India Act, 1935 has been incorporated in the Constitution of India in the year 1950 as Directive Principles of State Policy.

5 **Consider the following statements and choose the correct code.** *(Chap 4, Class-IX & X, Old NCERT)*

Statement-I The Executive, the Legislature and the Judiciary have to take cognisance of the Directive Principles.

Statement-II Though they are non-enforceable, the directives are the fundamental principles of governance.

Which one of the following is/are correct in respect of the above statements?
(a) Both Statement-I and Statement-II are correct and Statement-II is the correct explanation for Statement-I.
(b) Both Statement-I and Statement-II are correct and Statement-II is not the correct explanation for Statement-I.
(c) Statement-I is correct but Statement-II is incorrect.
(d) Statement-II is incorrect but Statement-II is correct.

Ans. *(a)*

Exp. Both Statement-I and Statement-II are correct and Statement-II is the correct explanation for Statement-I.

Directive Principle of State Policy are directions to the policy-makers of India therefore the Executive, the Legislature and the Judiciary have to take cognisance of the Directive Principles. Unlike Fundamental Right, the Directive Principles of State Policy (DPSP) are non-justiciable which means they are not enforceable by the courts for their violation. However, as per Article 37, the provision contained in part IV (DPSP) shall not be enforceable by any court, nevertheless, these principles are fundamental in the governance of the country and it shall be the duty of the state to apply these principles n making laws.

6 With reference to the provisions contained in Part IV of the Constitution of India, which of the following statements is/are correct?

(Chap 4, Class-IX, Old NCERT) (IAS Pre 2020)

1. They shall be enforceable by courts.
2. They shall not be enforceable by any court.
3. The principles laid down in this part are to influence the making of laws by the state.

Select the correct answer using the codes given below.

(a) Only 1 (b) Only 2 (c) 1 and 3 (d) 2 and 3

Ans. (d)

Exp. Statements (2) and (3) are correct. Part IV of the Indian Constitution deals with the Directive Principles of our State Policy (DPSP). It cannot be enforced by any court. The DPSP is fundamental in the governance of the country and it shall be the duty of the state to apply these principles in making laws. The Principles laid down in this part are to influence the making of laws by the state. Statement (1) is incorrect because in this part they shall not be enforceable by courts.

7 In essence, what does Due process of Law mean?

(Chap 2, Class-XI, New NCERT) (IAS Pre 2023)

(a) The principle of natural justice
(b) The procedure established by law
(c) Fair application of law
(d) Equality before law

Ans. (c)

Exp. Option (c) is correct with respect to due process of law. Due process of law ia a legal principle that requires governments to follow fair and reasonable procedures when depriving individuals of their life, liberty or property. It also requires governments to pass laws that are just, fair and reasonable. The Supreme Court of India has the power to declare laws unconstitutional if they violate due process of law.

Thie means that the Court can strike down laws that are unfair, unjust or unresonable. The phrase due process of law is not mentioned explicitly anywhere in the Indian Constitution, but it has been interpreted by the Supreme Court to be a Fundamental Right.

8 Under the Indian Constitution concentration of wealth violates

(Chap 4, Class-XI, New NCERT) (IAS Pre 2021)

(a) The Right of Equality
(a) The Directive Principles of State Policy
(b) The Right to Freedom
(c) The Concept of Welfare

Ans. (b)

Exp. Under the Indian Constitution, the concentration of wealth violates Directive Principles of State Policy.

Article 39 of the Indian Constitution requires the state to direct its policies towards securing for all its citizens the right to an adequate means of livelihood, availability of material resources and ensuring prevention of concentration of wealth, etc.

9 Which of the following statements with respect to directives relating to political policies is/are correct?

(Chap 4, Class-XI, Old NCERT)
(Unit 1, Class-XII, Tamil Nadu Board)

1. The State is required to take steps to organise Village Panchayats.
2. The State should endeavour to secure for the citizens a Uniform Civil Code throughout the territory of India.
3. The State is required to take steps to separate the Judiciary from the Executive in the public services of the State.

Codes

(a) 1, 2 and 3 (b) 2 and 3
(c) 1 and 2 (d) None of these

Ans. (a)

Exp. Statements (1), (2) and (3) are correct with respect to directives relating to political policies.

Article 40 of the Indian Constitution directs the State to take steps to organise Village Panchayat in order to enhance grassroots democracy.

Article 44 directs the State to secure a Uniform Civil Code throughout the territory of India in order to safeguard its secular character.

Article 50 directs the State to take steps to separate Judiciary from the Executive so that principle of separation of Judiciary is upheld as enshrined in the Constitution.

10 Match the following lists and choose the correct code. *(Chap 4, Class-XI, Old NCERT) (Chap 7, Module-2, NIOS)*

List I (DPSP)	List II (Policy Types)
A. Right to work	1. Political Policy
B. Protect monuments of artistic interest	2. Economic Policy
C. Encourage settlement of international disputes	3. Cultural Policy
D. Protect and improve the environment	4. Health Policy

Codes

	A	B	C	D		A	B	C	D
(a)	3	2	1	4	(b)	2	3	1	4
(c)	1	3	4	2	(d)	4	1	3	2

Ans. (b)

Exp. The correct matching is A-2, B-3, C-1, D-4.

Article 41 makes effective provision for securing the right to work under its **economic policy**.

Article 49 puts the obligation of the state to protect every monument or place or object of artistic or historic interest under its **cultural policy**.

Article 51 states that the State shall endeavour to encourage settlement of international disputes by arbitration under its **political policy**.

Article 48A states that the State shall endeavour to protect and improve the environment under its **health policy**.

11 As per the directives related to political policies, the State is required to do which of the following?

(Chap 4, Class-XI, Old NCERT)

1. Promote international peace and security.
2. Maintain just and honourable relations between nations.
3. Foster respect for international law and treaty obligations in the dealings of organised people with one another.

Codes

(a) 1 and 3 (b) 2 and 4
(c) 1 and 2 (d) All of these

Ans. (d)

Exp. As per the directives related to political policies, the state is required to do all the options mentioned in the question.

Article 51 deals with promotion of international peace and security. It also provides for maintaining just and honourable relations between nations, foster respect for international law and treaty obligations in the dealings of organised people with one another. It further provides for encouraging settlement of international disputes by arbitration.

12 Consider the following statements.

(Chap 4, Class-XI, Old NCERT)

1. The citizens, men and women equally, have the right to an adequate means of livelihood.
2. There is equal pay for equal work for both men and women.
3. Suitable provision is made for just and humane condition of work and for maternity relief.

The above given directives are related to which of the following policy?

(a) Political Policy
(b) Economic Policy
(c) Social Policy
(d) Cultural Policy

Ans. (b)

Exp. The directives given in the question are related to economic policy.

Article 39(a) and (d) are directives under economic policy through which the State shall direct its policy towards securing that the citizen, men and women equally, have the right to an adequate means of livelihood and that there is equal pay for equal work for both men and women.

Article 42 states that the State shall make provision for securing just and humane conditions of work and for maternity relief.

13 Consider the following statements with reference to Directive Principles of State Policy.

(Chap 5, Class-VII, Old NCERT)

1. Members of the Constituent Assembly devised it to assure more social and economic transformations.
2. To act as a guide for the newly independent Indian state in enacting laws and policies that will aid in the reduction of poverty among the people.
3. The motive behind the inclusion of DPSP is establishing political democracy.

How many of the statements given above is/are correct?

(a) Only one (b) Only two (c) All of these (c) None of these

Ans. (b)

Exp. Only two statements i.e., (1) and (2) are correct.

Directive Principles of State Policy were designed by the members of the Constituent Assembly to ensure greater social and economic reforms.

They act as a guide for the newly independent Indian state in enacting laws and policies that will aid in the reduction of poverty among the people.

Statement (3) is incorrect because the motive behind the inclusion of DPSP is not establishing political democracy rather, its about establishing social and economic democracy in the state.

14 With reference to the Constitution of India, the Directive Principles of State Policy constitute limitations upon which of the following function?

(Chap 2, Class-XI, New NCERT) (IAS Pre 2017)

1. Legislative function 2. Executive function

Select the correct answer using the code given below.

(a) Only 1 (b) Only 2
(c) Both 1 and 2 (d) Neither 1 nor 2

Ans. (d)

Exp. Neither (1) nor (2) are correct with reference to the Constitution of India. It is because the Directive Principles of State Policy does not constitute limitations upon legislative functions or executive functions.

The directive principles are in the nature of instruments of instruction to the government of the day to achieve certain ends by their actions. It guides them, not restricts them. It is the Fundamental Rights that constitute limitations upon state action (whether Legislative or Executive).

15 **Which of the following is not one of the three schools of thoughts under which the Directive Principles have been classified?**

(Chap 4, Class-XI, Old NCERT) (IAS Pre 2002)

(a) Idealism (b) Liberalism (c) Socialism (d) Gandhism

Ans. (a)

Exp. Idealism is not one of the three schools of thought under which the Directive Principles have been classified. Directive Principles of State Policy have been grouped into following categories

- Liberal intellectual principles
- Gandhian principles
- Socialistic and economic principles

While idealism is a label which covers a number of philosophical positions with quite different tendencies and implications.

16 **Which of the following has been done by the governments from time to time to give effect to Directive Principles of State Policy?**

(Chap 2, Class-XI, New NCERT)
(Unit 1, Class-XII, Tamil Nadu Board)

1. Mid-day meal scheme
2. Banks nationalisation
3. Reservation for the uplift of the Scheduled Castes and Scheduled Tribes
4. Right to Health

Codes

(a) 1 and 3 (b) 1, 2 and 3 (c) 2 and 4 (d) All of these

Ans. (b)

Exp. Statements (1), (2) and (3) are correct with respect to the work done by governments from time to time to give effect to DPSP.

Mid-day-meal scheme has been started to give effect to Article 45 which says that State shall endeavour to provide early childhood care and education for all children until they complete the age of six years.

Bank nationalisation has been done to give effect to Article 39 which directs State in its policies towards securing right to an adequate means of livelihood to all the citizens and the state shall avoid concentration of wealth in few hands.

Article 46 says that the State shall promote with special care the educational and economic interests of the weaker sections of the people such as Scheduled Castes and the Scheduled Tribes, and shall protect them from social injustice and all forms of exploitation.

17 **Which one of the following pairs is not matched correctly?** *(Unit 1, Class-XII, Tamil Nadu Board)*

	Subject		Related Articles
(a)	The separation of Judiciary from Executive	–	Article 50
(b)	The promotion of educational and economic interests of Scheduled Castes and Scheduled Tribes	–	Article 46
(c)	The promotion of Co-operative Societies	–	Article 43 (A)
(d)	The Organisation of Village Panchayats and enable them to function as the units of self-government.	–	Article 40

Ans. (c)

Exp. Pair (c) is not correctly matched because the 97th Amendment Act of 2011 added Article 43 (B) new Directive Principle relating to co-operative societies. It requires the State to promote voluntary formation, autonomous functioning, democratic control and professional management of co-operative societies Article 43 (B).

Article 43 (A) was added by 42nd Amendment and provides to take steps to secure the participation of workers in the management of industries.

Chapter 08

Fundamental Duties

Fundamental Duties

Basics of Fundamental Duties

- Added by 42nd Amendment Act, (1976)
- Recommended by Swarn Singh Committee
- Duties mentioned in the Constitution

Swaran Singh Committee

- Set-up in 1976
- During Internal Emergency (1975-77)
- Proposed to add a separate chapter in the Constitution
- Originally suggested 8 Fundamental Duties
- 42nd CAA added 10 Fundamental Duties were added in the Constitution

Significance of Fundamental Duties

- Ethical, social and economic importance
- Constant reminder to be aware of duties while enjoying rights
- Acts as a warning against activities disrespecting the nation
- Promotes a sense of discipline and commitment

Need for Fundamental Duties

- Promotes discipline and commitment to society
- Encourages adherence to democratic norms, emphasising the correlation between rights and duties

Fundamental Duties

11 Fundamental Duties for Citizens

- Article 51A provides that it shall be the duty of every citizen of India-
  - To abide by the Constitution and respect its ideals and institutions, the National Flag and National Anthem
  - To cherish and follow the noble ideals which inspired our national struggle for freedom
  - To uphold and protect the sovereignty, unity and integrity of India
  - To defend the country and render national service when called upon to do so
  - To promote harmony and the spirit of common brotherhood amongst all the people of India and to renounce practices derogatory to the dignity of women
  - To preserve the rich heritage of our composite culture
  - To protect and improve the natural environment
  - To develop the scientific temper and spirit of inquiry
  - To safeguard public property
  - To strive towards excellence in all spheres of individual and collective activity
  - Duty of every parent or guardian to provide opportunities for education of his child or ward between the age of 6 to 14 years

Enforcement, Criticism and Relation between FRs and FDs

Enforcement of Fundamental Duties

- Guide citizens and influence legislative and executive actions
- Legal utility of Fundamental Duties and Directive Principles are similar

Criticism of Fundamental Duties

- Critics find Fundamental Duties list not exhaustive, ineffective in court enforcement
- Some duties like respecting National Flag are performed automatically

Relation Between FRs and FDs

- Fundamental Duties, though not legally enforceable, represent's citizen's moral obligations
- Fundamental Duties should complement Fundamental Rights
- Article 21 guarantees Right to Education and Article 51 A (K) mandates parents to provide free and compulsory education during the age group of (6-14)
- Democracy cannot establish its deep roots in the society until citizens don't follow their Fundamental Rights with their Fundamental Duties

SOURCE ***New NCERT Class XI*** *(Rights in the Indian Constitution),* ***Old NCERT Class XI*** *(Fundamental Rights, Fundamental Duties and Directive Principles of State Policy)*

1 Consider the following statements with respect to Fundamental Duties. *(Chap 4, Class-XI, Old NCERT) (Unit 1, Class-XII, Tamil Nadu Board)*

1. Fundamental Duties were inserted by the 42nd Constitutional Amendment Act, 1976.
2. Originally, it contained a list of 11 Fundamental Duties.
3. Fundamental Duties enjoin upon a citizen among other things to follow noble ideas.

How many of the statements given above is/are incorrect?

(a) Only one (b) Only two (c) All three (d) None of these

Ans. *(a)*

Exp. Only one statement i.e., (2) is incorrect with respect to Fundamental Duties. Originally, there were 10 Fundamental Duties. However, a new Fundamental duty was added by 86th Constitutional Amendment Act, 2002, which provides for opportunities for education to children between 6 to 14 years.

2 Consider the following statements, with reference to Swaran Singh Committee. *(Chap 4, Class-XI, Old NCERT)*

1. It was set-up in 1979 to make recommendations about Fundamental Duties.
2. The need and necessity of Fundamental Duties was felt during the operation of internal emergency in 1975.
3. It suggested the inclusion of 10 Fundamental Duties in the Constitution.

How many of the statements given above is/are not correct?

(a) Only one (b) Only two (c) All three (d) None of these

Ans. *(b)*

Exp. Only two statements i.e., (1) and (3) are incorrect regarding Swaran Singh Committee because Sardar Swaran Singh Committee was set-up in 1976 to make recommendations about Fundamental Duties. It also suggested the inclusion of 8 Fundamental Duties in the Constitution but by 42nd Constitutional Amendment, 10 Fundamental Duties were added in Article 51(A) of the Constitution.

3 Which of the following duties have been prescribed by the Indian Constitution as Fundamental Duties? *(Chap 4, Class-XI, Old NCERT) (UPPSC Pre 2019)*

1. To defend the country.
2. To pay income tax.
3. To preserve the rich heritage of our composite culture.
4. To safeguard the public property.

Codes

(a) 1 and 2 (b) 2 and 4 (c) 1, 2 and 4 (d) 1, 3 and 4

Ans. *(d)*

Exp. To defend the country, to preserve the rich heritage of our composite culture and to safeguard the public property have been prescribed by the Indian Constitution as Fundamental Duties.

However, paying income tax is not a Fundamental Duty enshrined in the Constitution. It is rather a moral and economic liability of every citizen to pay rightful taxes on time for nation building.

4 Consider the following statements, with reference to Fundamental duties. *(Chap 4, Class-XI, New NCERT)*

Statement-I The inclusion of Fundamental Duties has not changed the status of the Fundamental Rights.

Statement-II Our Constitution does not make the enjoyment of rights dependent or conditional upon fulfilment of duties.

Codes

(a) Both Statement-I and Statement-II are correct and Statement-II is the correct, explanation for Statement-I.
(b) Both Statement-I and Statement-II are correct and Statement-II is not the correct explanation for Statement-I.
(c) Statement-I is correct but Statement-II is incorrect.
(d) Statement-I is incorrect but Statement-II is correct.

Ans. *(a)*

Exp. Both Statement-I and Statement-II are correct and Statement-II is the correct explanation for Statement-I. Fundamental Rights and Fundamental Duties are independent of each other. Fundamental Rights are justiciable and their violation is protected by the Constitution whereas non-performance of Fundamental Duties does not attract any punishment as they are non-justiciable.

5 Which of the following statements regarding Fundamental Duties is not correct? *(Chap 4, Class-XI, Old NCERT) (UPPSC Pre 2003)*

(a) They can be enforced by writs.
(b) They can be promoted only by constitutional methods.
(c) They can be used for interpreting ambiguous statues.
(d) The performance of any particular duties comes within the sphere of constitutional law which court has to decide.

Ans. *(a)*

Exp. Statement (a) they is not correct regarding Fundamental Duties because they cannot be enforced by the court of law. They can be promoted only by constitutional methods. However, it is useful in interpreting the various provisions of the Constitution.

6 Which of the following is/are among the Fundamental Duties of citizens laid down in the Indian Constitution? *(Chap 4, Class-XI, Old NCERT) (IAS Pre 2012)*

1. To preserve the rich heritage of our composite culture.
2. To protect the weaker sections from social injustice.
3. To develop scientific temper and spirit of inquiry.
4. To strive towards excellence in all spheres of individual and collective activity.

Which of the statements given above is/are correct?
(a) 1 and 2
(b) Only 2
(c) 1, 3 and 4
(d) 1, 2, 3 and 4

Ans. (c)

Exp. Statements (1), (3) and (4) are Fundamental Duties of citizens laid down in the Indian Constitution.

Statement (2) is incorrect because to protect the weaker sections from social injustice is not the Fundamental Duty laid down in our Constitution. It has been mentioned in Directive Principles of State Policy as well as Fundamental Rights.

7 Consider the following statements, with reference to the term 'Abide by the Constitution' as mentioned in Fundamental Duties. *(Chap 4, Class-XI, Old NCERT)*

1. Every citizen should act according to the provisions of the Constitution.
2. He should not do anything that is prohibited by the Constitution.
3. Some of the prohibitions by the Constitution are the practice of untouchability, traffic in human beings, etc.

How many statements given above is/are correct?
(a) Only one
(b) Only two
(c) All three
(d) None of these

Ans. (c)

Exp. All the given statements are correct regarding the term 'Abide by the Constitution'.

In Fundamental Duties, it has been mentioned that every citizen should act according to the provisions of the Constitution. It means that he should not do anything that is prohibited by the Constitution.

Some of the important prohibitions by the Constitution are the practice of untouchability (Article 17), Traffic in human beings (Article 23), abusing the health and strength of workers and tender age of children (Article 39) and slaughter of cows, calves and other milch and drought animals (Article 48).

8 Which of the following pairs is incorrectly matched? *(Chap 4, Class-XI, Old NCERT)*

	List I (Fundamental Duty)		List II (Implication)
(a)	Uphold Sovereignty of India	–	Priority to the national interest.
(b)	Defend the country	–	Every citizen should be ready to defend the country.
(c)	Renounce Practices Derogatory to Women	–	Renounce evil practices like teen talak, etc.
(d)	Protect and Improve Natural Environment	–	Reform our society through the spirit of inquiry.

Ans. (d)

Exp. Pair (d) is incorrectly matched because to protect and improve the natural environment including lakes, wildlife, rivers, forests, etc is an eco-friendly duty for the sustainable development and protection of our environment. The Fundamental Rights help to promote reform in our society through the spirit of inquiry.

9 Which of the following statements is/are correct regarding the utility of Fundamental Duties? *(Chap 4, Class-XI, Old NCERT)* *(Unit 1, Class-XII, Tamil Nadu Board)*

(a) Laws can be enacted to punish who disobey it.
(b) They can be useful in interpreting the various provisions of the Constitution.
(c) The executives can rely upon them to justify actions regarding the practical application of these duties.
(d) All of the above

Ans. (d)

Exp. All of the given statements are correct as Fundamental Duties are non-justiciable but the Legislature and Executive are empowered to enact laws for their disobedience.

Fundamental Duties are an integral part of the Constitution which can be helpful in interpreting other provisions of the Constitution.

Both Legislature and Executive take guidance from Fundamental Duties to justify actions regarding their practical application.

Chapter 09

Union Executive

Union Executive

President and Vice-President

President

- Executive Power vested in President (Article 52)
- Formal Head of Nation
- **Qualification** Article 58 and 59; Must be an Indian citizen, 35 years old and meet requirement for Lok Sabha membership
- **Oath or Affirmation by the President** Article 60; In presence of Chief Justice of India
- **Salary and Emoluments;** Decided by President's Emoluments and Pension Act, 1951; 5 Lakh per month
- **Powers of the President**
- **Executive Power**
  - Article 111 : Confers all Executive Powers
  - Article 75 : Prime Minister communicates with President regarding Union Council of Ministers
- **Legislative Power**
  - Article 111; Power Regarding Bill; Veto Power of President, etc
- **Financial Power**
  - Article 112, Money Bill are introduced in Lok Sabha
- **Judicial Power**
  - Article 143; Appoints Judge of Supreme Court and High Court

Vice-President

- Article 63; Second most important constitutional body
- **Election of the Vice-President**
  - Elected by a Electoral College comprising members of both Houses of Parliament
  - Proportional representation, with single transferable vote system
- **Qualifications**
  - Indian citizenship, age 35 years, eligible for Council of States (Rajya Sabha)
- **Tenure of Vice-President**
  - 5 years • Can resign any time by addressing President
- **Oath/Affirmation by the Vice-President**
- **Power and Functions of the Vice-President**
  - Serves as a ex-officio chairman of Rajya Sabha
  - Presides over Rajya Sabha, ensuring order, allowing members to speak and putting bills to vote

Prime Minister

Introduction

- Real executive authority (defacto executive)
- Head of Government, leader of Cabinet Ministers
- **Eligibility**
  - Indian citizen; Member of Lok Sabha or Rajya Sabha
  - 30 year for Rajya Sabha and 25 years for Lok Sabha
- **Oath, Term and Salary** Appointed by President, based on majority support in Lok Sabha
- **Power and Functions of the Prime Minister**
  - Powers with reference to Council of Ministers
  - Powers in Relation to the President
  - Powers in Reference to Parliament

Deputy Prime Minister

- Originally not mention in Constitution
- Appointed mainly for political reason
- **Attorney-General**
  - Appointed by President Under Article 76
  - Hold office at the pleasure of President
  - Must be qualified for Supreme Court Judge

Council of Ministers

Introduction

- Council of Ministers lead by Prime Minister serving as the real executive
- Article 74 : President shall have a Council of Ministers who must help the President exercise their functions
- **Power and Function of Council of Ministers**
  - Ministers of State have independent charge of ministries, performing functions and exercising powers like Cabinet Ministers
  - Ministers of State are not cabinet members
- **Appointment of Ministers**
  - Appointed by President on the recommendation of Prime Minister
  - Non-Member of Parliament (MP) can be appointed, but must get elected within 6 months
- **Oath and Salary**
  - President administers oath to ministers
  - Parliament determines minister's salary and allowances
- **Responsibilities of Ministers**
  - Collective Responsibilities
  - Collectively responsible to Lower House (Article 75)
- **Individual Responsibilities** Article 75 States Ministers hold office at the President's pleasure, President can remove ministers despite Lok Sabha confidence

SOURCE **Old NCERT Class VII** *(Who Execute Laws,* **New NCERT Class IX** *Working of Institutions),* **Old NCERT Class IX & X** *(Government),* **Old NCERT Class IX & X** *(Our Government at the Centre),* **New NCERT Class XI** *(Executive),* **Old NCERT Class XI** *(Features of Executive),* **Old NCERT Class XI** *(Executive of India),* **Old NCERT Class XI** *(Central Administration : Working and Organisation)*

The Executive

1 Consider the following statements with respect to the Executive. *(Chap 4, Class-XI, New NCERT)*

1. The organ of government that primarily looks after the function of implementation and administration is called the Executive.
2. It also extends to the administrative machinery (civil servants).
3. The official designations of the Executive are similar in all democracies.

Which of the statements given above is/are correct?

(a) Only 1
(b) Only 2
(c) 1, 2 and 3
(d) 1 and 2

***Ans.** (d)*

Exp. Statements (1) and (2) are correct with respect to Executive. Executive is a person or persons constituting the branch of government charged with executing or carrying out the laws and appointing officials, formulating and instituting foreign policy, and providing diplomatic representation.

The primary function of Executive is to enforce laws and to maintain law and order in the state.

Statement (3) is incorrect because the official designations of the Executive are not the same in all democracies. Some countries have Presidents, while others have Chancellors. However, it is not just about Presidents, Prime Ministers but also extends to the administrative structure.

2 Consider the following statements and choose the correct code. *(Chap 4, Class-XI, New NCERT)*

Statement-I In USA, the Executive powers are in the hands of the President.

Statement-II In Presidential system, the President is the head of the state only.

Codes

(a) Both Statement-I and Statement-II are correct and Statement-II is the correct explanation for Statement-I.
(b) Both Statement-I and Statement-II are correct and Statement-II is not the correct explanation for Statement-I.
(c) Statement-I is correct but Statement-II is incorrect.
(d) Statement-I is incorrect but Statement-II is correct.

***Ans.** (c)*

Exp. Statement-I is correct but Statement-II is incorrect because in USA, there is a Presidential form of government. The Executive powers are in the hands of the President.

In a Presidential form of government, President is the head of the state as well as the head of the government. In this system, the office of President is very powerful, both in theory and practice.

The President

3 Consider the following statements in respect of election to the President of India. *(Chap 5, Class-XI, Old NCERT) (IAS Pre 2023)*

1. The members nominated to either House of the Parliament or the Legislative Assemblies of State are also eligible to be included in the Electoral College.
2. Higher the number of elective Assembly seats, higher is the value of vote of each MLA of that State.
3. The value of vote of each MLA of Madhya Pradesh is greater than that of Kerala.
4. The value of vote of each MLA of Puducherry is higher than that of Arunachal Pradesh because the ratio of total population to total number of elective Puducherry is greater as compared to Arunachal Pradesh.

How many of the statements given above is/are correct?

(a) Only one
(b) Only two
(c) All three
(d) None of these

***Ans.** (a)*

Exp. Only one statement i.e., (4) is correct in respect of election to the President of India.

Statement (4) is correct as the vote value of each MLA of Puducherry is higher than that of Arunachal Pradesh as the ratio of total population to total elective seats in Puducherry is greater relative to that in Arunachal Pradesh. In 2022 Presidential election, the vote value of each MLA from Puducherry was 16 whereas the vote value of each MLA from Arunachal Pradesh came out to be 8.

Statements (1), (2) and (3) are incorrect because the elected members of the Upper and Lower Houses of Parliament that is the Rajya Sabha and the Lok Sabha as well as the elected members of the Legislative Assemblies of States and Union Territories (MLAs) comprise the Electoral College for the Presidential Election in India.

The value of vote of each MLA depends on the ratio of the State's population and the number of MLAs in its Legislative Assembly.

The vote value of each MLA of Madhya Pradesh is less than that of the vote value of each MLA of Kerala as the ratio of total population to total elective seats in Kerala is greater relative to that in Madhya Pradesh.

4 Which of the following statements is/are correct with respect to the Executive? *(Chap 5, Class-XI, Old NCERT)*

1. The Executive authority of the Union is vested in the President of India who exercises it directly or through the officers subordinate to him.
2. All the Executive functions of the Union Government are carried on in the name of the President.

Select the correct answer using the codes given below.

(a) Only 1 (b) Only 2
(c) Both 1 and 2 (d) Neither 1 nor 2

Ans. *(c)*

Exp. Both the statements (1) and (2) are correct with respect to the Executive.

Article 53 vests the President with Executive Power of the Union and such powers shall be exercised by him either directly or through officers subordinate to him in accordance with the Constitution.

All the Executive functions of the Union Government are carried on in the name of the President as he/she is the head of Union Executive.

5 Consider the following statement with reference to the constitutional/discretionary powers of President of India. *(Chap 4, Class-XI, New NCERT)* *(Unit 3, Class-XII, Tamil Nadu Board)*

1. The President has a right to be informed of all important matters and deliberations of the Council of Ministers.
2. The Prime Minister is obliged to furnish all the information that the President may call for.
3. The President can appoint anyone as the Prime Minister in case of Hung Parliament.

How many of the statements given above is/are incorrect?

(a) Only one (b) Only two
(c) All three (d) None of these

Ans. *(a)*

Exp. Only one statement i.e., (3) is incorrect because the power mentioned in constitutional/discretionary power vested in President of India. When no party or pre-poll alliance is able to secure a majority in the elections, this situation leads to a Hung Parliament.

In such case, the President can invite the leader of the single largest party/alliance in the House to try to secure the confidence of the House.

6 Consider the following Assertion (A) and Reason (R) and choose the correct code. *(Chap 5, Class-XI, Old NCERT) (UPPSC Mains 2012)*

Assertion (A) The Supreme Command of the defence forces is vested in the President.

Reason (R) The President's powers as Commander-in-Chief are independent of Legislative control.

Codes

(a) Both A and R are true and R is the correct explanation of A.
(b) Both A and R are true, but R is not the correct explanation of A.
(c) A is true, but R is false.
(d) A is false, but R is true.

Ans. *(c)*

Exp. Assertion (A) is true, but Reason (R) is false.

The Supreme Command of the defence forces is vested in the President. The power (military) exercised by the President is to be regulated by law. The Parliament can make any law with regard to navy, army, air force and any other armed forces of the Union. The President cannot declare war or deploy forces of the country without the sanction of the Parliament.

7 Consider the following statements about the President of India. *(Chap 5, Class-XI, Old NCERT)* *(UP Lower Sub Pre 1998)*

1. He should be a citizen of India by birth.
2. He should have completed the age of 35 years.
3. He should be qualified for election as a member of Parliament.

Which of the statements given above is/are correct?

(a) Only 1 (b) Only 2 (c) 1 and 2 (d) 1 and 3

Ans. *(b)*

Exp. Only statement (2) is correct about the President of India. Following are the qualifications for becoming the President of India are

He should be a citizen of India.
He should have completed the age of 35 years.
He should have to be qualified for election as a member of Lok Sabha.
He should not hold office of profit under the Government of India or Government of any state or under any local authority.

8 Which of the following is not included in the Electoral College for the election of President of India? *(Chap 5, Class-XI, Old NCERT)* *(UPPSC Pre Re-exam 2015)*

(a) Elected members of State Legislative Council.
(b) Elected members of State Legislative Assembly.
(c) Elected members of Lok Sabha.
(d) Elected members of Rajya Sabha.

Ans. *(a)*

Exp. Elected members of State Legislative Council are not included in the Electoral College as according to Article 55, the President of India is indirectly elected by means of an Electoral College. This college consists of the elected members of the Parliament of India and the Legislative assemblies of the states of India and the Union Territories (having an elected assembly).

9 With reference to the election of the President of India, consider the following statements. *(Chap 5, Class-XI, Old NCERT) (IAS Pre 2018)*

1. The value of the vote of each MLA varies from state to state.
2. The value of the vote of MPs of the Lok Sabha is more than the value of MPs of the Rajya Sabha.

Which of the statements given above is/are correct?

(a) Only 1 (b) Only 2
(c) Both 1 and 2 (d) Neither 1 nor 2

Ans. (a)

Exp. Only statement (1) is correct with reference to the election of the President of India.

The election of President of India is held in accordance with the system of proportional representation by means of single transferable vote system.

The value of a vote casted by an elected member of a State Legislative Assembly is determined by dividing the population of a state by the total number of the elected members of that state.

Statement (2) is incorrect because the value of the vote of MPs of the Lok Sabha is equal to the value of the vote of MPs of the Rajya Sabha. It can be calculated as follows

Vote Value of Member of Parliament

$$= \frac{\text{Sum of vote value of elected members of all State Legislative Assemblies}}{\text{Number of elected members of both the Houses (Lok Sabha + Rajya Sabha) of the Parliament}}$$

10 With respect to the election of President of India, consider the following statements.

(Chap 5, Class-XI, Old NCERT)

1. The election is held in accordance with the system of First Past the Post System.
2. The Parliament provides a special procedure to determine the value of a vote casted by each elector.
3. Article 55 deals with the method of the President's election.

How many of the statements given above is /are incorrect?

(a) Only one
(b) Only two
(c) All three
(d) None of these

Ans. (b)

Exp. Only two statements i.e., (1) and (2) are incorrect with respect to the election of the President of India because these elections are held in accordance of proportional representation by means of single transferable vote system.

The system assigns varying numbers of votes to these electoral college members, such that the total weight of MPs and those of MLAs is roughly equal and that the voting power of states and territories are proportional to their population.

11 The President holds office for a term of five years from date on ***(Chap 5, Class-XI, Old NCERT)***
(RAS/RTS Pre 1996)

(a) which he/she is elected.
(b) which is decided by the Parliament.
(c) which he enters upon his office / holds his office.
(d) which is decided by Election Commission.

Ans. (c)

Exp. The President holds office for a term of five years from the date on which he enters upon his office. However, before entering upon his office, the President is required to take an oath in a prescribed form in the presence of Chief Justice or the senior most Judge of the Supreme Court of India.

12 Consider the following pairs.

(Chap 5, Class-XI, Old NCERT)

	Description	Powers of the President
1.	Prior recommendation for Money Bill	Financial power
2.	Supreme Command of Defence Forces	Military power
3.	International treaties and agreements in his name	Diplomatic power
4.	Declaration of Financial Emergency	Financial power

How many of the pairs given above is/are not correctly matched?

(a) Only one (b) Only two (c) Only three (d) All four

Ans. (a)

Exp. Only one pair i.e., (4) is not correctly matched because the Declaration of Financial Emergency (Article 360) comes under the emergency power of the President and not the financial power of the President. Some of the financial powers of the President are as follows

- Annual financial statement is laid down by the Finance Minister every year on behalf of the President.
- A Money Bill cannot be introduced or moved in Lok Sabha except on the recommendation of the President.
- No demand for a grant can be made except on the recommendation of the President.

13 With reference to the election of the President of India, consider the following statement.

(Chap 4, Class-XI, New NCERT)

1. A person above the age of 35 years is eligible for election as the President of India.
2. The President of India is eligible for re-election for more than one term.
3. A person is not eligible for election as the President of India if the person holds and office of profit.

How many of the statements given above is/are correct?

(a) Only one
(b) Only two
(c) All three
(d) None of these

Ans. (c)

Exp. All the three statements i.e., (1), (2) and (3) are correct in reference to the election of the President of India. According to Article 58 of the Indian Constitution, a person should be at least 35 years old to be eligible for the presidency. According to Article 57 of the Indian Constitution, there is no limit on the numbers of terms a President can serve.

The President can be re-elected for multiple terms. According to Article 58 of the Indian Constitution, a person holding any office of profit under the government of India or any State Government is not eligible for election as President.

14 Which of the following statements provides the Executive Powers of the President?

(Chap 8, Class-VII, Old NCERT)

1. He appoints ministers and distributes portfolios amongst them on the advice of the Council of Ministers.
2. He appoints Attorney-General, Comptroller and Auditor-General, Chairman and members of the Union Public Service Commission.
3. He also appoints Inter-State Council.

Codes

(a) 1 and 2 (b) 2 and 3
(c) 1 and 3 (d) All of these

Ans. *(b)*

Exp. Statements (2) and (3) provides the Executive Powers of the President.

President appoints the Constitutional positions such as Attorney-General, Comptroller and Auditor-General, Chairman and members of UPSC as he is the head of the state and is empowered under the Constitution to appoint such members.

Article 263 empowers President to establish Inter-State Council if at any time it appears to the President that the public interests would be served by the establishment of a Council.

Statement (1) does not provides executive powers of the President because the President appoint ministers and distributes portfolios amongst them on the advice of the Prime Minister and not on the advice of the Council of Ministers.

15 Which of the following statements is/are correct?

(Chap 5, Class-XI, Old NCERT) (Chap 10, Module-3, NIOS)

1. President, Vice-President, the Governor of any State or a Cabinet Minister is debarred from becoming a candidate for contesting the election for the office of the President.
2. The President is required to take an oath in a prescribed form in the presence of the Chief Justice or the senior most Judge of the Supreme Court of India.

Codes

(a) Only 1 (b) Only 2
(c) Both 1 and 2 (d) Neither 1 nor 2

Ans. *(b)*

Exp. Statement (2) is correct as according to Article 60, every President and every person acting as President or discharging the functions of the President shall before entering upon his office is required to take an oath in a prescribed form.

This oath is taken in the presence of the Chief Justice of India or in his absence, the seniormost Judge of the Supreme Court affirmates oath to preserve, protect and defend the Constitution and the law.

Statement (1) is incorrect because President, Vice-President, the Governor of any State or a Cabinet Minister, whether at the centre or state, is not debarred from becoming a candidate for contesting the election for the office of the President.

16 Consider the following statements.

(Chap 5, Class-XI, Old NCERT)

1. If the election of the President of India is declared void by the Supreme Court of India, all acts done by him/her in the performance of duties of his/her office of President before the date of decision become invalid.
2. Election for the post of the President of India can be postponed on the ground that some Legislative Assemblies have been dissolved and elections are yet to take place.
3. When a Bill is presented to the President of India, the Constitution prescribes time limits within which he/she has to declare his/her assent.

How many of the statements given above is/are correct?

(a) Only one (b) Only two
(c) All three (d) None of these

Ans. *(d)*

Exp. None of these statements are correct. If the election of a person as President is declared void by the Supreme Court, acts done by him before the date of such declaration of the Supreme Court are not invalidated and continue to remain in force.

The Supreme Court in 1974 held that the dissolution of State Legislative Assembly will not be a ground for preventing the holding of the elction on the expiry of the term of the President.

The Constitution of India does not prescribe any time-limit within which the President has to take decision with respect to a Bill presented to him/her fot his/her assent.

17 With reference to the legislative power of the President of India, consider the following statement.

(Chap 4, Class-XI, New NCERT)

1. Summoning, proroguing and dissolving the two houses of Parliament.
2. Addressing the Joint Session of the two houses.
3. Assenting the Bills passed by the two houses.
4. Promulgation of an ordinance.

How many of the statements given above is/are incorrect?

(a) Only one (b) Only two
(c) Only three (d) All of these

Ans. *(a)*

Exp. Only one statement i.e., (1) is incorrect with reference to the legislative power of the President of India. According to Article 86 of the Constitution, the President summons both the houses (Lok Sabha and Rajya Sabha) of the Parliament and prorogues them. However, he can dissolve only the Lok Sabha and not the Rajya Sabha as Rajya Sabha is a permanent house and not subject to dissolution.

18 Consider the following statements regarding the ordinance promulgated by the President of India.

(Chap 6, Class-IX & X, Old NCERT)

1. The President can promulgate ordinances when both the houses of Parliament are in session.
2. It has the same force and effect as an act passed by the Parliament under its legislative powers.
3. An ordinance promulgated by the President needs to be approved within six weeks of reassembly of both the houses of Parliament.

Which of the statements given above is/are incorrect?

(a) 1 and 2 (b) 2 and 3
(c) 1 and 3 (d) 1, 2 and 3

Ans. (c)

Exp. Statements (1) and (3) are incorrect regarding the ordinance promulgated by the President of India.

The President can promulgate ordinances when either of the houses of Parliament is not in session.

An ordinance remains valid for not more than 6 weeks from the date Parliament is convened unless approved by it earlier. If the houses of Parliament are summoned to reassemble on different dates, the period of six weeks is calculated from the later of those dates.

19 With reference to the powers of the President of India, consider the following statements.

(Chap 6, Class-XI, Old NCERT)
(Unit 3, Class-XII, Tamil Nadu Board)

1. The President can direct that any matter on which decision has been taken by a minister should be placed before the Council of Ministers.
2. The President can call all information relating to proposals for Legislation.
3. The President has the right to address and send messages to either house of the Parliament.
4. All decisions of the Council of Ministers relating to the administration of Union must be communicated to the President.

How many of the statements given above is/are not correct?

(a) Only one (b) Only two (c) Only three (d) All four

Ans. (d)

Exp. All four statements i.e., (1), (2), (3) and (4) are correct with reference to power of President of India. The President is the Chief Executive of the Union and integral part of the Parliament and enjoys certain legislative powers.

The Prime Minister of India has a duty to communicate to the President all decisions of the Council of Ministers relating to the administration of the affairs of the Union and proposals for legislation.

It is the duty of the Prime Minister to furnish such information relating to the administration of affairs of the union and proposals for legislation as the President.

According to Article 78 if the President requires to submit for the consideration of the Council of Ministers on any matter on a decision has been taken but not considered by the Council. According to Article 86 the President has the right to address and send messages to the house of Parliament relating to bills pending or other topics.

20 Consider the following statements.

(Chap 4, Class-XI, New NCERT) (Chap 10, Module-3, NIOS)

1. The President of India can summon a session of the Parliament at such place as he/she thinks fit.
2. The Constitution of India provides for three sessions of the Parliament in a year, but it is not mandatory to conduct all three sessions.
3. There is no minimum number of days that the Parliament is required to meet in a year.

How many of the statements given above is/are correct?

(a) Only one (b) Only two
(c) All three (d) None of these

Ans. (b)

Exp. Only two statements i.e., (1) and (3) are correct.
Article 85(1) of the Indian Constitution states that the President shall from time to time summon each house of Parliament to meet at such time and place and the date appointed for its first sitting in the West session and there is no provision of the minimum number of days that the Parliament is required to meet in a year.

Statement (2) is incorrect because the Constitution does not state that three session of the Parliament should be called in a year.

21 The President cannot declare war or deploy forces of the country without the sanction or in anticipation of the sanction of which of the following?

(Chap 5, Class-XI, Old NCERT)

(a) Council of Ministers
(b) Prime Minister
(c) Parliament
(d) None of the above

Ans. (c)

Exp. The President cannot declare war or deploy forces of the country without the sanction or in anticipation of the sanction of Parliament. The President is the Supreme Commander of the Indian Armed Forces.

The President can declare war or conclude peace, on the advice of the Union Council of Ministers headed by the Prime Minister which is the Executive and part of Parliament.

22 **In which of the following cases, the President can exercise its pardoning power?**

(Chap 5, Class-XI, Old NCERT)

1. In all cases where the punishment or sentence is by a Court Martial.
2. In all cases where the punishment or sentence is for an offence against any law relating to a matter to which the Executive Power of the Union extends.
3. In all cases where the sentence is a sentence of death.

Codes

(a) 1 and 2 (b) 2 and 3 (c) 1 and 3 (d) All of these

Ans. (d)

Exp. In all of the given cases, the President can exercise its pardoning power. As mentioned in Article 72 of the Indian Constitution, the President is empowered with the powers to grant pardons in the following situations

- Punishment is for an offence against Union Law.
- Punishment is by a Military Court.
- Sentence of death.

The President of India grants, pardons, reprieves or remissions of punishment to any person who has been convicted by a Court of Law.

23 **Which of the following are not included in the power 'to pardon' of President?**

(Chap 1, Class-XI, Old NCERT) (CGPSC Pre 2016)

1. Pardon 2. Commutation 3. Remission
4. Respite 5. Reprieve 6. Detention
7. Continuation

Codes

(a) Only 1 (b) 2 and 3
(c) 6 and 7 (d) 1, 2, 3, 4 and 5

Ans. (c)

Exp. 'Detention' and 'Continuation' are not included in the power 'to pardon' of President. The pardoning powers of President consist of pardon, commutation, remission, respite, reprieve.

Article 72 empowers the President to grant pardens to persons. There pardoning power are Executive Power and are independent of the Judiciary.

24 **Consider the following statements with reference to powers regarding foreign affairs of the President.**

(Chap 5, Class-XI, Old NCERT)

1. All the diplomatic businesses are conducted in the name of President.
2. He appoints ambassadors and other diplomatic agents of India accredited to other countries.
3. All international treaties and agreements conducted in his name need not to be ratified by Parliament.

Which of the statements given above is/are correct?

(a) 1 and 2 (b) 1 and 3 (c) 2 and 3 (d) 1, 2 and 3

Ans. (a)

Exp. Statements (1) and (2) are correct with reference to powers regarding foreign affairs of the President.

All the diplomatic businesses are conducted in the name of the President. He appoints ambassadors and other diplomatic agents of India accredited to other countries. Diplomatic agents accredited to India present their credentials to the President.

Statement (3) is incorrect because all international treaties and agreements are also conducted in his name but they are to be ratified by the Parliament later on.

25 **Consider the following pairs.**

(Chap 5, Class-XI, Old NCERT)

Emergency Power		Article
1. National Emergency	–	Article 351
2. State Emergency	–	Article 352
3. Financial Emergency	–	Article 356

How many pairs given above is/are correctly matched?

(a) Only one (b) Only two
(c) All three (d) None of these

Ans. (d)

Exp. None of the pair given above is correctly matched. National Emergency, when the President feels satisfied that the security of India or any part thereof is threatened or there is an imminent danger of such a threat by war or external aggression or by armed rebellion, he can proclaim an emergency, known as National Emergency. under Article 352.

State Emergency If a President is satisfied that it is not possible to carry on the government of that State according to the provisions of the Constitution, State Emergency or President's rule can be imposed by him, under Article 356.

Financial Emergency If the President is satisfied that a situation has arisen whereby the financial stability or credit of India or any of its part is threatened, he may proclaim a Financial Emergency under Article 360.

The Vice-President

26 **Which of the following statements is/are correct about the Vice-President of India?**

(Chap 5, Class-XI, Old NCERT)

1. When the office of the President is vacant by reason of his death, resignation or removal, the Vice-President discharges his functions as officiating President.
2. When the President is unable to discharge his functions due to absence or illness, the Vice-President becomes the acting President.

Codes

(a) Only 1 (b) Only 2
(c) Both 1 and 2 (d) Neither 1 nor 2

Ans. (c)

Exp. Both the statements (1) and (2) are correct about the Vice-President of India. Article 65 of the Indian Constitution says that the Vice-President of India will have to discharge the duties of the President, if the office falls vacant due to any reason other than the expiry of the term.

In this case, Vice-President discharges functions as the acting President. The Vice-President reverts to his office when a new President is elected and enters office.

When the President is unable to act because of absence, illness or any other cause, the Vice-President discharges the President's functions as officiating President until the President resumes the duties.

27 Who amongst the following elects the Vice-President of India? *(Chap 5, Class-XI, Old NCERT)* *(UPPSC Pre 2012)*

1. Members of Lok Sabha
2. Members of Rajya Sabha
3. Members of Legislative Assemblies
4. Members of Legislative Councils

Codes

(a) 1 and 2 (b) 1 and 3
(c) 1, 2 and 3 (d) 1, 2, 3 and 4

Ans. (a)

Exp. Members of Lok Sabha and Rajya Sabha elects the Vice-President of India. The Vice-President is elected by the members of both the houses of Parliament (i.e Lok Sabha and Rajya Sabha) assembled at a joint meeting.

The election is held in accordance with the system of proportional representation by means of single transferable votes.

28 Which of the following statements is incorrect regarding the Vice-President of India? *(Chap 5, Class-XI, Old NCERT)*

(a) The Vice-President is elected by the members of both the houses of Parliament.
(b) All doubts and disputes related to the election of a Vice-President shall be decided by the Supreme Court.
(c) He presides over the meetings of Rajya Sabha and conducts all its proceedings except when the resolution for his removal is under consideration.
(d) He can be removed from his office by a resolution of Rajya Sabha on the ground of violation of the Constitution.

Ans. (d)

Exp. Statement (d) is incorrect regarding the Vice-President of India. Article 67(b) of the Constitution states that "the Vice-President can be removed by a resolution of the Rajya Sabha passed by an effective majority and agreed by the Lok Sabha with simple majority". However, such a resolution can be moved only by giving at least fourteen days' notice. The Constitution does not list grounds for removal.

29 Who among the following Vice-Presidents have worked as the Acting President of India? *(Chap 4, Class-XI, New NCERT)*

1. Zakir Hussain
2. VV Giri
3. BD Jatti
4. Gopal Swarup Pathak

Codes

(a) 2 and 3 (b) 2 and 4 (c) 3 and 4 (d) 1, 2 and 3

Ans. (a)

Exp. VV Giri and BD Jatti are the Vice-Presidents who have worked as the Acting President of India.

After the death of President Zakir Hussain in office on 3rd May, 1969, VV Giri became acting President of India.

BD Jatti was acting President of India from 11th February to 25th July, 1977 following the death of President Fakhruddin Ali Ahmed.

Prime Minister and Council of Ministers

30 Consider the following statements. *(Chap 4, Class-XI, New NCERT)*

1. Article 79 of our Constitution provides for a Council of Ministers, with Prime Minister as its head, to aid and advice the President.
2. The President first appoints Council of Ministers and then Prime Minster on their advice.

Which of the statements given above is/are correct?

(a) Only 1 (b) Only 2
(c) Both 1 and 2 (d) Neither 1 nor 2

Ans. (d)

Exp. Neither statement (1) nor (2) is correct.

Article 74 of the Constitution provides for a Council of Ministers, with Prime Minister as its head, to aid and advice the President. The President is required to act according to its advice.

The President first appoints the Prime Minister and then on his advice appoints other ministers. He appoints such a person as Prime Minister about whom he feels that he would be able to get support of the majority of members of Lok Sabha.

31 With reference to the appointment of the Prime Minister, consider the following statement. *(Chap 5, Class-XI, Old NCERT)*

1. Need not necessarily be a member of one of the houses of Parliament but must become a member of one of the houses within six months.
2. Need not necessarily be a member of one of the houses of Parliament but must become a member of the Lok Sabha within six months.
3. Must be either a nominated or elected member of one of the houses of Parliament.

Which of the statements given above is/are incorrect?

(a) 1 and 2 (b) Only 1 (c) Only 2 (d) 2 and 3

Ans. (d)

Exp. Statements (2) and (3) are incorrect with reference to the appointment of the Prime Minister. He/she can be member of either house of Parliament, Rajya Sabha/Lok Sabha . It is not necessary to be a member of Lok Sabha only. It is not necessary to be a member of either house at the time of appointment. He/she must be a member of either house within six month after appointment.

32 The power wielded by the Prime Minister flows from which of the following sources? ***(Chap 4, Class-XI, New NCERT)***

1. Control over the Council of Ministers
2. Leadership of the Lok Sabha
3. Command over the bureaucratic machine
4. Access to media

Codes

(a) 1 and 3 (b) 1, 2 and 3 (c) 2 and 4 (d) All of these

Ans. *(d)*

Exp. The power wielded by the Prime Minister flows from all of the given sources. Some powers wielded by Prime Minister are as follows

- The Prime Minister has full control over the Council of Ministers. He presides over the meeting of Council of Minister and also influences its decisions.
- He is the leader of Lok Sabha and announces the government policies on the floor of the house.
- He has full command over the bureaucratic machinery. He plays an instrumental role in appointing these machineries.
- He has access to media.

33 Consider the following statements. ***(Chap 5, Class-XI, Old NCERT)***

1. There are three categories of ministers-Cabinet Ministers, Ministers of State and Deputy Ministers.
2. The ministers of state are of two categories.

Which of the statements given above is/are correct?

(a) Only 1 (b) Only 2
(c) Both 1 and 2 (d) Neither 1 nor 2

Ans. *(c)*

Exp. Both the statements (1) and (2) are correct.

There are three categories of ministers i.e. Cabinet Minister, Ministers of State and Deputy Ministers.

Cabinet is a small body of ministers who occupies the prominent position in the party and holds important portfolios. Deputy Ministers work under the supervision of either a Cabinet Minister or a minister of state.

The ministers of state are of two categories. Some of the ministers of state have an independent charge of their ministry. The second category of the minister of state acts under the supervision of a Cabinet Minister. Sometimes, they may be called to attend the meetings of the Cabinet when an important meeting pertaining to their department is discussed.

34 Consider the following statements and choose the correct code. ***(Chap 4, Class- XI, New NCERT)***

Statement-I A vote of no confidence even against a single minister leads to the resignation of the entire Council of Ministers.

Statement-II Collective responsibility is based on the principle of the solidarity of the Cabinet.

Codes

(a) Both Statement-I and Statement-II are correct and Statement-II is the correct explanation for Statement-I.
(b) Both Statement-I and Statement-II are correct and Sstatement-II is not the correct explanation for Statement-I.
(c) Statement-I is correct, but Statement-II is incorrect.
(d) Statement-I is incorrect, but Statement-II is correct.

Ans. *(a)*

Exp. Both Statement-I and Statement-II are correct and Statement-II is the correct explanation for Statement-I.

A formal vote by which the members of a Legislature indicate that they no longer support a leader, government, etc. results in resignation of the entire Council of Ministers.

Cabinet collective responsibility, also known as collective ministerial responsibility, is a constitutional convention in Parliamentary systems that members of the Cabinet must publicly support all governmental decisions made in Cabinet meeting even if they do not privately agree with them.

35 Consider the following statements. ***(Chap 4, Class-XI, New NCERT) (UPPSC Mains 2012)***

1. The Council of Ministers is collectively responsible to the house of the people.
2. The Council of Ministers is collectively responsible under a Constitutional obligation.
3. The Council of Ministers is collectively responsible as per Article 75(3).
4. The Council of Ministers is collectively responsible as per Article 74(3).

Which of the statements given above is/are correct?

(a) 1 and 2
(b) 1, 2 and 3
(c) 1, 3 and 4
(d) 1, 2, 3 and 4

Ans. *(b)*

Exp. Statements (1), (2) and (3) are correct.

The Council of Ministers is collectively responsible to the house of the people and it also responsible under a constitutional obligation. Article 75(3) of our Constitution provides that Council of Ministers shall be collectively responsible to the house of people. It is a Constitutional obligation.

Statement (4) is incorrect because Article 74(3) is not provided in our Constitution.

36 **With reference to the Constitution of India, consider the following statements.**

(Chap 4, Class-XI, New NCERT)

1. The Council of Ministers of the Union are responsible to both the house of Parliament.
2. The President of India cannot appoint anyone as Union Minister not recommended by Prime Minister.
3. The Prime Minister in the Council of Ministers shall not exceed 15% of the total strength of the Lok Sabha.

Which of the statements given above is/are correct?

(a) Only 1 (b) Only 2
(c) Both 2 and 3 (d) None of these

Ans. (c)

Exp. Both statements (2) and (3) are correct.

According to Article 75, the President of India cannot appoint anyone as Union Minister and the other ministers shall be appointed by the President on the advice of the Prime Minister. As per 91st Amendment Act of 2003, the total number of Minister including the Prime Minister in the Council of Ministers shall not exceed 15% of the total strength of the Lok sabha.

Statement (1) is incorrect because according to Article 75 Clause 3, the Council of Ministers shall be collectively responsible to the Lok Sabha not to both of the house of Parliament.

37 **Which of the following statements is incorrect regarding the Prime Minister of India?**

(Chap 4, Class-XI, New NCERT)

(a) The Prime Minister enjoys a pre-eminent place in the government.
(b) The Council comes into existence only after the Prime Minister has taken the oath of office.
(c) The death or resignation of the Prime Minister does not automatically bring about the dissolution of the Council of Ministers.
(d) The Prime Minister acts as a link between the Council of Ministers on the one hand and the President as well as the Parliament on the other.

Ans. (c)

Exp. Statement (c) is incorrect regarding the Prime Minister of India. The death or resignation of the Prime Minister automatically brings about the dissolution of the Council of Ministers. However, dismissal or resignation of a minister only creates a ministerial vacancy. The Prime Minister acts as a link between the Council of Ministers on the one hand and the President as well as Parliament on the other.

38 **Consider the following statements.**

(Chap 5, Class-XI, Old NCERT)

1. The Cabinet takes all the major policy decisions.
2. In case of difference of opinion, the Council of Ministers can refuse to take the responsibility for those decisions.
3. An individual minister may differ on a particular decision and he cannot express it publicly even after resignation.

Which of the statements given above is/are correct?

(a) 1 and 2 (b) Only 1 (c) 2 and 3 (d) All of these

Ans. (b)

Exp. Statement (1) is correct as the Cabinet is a body of high-ranking state officials, typically consisting of the executive branch's top leaders.

Members of a Cabinet are usually called Cabinet Ministers and take all important and major policy decisions. It is a collegiate decision-making body with collective responsibility.

Statements (2) and (3) are incorrect. The Council of Ministers takes the responsibility of all the decisions taken by Cabinet.

Also an individual minister may differ on a particular decision but he cannot publish it publicly unless he first submits his resignation from the Council of Ministers.

39 **The Prime Minister of India, at the time of his/her appointment** *(Chap 4, Class-XI, New NCERT) (IAS Pre 2012)*

(a) need not necessarily be a member of one of the houses of the Parliament but must become a member of one of the houses within six months.
(b) need not necessarily be a member of one of the houses of the Parliament but must become a member of the Lok Sabha within six months.
(c) must be a member of one of the houses of the Parliament.
(d) must be a member of Lok Sabha.

Ans. (a)

Exp. As per Article 75 (5), the Prime Minister or any minister of India, at the time of his/her appointment not necessarily needed to be a member of one of the houses of the Parliament but must become a member of one of the houses within six months (by election or by nomination).

40 **With reference to the function of Council Ministers, consider the following statements.**

(Chap 5, Class-XI, Old NCERT)

1. It supervises the execution of all policy decisions.
2. It introduces a censure motion against the member of Parliament of the opposition party.
3. It prepares bills and pilots them in the two houses of Parliament so that they become laws.

How many of the statements above given is /are incorrect?

(a) Only one (b) Only two
(c) All three (d) None of these

Ans. (a)

Exp. Only one statement i.e., (2) is incorrect because it is not one of the function of the Council of Minister.

A censure motion can be moved in the Parliament or in a State Assembly in India. It is moved by the opposition against a specific policy of the government or against a minister or against the whole Council of Ministers.

41 Arrange the following offices of Central Administration in the correct hierarchical order.

(Chap 8, Class-XI, Old NCERT)

1. Secretary
2. Joint Secretary
3. Additional Secretary
4. Deputy Secretary
5. Under Secretary

Codes

(a) 1, 2, 3, 4, 5 (b) 5, 4, 2, 3, 1
(c) 1, 2, 3, 5, 4 (d) 5, 1, 2, 3, 4

Ans. (b)

Exp. The correct hierarchical order of positions and designations held by IAS officer in their career are 5, 4, 2, 3, 1 i.e., under Secretary, Deputy Secretary, Joint Secretary (post under the central staffing scheme and the third highest non-political executive rank in Government of India), Additional Secretary (post and a rank under the central staffing scheme of the Government of India) and Secretary (post and a rank under the central staffing scheme of the Government of India).

The authority for the creation of this post solely rests with the Union Council of Ministers heading a ministry or a department.

42 Consider the following statements with respect to Cabinet Secretariat. *(Chap 8, Class-XI, Old NCERT)*

1. Cabinet Secretary heads the Cabinet Secretariat.
2. The office has its origin in the British era.
3. The efficiency of the Cabinet depends largely on the working of the Secretariat.

Which of the statements given above is/are correct?

(a) 1 and 3 (b) 2 and 3 (c) 1, 2 and 3 (d) 1 and 2

Ans. (c)

Exp. All the given statements (1), (2) and (3) are correct with respect to Cabinet Secretariat.

The head of Cabinet Secretariat is Cabinet Secretary. He is usually the seniormost civil servant of the country. The official precedence gives him the first place among the civil servants.

The origin of the Cabinet Secretariat can be traced back from the time of British period. When the work of the Government of India expanded, the Governor-General distributed the work of different departments among various members of Executive Council. Thus, office of Cabinet Secretariat originated.

The efficiency of the Cabinet depends largely on the working of the Secretariat.

43 With reference to the Union Government, consider the following statements.

(Unit 3, Class-XII, Tamil Nadu Board)

1. N. Gopalaswami Ayyangar Committee suggested that a minister and a secretary be designated solely for pursuing the subject of administrative reform and promoting it.
2. In 1970, the Department of Personnel was constituted on the Reforms Commission, 1966, and this was placed under the Prime Minister's charge.

Which of the statements given above is/are correct?

(a) Only 1 (b) Only 2
(c) Both 1 and 2 (d) Neither 1 nor 2

Ans. (c)

Exp. Both the statements (1) and (2) are correct. In 1954, on the recommendation of Paul H. Appleby report, an Organisation and Methods (O&M) Division was set up in the Cabinet Secretariat. In 1964, the O&M Division was transferred to the Ministry of Home Affairs, under the newly created Department of Administrative Reforms. In 1970, on the basis of the recommendations of the Administrative Reforms Commission, the Department of Personnel was set up in the Cabinet Secretariat. Since Cabinet secretariat falls under the Prime Minister,

In 1949, the Gopalaswami Ayyangar Committee while recommending restructuring of the Central Secretariat, suggested that a Department should be identified with a Secretary's charge and a Ministry should be identified with a Minister's charge.

Chapter 10

Union Legislature

Union Legislature

Legislature and Structure of Parliament

Legislature
- Makes legal rule for general application
- Rules made by elected members on behalf of constituents
- Central Legislature in India is called Parliament
- **Functions and Powers of Parliament**
  - Legislative Functions and Powers
  - Financial Power and Functions
  - Power to Control the Executive
  - Judicial Power and Functions
  - Electoral Functions
  - Power to Amend the Constitution

Structure of Parliament
- Parliament consists the President and two Houses (Lok Sabha and Rajya Sabha)
- President integral part but not a member of House
- **Unicameral and Bicameral System of Parliament**
  - Two types of Parliament : Unicameral and Bicameral
  - Bicameral System : India, Britain
  - Unicameral System : China, Nepal

Rajya Sabha & Lok Sabha

Rajya Sabha
- Members elected by State Legislatures
- Proportional representation, Single-Transferable Vote System
- **Structure of Rajya Sabha**
  - Permanent body
  - Maximum 250 members; State representation depends on population size
- **Qualification of the Member** Citizen of India, age 30 years
- **Tenure** Six years; 1/3rd retire every two years, eligible for re-election
- **Functions and Powers of Rajya Sabha**
  - Legislative Powers; Financial Powers; Electoral Powers; Amendment Powers; Executive Powers
- **Special Power of Rajya Sabha**
  - Article 249 allows Rajya Sabha to declare State List 1 subject as national importance with 2/3rd majority
  - Article 312 grants Rajya Sabha power to create All India Services with 2/3rd majority for National Interest

Lok Sabha
- Lower House; Elected by Universal Adult Franchise
- **Structure of Lok Sabha**
  - Maximum 550 members
  - 530 from states, 20 from UTs
- **Qualification** Indian citizen Minimum age 25 years; Voter registration in any Indian Constituency
- **Tenure**
  - Five years; Dissolution possible before five years with President's advice; Extension during national emergency upto 1 year
- **Allocation of Seats** Allocation based on population Article 81 (2)A
- **Powers and Functions of Lok Sabha**
  - Legislative Powers
  - Executive Powers
  - Financial Powers
- **Special Powers**
  - Leader of the House
  - Leader of Opposition

Budget and Parliament Commitee

Budget in Parliament and Financial Process
- Article 112 as the Annual Financial System
- **Stages of Enactment of Budget**
  - Presentation of Budget
  - General Discussions
  - Scrutiny by Dept Committees
  - Voting on Demand for Grants
  - Appropriation Bill and Finance Bills

Funds of Government of India
- Consolidated Fund of India (Article 266 (1)
- Contingency Fund of India (Article 267)
- Public Accounts of India (Article 266 (i)

Parliamentary Committee
- Ad Hoc Committees.
- Joint Parliamentary committees
- Standing Committees
- **Public Account Committee**
  - Total 22 members
  - 15 from Lok Sabha and 7 from Rajya Sabha
- **Estimates Committee**
  - Total 30 members
  - All from Lok Sabha

Committee on Public Undertaking
- Total 22 members
- 15 from Lok Sabha and 7 from Rajya Sabha

SOURCE ***Old NCERT Class VII*** *(Our Parliament in Action),* ***New NCERT Class VIII*** *(Why do we Need a Parliament?),* ***Old NCERT Class IX & X*** *(Our Government at the Centre),*
New NCERT Class XI *(Legislature),* ***Old NCERT Class XI*** *(Features of Legislature, Legislature of India, Legislative and Financial Processes at Centre and State Level, Our Government at the Centre)*

1 With reference to the legislature, consider the following statements. *(Chap 3, Class- VIII, New NCERT)*

1. The Legislative authority of the Union is vested in the Parliament of India.
2. The Parliament consists of the President and the two Houses, the Rajya Sabha (Council of States) and the Lok Sabha (House of the People).
3. It is recognised as one of the most democratic and open forums of debate.

How many of the statements given above is/are correct?

(a) Only one (b) Only two (c) All three (d) None of these

***Ans.* (c)**

Exp. All three statements i.e., (1), (2) and (3) are correct with respect to the legislature.

The Legislative authority of the Union is vested in the Parliament of India.

As per Article 79 of the Constitution of India, the Council of the Parliament of the Union consists of the President and two Houses known as the Council of States (Rajya Sabha) and the House of the People (Lok Sabha).

Primarily, it serves to represent the population or electorate, making laws and subsequently enacting them. Hence, it is described as one of the most democratic and open forums of debate.

2 Consider the following statements about the legislature. *(Chap 5, Class- XI, New NCERT)*

1. It is a law-making body.
2. It is the centre of all democratic political process.
3. A genuine democracy is inconceivable without a representative, efficient and effective legislature.

Which of the statements given above is/are correct?

(a) Only 1 (b) Only 2
(c) Only 3 (d) All are correct

***Ans.* (d)**

Exp. All the given statements are correct regarding legislature.

Law-making is one of the functions of legislature. It is not merely the law-making body. It is the centre of all democratic process. It is packed with actions, such as walkouts, protests, demonstration, unanimity, concern and co-operation.

A genuine democracy is inconceivable without a representative, efficient and effective legislature. Legislature also helps people in holding the representatives accountable.

3 With reference to a Bicameral Legislature, consider the following statements. *(Chap 2, Class-XI, Old NCERT)*

1. It embodies unitary principle or the will of the states in a federation.
2. It affords a chance to able men to enter the legislature.
3. It prevents the passage of hasty and ill-considered legislation by a single house.
4. It gives representation to special interests or groups or sections of people in a state.

How many of the statements given above is/are incorrect?

(a) Only one (b) Only two
(c) Only three (d) All of these

***Ans.* (a)**

Exp. Only one statement i.e., (1) is incorrect with reference to a Bicameral Legislature. It embodies federal principle with representation of federal units in the form of Upper House which is a permanent house.

By dividing power within the legislative branch, bicameralism helps prevent the legislative branch from having too much power.

4 Consider the following statements with respect to the qualifications of Member of Parliament.

1. Citizen of India. *(Chap 3, Class-IX & X, Old NCERT)*
2. 30 years in the case of Lok Sabha.
3. 25 years in the case of Rajya Sabha.

Which of the statements given above is/are incorrect?

(a) Only 1 (b) Only 2 (c) 2 and 3 (d) 1, 2 and 3

***Ans.* (c)**

Exp. Statements (2) and (3) are incorrect with respect to the qualifications of Member of Parliament.

According to Article 84(b), qualifications of Member of Parliament in terms of age is not less than 30 years of age for Rajya Sabha and not less than 25 years of age for Lok Sabha.

5 Which of the following statements with respect to the Parliament is/are correct? *(Chap 3, Class-XI, Old NCERT)*

1. Every member of either house has to take an oath before taking his/her seat.
2. 50 members constitute the quorum of the Houses of Parliament.

Select the correct answer from the codes given below.

(a) Only 1 (b) Only 2 (c) Both 1 and 2 (d) Neither 1 nor 2

***Ans.* (a)**

Exp. Statement (1) is correct with respect to the Parliament as according to Schedule 3 of Indian Constitution, a Member of Parliament has to take an oath to bear true faith and allegiance to the Constitution of India before taking his/her seat in the house.

Statement (2) is incorrect as one-tenth of the total number of members forms the quorum of any meeting of the house.

6 Consider the following statements about the oath of members of Parliament. *(Chap 11, Module-3, NIOS)*

1. Members of Parliament are administered oath by the President as provided under the Fourth Schedule of the Constitution.
2. A Member of Parliament subscribes to the oath 'To preserve, protect and defend the Constitution and the law'.

3. A person can be disqualified from the House of the Parliament, if he sits or votes as a member in the House without taking and subscribing to the prescribed oath or affirmation.

Which of the statements given above is/are incorrect?

(a) Only 1 (b) Only 2
(c) Both 2 and 3 (d) 1, 2 and 3

Ans. (d)

Exp. All the statements (1), (2) and (3) are incorrect about the oath of members of Parliament.

Members of Parliament are not administered the oath by the President. They take the oath or affirmation in the respective Houses of Parliament. The President's oath is specified in Article 60 of the Constitution.

The oath or affirmation taken by Members of Parliament includes the commitment 'To bear true faith and allegiance to the Constitution of India'.

A person can not be disqualified from the House of Parliament if he/she sits or votes without taking and subscribing to the prescribed oath or affirmation.

Rajya Sabha

7 Consider the following statements with respect to the Rajya Sabha. *(Chap 5, Class-XI, Old NCERT) (Chap 11, Module-2, NIOS)*

1. It consists of 12 members nominated by the President from the field of literature, science, art and social service.
2. The representatives of each State are elected by the members of the Legislative Assembly of that State.

Which of the statements given above is/are incorrect?

(a) Only 1 (b) Only 2
(c) Both 1 and 2 (d) Neither 1 nor 2

Ans. (d)

Exp. Neither statements (1) nor (2) are incorrect with respect to Rajya Sabha.

Rajya Sabha consists of 12 members nominated by the President from the field of literature, science, art and social services.

The representative of each states are elected by the elected members of the Legislative Assembly of that State in accordance with the system of proportional representation by means of single transferable vote system. The representatives of each Union Territory are chosen in such a manner as Parliament by law prescribes.

8 Consider the following statements with respect to qualification to become the member of Rajya Sabha. *(Chap 5, Class-XI, Old NCERT) (MPPSC Pre 2005)*

1. Should be at least 30 years of age.
2. Should be registered as a voter on the list of voters in the state from which the candidate is to be elected.
3. Should not hold office of profit under the state.

Which of the statements given above are correct?

(a) 1 and 2 (b) 1 and 3 (c) 2 and 3 (d) 1, 2 and 3

Ans. (b)

Exp. Statements (1) and (3) are correct with respect to qualification to become the member of Rajya Sabha.

Following are some of the qualifications to become the member of Rajya Sabha i.e.,

He must be a citizen of India.

He must not be less than 30 years.

He should not hold any office of profit (excepting of a minister under the Government of India, any State, Union Territory).

He should not be of unsound mind.

He should not be insolvent.

Statement (2) is incorrect because prior to 2003, it was necessary that a candidate of Rajya Sabha must be enrolled in the voter list of that state from which he / she is elected. But after the amendment, this criteria was removed.

9 According to which of the following schedules to the constitution provides for allocation of seats to the States and Union territories of Rajya Sabha? *(Chap 5, Class-XI, New NCERT)*

(a) Second Schedule
(b) Third Schedule
(c) Fifth Schedule
(d) Fourth Schedule

Ans. (d)

Exp. Fourth Schedule (4) of the Indian Constitution provides for allocation of seats to the States and Union Territories in Rajya Sabha. The allocation of seats is made on the basis of the population of each state.

10 With reference to the special powers of the Rajya Sabha, consider the following statements. *(Chap 5, Class-XI, New NCERT)*

1. It can alone initiate the procedure for removal of the President.
2. Any matter that affects the states must be referred to it for its consent and approval.
3. If the Union Parliament wishes to remove a matter from the State list to either the Union List or Concurrent List in the interest of the nation, the approval of the Rajya Sabha is necessary.

How many of the statements given above is/are not correct?

(a) Only one (b) Only two (c) All three (d) None of these

Ans. (a)

Exp. Only one statement i.e., (1) is not correct with reference of the special powers of the Rajya Sabha. According to Article 61, the President may be removed before the expiry of the term through impeachment for violating the Constitution of India by the Parliament of India. The process may start in either of the two houses of the Parliament i.e, Lok Sabha and Rajya Sabha.

11 Which of the following statements is/are incorrect?
(Chap 5, Class-XI, New NCERT)
(Unit 2, Class-XII, Tamil Nadu Board)

1. Members of the Rajya Sabha are elected for a term of six years.
2. Every two years, half the members of the Rajya Sabha complete their term and elections are held for those seats only.

Select the correct answer using the codes given below.
(a) Only 1
(b) Only 2
(c) Both 1 and 2
(d) Neither 1 nor 2

Ans. *(b)*
Exp. Statement (2) is incorrect as according to Article 83(1), every second year, one-third of the members retire and vacancies are filled up by fresh elections.

12 Rajya Sabha has equal powers with Lok Sabha in
(Chap 5, Class-XI, New NCERT) (IAS Pre 2020)

(a) the matter of creating new All India Services.
(b) amending the Constitution.
(c) the removal of the government.
(d) making cut motions.

Ans. *(b)*
Exp. Rajya Sabha has equal powers with Lok Sabha in amending the Constitution. Besides it, Rajya Sabha and Lok Sabha are co-equal in passing of non-money bills, impeaching the President and removing the Vice-President of India.
The matter of creating new All India Services is initiated in Rajya Sabha. The Council of Ministers is responsible to the Lok Sabha and not Rajya Sabha.
Therefore, Rajya Sabha can only criticise the government and cannot remove it. Cut motions are special privilege of Lok Sabha.

13 With reference to Finance Bill and Money Bill in the Indian Parliament, consider the following statements. *(Chap 5, Class-XI, Old NCERT) (IAS Pre 2023)*

1. When the Lok Sabha transmits Finance Bill to the Rajya Sabha, it can amend or reject the Bill.
2. When the Lok Sabha transmits Money Bill to the Rajya Sabha, it cannot amend or reject the Bill, it can only make recommendations.
3. In the case of disagreement between the Lok Sabha and the Rajya Sabha, there is no joint sitting for Money Bill, but a joint sitting becomes necessary for Finance Bill.

How many of the statements given above is/are correct?
(a) Only one
(b) Only two
(c) All three
(d) None of the above

Ans. *(a)*
Exp. Only one statement i.e., (2) is correct with reference to Finance Bill and Money Bill in the Indian Parliament as when the Lok Sabha transmits Money Bill to the Rajya Sabha, it cannot amend or reject the bill, it can only make recommendations.
Statements (1) and (3) are incorrect because the Rajya Sabha can only recommend amendments in the bill. The bill has to be passed by the Parliament within 75 days of its introduction.
In the case of disagreement the Lok Sabha and the Rajya Sabha, there is no joint sitting for Money bill and no joint sitting of the two Houses is allowed with regard to a Finance Bill under Article 108.

Lok Sabha

14 Consider the following statements with reference to Lok Sabha. *(Chap 7, Class- VII, New NCERT)*

1. It consists of not more than 530 members elected directly by the people of the States and Union Territories.
2. Seats shall be reserved for the Scheduled Castes and the Scheduled Tribes in proportion to their population.
3. Each state is allotted a number of seats in proportion to its population.
4. The members of Lok Sabha are elected on the basis of Universal Adult Franchise.

Which of the statements given above is/are incorrect?
(a) Only 1
(b) Only 3
(c) Both 2 and 3
(d) Both 1 and 4

Ans. *(a)*
Exp. Statement (1) is incorrect with reference to Lok Sabha as Article 81(a) and (b) of the Constitution defines the composition of the House of the People or Lok Sabha. It states that the House shall not consist of more than 550 elected members of whom not more than 20 will represent Union Territories.

15 For election to the Lok Sabha, a nomination paper can be filed by *(Chap 5, Class-XI, Old NCERT) (IAS Pre 2017)*

(a) anyone residing in India.
(b) a resident of the constituency from which the election is to be contested.
(c) any citizen of India whose name appears in the electoral roll of a constituency.
(d) any citizen of India.

Ans. *(c)*
Exp. For election to Lok Sabha, a nomination paper can be filed by any citizen of India whose name appears in the electoral roll of a constituency. Beside it, he must possess the following qualifications for being elected as the member of Parliament.
He must be a citizen of India.
He must not be less than twenty-five years of age.
he must be of sound mind.

16 **Which of the following statements is/are correct ?**

(Chap 5, Class-XI, Old NCERT)
(Unit 2, Class-XII, Tamil Nadu Board)

1. The tenure of the Lok Sabha is five years but the President is empowered to dissolve it earlier also.
2. While a Proclamation of Emergency is in operation, the term of the Lok Sabha can be extended by the Parliament for a period of six months at a time.

Select the correct answer using the codes given below.

(a) Only 1 (b) Only 2
(c) Both 1 and 2 (d) Neither 1 nor 2

Ans. (a)

Exp. Statement (1) is correct as the President summons both the Houses (the Lok Sabha and the Rajya Sabha) of the Parliament and prorogues them. They also have the power to dissolve the Lok Sabha pursuant to Article 85(2)(b).

Statement (2) is incorrect as under Article 352 of the Indian Constitution, Lok Sabha can be extended during the time of National Emergency for one year at a time. In any case of extension, it can't continue beyond the period of six months after the emergency has ceased to operate.

17 **With reference to the powers of Lok Sabha, consider the following statements.** *(Chap 5, Class-XI, New NCERT)*

1. A money bill can only be introduced in the Lok Sabha.
2. The Council of Ministers is responsible to the Lok Sabha and not Rajya Sabha.
3. Approves proposals for taxation, budgets and annual financial statements.
4. The number of constituencies has not changed since the 2001 Census.

How many of the statements given above is/are incorrect?

(a) Only one (b) Only two (c) Only three (d) All four

Ans. (a)

Exp. Only one statement i.e., (4) is incorrect with reference to the powers of Lok Sabha because the number of constituencies of Lok Sabha has not changed since 1971 Census. At present, there are 543 constituencies in Lok Sabha. The number of constituencies of Lok Sabha will remain same till 2026. In 2008, Delimitation was done based on 2001 Census, but the total number of seats in the Assemblies and Parliament as per 1971 Census was not changed.

18 **Consider the following statements regarding the office of the Lok Sabha Speaker.**

(Chap 5, Class-XI, Old NCERT)

1. He/she holds the office during the pleasure of the President.
2. He/she need not be a member of House at the time of his/her election but has to become a member of the House within six months from the date of her/his election.
3. If he/she intends to resign, the letter of his/her resignation has to be addressed to the Deputy Speaker.

Which of the statements given above is/are incorrect?

(a) 1 and 2 (b) Only 3 (c) 1, 2 and 3 (d) None of these

Ans. (a)

Exp. Statements (1) and (2) are incorrect regarding the office of the Lok Sabha Speaker.

The House of People choose the speaker among themselves, who conducts its business. He/she does not hold the office during the pleasure of the President. Since, he is elected within the members of House of people and hence he needs to be a member of that house at the time of election.

19 **With reference to the removal of the Speaker of the Lok Sabha, consider the following statements.**

(Chap 5, Class-XI, New NCERT) (Chap 11, Module-3, NIOS)

1. The motion of removal of the Speaker of Lok Sabha can be considered and discussed only when 50 members support it.
2. He/she can be removed only by a resolution passed by the Lok Sabha by an effective majority.
3. He/she does not have the right to speak in the proceeding of the resolution of his removal.

Which of the statements given above is/are correct?

(a) Only 1 (b) 1 and 2 (c) 1, 2 and 3 (d) 2 and 3

Ans. (c)

Exp. All the statements are correct with reference to the removal of the Speaker of the Lok Sabha.

The motion for the removal of the Speaker of the Lok Sabha can be considered and discussed only if it is supported by at least 50 members of Lok Sabha.

The Speaker can be removed only by a resolution passed by the Lok Sabha, and for this resolution effective majority requires, which needs to be passed by a majority of the total membership of the House.

The Speaker, during the proceeding of the resolution for his/her removal, does not have the right to speak.

20 **Match the following lists correctly and choose the correct code.** *(Chap 5, Class-XI, Old NCERT)*

List I (Functions of Lok Sabha)	List II (Description)
A. Electoral functions	1. Removal of President, Vice-President
B. Financial functions	2. Election of the President and Vice- President of India
C. Judicial functions	3. Grant of resources to the government
D. Constitutional functions	4. Constitutional amendments

Codes

	A	B	C	D		A	B	C	D
(a)	3	2	1	4	(b)	2	3	1	4
(c)	1	3	4	2	(d)	4	1	3	2

Ans. (b)

Exp. The correct matching is A-2, B-3, C-1 and D-4.

Electoral function Election of President and Vice-President is an electoral function of Election Commission of India conducted under the aegis of Parliament under Article 54 and 61 respectively.

Financial function Parliament has the financial function of granting resources to the government under Article 110.

Judicial function Parliament has the judicial function of removal of President and Vice-President under Article 61 and 71(1) respectively.

Constitutional function Parliament has the constitutional function to amend the Constitution under Article 368.

Law-making Process/ Parliamentary Procedure

21 Which of the following statements is/are incorrect with respect to Parliament? *(Chap 5, Class-XI, Old NCERT)*

1. It has an exclusive power to legislate on the subjects mentioned in the Union List as well as all the residuary subjects.
2. If there is a conflict between the laws passed by the Parliament and that of a State Legislature, the law of the Parliament prevails to the extent of inconsistency.

Select the correct answer using the codes given below.

(a) Only 1
(b) Only 2
(c) Both 1 and 2
(d) Neither 1 nor 2

Ans. (d)

Exp. Neither statements (1) nor (2) are incorrect with respect to Parliament. According to Article 248, the Parliament has exclusive power to make any law with respect to any matter not enumerated in the Concurrent List or the State List.

Also, in case of inconsistency between a state law and a Parliamentary law, the latter is to prevail. Such a law can be amended or repealed only by the Parliament and not by the legislatures of the concerned states.

22 Consider the following statements with reference to the ordinary bills. *(Chap 5, Class-XI, New NCERT)*

1. An ordinary bill can be introduced in either of the two Houses.
2. The draft of the proposed bill has to be sent to the Secretariat of the House.
3. It has to be passed by both Houses for enactment.
4. If there is disagreement between the two Houses on the proposed bill, the bill lapses.

Which of the statements given above is/are not correct?

(a) Only 1
(b) 1 and 2
(c) Only 4
(d) 3 and 4

Ans. (c)

Exp. Statement (4) is not correct regarding the ordinary bills as in case of ordinary bill, the powers of Lok Sabha and Rajya Sabha are equal.

If there is disagreement between both the Houses on the passage of the bill, then the President may call for a joint sitting which is presided over by the Speaker of Lok Sabha. Article 108 of Constitution deals with the provision of the joint sitting.

23 Consider the following statements with reference to the Money Bills. *(Chap 5, Class-XI, New NCERT)*

1. The Rajya Sabha can either approve the bill or suggest changes but cannot reject it.
2. Amendments in the Money Bill as suggested by Rajya Sabha must be accepted by the Lok Sabha within 14 days.
3. A Money Bill shall not be introduced in the Council of States.
4. Procedure with respect to the Money Bills is given under Article 109 of the Indian Constitution.

How many of the statements given above is/are not correct?

(a) Only one
(b) Only two
(c) Only three
(d) All of these

Ans. (a)

Exp. Only one statement i.e., (2) is not correct about the Money Bills. Procedure with respect to Money Bill has been mentioned in Article 109 of the Constitution as per Article 109, a Money Bill shall not be introduced in Council of States (Rajya Sabha).

After the Money Bill is passed by the House of People (Lok Sabha) it shall be transmitted to the Council of States for its recommendations and Council of States has to return the bill within 14 days from the date of its receipt. However, Lok Sabha is free to pass the bill with or without considering its recommendations.

24 A deadlock between the Lok Sabha and the Rajya Sabha calls for a joint sitting of the Parliament during the passage of

(Chap 5, Class-XI, New NCERT) (IAS Pre 2012)

1. Ordinary Legislation
2. Money Bill
3. Constitutional Amendment Bill

Codes

(a) Only 1
(b) 1 and 3
(c) 2 and 3
(d) 1, 2 and 3

Ans. (a)

Exp. A deadlock between the Lok Sabha and Rajya Sabha calls for a joint sitting of the Parliament during the passage of Ordinary Legislation.

Article 108 of our Constitution provides for joint sitting of Parliament. It provides that when there is a deadlock between the two Houses of Parliament then joint sitting is summoned by the President. It is mainly called to resolve the deadlock in the case of ordinary bill.

Money Bill can only be introduced in Lok Sabha and hence there is no provision of joint sitting.

In case of Constitutional Amendment Bill, each house has to pass it separately and hence there is also no provision of joint sitting. Joint sitting is presided by the Speaker of Lok Sabha.

25 Which of the following does not form the part of expenditure charged upon the Consolidated Fund of India? *(Chap 5, Class-XI, Old NCERT)*

(a) Emoluments and allowances of President of India.
(b) Salaries and allowances of the Chairman and Deputy Chairman of Rajya Sabha.
(c) Salaries and allowances of Speaker and Deputy Speaker of the Lok Sabha.
(d) Salaries and allowances of Members of Parliament.

Ans. (d)

Exp. Salaries and allowances of the Members of Parliament does not form the part of expenditure charged upon the Consolidated Fund of India.

The Consolidated Fund of India was created under Article 266 (1).

26 Consider the following statements about difference between Public Bill and Private Bill in the Parliament. *(Chap 5, Class-XI, New NCERT)*

1. Introduction of a Private member's Bill in the house requires one month's notice, whereas Public Bill requires only seven days' notice.
2. A Public Bill can be introduced and discussed on any day, a Private Bill can only be introduced and discussed on Fridays.
3. The Public Bill can propose a constitutional amendment, but the Private Bill cannot do this.

Which of the statements given above is/are correct?

(a) Only 1
(b) 1 and 3
(c) 2 and 3
(d) l, 2 and 3

Ans. (b)

Exp. Statements (1) and (3) are correct. A private member's bill in the house requires one month's notice,whereas public bill requires only seven days' notice. Private Member's Bills, those introduced by members who are not part of the government, generally require a longer notice period compared to Public Bills.

Both Public Bills and Private Bills can propose Constitutional Amendments. There is no restriction on the type of bill that can propose a Constitutional Amendment.

Statement (2) is incorrect because both Public Bills and Private Bills can be introduced and discussed on any day when the House is in session. There is no restriction that Private Bills can only be introduced and discussed on Fridays.

27 Arrange the following stages of enactment of a bill in correct order. *(Chap 5, Class-XI, Old NCERT)*

1. The draft of the proposed Bill has to be sent to the Secretariat.
2. Second Reading
3. First Reading
4. Refer the Bill to a selected committee

Codes

(a) 1, 2, 3, 4
(b) 1, 3, 2, 4
(c) 2, 1, 3, 4
(d) 3, 2, 4, 1

Ans. (b)

Exp. The correct order of the stages of enactment of a bill is the draft of the Proposed Bill has to be sent to the Secretariat-First Reading-Second Reading- Refer the Bill to a selected committee.

After the introduction of Ordinary Bill, the draft of the proposed bill has to be first sent to the Secretariat of the House. The presiding officers of the concerned house, after consulting the Business Advisory Committee determines the day and time, when the bill is to be moved.

In the first reading, the bill is introduced in the house. At this stage, no discussion takes place. In the second reading, bill is discussed clause and in the third reading, a brief general discussion of the billl takes place and bill is finally passed. When the bill is passed by one house, it is sent to the other house for its consideration.

28 Consider the following statements about Adjournment motion in the Parliament. *(Chap 4, Class-XI, Old NCERT)*

1. It is introduced in the House to draw attention of the House to a definite matter of urgent public importance.
2. It can be introduced in Lok Sabha only.
3. During the discussion on Adjournment motion, the Speaker has no power to adjourn the House for the day.

Which of the statements given above is/are correct?

(a) Only 1
(b) Only 1 and 2
(c) Only 2 and 3
(d) 1, 2 and 3

Ans. (b)

Exp. Statements (1) and (2) are correct. Adjournment motion is introduced only in the Lok Sabha to draw the attention of the House to a definite matter of urgent public importance.

It involves an element of censure against the government; therefore Rajya Sabha is not permitted to make use of this device.

Statement (3) is incorrect because during the discussion on an Adjournment motion, the Speaker has the power to adjourn the House if he/she is of the opinion that the matter is not of urgent public importance.

29 **Which of the following statements is incorrect regarding No-Confidence Motion?** *(Chap 11, Module-3, NIOS)*

(a) No-Confidence Motion is mentioned in the Constitution under Article 75.
(b) The Ministry stays in office till they enjoy the confidence of the majority of the members of the Lok Sabha.
(c) It can be moved only in Lok Sabha and not in Rajya Sabha.
(d) It is moved only against the entire Council of Minister and if passed, the Council of Minister must resign from office.

Ans. *(a)*

Exp. Statement (a) is incorrect regarding No-Confidence Motion.

The No-Confidence Motion is not specifically mentioned in the Constitution under Article 75. It is based on parliamentary conventions and practices.

30 **Consider the following statements and choose the correct code.** *(Chap 4, Class-XI, Old NCERT)*

Statement-I The powers of the Council of States in respect of financial matters are lesser than those conferred upon the House of People.

Statement-II The Council does not possess the right of voting grants.

Codes

(a) Both Statement-I and Statement-II are correct and Statement-II is the correct explanation for Statement-I.
(b) Both Statement-I and Statement-II are correct and Statement-II is not the correct explanation for Statement-I.
(c) Statement-I is correct, but Statement-II is incorrect.
(d) Statement-I is incorrect, but Statement-II is correct.

Ans. *(b)*

Exp. Both Statement-I and Statement-II are correct and Statement-II is not the correct explanation for Statement-I.

The powers of the Council of States in respect of financial matters are lesser than those conferred upon the House of People. As Money Bills and Financial Bills under Articles 110 and 117 can be introduced only in House of People, Rajya Sabha does not have any voting rights with respect to voting grant as it is passed by the Lower House.

31 **With reference to the budget, consider the following statements.** *(Chap 4, Class-XI, Old NCERT)*

1. No demand for grant is made except on the recommendation of the Lok Sabha.
2. No money shall be withdrawn from the consolidated fund except under appropriation made by the Appropriation Act.
3. Cut motions can be introduced in response to the demand for grants.
4. The Finance Bill incorporates all proposals of new taxes as well as the changes in rate of existing taxes.

How many of the statements given above is/are incorrect?

(a) Only one (b) Only two
(c) All three (d) None of these

Ans. *(a)*

Exp. Only one statement i.e., (1) is incorrect with reference to the budget. According to Article 113(III), budget as no demand for grant is made in Lok Sabha except on the recommendation of the President.

Under Article 113, the Lok Sabha has the power to give or refuse its ascent to a demand for grants or it can reduce the amount specified in the demand.

32 **Which of the following conditions gives scope to delegated legislation?** *(Chap 3, Class-XI, Old NCERT)*

1. Subjects of legislation sometimes are of technical nature.
2. Emergency and urgent situation requiring prompt legislative action.

Select the correct answer using the codes given below.

(a) Only 1 (b) Only 2
(c) Both 1 and 2 (d) Neither 1 nor 2

Ans. *(c)*

Exp. The conditions mentioned in statements (1) and (2) give scope to delegated legislation. When the legislature enacts a law, it leaves the details to be worked out by the executive through rules and regulations subject to the approval of legislature. This arrangement is called delegated legislation or Subordinate legislation.

When the subject matter under the Act is completely technical in nature, then consultation of expert is needed. This leads towards delegated legislation.

Delegated legislation is very important in dealing with an emergency situation as it arises without waiting for an Act to be passed by Parliament to resolve the particular situation.

Parliamentary Privileges and Immunities

33 **Consider the following points, with reference to the Individual Parliamentary Privileges.** *(Chap 3, Class-XI, Old NCERT)*

1. Freedom of speech
2. Freedom from arrest
3. Freedom from attendance as witness
4. Right to publish debate and proceedings

Which of the given above is not one of the individual Parliamentary Privileges?

(a) Only 1 (b) Only 2
(c) Only 4 (d) Both 2 and 4

Ans. *(d)*

Exp. Both (2) and (4) are not the points with reference to the Individual Parliamentary Privileges.

Freedom from arrest and Right to publish debate and proceedings is not one of the individual parliamentary privileges.

Parliamentary privileges are defined in Article 105 of the Indian Constitution.

The Members of Parliament are exempted from any civil or criminal liability for any statement made or act done in the course of their duties under parliamentary privileges.

The privileges given to the members are necessary for exercising constitutional functions.

Right to publish debate and proceedings of the House comes under Freedom of Speech and Expression under Article 19.

34 Consider the following statements. *(Chap 3, Class-XI, Old NCERT)*

1. Right to regulate the internal affairs of the house.
2. Right to punish any person for breach of its privileges.
3. Right to punish any person for Parliamentary behaviour.

Which of the statements given above is/are the collective parliamentary privileges?

(a) 1 and 2 (b) Only 1 (c) 2 and 3 (d) All of these

Ans. (a)

Exp. Both the statements (1) and (2) are the collective Parliamentary privilege as under Article 118, each house of Parliament has the power to make rules for regulating its proceeding and conduct its business.

The Indian Parliament has the power to punish any person whether strangers or any member of the house for any breach or contempt of the house. When any breach is committed by the member of the house, he/she is expelled from the house.

Statement (3) is not a collective parliamentary privilege as a person can be punished only when he is indulged in some non-Parliamentary activities.

35 With respect to Question Hour, consider the following statements. *(Chap 4, Class-XI, Old NCERT)*

1. Most of the questions aim at eliciting information from the government on issues of public interest.
2. The Question hour is the second item of business after the Zero Hour in Lok Sabha.
3. The starred questions are answered orally.
4. The upstarted questions are meant for written reply.

Which of the statements given above is/are not correct?

(a) Only 1 (b) Both 1 and 2
(c) Only 2 (d) Both 3 and 4

Ans. (c)

Exp. Only statement (2) is not correct with respect to Question Hour. It is the first hour of a sitting session of Lok Sabha. It is devoted to questions that Members of Parliament raise about any aspect of administrative activity.

Parliamentary Committees

36 Consider the following statements with respect to parliamentary committees. *(Chap 5, Class-XI, Old NCERT)*

1. The Standing Committee is appointed as and when the need arises, they cease to exist as soon as they complete the work assigned to them.
2. The Ad hoc Committee is elected or appointed every year or periodically and their work goes on more or less on a continuous basis.

Which of the statements given above is/are correct?

(a) Only 1
(b) Only 2
(c) Both 1 and 2
(d) Neither 1 nor 2

Ans. (d)

Exp. Neither statement (1) nor (2) are correct with respect to parliamentary committees. Standing Committee is permanent and regular committee which is constituted from time to time in pursuance of the provisions of an Act of Parliament.

On the other hand, Ad hoc Committee is formed for a limited period of time to address a specific need. When the work of the Ad hoc Committee is completed, the committee is dissolved.

37 Which of the following are financial committees of Indian Parliament? *(Chap 5, Class-XI, Old NCERT) (RAS/RTS Pre 2018)*

1. Estimates Committee
2. Public Accounts Committee
3. Committee on Public Undertakings
4. Joint Committee on Salaries and Allowances for Members of Parliament.

Select the correct answer using the codes given below.

(a) 1, 3 and 4
(b) 1, 2 and 4
(c) 1, 2 and 3
(d) 2, 3 and 4

Ans. (c)

Exp. Estimates Committee, Public Accounts Committee and Committee on Public Undertakings are the financial committees of Indian Parliament. These are permanent (standing) committees of Parliament. These committees constitute a distinct class, which keep vigilance over government expenditure.

On the other hand, Joint Committee on Salaries and Allowances for Members of Parliament is one of the Housekeeping Committee.

38 Which of the following statements is correct about the Public Accounts Committee?

(Chap 5, Class-XI, Old NCERT) (IAS Pre 2013)

(a) It consists of 15 members elected by Lok Sabha and 7 elected by Rajya Sabha for a period of one year.
(b) It scrutinises the appropriation accounts of the Government of India and the reports of the Attorney-General of India.
(c) It calls attention to cases of waste, extravagance, loss or nugatory expenditure or lack of financial integrity in public services.
(d) Both a and c

***Ans.** (d)*

Exp. Statements (a) and (c) are correct about Public Accounts Committee.

The Public Accounts Committee consists of not more than 22 members, 15 elected by Lok Sabha, the Lower house of the Parliament, and not more than 7 members of Rajya Sabha, the Upper house of the Parliament. The members are elected every year from amongst its members of respective houses according to the principle of proportional representation by means of Single Transferable Vote.

It also ensures that public money is spent in accordance with Parliament's decisions and calls attention to cases of waste, extravagance, loss or nugatory expenditure or lack of financial integrity in public services.

Statement (b) in incorrect because the primary function of the PAC is to examine the audit report of Comptroller and Auditor-General (CAG) after it is laid in the Parliament.

39 Consider the following statements regarding the Estimates Committee. *(Chap 5, Class-XI, Old NCERT)*

1. It consists of 30 members elected by Lok Sabha every year.
2. The Chairman of the Committee is appointed by the Speaker from amongst its members.
3. It also examines whether the money is laid out within the limits of the estimates.
4. It cannot suggest alternative policies to the government.

How many of the statements given above is/are incorrect?

(a) Only one
(b) Only two
(c) All four
(d) None of the above

***Ans.** (a)*

Exp. Only one statement i.e., (4) is incorrect regarding the Estimates Committee because it functions include reporting on potential savings, organisational improvements, efficiency gains and administrative reforms that are consistent with the policy implied in the estimates and also suggesting alternative policies to achieve efficiency and economy in administration.

40 Which of the following statements with respect to the Committee on Public Undertakings is /are correct? *(Chap 5, Class-XI, Old NCERT)*

1. The Committee checks the accounts of public undertakings and examines their working and other financial matters and the reports of Comptroller and Auditor-General of India.
2. This Committee consists of twenty members, out of which fifteen are elected by members of Lok Sabha and five from Rajya Sabha.

Select the correct answer using the codes given below.

(a) Only 1
(b) Only 2
(c) Both 1 and 2
(d) Neither 1 nor 2

***Ans.** (a)*

Exp. Statement (1) is correct with respect to the Committee on Public Undertakings as their functions are to examine the reports and accounts of public undertakings specified in the Fourth Schedule to the Rules of Procedure and Conduct of Business in Lok Sabha and to examine the reports of the Comptroller and Auditor-General of India on the Public Undertakings.

Statement (2) is incorrect because the committee consists of twenty-two members, where fifteen were elected by Lok Sabha and not more than seven members by Rajya Sabha. Its chairman is appointed by the Speaker.

Chapter 11

State Executive

State Executive

Constitutional Provisions

Constitutional Provisions and State Executive

- Articles 153 to 167 in Part-VI deal with State Executive
- **Parts of State Executive**
  - Governor
  - Chief Minister
  - Council of Ministers
  - Advocate-General

Governor

- **Appointment**
  - Under Article 155
  - By President
  - Term Five years
- **Qualification**
  - Citizen of India
  - Age 35 years
  - Not a Member of either House of Parliament or Legislature
- **Oath** Chief Justice or seniormost Judge of High Court

Powers and Functions

- **Executive Power**
  - Article 154
  - Appoints Chief Minister and other ministers
  - Appoints Advocate-General, Chairman and members of SPSC

Legislative Power

- Article 174; Dissolving Legislative Assembly
- Article 171 (3) nominate 1/6th members of Legislative Council

Financial Power

- Article 202
- Money Bill on recommendation of Governor
- Demand for grant on recommendation of Governor

Judicial Power

- Power to grant pardons, reprieves, remissions of Punishment; Appointment of Judges of concerned states High Court

Chief Minister

Chief Minister

- Real Head of the Government
- Responsible to the people
- **Appointment**
  - Article 164 (1)
  - Appointed by Governor
  - In case of alliance, leader of such group is called to assume the office of Chief Minister
- **Qualification**
  - Must be citizen of India
  - Age 25 or more
  - Should be member of either State Legislative or State Council (if exists)
- In case if not a member of either Houses, he should be a member within six months
- **Oath** In presence of Governor

Powers and Functions of CM

- Article 163
- Takes all financial decision
- Chief spokesperson of the government
- Can remove a minister from his post
- Presides over meeting of the CM
- Can re-shuffle the Council of Ministers

State Council of Minister

Structure

- Cabinet Minister
- Minister of State
- Deputy Minister
- **Appointment**
  - Pleasure of the Governor
  - Appointed by Governor
- **Size** Must not exceed 15% of the total members of the House
- **Qualification**
  - Citizen of India
  - Age 25 or more
  - Should be Member of Legislative Assembly or Council (If exists)
- **Oath** In presence of Governor

Advocate-General

- Legal Advisor of State Government
- Constitutional Body
- Appointed by Governor
- Qualification similar to Judges of High Court
- No fixed tenure

Administration of Union Territories

- Articles 239 to 241 in Part VIII
- Article 239 Administration of Union Territories
- Administered by President (Lieutenant Governor or Chief Commissioner)
- Currently, 8 Union Territories

Chief Secretary

- Controls all Secretariat Departments
- Tenure not fixed

Function of Chief Secretary

- Principal adviser to the Chief Minister
- Prepares agenda for cabinet meetings
- Head of the State Civil Services

SOURCE *Old NCERT Class IX & X* (Our Government at the State), ***New NCERT Class IX*** (Working of Institutions), ***Old NCERT Class XI*** (State Government), ***Old NCERT Class XI*** (Executive of India), ***Old NCERT Class XI*** (Indian Administration : Working and Organisation)

The Governor

1 Consider the following statements, with reference to the Governor. *(Chap 4, Class-XI, New NCERT)*

1. The executive authority of a state is vested in the Governor of the State who exercises all powers directly.
2. The President of India appoints the Governor of a State for a term of five years.
3. He can be removed only after a resolution passed by the Parliament to such effect.

Which of the statements given above is/are correct?

(a) Only 1
(b) Both 1 and 2
(c) Only 2
(d) Both 2 and 3

Ans. (c)

Exp. Only statement (2) is correct with reference to the Governor. According to Article 155, President appoints Governor on advice of Council of Ministers for the term of five years.

Statements (1) and (3) are incorrect because the executive authority of a state is vested in the Governor of the State. It is exercised by him either directly or through officers subordinate to him in accordance with Constitution of India (Article 154).

He works at the pleasure of the President which means he can be removed any time by the President on the recommendation of Council of Ministers headed by Prime Minister.

2 Consider the following statements about the Governor. *(Chap 13, Module-3, NIOS)*

1. The same person cannot be appointed as Governor for two or more states at the same time.
2. No procedure has been laid down in the Constitution of India for the removal of a Governor from his post.
3. The Governor should be a member of either House of the Parliament.
4. The Governor appoints the Chancellors of the Universities in the state.

Which one of the statements given above is/are correct?

(a) Only 1 (b) Only 2
(c) Both 2 and 3 (d) Both 1 and 4

Ans. (b)

Exp. Only statement (2) is correct with reference to Governor. The Constitution does not lay down any grounds upon which a Governor may be removed by the President. It only says that Governor holds office during the pleasure of the President. Statements (1), (3) and (4) are incorrect because there is a Governor for each state, but the 7th Constitutional Amendment Act of 1956, facilitated the appointment of the same person as a Governor for two or more states. Governor should not be a member of either House of Parliament or a House of the State Legislature. Governor himself is Ex-officio Chancellor of the State Universities.

3 Which of the following statements is not correct with respect to the powers of the Governor? *(Chap 6, Class-XI, Old NCERT) (IAS Pre 2014)*

(a) He calls the leader of the majority party or an alliance of parties to form the Ministry.
(b) He distributes portfolios amongst the ministers on the advice of the Council of Ministers.
(c) The Governor has a right to be informed of all the affairs of the State Government.
(d) None of the above

Ans. (b)

Exp. Only statement (b) is not correct with respect to the powers of the Governor because Article 164 states that Governor appoints the Council of Ministers on the aid and advice of Chief Minister who allocates portfolios amongst the ministers who works at the pleasure of the Governor.

4 Consider the following statements. *(Chap 6, Class-XI, Old NCERT) (UPPSC Pre 2017)*

1. The Governor does not have the power to appoint the Judge of a State High Court.
2. He is not a part of the Legislature.
3. He has the power to nominate some members in the Legislative Council.
4. He has no Judicial Power.

Which of the statements given above are correct?

(a) 1 and 2 (b) 1 and 3 (c) 2 and 4 (d) All of these

Ans. (b)

Exp. Statements (1) and (3) are correct as the Governor does not have the power to appoint the Judge of a State High Court. According to Article 217(1), the judges of State High Court are appointed by the President of India, after consultation with the Chief Justice of India, Governor of the State and the Chief Justice of that High Court.

The Governor of State has the powers to nominate some members in Legislative Councils.

Statements (2) and (4) are incorrect because the Governor is an inseparable part of the Legislature as he possesses certain Legislative Powers. The Governor also possesses the judicial powers by granting pardons, reprieves, respites on remissions, etc. to the offender.

5 Consider the following statements. *(Chap 7, Class-IX & X, Old NCERT)*

1. The President must appoint a Governor for each state.
2. Normally, the Governor should not belong to as state to which she/he has been appointed as Governor.

Which of the statements given above is/are incorrect?

(a) Only 1 (b) Only 2 (c) Both 1 and 2 (d) Neither 1 nor 2

Ans. (d)

Exp. Neither statements (1) nor (2) are incorrect with respect to Governor.

The President must appoint a Governor for each state for a term of 5 years and hold office during his pleasure.

The Governor should not belong to the state to which he/she has been appointed. However, this is a convention which is not mentioned in the Constitution.

6 Which of the following is/are the Legislative Powers of the Governor? *(Chap 6, Class-XI, Old NCERT)*

1. He is an inseparable part of the State Legislature.
2. Summoning, proroguing and dissolving the Legislative Assembly.
3. He can send messages to either or both the Houses of Legislature.

Select the correct answer using the codes given below.

(a) Only 1 (b) Only 2
(c) 1 and 3 (d) 1, 2 and 3

Ans. (d)

Exp. All the given statements (1), (2) and (3) are correct regarding the Legislative Powers of the Governor.

Article 168 clearly states that for every state, there shall be a Legislature, which shall consist of the Governor. Hence, he is an inseparable part of the State Legislature.

Article 174 gives power to Governor to summon the house or each House of the Legislature of the state to meet at such time and place as he thinks fit within six months, prorogue the house or either house and dissolve the Legislative Assembly.

7 Consider the following statements and choose the correct code. *(Chap 6, Class-XI, Old NCERT)*

Statement-I The Constitution (Fourty-Second Amendment) Act, 1976 made mandatory for the President to act on the advice of the Council of Ministers but not so in the case of the Governor.

Statement-II The Central Government did not want to loosen its grip on the State Governments.

Codes

(a) Both Statement-I and Statement-II are correct and Statement-II is the correct explanation for Statement-I.
(b) Both Statement-I and Statement-II are correct and Statement-II is not the correct explanation for Statement-I.
(c) Statement-I is correct, but Statement-II is incorrect.
(d) Statement-I is incorrect, but Statement-II is correct.

Ans. (a)

Exp. Both Statement-I and Statement-II are correct and Statement-II is the correct explanation for Statement-I.

The Constitution (Fourty-Second Amendment) Act, 1976 made mandatory for the President to act on the advice of the Council of Ministers but not so in the case of the Governor because Governor serves as a bridge between Central and State Government.

The Governor has to ensure that stable government is formed in the state and also look into the legal validity of the law passed by State Legislature and recommend President rule in the state, if there is a breakdown of constitutional machinery.

Therefore, this is the reason Central Government did not want to loosen its grip on the State Government.

8 Article 156 of the Constitution of India provides that a Governor shall hold office for a term of five years from the date on which he enters upon his office. Which of the following statement is correct regarding this? *(Chap 6, Class-XI, Old NCERT) (IAS Pre 1995)*

1. No Governor can be removed from office till the completion of his term.
2. No Governor can continue in office beyond the expiration of a period of five years.

Select the correct answer using the codes given below.

(a) Only 1 (b) Only 2
(c) Both 1 and 2 (d) Neither 1 nor 2

Ans. (d)

Exp. Neither statements (1) nor (2) are correct regarding the holding of office by the Governor.

Article 156 deals with the term of office of Governor. As per this Article, Governor shall hold office during the pleasure of the President. However, the Governor may resign from his office by writing to the President.

The Governor, notwithstanding the expiration of the term, continues to hold the office until his successor enters upon his office.

9 Consider the following statements. *(Chap 6, Class-XI, Old NCERT)*

1. He must have completed 30 years of age.
2. He must not hold any office of profit.
3. He must not be a Member of Parliament.
4. He must not be a Member of State Legislature.

Which of the following is not one of the qualifications for the appointment of the Governor?

(a) Only 1 (b) Only 2
(c) Both 2 and 3 (d) Both 3 and 4

Ans. (a)

Exp. Statement (1) is not one of the qualifications for the appointment of the Governor of India.

Article 157 states that no person shall be eligible for appointment as Governor unless he is a citizen of India and has completed the age of 35 years.

The Governor shall not be a member of either House of Parliament or Legislature of a State.

If any member of these houses is appointed as Governor, he shall be deemed to have vacated such membership on the date on which he assumes charge of governorship.

The Governor must not hold any office of profit under the Government of India or Government of State or under any local authority.

10 Consider the following Assertion (A) and Reason (R) and choose the correct code.

(Chap 6, Class-XI, Old NCERT)

Assertion (A) The Governor is a constitutional head of the state.

Reason (R) The real and effective authority with respect to administration of the state is exercised by him.

Codes

(a) Both A and R are true and R is the correct explanation of A.
(b) Both A and R are true, but R is not the correct explanation of A.
(c) A is true, but R is false.
(d) A is false, but R is true.

Ans. *(c)*

Exp. Assertion (A) is true, but Reason (R) is false. According to Article 154, Executive Powers of the State are vested in the Governor and thus he/she is the Constitutional head of the state but the real and effective authority of the state is vested in the Council of Ministers headed by Chief Minister as provided in Article 163 (1).

11 Consider the following statements about the pardoning power of the Governor.

(Chap 6, Class-XI, Old NCERT)

1. The Governor has the power to grant pardons, reprieves, respites, commutation or remissions of punishment of any person convicted of any offence relating to the Executive Power of the State.
2. Like the President, he can also grant pardon in case of a death sentence.

Which of the statements given above is/are incorrect?

(a) Only 1 (b) Only 2 (c) Both 1 and 2 (d) Neither 1 nor 2

Ans. *(b)*

Exp. Only statement (2) is incorrect about the pardoning power of the Governor because Governor cannot pardon death sentences; he can only commute them.

Article 161, states that, the Governor of a State shall have the power to grant pardons, reprieves, respites or remissions of punishment or to suspend, remit or commute the sentence of any person convicted of any offence against any law relating to a matter to which the Executive Power of the State extends except pardoning death sentences as he can only commute the death sentences.

12 With reference to the discretionary power of the Governor, consider the following statements.

(Chap 6, Class-XI, Old NCERT)
(Unit 2, Class-XII, Tamil Nadu Board)

1. Appointment of Chief Minister when no party commands majority.
2. Reservation of State Bills for consideration of the President.
3. Sending a report to the President regarding President rule.
4. Exercising power of suspension veto.

Which of the statements given above is/are incorrect?

(a) Only 1 (b) Only 2 (c) 2 and 3 (d) Only 4

Ans. *(d)*

Exp. Only statement (4) is incorrect with reference to discretionary power of Governor.

Exercising power of suspension veto is not a discretionary power of the Governor. The Governor uses his suspension veto usually when he returns the bill to the Legislature for its consideration. But his suspension veto can be overridden by the repassage of the bill by the Legislature. Hence, it is not the discretionary power of the Governor.

13 Which of the following pairs is incorrectly matched?

(Chap 5, Class-XI, Old NCERT)

Description	Power
(a) Prior Recommendation for Money Bill	– Financial Power
(b) Administering adjoining Union Territory	– Discretionary Power
(c) Power to grant pardons	– Judicial Power
(d) Promulgation of ordinance	– Legislative Power

Ans. *(b)*

Exp. Pair (b) is incorrectly matched.

Administering adjoining Union Territory is not a discretionary power of the Governor. He works at the pleasure of the President and can be entrusted at times the duties of administration of Union Territories on the direction of President.

14 Consider the following statements regarding the Governor of State. *(Chap 6, Class-XI, Old NCERT)*

1. No Money Bill can be introduced in the Legislative Assembly without the recommendation of the Governor.
2. He sees that the budget is laid before the State Legislature every year.
3. He has no veto power in case of Money Bills.

How many of the statements given above is/are incorrect?

(a) Only one (b) Only two
(c) All three (d) None of these

Ans. *(d)*

Exp. None of the given statements i.e., (1), (2) and (3) are incorrect about the Governor of State. According to Article 207, a Bill or amendment-making provision for any of the matters specified in Sub-clauses (a) to (f) of Clause (1) of Article 199 (Money Bill) shall not be introduced or moved except on the recommendation of the Governor.

Article 202 provides that the Governor shall in respect of every financial year cause to be laid before the House or Houses of the Legislature of the State a statement of the estimated receipts and expenditure of the state.

15 The Governor enjoys certain discretionary powers to safeguard the tribal ways of life in which of the following state/states? *(Chap 6, Class-XI, Old NCERT)*

1. Assam
2. Meghalaya
3. Tripura
4. Mizoram

Codes.

(a) 1 and 2
(b) 2 and 3
(c) 3 and 4
(d) 1, 2, 3 and 4

Ans. (d)

Exp. The Governor enjoys certain discretionary powers to safeguard the tribal ways of life in states of Assam, Meghalaya, Tripura and Mizoram. The tribal areas in these four states have been constituted as autonomous districts. It has been mentioned in the Sixth Schedule of the Indian Constitution under Article 244(2) and Article 275(1).

The Governor is empowered to organise and reorganise the autonomous districts. He can increase or decrease their areas or change their names or define their boundaries.

16 With reference to the Advocate-General, consider the following statements. *(Chap 6, Class -XI, Old NCERT)*

1. The Governor appoints the Advocate-General.
2. The remuneration of Advocate-General is determined by the concerned State Legislature.
3. There is a fixed term of office and age limit of 55 years for Advocate-General.

How many of the statements given above is/are correct?

(a) Only one
(b) Only two
(c) All three
(d) None of these

Ans. (a)

Exp. Only statement (1) is correct about the Advocate-General. The Governor of each state shall appoint a person who is qualified to be appointed as Advocate-General.

Statements (2) and (3) are incorrect because the remuneration of Advocate-General is determined by the Governor and there is no fixed term of office and no upper age limit mentioned for the Advocate-General.

17 Consider the following statements and choose the correct code. *(Chap 6, Class-XI, Old NCERT)*

Statement-I The Governor enjoys wider discretionary power as compared to President.

Statement-II It is the Governor himself who decides, at his discretion, as to in which sphere he shall act at his discretion, as to in which sphere he shall act at his discretion and in which field he shall act on the advice of the Council of Ministers.

Codes

(a) Both Statement-I and Statement-II are correct and Statement-II is the correct explanation for Statement-I.
(b) Both Statement-I and Statement-II are correct, and Statement-II is not the correct explanation for Statement-I.
(c) Statement-I is correct., but Statement-II is incorrect.
(d) Statement-I is incorrect, but Statement-II is correct.

Ans. (a)

Exp. Both Statement-I and Statement-II are correct and Statement-II is the correct explanation for Statement-I.

The Governor of State, unlike the President of India, is conferred with power to act at his own discretion. There are two categories of discretion for the Governor. One is Constitutional discretion and the other is situational Discretion. Thus, Governor's discretion is constitutionally valid. Governor is not bound to abide the advice of the Council of Ministers when there is any action taken at his discretion.

Chief Minister and Council of Ministers

18 With respect to the Chief Minister and his Council of Minister, consider the following statements. *(Chap 6, Class-XI, Old NCERT)*

1. Whenever there arises a conflict between a Minister and the Chief Minister, the Minister has to give way to the Chief Minister.
2. The Governor may ask any Minister to resign from his post.
3. The Governor has to appoint such persons as ministers, who have been so recommended by the Chief Minister.
4. If a party commands absolute majority in the Legislative Assembly and elects its own leader, the Governor has to appoint him as the Chief Minister.

Which of the statement is/are incorrect in respect to the Chief Minister and his Council of Ministers?

(a) Only 1 (b) Only 2 (c) 2 and 3 (d) 3 and 4

Ans. (b)

Exp. Only statement (2) is incorrect because it is the Chief Minister who advises the Governor to ask any Minister to resign from his post. Governor on its own cannot ask any Minister to resign from his post.

19 Which of the following statements is incorrect? *(Chap 6, Class-XI, Old NCERT)*

1. The Chief Minister presides over the meetings of the Council of Ministers.
2. It is he who communicates the decision of the Council of Ministers to the Governor.
3. Whenever the Governor wants to communicate to the Chief Minister, he does so through the Council of Ministers.
4. The Chief Minister is the chief spokesman of the government.

Codes

(a) 1 and 2 (b) 2 and 3
(c) Only 3 (d) Only 1

Ans. (c)

Exp. Only statement (3) is incorrect as according to Article 167(A), it shall be the duty of the Chief Minister of each State to communicate to the Governor of the State all decisions of the Council of Ministers relating to the administration of the affairs of the State and proposals for legislation. Chief Minister is the chief spokesman of the government.

20 Consider the following statements about the function of State Council of Ministers.

(Chap 6, Class-XI, Old NCERT)

1. It takes policy decisions on all matters of administration.
2. It supervises the execution of all the policy decisions.
3. It prepares bills and pilots them in the Legislature so that they become laws.

How many of the statements given above is/are correct?

(a) Only one (b) Only two
(c) All three (d) None of these

Ans. (c)

Exp. All three statements i.e., (1), (2) and (3) are correct with reference to the functions of the State Council of Ministers. The Council of Ministers constitutes the real executive in the state. Although, the administration is carried on in the name of the Governor, actual decisions are normally made by Ministers.

The Ministers formulate the policies of the government.

The Cabinet takes decisions on all policy matters. When it formulates a policy, the appropriate department carries it out.

Most of the Bills passed by the Legislature are Government Bills, prepared in the Ministries. They are introduced, explained and defended in the State Legislature by the Ministers.

21 The Constitution of India provides that

(Chap 6, Class-XI, Old NCERT) (IAS Pre 2008)

1. the Legislative Assembly of each state shall consist of not more than 450 members chosen by the direct election from territorial constituencies in the state.
2. a person shall not be qualified to be chosen to fill a seat in the Legislative Assembly of a State if he/she is less than 25 years of age.

Which of the statements given above is/are incorrect?

(a) Only 1 (b) Only 2
(c) Both 1 and 2 (d) Neither 1 nor 2

Ans. (a)

Exp. Only statement (1) is incorrect because according to Article 170(1) of the Indian Constitution, the Legislative Assembly of each state consists of not more than 500 and not less than 60 members elected by direct election from territorial constituencies of the state. For this purpose, each state is divided into territorial constituencies in such manner that the ratio between the population of each constituency and the number of seats allotted to it is almost the same throughout the state.

22 Which Legislative Committees keep a check on the State and Union Executive?

(Chap 6, Class-XI, Old NCERT)

1. Public Account Committee
2. Estimates Committee
3. Committee on Government Assurance

Codes.

(a) 1 and 2 (b) 2 and 3 (c) 1 and 3 (d) All of these

Ans. (d)

Exp. All the given Legislative Committees keep a check on the State and Union Executive.

Public Account Committee keeps a check by auditing the revenue and expenditure of the State Executive.

Estimates Committee scrutinises the functioning of government ministries and departments in terms of expenditure and utilisation of funds.

Committee on Government Assurance scrutinises the assurances, promises, undertakings, etc.

State Administration

23 With respect to the Chief Minister, consider the following statements. *(Unit 2, Class-XII, Tamil Nadu Board)*

1. The offices of the Chief Minister and the Deputy Chief Minister are constitutionally created.
2. The Constitution says nothing about the qualifications of the Chief Minister.

Codes

(a) Only 1 (b) Only 2
(c) Both 1 and 2 (d) Neither 1 nor 2

Ans. (b)

Exp. Only statement (2) is correct as the Constitution does not explicitly mentions any qualifications for the Chief Minister.

The Governor appoints the leader of majority party in the State Legislature Assembly as Chief Minister.

Governor can also appoint a person who is not a member of State Legislature as the Chief Minister, but for a maximum period of six months.

Statement (1) is incorrect because the Constitution of India does not mention any post or office of Deputy Chief Minister. It only states that there shall be a Council of Ministers with Chief Minister as the head to aid and advise the Governor.

24 **With reference to the Advocate-General, consider the following statements.** *(Chap 13, Module-3, NIOS)*

1. The Advocate-General of the State in India is appointed by the President of India on the recommendation of the Governor of the concerned state.
2. According to the provisions of the Code of Civil Procedure, the High Courts at the state level have original, appellate and advisory Jurisdiction.

Which of the statements given above is/are correct?

(a) Only 1 (b) Only 2 (c) Both 1 and 2 (d) Neither 1 nor 2

Ans. (d)

Exp. Neither statements (1) nor (2) are correct because according to Article 165, the Advocate-General of the State is appointed by the Governor of the State and not by the President. According to the provisions of the Code of Civil Procedure, the Jurisdiction of the High Courts at the state level is original and appellate. The Advisory Jurisdiction rests with the Supreme Court.

25 **Consider the following statements about the State Administration.** *(Chap 8, Class-XI, Old NCERT)*

1. The secretariat department is ordinarily headed by a Secretary who is a specialist.
2. An executive department is ordinarily headed by a director who is a generalist.
3. The secretariat department assists the minister in the process of policy-making.
4. The state administrative departments are of three categories.

Which of the statements given above is/are correct?

(a) Only 1
(b) Only 3
(c) Both 1 and 2
(d) Both 3 and 4

Ans. (b)

Exp. Only statement (3) is correct regarding the State Administration as the State Secretariat helps the ministers in their individual and collective capacity to formulate policies on all matters of state administration.

Statements (1), (2) and (4) are incorrect because a secretariat department is ordinarily headed by a secretary who is a generalist.

An executive department is usually headed by a director who is specialist.

The state administrative departments are of two types i.e., secretariat department and executive department.

26 **Consider the following statements with respect to the Chief Secretary.** *(Chap 8, Class-XI, Old NCERT)*

1. The Chief Secretary in a state is appointed by the Governor of that State.
2. The Chief Secretary in a state has a fixed tenure.
3. The Chief Secretary does not controls all secretariat departments.

Which of the statements given above is/are correct about the chief Secretary?

(a) Only 1 (b) Only 2
(c) Both 2 and 3 (d) None of these

Ans. (a)

Exp. Only statement (1) is correct as the Chief Secretary is chosen by Chief Minister and appointed by the Governor of a State. It depends upon his administrative fact, experience, rapport with the Chief Minister and, to a large extent, on his capacity to take an objective stand on sensitive matters.

Statements (2) and (3) are not correct because the Chief Secretary in a state has no fixed tenure. The Chief Secretary would normally retire from the same position or move to the Union Government to take higher position.

Every state has a Chief Secretary and he/she controls all secretariat departments.

27 **With reference to the roles of Chief Secretary, consider the following statements.** *(Chap 8, Class-XI, Old NCERT)*

1. He is an Ex-officio Secretary of the Cabinet and attends all the Cabinet meetings.
2. He acts as the main source of information and advice to the Governor.
3. He supervises the follow-up action for the implementation of the decisions taken at the Cabinet meeting.
4. He deals with the matters relating to inter-state disputes.

Which of the statements given above is/are incorrect?

(a) Only 1 (b) Only 2 (c) 2 and 3 (d) 3 and 4

Ans. (b)

Exp. Only statement (2) is incorrect regarding the roles of Chief Secretary as it is the Council of Ministers headed by Chief Minister which is the main source of information and advice to the Governor as provided in Article 167 of the Indian Constitution. But the Chief Secretary acts as the main source of information and advisor to the Chief Minister.

Chapter 12

State Legislature

State Legislature

Constitutional Provisions

Introduction

- Part VI of Article 168 to 212
- State Legislature is a law making body
- Can be Unicameral or Bicameral

Composition of the State Legislature

- Legislative Assembly (Vidhan Sabha)
  - Lower House
  - Represent people of State
  - Members are directly elected
  - Election held on the basis of Adult Franchise
  - Citizens age 18 or above are eligible to vote
- **Eligibility and Composition**
  - Should be Citizen of India
  - Age 25 years
  - Not hold office of profit
  - Tenure 5 years
- **Legislative Council** (Vidhan Parishad)
  - Upper House
  - Article 168 to 212
  - Article 169, creation or abolition of Legislative Council
  - Parliament can create or abolish
  - State must pass a resolution by a majority of total membership and not less than 2/3rd of the members of the assembly present and voting
  - Currently, 6 states have Legislative Council (Andhra Pradesh, Karnataka, Maharashtra, Telangana, Bihar and Uttar Pradesh)
- **Eligibility and Composition**
  - Total members should not exceed 1/3rd of the Vidhan Sabha, but not less than 40
  - Citizen of India, Age 30 years, not hold office of profit
  - Members are Partly Elected and Partly Nominated
  - Election method single transferable

Disqualification of the Houses

- Hold any office of profit
- Undischarged insolvent
- Under any law made by Parliament
- Article 191 (2) : Anti-defection law

Session of the State Legislature

- Meets atleast twice a year
- Six month gap between two sessions
- Governor can summon and prorogues sessions
- Governor address both House at commencement of the first session after each General Election

Powers and Functions of the State Legislature

- **Law-making Functions**
  - Right to make laws on State and Concurrent List
  - Bills are introduced in either Houses
  - Governor can issue Ordinance (213)
  - Ordinance expires after six weeks
- **Financial Power**
  - Keeps control over State Finance
  - Money Bill certified by Speaker
  - Vidhan Parishad has no power on Money Bill
  - Governor cannot withhold Money Bill
- **Control over the Executive**
  - Council of Ministers is responsible to Vidhan Sabha collectively
  - Dissolution of Houses after passed No-confidence Motion

Officers of the State Legislature

- Article 178 to 187
- **Speaker of Assembly**
  - Elected among members
  - Tenure : till the tenure of House
  - Resignation to Deputy Speaker
- **Deputy Speaker**
  - Elected among members
  - Perform duties in the absence of Speaker

Legislative Procedure in State Legislature

Ordinary Bill (Article 196)

- Expenditure from the consolidated fund of the state
- Can be introduced either Houses of State
- Article 197, conflict in the two Houses of the State Legislature
- No provision for Joint sitting

Money Bill (Article 199)

- Only introduced in Legislative Assembly
- Need prior recommendation of Governor

Privileges of State Legislature

- Can make rules to regulates its own procedure
- Courts are prohibited to enquire into the proceeding of the Houses
- **Collective Privileges**
  - Right to publish its reports, debates and proceedings
  - Right to immediate information of arrest, detention, conviction, etc
  - No person can be arrested within the precincts of House without permission of the Presiding Officer
- **Individual Privileges**
  - Cannot arrested during the session and 40 days before beginning and 40 days after the end of session
  - Freedom of speech in Legislature
  - Exempted from jury service

Session of the State Legislature

- **Summoning** Governor summons each Hours of State Legislature to meet
- **Adjournment** Suspends the work
- **Prorogation** Presiding officer declares the House adjourned
- **Dissolution** New house is constituted
- **Quorum** 1/10th of the total number of members

SOURCE *Old NCERT Class IX & X* (*Our Government at the State*), *Old NCERT Class XI* (*State Government, Legislature of India, Constitutional and Financial Processes at Central and State Level*)

1 **With reference to the legislature of states, consider the following statements.** *(Chap 3, Class- XI, New NCERT)*

1. The system of legislature in states closely follows the pattern of Union Parliament.
2. The State Legislature consists of the Governor and one or two Houses of legislature.
3. The Lower House is known as Legislative Assembly and the Upper House is known as Legislative Council.

How many of the statements given above is/are correct?

(a) Only one
(b) Only two
(c) All three
(d) None of the above

***Ans.** (c)*

Exp. All three statements i.e., (1), (2) and (3) are correct with respect to the Legislature of States.

India has a Parliamentary system of Government with a bicameral legislature at the Centre. Some states have a bicameral legislative system while other have a unicameral one.

At the state level, the legislature is composed of the Legislative Assembly, the Legislative Council (only in 6 states currently) and the Governor of the State.

The State Legislature which has only one House is known as the Legislative Assembly and in the State which has two houses, the Upper House is known as the Legislative Council and the Lower House is known as the Legislative Assembly.

2 **As per Indian Constitution, Legislature of States consists of** *(Chap 14, Module-3, NIOS) (BPSC Pre 1996)*

1. Legislative Council and Governor.
2. Legislative Assembly and Legislative Council.
3. Legislative Assembly and Governor.
4. Governor, Legislative Assembly and Legislative Council where it exists.

Select the correct answer using the codes given below:

(a) Only 3 (b) 2 and 3
(c) 3 and 4 (d) Only 4

***Ans.** (c)*

Exp. Statements (3) and (4) are correct as the Constitution of India provides for a State Legislature in every state. It can either be bicameral or unicameral and it also includes the Governor of the State as well. The state which have a Bicameral Legislature consists of two houses namely as the Legislative Assembly (Lower house of state or Vidhan Sabha) and the Legislative Council (Upper house of state or the Vidhan Parishad). The state having a Unicameral Legislature have just one house i.e. Legislative Assembly.

3 **With reference to the legislative procedure of states, consider the following statements.** *(Chap 6, Class-XI, Old NCERT)*

1. When the legislature is not in session, the Governor may issue an ordinance that has the same force and effect as that of an Act of the Legislature.
2. The ordinance has to be laid before the legislature and approved by it within six weeks of its Assembly.
3. If the ordinance is not approved within six weeks it shall cease to operate.
4. At the end of the last session of each year, the Governor addresses the legislature and informs it of the causes of its summons.

How many of the statements given above is/are incorrect?

(a) Only one (b) Only two
(c) Only three (d) All of these

***Ans.** (a)*

Exp. Only one statement i.e., (4) is incorrect about the legislative procedure of states. According to Article 176, at the start of the session of each year, the Governor addresses the legislature and informs about the causes of the summons. This is the special address given by the Governor.

Legislative Assembly

4 **Which of the following statements is/are incorrect?** *(Chap 6, Class-XI, Old NCERT)*

1. The Legislative Assembly of each State consists of not more than five hundred and not less than 75 members elected by direct election.
2. Each State is divided into territorial constituencies in such a manner that the ratio between the population of each Constituency and the number of seats allotted to it, is almost the double throughout the State.

Select the correct answer using the codes given below.

(a) Only 1 (b) Only 2
(c) Both 1 and 2 (d) Neither 1 nor 2

***Ans.** (c)*

Exp. Both the statements (1) and (2) are incorrect.

According to Article 170(1), the Legislative Assembly of each state shall consist of not more than five hundred and not less than sixty members chosen by direct election from territorial constituencies in the State.

According to Article 170(2), each State shall be divided into territorial constituencies in such manner that the ratio between the population of each constituency and the number of seats allotted to it shall, so far as practicable, be the same throughout the state.

5 **With reference to the Speaker of the Legislative Assembly, consider the following statements.**
(Chap 14, Module-3, NIOS) (IAS Pre 2018)

1. The Speaker of the Legislative Assembly shall vacate his/her office if he/she ceases to be a member of Assembly.
2. Whenever the Legislative Assembly is dissolved, the speaker shall vacate his/her office immediately.

Which of the statements given above is/are correct?
(a) Only 1 (b) Only 2
(c) Both 1 and 2 (d) Neither 1 nor 2

Ans. *(a)*
Exp. Only statement (1) is correct as under Article 179, the Speaker of the Legislative Assembly shall vacate his/her office if he /she ceases to be a member of the Assembly. A member holding office as Speaker or Deputy Speaker of an Assembly;
(a) shall vacate his office if he ceases to be a member of the Assembly;
(b) may at any time by writing under his hand addressed, if such member is the Speaker, to the Deputy Speaker and if such member is the Deputy Speaker, to the Speaker, resign his office; and
(c) may be removed from his office by a resolution of the Assembly passed by a majority of all the then members of the Assembly.

Statement (2) is incorrect because the Speaker does not have to vacate his/her office immediately upon dissolution of the Legislative Assembly.

The Speaker continues to hold office till the newly elected Assembly meets.

6 **Consider the following statements regarding the reservation in State Legislative Assembly.**
(Chap 6, Class-XI, Old NCERT)

1. The Constitution provides for reservation of seats for the Scheduled Castes, Scheduled Tribes and women in the Legislative Assembly of each State in proportion to their population.
2. The members of the Legislative Assembly are elected on the basis of Universal Adult Franchise.
3. The tenure of the Legislative Assembly is five years but the Governor is empowered to dissolve it earlier also.

How many of the statements given above is/are incorrect?
(a) Only one (b) Only two (c) All three (d) None of these

Ans. *(a)*
Exp. Only one statement i.e., (1) is incorrect regarding the reservation in State Legislative Assembly as Article 332 of the Constitution of India provides for reservation of seats for Scheduled Castes and Scheduled Tribes in the Legislative Assemblies of the States, but there is not reservation for women in State Legislative Assembly.

7 **Which of the following is/are the qualifications for becoming a member of the Legislative Assembly?**
(Chap 7, Class-IX & X, Old NCERT)

1. Citizen of India
2. 25 years of age
3. Must not hold an office of profit
4. Such other qualifications as may be prescribed by or under any law made by the Parliament.

Codes
(a) 1 and 2
(b) 2 and 3
(c) 1, 2 and 3
(d) 1, 2, 3 and 4

Ans. *(d)*
Exp. All the conditions mentioned are the qualifications required to become a member of the Legislative Assembly. According to Article 173, the qualifications to become a member of the Legislative Assembly are
- the person should be a Citizen of India, not less than 25 years of age.
- he must not hold an office of profit under the Government of India.
- individual is a voter from any constituency of the State.
- Other such qualification as may be prescribed by or under any law made by Parliament.

8 **With reference to the officers of the State Legislative Assembly, consider the following statements.** ***(Chap 6, Class-XI, Old NCERT)***

1. The House elects its own presiding officer, called Speaker, who conducts its business.
2. During the absence of Speaker from any sitting of the Assembly, the Deputy Speaker, acts as a Speaker.
3. The Speaker presides over all the meetings of,the Legislative Assembly except when the resolution for his removal is under consideration.

Which of the statements given above is/are correct?
(a) Only 1
(b) Both 1 and 2
(c) Only 3
(d) All of the above

Ans. *(d)*
Exp. All the given statements are correct about officers of the State Legislative Assembly.

Article 178 provides that every Legislative Assembly of a State shall, choose two members of the Assembly to be respectively Speaker and Deputy Speaker.

Article 180 provides that while the office of Speaker is vacant, the duties of the office shall be performed by the Deputy Speaker.

Article 181 provides that the Speaker or the Deputy Speaker preside over all the meetings while a resolution for his removal from office is under consideration.

9 Consider the following statements with reference to the powers of the Speaker of the Legislative Assembly. *(Chap 6, Class-XI, Old NCERT)*

1. He disqualifies members on the recommendation of the Election Commission.
2. He maintains order and discipline in the House and prevents the use of unparliamentary language in the house.
3. He decides whether and adjournment motion moved by a member is admissible or not.
4. He decides whether a Bill is a Money Bill or not.

How many of the above statements is not one of the powers of the Speaker of the Legislative Assembly?
(a) Only one (b) Only two (c) Only three (d) All four

Ans. (a)

Exp. Only one statement i.e., (1) is not correct with reference the powers of the Speaker of the Legislative Assembly. Under representation of People's Act 1951, the Governor is the authority who decides in consultation with the Election Commissioner of the State, regarding the disqualifications of the member of the Legislature. The decision of the Governor is final.

10 Consider the following statements, the Constitution of India provides that *(Class-XI, Old NCERT)* *(IAS Pre 2008)*

1. the Legislative Assembly of each State shall consist of not more than 450 members chosen by direct election from territorial constituencies in the state.
2. a person shall not be qualified to be chosen to fill a seat in the Legislative Assembly of a State, if he/she is less than 25 years of age.

Which of the statements given above is/are correct?
(a) Only 1 (b) Only 2 (c) Both 1 and 2 (d) Neither 1 nor 2

Ans. (b)

Exp. Only statement (2) is correct as a person shall not be qualified to be chosen to fill a seat in the Legislative Assembly of a State, if he/she is less than 25 years of age.

Statement (1) is incorrect because the Legislative Assembly consists of representatives directly elected by the people on the basis of Universal Adult Franchise. Article 170 states that the Legislative Assembly can have maximum strength of 500 and minimum strength of 60.

11 Consider the following statements regarding the Speaker of the Legislative Assembly. *(Chap 14, Module-3, NIOS)*

1. He shall vacate his office if he ceases to be a member of the Assembly.
2. He may at any time by writing under his hand addressed to the Governor resign his office.
3. He may be removed from his office by a majority of the members present and voting.
4. No resolution for removal shall be moved unless at least one month's notice has been given of the intention to move the resolution.

Which of the statements given above is/are correct?
(a) 1, 2 and 3 (b) 2 and 3 (c) Only 1 (d) 1, 2 and 4

Ans. (c)

Exp. Only statement (1) is correct about the Speaker of Legislative Assembly. Usually, the Speaker remains in the office during the life of the Assembly. However, he vacates his office earlier if he ceases to be a member of the Assembly.

Statements (2), (3) and (4) are incorrect because the Speaker vacates his office if he resigns by writing to the Deputy Speaker.

The Speaker vacates his office if he is removed by a resolution passed by a majority of all the then members of the Assembly. Such a resolution can be moved only after giving 14 days advance notice.

12 With reference to the distribution of seats in State Legislative Assembly, consider the following pairs. *(Class-XI, Old NCERT)*

States	No. of seat
1. Bihar	243
2. Assam	129
3. Rajasthan	192
4. Tamil Nadu	238

How many of the pairs given above is/are incorrectly matched?
(a) Only one (b) Only two
(c) Only three (d) All of these

Ans. (c)

Exp. Only three pairs i.e., (2), (3) and (4) are incorrectly matched because the distribution of seats in Assam Legislative Assembly is 126 not 129. Rajasthan has 200 seats in Legislative Assembly not 192 and Tamil Nadu has 234 seats not 238 in Legislative Assembly.

Legislative Council

13 Which of the following is the qualification of Member of Legislative Council? *(Chap 6, Class-XI, Old NCERT)*

1. Citizen of India
2. 30 years of age
3. Any other qualification as prescribed by the State Legislature

Select the correct answer using the codes given below.
(a) Only 1 (b) Only 3
(c) 1 and 2 (d) 1, 2 and 3

Ans. (c)

Exp. Statements (1) and (2) posses the qualification of Member of Legislative Council.

A person who wants to become the member of State Legislative Council must be a citizen of India and also should be at least 30 years of age.

Statement (3) is incorrect because the Parliament is empowered to make any other qualification for becoming the member of Legislative Council.

14 **Consider the following statements.**

(Chap 6, Class-XI, Old NCERT) (IAS Pre 2015)

1. The Legislative Council of a state in India can be larger in size than half of the Legislative Assembly of that particular state.
2. The Governor of a state nominates the Chairman of Legislative Council of that particular state.

Which of the statements given above is/are correct?

(a) Only 1 (b) Only 2
(c) Both 1 and 2 (d) Neither 1 nor 2

***Ans.** (d)*
Exp. Neither statements (1) nor (2) are correct.

As per Article 171(1) of the Constitution, the total number of members in the State Legislative Council shall not exceed one-third of the total number of members in Legislative Assembly. But the total number of members in the Legislative Council shall in no case be less than forty.

As per Article 182 of the Constitution, the Chairman and Deputy Chairman of the Legislative Council shall be chosen by the members of the Legislative Council of the state.

15 **In any state of India, Legislative Council can be created or can be abolished by**

(Chap 6, Class-XI, Old NCERT) (BPSC Pre 1995)

(a) the President on the recommendation of the Governor of the State.
(b) the Parliament.
(c) the Parliament as per resolution passed by the Legislative Assembly of the State.
(d) the Governor on the recommendation of the Council of Ministers.

***Ans.** (c)*
Exp. In any state of India, Legislative Council can be created or can be abolished by the Parliament as per resolution passed by the Legislative Assembly of the State under Article 169. As per this Article, Parliament may by law provide for the abolition or creation of Council of states, if the Legislative Assembly of the State passes a resolution to that effect by a majority of the total membership of the Assembly and a majority of not less than two-third of the members of the Assembly present and voting.

16 **Consider the following statements with respect to the State Legislative Council.**

(Chap 6, Class-XI, Old NCERT)

1. The elections are held in accordance with the system of proportional representation by means of Single Transferable Vote System.
2. The tenure of every member of the Council is six years but their membership lapses in case of premature dissolution.

Which of the statements given above is/are incorrect?

(a) Only 1 (b) Only 2
(c) Both 1 and 2 (d) Neither 1 nor 2

***Ans.** (b)*
Exp. Only statement (2) is incorrect with respect to the State Legislative Council as the tenure of the Members of Legislative Council is six years. One-third members of the State Legislative Council retire after every two years. Thus, their membership does not lapse in case of premature dissolution. This arrangement is similar to that of Rajya Sabha.

17 **Consider the following statements with respect to the election of the members of the State Legislative Council.**

(Chap 6, Class-XI, Old NCERT)

1. One-third of the total number of members of the Council arc elected by electorates consisting of members of Municipalities, District Boards, etc.
2. One-third are elected by members of the Legislative Assembly of the State.
3. One-sixth are elected by graduates of three years standing.
4. One-sixth are nominated by the Governor of the State.

Which of the statements given above is/are incorrect?

(a) Only 1 (b) 1 and 2
(c) Only 3 (d) 3 and 4

***Ans.** (c)*
Exp. Only satements (3) is incorrect regarding the election of the members of the State Legislative Council. One-twelfth of the members are elected by persons who are graduates of three years' residing in that state through the system of proportional representation by means of Single Transferable Vote System.

18 **With reference to the State Legislative Council, consider the following statements.**

(Chap 14, Module-3, NIOS)

1. Its tenure is 6 years.
2. It is a permanent house.
3. It can not be dissolved.
4. One-sixth members are elected by local institutions.
5. One-sixth members are elected by Legislative Assembly.
6. On each two years, one-third members are retired.
7. Deputy Governor is the Chairman of House.

Which of the statements given above is/are correct?

(a) 1, 3, 4 and 5 (b) 3, 6, 7 and 8
(c) 1, 2, 3 and 6 (d) 2, 5, 6 and 8

***Ans.** (c)*
Exp. Statements (1), (2), (3) and (6) are correct about the State Legislative Council.

Like the Rajya Sabha, the Legislative Council is a continuing chamber, i.e., it is a permanent body and is not subject to dissolution. One-third of its members retire every two years. So, tenure of its members is six years.

Statements (4), (5) and (7) are incorrect because one-third members are elected by local institution not one-sixth. One-third are elected by the members of the Legislative Assembly of the State from amongst the persons who are not members of the Assembly. There is no such post of the Deputy Governor. The Chairman is elected by the Council itself from amongst its members.

19 With reference to the Chairperson and Deputy Chairperson of the State Legislative Council, consider the following statements.

(Chap 6, Class-XI, Old NCERT)

1. The Legislative Council chooses two of its members as Chairman and Deputy Chairman respectively.
2. A member holding office as Chairman or Deputy Chairman vacates his office if he ceases to be a member of the Council.
3. He may be removed from his office by a resolution of the Council passed by a majority of 2/3rd members present and voting.
4. The Chairman and the Deputy Chairman are paid such salaries and allowances as are fixed by the Legislature.

How many of the statements given above is/are not correct?

(a) Only one (b) Only two
(c) Only three (d) All of these

Ans. (a)

Exp. Only one statement i.e., (3) is not correct regarding the Chairperson and Deputy Chairperson of the State Legislative Council. According to Article 183(c), a member holding office as Chairman or Deputy Chairman may be removed from his office by a resolution of the Council passed by a simple majority of all the then members of the Council. Before moving such a resolution, fourteen days notice must be given.

20 Which of the following is/are correct regarding the powers of the State Legislative Council with respect to the passage of bills?

(Chap 6, Class-XI, Old NCERT)

1. It can reject the Bill or send it back with its recommendations.
2. It cannot sleep over the Bill for more than three months when it is sent for the first time.
3. If the Legislative Assembly passes the Bill again with or without changes, the Council cannot reject it.

Select the correct answer using the codes given below.

(a) 1 and 2 (b) 2 and 3
(c) 1 and 3 (d) 1, 2 and 3

Ans. (a)

Exp. Statements (1) and (2) are correct regarding the powers of the State Legislative Council with respect to the passage of bills.

Article 197 says that if a Bill has been passed by the Legislative Assembly of a state having a Legislative Council and transmitted to the Legislative Council, then Council can reject the Bill with or without recommendation.

State Legislative Council cannot sleep over the Bill for more than three months from the date on which bill is laid before the Council for the first time.

Statement (3) is incorrect because Council can reject the Bill for the second time as well but the Bill will be deemed to be passed by the Legislative Assembly for the second time with or without amendments. It must be passed within one month or deemed to be passed by both the houses.

Powers and Functions of State Legislature

21 Which of the following statements is/are incorrect regarding the State Legislature?

(Chap 6, Class-XI, Old NCERT)

1. It has an exclusive power to legislate on the subjects mentioned in the State List.
2. If there is a conflict between the laws passed by the Parliament and that of a State Legislature, the law of the Parliament prevails to the extent of inconsistency.

Select the correct answer using the codes given below.

(a) Only 1 (b) Only 2
(c) Both 1 and 2 (d) Neither 1 nor 2

Ans. (d)

Exp. Neither statements (1) nor (2) are incorrect regarding the State Legislature.

The State Legislature can make laws on the subjects of the State List and the Concurrent List. It can enact any bill on any subject of State List, which becomes an Act with the signatures of the Governor.

If both the Union Parliament and State Legislature pass a law on the same subject of the Concurrent List and there is an inconsistency between the two, the law passed by the Union Parliament gets precedence over the corresponding state law.

22 With reference to the Legislative Assembly of a state in India, consider the following statements.

(Chap 6, Class-XI, Old NCERT) (IAS Pre 2019)

1. The Governor makes a customary address to members of the House at the commencement of the first session of the year.
2. When a State Legislature does not have a rule on a particular matter, it follows the Lok Sabha rule on that matter.

Which of the statements given above is/are correct?

(a) Only 1 (b) Only 2
(c) Both 1 and 2 (d) Neither 1 nor 2

Ans. (c)

Exp. Both the statements (1) and (2) are correct with reference to the Legislative Assembly of a state in India. At the commencement of the first session after the general election to the Legislative Assembly and at the commencement of the first session of each year, the Governor addresses the Legislature and informs it about the causes of the summons. When State Legislature does not have a rule on a particular matter, they follow the Lok Sabha rules on that matter.

23 Consider the following statements about the Money Bills in State Legislature. *(Chap 4, Class-XI, New NCERT)*

1. The Legislative Council can either approve the Bill or suggest changes but cannot reject it.
2. Amendments to the Bill, suggested by the Legislative Council must be accepted by the Legislative Assembly in order to get it passed.
3. A Money Bill shall not be introduced in the State Legislative Council.
4. Procedure with respect to the Money Bills is given under Article 198 of the Indian Constitution.

Which of the statements given above is/are not correct?

(a) Only 1 (b) Only 2 (c) 1 and 3 (d) 3 and 4

Ans. (b)

Exp. Only statement (2) is not correct about the Money Bills in State Legislature. At State Legislature, Money Bills shall be introduced in the Legislative Assembly as per Articles 198, 199 and 207 on the recommendation of the Governor. In case of Money Bill, State Legislative Council has no power to reject or amend it. However, it call only make recommendations. It is upto State Legislative Assembly to accept or reject the recommendation of Legislative Council.

24 Consider the following statements. *(Chap 4, Class-XI, Old NCERT)*

1. Emoluments and allowances of Governor of States.
2. Salaries and allowances of the Chairman and Deputy Chairman of Legislative Council.
3. Salaries and allowances of Speaker and Deputy Speaker of the Legislative Assembly.
4. Pension of the judges of High Court.

Which of the statements does not form the part of expenditure charged upon the consolidated fund of state?

(a) Only 1 (b) Only 4 (c) 2 and 3 (d) None of these

Ans. (b)

Exp. Only statement (4) is incorrect regarding expenditure charge on consolidated fund of India. The pension of a retired judge of High Court does not form the part of expenditure charged upon the consolidated fund of state. It is charged on the consolidated fund of India according to Article 112(3) of the Constitution of India but salaries and allowances of a judge of High Court are charged on consolidated fund of state.

25 Consider the following statements and choose the correct code. *(Chap 6, Class-XI, Old NCERT)*

Statement-I The Legislative Council is empowered to pass a vote of censure against the Ministry.

Statement-II Whenever a censure motion is passed, the ministry has to resign.

Codes

(a) Both Statement-I and Statement-II are correct and Statement-II is the correct explanation for Statement-I.
(b) Both Statement-I and Statement-II are correct and Statement-II is not the correct explanation for Statement-I.
(c) Statement-I is correct but Statement-II is incorrect.
(d) Both Statement-I and Statement-II is incorrect.

Ans. (d)

Exp. Both Statement-I and Statement-II is incorrect because a censure motion can be moved only in the State Assembly and not in Council. It is moved by the opposition against a specific policy of the government or any minister or the Council of Ministers.

In case any censure motion has been passed, the Government immediately needs to seek the confidence of the house after it is passed and on failure of getting the confidence of the house, entire ministry has to resign.

26 Consider the following statements. *(Chap 6, Class-XI, Old NCERT)*

1. No demand for grant can be made in the Legislative Assembly except on the recommendation of Council of Ministers.
2. Both the Houses exercise control over the executive through asking questions, supplementary questions etc.

Which of the statements given above is/are correct?

(a) Only 1 (b) Only 2
(c) Both 1 and 2 (d) Neither 1 nor 2

Ans. (b)

Exp. Only statement (2) is correct. Both the Houses exercise control over the executive through asking questions, supplementary questions, discussing matter of urgent public importance, moving call-attention notices, and adjournment motion.

Statement (1) is incorrect because as per Article 203(3), no demand for grant shall be made except on the recommendation of the Governor. Demand for grants is the form in which the estimates of the expenditure from the Consolidated Fund, included in annual financial statement and required to be voted.

27 Consider the following statements regarding State Legislature. *(Chap 6, Class-XI, Old NCERT)*

1. The expenditure charged on the Consolidated Fund of State can be discussed only.
2. The general discussion on Budget is followed by the Budget speech, by the Finance Minister.

Which of the statements given above is/are correct?

(a) Only 1 (b) Only 2
(c) Both 1 and 2 (d) Neither 1 nor 2

Ans. (a)

Exp. Only statement (1) is correct regarding State Legislature. The expenditure charged on Consolidated Fund of State can be discussed only and not voted upon. On the other hand, the expenditure made from the Consolidated Fund of State can be discussed as well as voted upon.

Statement (2) is incorrect because the Budget Speech by the Finance Minister is followed by a general discussion on the Budget as a whole. After the discussion is over, the Legislative Assembly proceeds to the voting of demands.

28 Consider the following statements.

(Chap 6, Class-XI, Old NCERT)

1. In the beginning of every financial year an Annual Financial Statement showing the receipts and expenditure, is laid down before the State Legislature.
2. The Budget shows the expenditure charged on the Consolidated Fund of India.

Which of the statements given above is/are correct?

(a) Only 1
(b) Only 2
(c) Both 1 and 2
(d) Neither 1 nor 2

Ans. (a)

Exp. Only statement (1) is correct as according to Article 202(1), the Governor, in the beginning of every financial year shall lay before the House an Annual Financial Statement showing the receipts and expenditure.

Statement (2) is incorrect as according to Article 202(2), the Annual Financial Statement shows both the sums required to be charged and expenses proposed to be made from the Consolidated Fund of State.

29 Consider the following statements.

(Chap 14, Module-3, NIOS)

1. Under Article 200, the Governor may reserve the bill for the consideration of the President.
2. President may direct the Governor to return the bill for the reconsideration of the State Legislature.
3. If the bill is passed again by the State Legislature with or without amendments and presented again to the President for his assent, the President is bound to give his assent to the bill.
4. The Constitution has not prescribed any time limit within which the President has to take decision with regard to a bill reserved by Governor for his consideration.

Which of the statements given above is/are not correct?

(a) Only 1 (b) Both 1 and 2
(c) Only 3 (d) Both 3 and 4

Ans. (c)

Exp. Only statement (3) is not correct because Article 200 of the Constitution of India deals with the powers of Governor with regard to assent given to bills passed by the State Legislature and other powers of the Governor such as reserving the bill for the President's consideration. If the bill is passed again by State Legislature with or without amendments and presented to the Governor for assent, the Governor shall not withhold assent.

Chapter 13

Judiciary

Judiciary

Supreme Court

Introduction
- Established on 26th January, 1950
- Part V of Article 127 to 147

Composition of Supreme Court
- Chief Justice and several other Judges
- At present 34 Judges, including CJI

Appointment of Judges
- Article 124 (2); By President
- Senior most Judge is appointed as CJI

Eligibility of Judges
- Article 124 (3); Citizen of India, Judge of High Court atleast 5 years, Advocate of High Court atleast 10 years

Salaries of Judges
- Determined by Parliament
- CJI - 2.80 lakh per month
- Other Judges - 2.50 lakh per month

Oath and Tenure of Judges
- In presence of President
- Tenure- until he/she attains the age of 65 years

Removal of Judges
- Article 124 (4); Can be removed by President ; On the ground of Misbehaviour an incapacity

Other Powers of Supreme Court
- Review of Judgement
- Enforcement of Supreme Courts Order
- Guardian of the Constitution
- Court of Record

High Court and Subordinate Court

High Court
- Article 214 to 231 of Part VI
- First three High Court in India-Calcutta, Bombay, Madras (1862)
- Currently 25 High Courts
- **Composition and Appointment**
  - Chief Justice and other Judges
  - Appointed by President
- **Qualification** Citizen of India, hold Judicial office atleast 10 years; Advocate of High Court atleast 10 years
- **Salaries and Privileges**
  - Determined by Parliament time to time; Parliament cannot do any change after their appointment
- **Tenure of Judges**
  - Until he/she attains the age of 62 years
  - Resignation to the President
  - Can be removed from office similar to Supreme Court Judge
  - Can practice in the Supreme Court and in any other High Court
- **Appointment of Acting Chief Justice**
  - Article 233 • President can appoint as acting Judge
- **Appointment of Retired Judges**
  - Chief Justice of High Court, with the consent of the President, can reappoint any retired Judge
- **Jurisdiction of High Court**
  - **Original Jurisdiction** Every High Court is empowered to issue directions, order or writs particularly the writs of Habeas Corpus, Mandamus, Prohibition, Certiorari, Quo Warranto
  - **Appellate Jurisdiction** It hears appeals against the Judges of Subordinate Courts
  - **Supervisory Jurisdiction** Power to transfer the cases from other Subordinate Courts (Article 227)
  - **Writ Jurisdiction**
    - (a) Article 226; Enforcement of the Fundamental Rights of the people as well as other purposes
    - (b) High Court can issue all kind of writs as issued by the Supreme Court
  - **Judicial Review** By using Judicial review, the Supreme Court or High Court can declare any law made by the Parliament or the State Legislature invalid

Subordinate Courts
- Article 233 to 237 of Part VI
- Appointment : By Governor
  - Should be advocate for 7 years
  - As per Article 234, appointment of persons other than District Judges to the Judicial Service of a State shall be made by the Governor of State

Other Courts
- Civil Court
- Revenue Court
- Family Court
- Gram Nyayalay
- Criminal Court
- Mobile Court
- Lok Adalat

SOURCE ***Old NCERT Class VII*** *(Our Courts),* ***New NCERT Class VIII*** *(Judiciary),* ***New NCERT Class VIII*** *(Understanding Our Criminal Justice System),* ***Old NCERT Class IX & X*** *(Our Courts),* ***New NCERT Class XI*** *(Judiciary),* ***Old NCERT Class XI*** *(Judiciary in India)*

Supreme Court

1 'In India, we have an integrated judicial system'. Which of the following can be inferred from this statement? *(Chap 5, Class-VIII, New NCERT)*

1. A person cannot appeal to higher courts in case he is not satisfied by decision of lower court.
2. The decisions made by higher courts are binding on the lower courts.

Select the correct answer using the codes given below.

(a) Only 1 (b) Only 2 (c) Both 1 and 2 (d) Neither 1 nor 2

Ans. *(b)*

Exp. Only statement (2) can be inferred from this statement given in the question as decisions of superior courts are binding on lower courts because of an integrated judicial system in India.

Statement (1) is not correct because the person can appeal to a higher court if they believe that the judgement passed by lower court is not justified.

2 Consider the following statements. *(Chap 5, Class-VIII, New NCERT)*

1. The Supreme Court was established on 24th January, 1950.
2. Unlike its predecessor, the Federal Court of India, which was situated at Central Hall, the Supreme Court was earlier located in the Chamber of Princes in the Parliament House.

Which of the statements given above is/are correct?

(a) Only 1 (b) Only 2
(c) Both 1 and 2 (d) Neither 1 nor 2

Ans. *(d)*

Exp. Neither statements (1) nor (2) are correct. The Supreme Court of India was established on 26th January, 1950. The Supreme Court initially had its seat at the Chamber of Princes in the Parliament building where the former Federal Court of India had sat from 1937 to 1950.

3 Consider the following statements about the Collegium System. *(Chap 12, Module-3, NIOS) (BPSC Pre 2023)*

1. The Supreme Court Collegium is a five member body, which is headed by the incumbent Chief Justice of India (CJI) and comprises four other senior most judges of the Court at that time.
2. The Parliament by law has evolved the Collegium System.
3. The judges of the Supreme Court and High Courts are appointed only through the Collegium System.
4. The Collegium System was introduced in the year 1993 by Justice PN Bhagwati in the landmark first Judges case.

Which of the statements given above is/are correct?

(a) Only 1 (b) 1 and 2 (c) 3 and 4 (d) 1 and 3

Ans. *(d)*

Exp. Statements (1) and (3) are correct as the Supreme Court Collegium is a five member body headed by the Chief Justice of India (CJI) and comprising the four senior most judges of the Court.

The judges of the Supreme Court and High Courts are appointed only through the Collegium System. The Government of India has no role in the selection of judges, except to formally appoint the judges recommended by the collegium.

Statements (2) and (4) are incorrect because the Collegium System was not evolved by Parliament through law.

Instead, it was evolved through a series of Supreme Court judgements, collectively known as the 'three Judges Cases'.

The Collegium System was not introduced by Justice PN Bhagwati in the first Judges Case.

In fact, the first Judges Case (1981) did not even mention the term 'Collegium'.

The Collegium System was first established in the second Judges Case.

4 Consider the following statements. *(Chap 2, Class-XI, New NCERT) (IAS Pre 2023)*

Statement-I The Supreme Court of India has held in some judgements that the reservation policies made under in Article 16(4) of the Constitution of India would be limited by Article 335 for the maintenance of efficiency of administration.

Statement-II Article 335 of the Constitution of India defines the term 'efficiency of administration'.

Which one of the following is correct in respect of the above statements?

(a) Both Statement-I and Statement-II are correct and Statement-II is the correct explanation for Statement-I.
(b) Both Statement-I and Statement-II are correct and Statement-II is not the correct explanation for Statement-I.
(c) Statement-I is correct, but Statement-II is incorrect.
(d) Statement-I is correct, but Statement-II is correct.

Ans. *(c)*

Exp. Statement-I is correct, but Statement-II is incorrect.

The Supreme Court of India has upheld in several judgements that the reservation policies articulated in Article 16(4) of the Indian Constitution are subject to Article 335, which calls for maintaining the efficiency of administration. A notable instance of this is the Indra Sawhney vs. Union of India Case (1992), where the Supreme Court ruled that the reservation under Article 16(4) could not exceed 50% except in extraordinary situations. This is to ensure that the efficiency of administration is not adversely affected.

However, Article 335 of the Indian Constitution does not explicitly define the term 'efficiency of administration'.

Article 335 of the Indian Constitution states the claims of the members of the Scheduled Castes and the Scheduled Tribes shall be taken into consideration, consistently with the maintenance of efficiency of administration, in the making of appointments to services and posts in connection with the affairs of the Union or of a State.

5 Consider the following statements with respect to the appointment of the Chief Justice of India.

(Chap 6, Class-XI, New NCERT)

1. A convention has developed whereby the seniormost judge of the Supreme Court is appointed as the Chief Justice of India.
2. This convention has never been broken in the history of the Supreme Court.

Which of the statements given above is/are correct?

(a) Only 1
(b) Only 2
(c) Both 1 and 2
(d) Neither 1 nor 2

***Ans.** (a)*

Exp. Only statement (1) is correct with respect to the appointment of the Chief Justice of India (CJI). As the Constitution does not prescribe any specific criterion for appointing the CJI but the seniormost judge of the Supreme Court gets an opportunity to become the CJI. Statement (2) is incorrect because this convention has been broken at some occasion. For instance, in 1973 AN Ray was appointed as CJI superseding three senior judges. It was again broken in 1977 when Justice MH Beg was appointed superseding Justice HR Khanna.

6 Consider the following statement(s) regarding the removal of a Supreme Court judge.

(Chap 6, Class-XI, New NCERT)

1. A judge of the Supreme Court or High Court can be removed only on the ground of violation of the Constitution.
2. A motion containing the charges against the judge must be approved by special majority in both Houses of the Parliament.
3. There have never been any proposals initiated for the removal of any Supreme Court judge in India.

Which of the statements given above is/are incorrect?

(a) Only 1
(b) 2 and 3
(c) 1 and 3
(d) None of the above

***Ans.** (c)*

Exp. Statements (1) and (3) are incorrect regarding the removal of a Supreme Court judge because as per Article 124(4) of the Constitution, President can remove a judge on the ground of proved misbehaviour or incapacity. Veeraswami Ramaswami was a judge of the Supreme Court of India and the first judge against whom removal proceedings were initiated in independent India.

7 Consider the following statements.

(Chap 6, Class-XII, New NCERT)(IAS Pre 2019)

1. The motion to impeach a judge of the Supreme Court of India cannot be rejected by the Speaker of the Lok Sabha as per the Judges (inquiry) Act, 1968.
2. The Constitution of India defines and gives details of what constitutes 'incapacity and proved misbehaviour of the judges of the Supreme Court of Indian.
3. The details of the process of impeachment of the judges of the Supreme Court of India are given in the Judges (Inquiry) Act, 1968.
4. If the motion for the impeachment of a judge is taken up for voting, the law requires the motion to be backed by each House of the Parliament and supported by each House of the Parliament and supported by a majority of total membership of that House and by not less than two - thirds of total members of that House present and voting.

Which of the statements given above is/are correct ?

(a) 1 and 2
(b) Only 3
(c) 3 and 4
(d) 1, 3 and 4

***Ans.** (c)*

Exp. Statements (3) and (4) are correct as the details of the process of impeachment of the judges of the Supreme Court of India are given in the Judges (Inquiry) Act, 1968.

If the motion is admitted, the Speaker or Chairman (who receives it) will constitute a three-member committee to investigate the complaint. It will comprise :

- a Supreme Court Judge
- Chief Justice of a High Court and
- a distinguished jurist

Statements (1) and (2) are incorrect because the Constitution of India does not defines or provide any details of what constitutes incapacity and proved misbehaviour. A removal motion signed by 100 members (in the case of Lok Sabha) or 50 members (in the case of Rajya Sabha) is to be given to the Speaker/Chairman. The Speaker/Chairman may admit the motion or refuse to admit it.

8 With respect to the judges of the Supreme Court, consider the following statements.

(Chap 6, Class-XI, New NCERT)

1. The judges of the Supreme Court are paid such salaries as are determined by the President.
2. A person who has held office as a Judge of the Supreme Court cannot plead or act in any court in any conditions.
3. Every person to be appointed as a judge of the Supreme Court is required to take an oath or affirmation before entering upon his office, before the President.

Which of the statements given above is/are correct?
(a) Only 1 (b) Only 3 (c) 1 and 2 (d) None of these

Ans. (b)

Exp. Only statement (3) is correct with respect to the judges of the Supreme Court. As per Article 124 and the third Schedule of the Constitution, the Chief Justice (or a judge) of the Supreme Court of India is required to make and subscribe in the presence of the President an oath or affirmation.

Statements (1) and (2) are not correct because the salaries, allowances, privileges, leave and pension of the judges of the Supreme Court are determined from time to time by the Parliament.

According to Article 128 of the Constitution, the Chief Justice of India, at any time, with the previous consent of the President, request any person who has held the office of Judge of the Supreme Court to sit and act as a Judge of the Supreme Court.

9. Consider the following statement with reference to provisions related to the Supreme Court. *(Chap 5, Class-XI, Old NCERT)*

1. The Chief Justice of India may request any retired judge of the Supreme Court or that of a High Court to sit and act as a judge of the Supreme Court.
2. If at any time there is no quorum in the Supreme Court for performing its duties, the Chief Justice may request one of the judges of a High Court to work as its Ad Hoc judge.
3. When the office of the Chief Justice of India is vacant, his duties shall be performed by one of the other judges as the Parliament may appoint for the purpose.

How many of the statements given above is/are not correct?
(a) Only one (b) Only two
(c) All three (d) None of these

Ans. (a)

Exp. Only one statement i.e., (3) is not correct with regard to the provisions related to the Supreme Court. When the office of the Chief Justice of India is vacant or when the Chief Justice is by reason of absence or otherwise unable to perform his duties, the same shall be performed by one of the other judges as the President may appoint for the purpose. Parliament has no role to play in it.

10 Ad Hoc judges are appointed in the Supreme Court when *(Chap 5, Class-XI, Old NCERT) (IAS Pre 2000)*

(a) some judges go on long leave.
(b) no one is available for permanent appointment.
(c) there is an abnormal increase in cases pending before the court.
(d) there is no quorum of the judges available to hold.

Ans. (d)

Exp. Only statement (d) is correct as per Ad Hoc judges appointment. Ad Hoc judges are appointed in the Supreme Court when there is no quorum of the judges available to hold. Article 127(1) of our Constitution provides for the appointment of Ad Hoc judges.

As per this article, when there is a lack of quorum of the permanent judges to hold or continue any session of the Supreme Court, the Chief Justice of India can appoint a judge of High Court as an Ad Hoc judge of the Supreme Court for temporary period. The judge so appointed should be qualified for appointment as a judge of the Supreme Court.

11 Consider the following statements regarding the jurisdiction of the Supreme Court. *(Chap 6, Class-XI, New NCERT)*

1. Original Jurisdiction means cases that can be directly considered by the Supreme Court without going to any court.
2. The Original Jurisdiction of the Supreme Court establishes it as an umpire in all disputes regarding federal matters.
3. Through writ jurisdiction, the Court can give orders to the executive to act or not to act in a particular way.

Which of the statements given above is/are incorrect?
(a) Only 1 (b) Only 2 (c) 2 and 3 (d) None of these

Ans. (d)

Exp. None of the given statements are incorrect regarding the jurisdiction of the Supreme Court.

As per Article 131, the Original Jurisdiction of the Supreme Court is authorised whereby the Supreme Court can decide matters at the first instance. For example, dispute between centre and states or among states.

Under Article 32, the Supreme Court enjoy writ jurisdiction under which it can issue writ of mandamus to the executive to do or not to do in a particular way.

12 Consider the following pairs. *(Chap 6, Class-XI, New NCERT)*

	Jurisdiction		Matter
1.	Special Leave	–	Disputes between states
2.	Original	–	Trials from Lower Courts
3.	Appellate	–	Appeal from any judgement

How many pairs given above is/are correctly matched?
(a) Only One (b) Only two
(c) All three (d) None of these

Ans. (d)

Exp. None of above given pair are correct.

Article 136 deals with the special leave to appeal from any judgement to the Supreme Court.

As per Article 131, under the Original Jurisdiction, the Supreme Court settles disputes between states.

Articles 132, 133 and 134, provides for the Appellate jurisdiction of the Supreme Court to settle trials from lower courts.

13 With reference to the Constitution of India, prohibitions or limitations or provisions contained in ordinary laws cannot act as prohibitions or limitations on the Constitution's power under Article 142. It could mean which one of following?

(Chap 5, Class-XI, Old NCERT) (IAS Pre 2019)

(a) The decision taken by the Election Commission of India while discharging its duties cannot be challenged in any court of law.
(b) The Supreme Court of India is not constrained in the exercise of its powers by laws made by Parliament.
(c) In the event of grave financial crisis in the country, the President of India can declare Financial Emergency without consulting the Cabinet.
(d) State Legislatures cannot make the laws on certain matters without the concurrence of Union Legislature.

Ans. (b)

Exp. Only statement (b) is correct with reference to the above situation.

Article 142 of the Constitution provides for enforcement of decrees and orders of Supreme Court and orders as to discovery, etc.

The Supreme Court in exercise of its jurisdiction may pass such decree or make such order as is necessary for doing complete justice in any case or matter pending before it.

14 Consider the following statements regarding the advisory jurisdiction of the Supreme Court.

(Chap 6, Class-XI, New NCERT)

1. The President of India can refer any matter that is of public importance or that which involves interpretation of the Constitution to the Supreme Court for advice.
2. The President is bound to accept such advice.
3. It allows the government to seek legal opinion on a matter of importance before taking action on it.
4. In the light of the advice of the Supreme Court, the Government can make suitable changes in its action or legislation.

Which of the statements given above is/are not correct?

(a) Only 1
(b) Only 2
(c) Both 2 and 3
(d) Only 4

Ans. (b)

Exp. Only statement (2) is not correct regarding the advisory jurisdiction of the Supreme Court.

Under this jurisdiction, the President of India can refer any matter that is of public importance or which involves interpretation of Constitution to Supreme Court for advice. However, Supreme Court is not bound to give such advice and the President is also not bound to accept such an advice.

15 'The Supreme Court is a Court of Record'. Which of the following inferences can be drawn from this statement? *(Chap 8, Class-IX & X, Old NCERT)*

1. The judgements of the Supreme Court are recorded and considered authoritative and serve as cases, laws or precedents.
2. The court can punish anyone who does not abide by the decision of the Supreme Court.

Select the correct answer using the codes given below.

(a) Only 1 (b) Only 2
(c) Both 1 and 2 (d) Neither 1 nor 2

Ans. (c)

Exp. Both the statements (1) and (2) can be inferred from the statement given in question.

Supreme Court is a court of record and the law-making power of the Supreme Court is given under Article 141 of the Constitution.

Law declared by Supreme Court is binding on all courts and any action or decision contrary to that attracts punishment for contempt of court.

16 Consider the following Assertion (A) and Reason (R) and choose the correct code.

(Chap 8, Class-IX & X, Old NCERT)

Assertion (A) Only Supreme Court of India has exclusive jurisdiction regarding the constitutional validity of central laws.

Reason (R) The Supreme Court is the Guardian of the Indian Constitution.

Codes

(a) Both A and R are true and R is the correct explanation of A.
(b) Both A and R are true, but R is not the correct explanation of A.
(c) A is true, but R is false.
(d) A is false, but R is true.

Ans. (d)

Exp. Assertion (A) is false, but Reason (R) is true. Not only Supreme Court but High Court also have jurisdiction regarding the Constitutional validity of Central laws.

The Supreme Court (under Article 32) and High Courts (Under Article 226) have the power to issue writs to protect the fundamental validity.

The principal function of the Supreme Court is to act as the guardian of the Constitution particularly related to the Fundamental Rights guaranteed to the citizens.

17 Which of the following two provisions of the Constitution establish the Supreme Court as the interpreter of the Constitution of the citizen on one hand and protector of Fundamental Rights on the other? *(Chap 6, Class-XI, New NCERT)*

(a) Article 19 and Article 21 (b) Article 13 and Article 32
(c) Article 14 and Article 21 (d) Article 14 and Article 32

Ans. (b)

Exp. Option (b) is correct regarding provision of the Constitution. Article 13 and Article 32 of the Indian Constitution establish the Supreme Court as the protector of Fundamental Rights of the citizen and interpreter of the Constitution respectively.

Article 13(3)(a) gives the Supreme Court the power to interpret any law in confirmation of the Constitutional ethos.

Article 32 empowers the Supreme Court to issue writs for the violation of Fundamental Rights.

18 With respect to the Supreme Court, consider the following statements. *(Chap 6,Class-XI, Old NCERT)*

1. The Supreme Court cannot interfere with the delimitation of constituencies.
2. The Supreme Court cannot question the detention or arrest of a person, if it has been made in accordance with the procedure established by law.
3. The Supreme Court cannot declare unconstitutional a law passed by the Parliament.
4. The Supreme Court cannot question the decision of the Speaker as to whether a bill is a Money Bill or not.

Select the correct answer using the codes given below.

(a) 2, 3 and 4 (b) 1, 2 and 4 (c) 1, 2 and 3 (d) 1, 2, 3 and 4

Ans. (b)

Exp. Statements (1), (2) and (4) are correct with respect to the Supreme Court. Delimitation Commission orders on delimitation of constituencies have the force of law and cannot be challenged in any court. As per Article 21, no person shall be deprived of his life or personal liberty except according to a procedure established by law, so if anyone is arrested in accordance to law, then Supreme Court cannot question the arrest of that person.

The decision of Speaker as to whether a bill is a Money Bill or not is final. Speaker's decision in this regard cannot be questioned in any court of law or in the either House of Parliament or even the President.

Statement (3) is incorrect because the Supreme Court can declare a law passed by the Parliament as unconstitutional.

19 Consider the following statements and choose the correct code. *(Chap 6, Class-XI, Old NCERT)*

Statement-I The Supreme Court of India has exclusive Jurisdiction regarding constitutional validity of Central laws.

Statement-II The Supreme Court is the guardian of the Indian Constitution.

Codes

(a) Both Statement-I and Statement-II are correct and Statement-II is the correct explanation for Statement-I.

(b) Both Statement-I and Statement-II are correct and Statement-II is not the correct explanation for Statement-I.

(c) Statement-I is correct, but Statement-II is incorrect.

(d) Statement-I is incorrect, but Statement-II is correct.

Ans. (d)

Exp. Statement-I is incorrect, but Statement-II is correct. The High Court and Supreme Court of India have Jurisdiction regarding Constitutional validity of Central laws. The Supreme Court (Under Article 32) and High Court (Under Article 226) can issue Writs to protect the Fundamental Rights of the people. The Supreme Court is the guardian of the Indian Constitution.

20 With reference to Indian Judiciary, consider the following statements. *(Chap 12, Module-3, NIOS) (IAS Pre 2021)*

1. Any retired judge of the Supreme Court of India can be called back to sit and act as a Supreme Court judge by the Chief Justice of India with prior permission of the President of India.
2. A High Court in India has the power to review its own judgement as the Supreme Court does.

Which of the statements given above is/are correct?

(a) Only 1 (b) Only 2
(c) Both 1 and 2 (d) Neither 1 nor 2

Ans. (a)

Exp. Only statement (1) is correct as per Article 128 of the Indian Constitution, any person who has served as a judges of the Supreme Court can be appointed again as a judge of the Supreme Court, but only after consultation with the Chief Justice of India and with the approval of the President of India. This provision allows retired judges to be called back to serve as Ad Hoc judges of the Supreme Court for a temporary period.

Statement (2) is incorrect because unlike the Supreme Court, a High Court in India does not have the power to review its own judgement.

However, it has the power to review the judgements passed by the Subordinate Courts under its jurisdiction. The power of review of a High Court is provided under Article 226 of the Indian Constitution.

21 Consider the following pairs. *(Chap 6, Class-XI, Old NCERT)*

1.	Court directs the detaining authority to produce the detained in the court and justify the cause of detention.	–	Writ of Habeas Corpus
2.	Order to court to an inferior authority to transfer the matter to it or to some other authority for its proper consideration.	–	Writ of Certiorari
3.	Court prohibits an inferior authority from doing an act which does not fall within its jurisdiction.	–	Writ of Prohibition
4.	Court restrains a person from acting in a public office to which he is not entitled.	–	Writ of Quo Warranto

How many pairs given above is/are correctly matched?

(a) Only one (b) Only two
(c) Only three (d) All four

Ans. (d)

Exp. All the pairs above are correct.

In the Writ of Habeas Corpus, the court directs the detaining authority to produce the detained in the court and justify the cause of detention.

In the Writ of Certiorari, the court's order to an inferior authority to transfer the matter to it or to some other authority for its proper consideration.

In the Writ of Prohibition, the court prohibits an inferior authority from doing an act which does not fall within its jurisdiction.

In the Writ of Quo Warranto, the court restrains a person from acting in a public office to which he is not entitled.

22 Consider the following statements and select the correct answer from the codes given below.

(Chap 6, Class-XI, Old NCERT) (IAS Pre 1997)

Statement-I Willful disobedience or nor-compliance of court orders and use of derogatory language about Judicial behaviour amount to contempt of court.

Statement-II Judicial activism cannot be practiced without arming the judiciary with punitive powers to punish contemptuous behaviour.

Codes

(a) Both Statement-I and Statement-II are correct and Statement-II is the correct explanation for Statement-I.
(b) Both Statement-I and Statement-II are correct and Statement-II is not the correct explanation for Statement-I.
(c) Statement-I is correct, but Statement-II is incorrect.
(d) Statement-I is incorrect, but Statement-II is correct.

Ans. *(b)*

Exp. Both Statement-I and Statement-II are correct and Statement-II is not the correct explanation for Statement-I.

Under the Contempt of Courts Act, 1971, Indian law defines the contempt of court as any action or behaviour that undermines the authority or dignity of a court. It can be classified into two categories i.e., civil and criminal contempt.

Civil contempt refers to the willful disobedience of a court's judgement, order or direction.

On the other hand, criminal contempt involves actions that tend to disrepute the court or interfere with the administration of justice.

High Courts

23 Consider the following statements regarding the High Courts. *(Chap 5, Class-VIII, New NCERT)*

1. High Courts were first established in the three Presidencies of Calcutta, Bombay and Madras in 1862.
2. Andhra Pradesh and Telangana share a common High Court.
3. Punjab and Haryana share a common High Court at Chandigarh.

Which of the statements given above is/are incorrect?

(a) Only 1 (b) Only 2 (c) 1 and 3 (d) Only 3

Ans. *(b)*

Exp. Only statement (2) is incorrect regarding the High Courts as on 26th December, 2018, the order for bifurcation of the High Courts of Andhra Pradesh and Telangana was issued by the President of India.

At present, the High Court of Telangana is located in Hyderabad and High Court of Andhra Pradesh is located in Amravati. The bifurcation and Constitution of separate High Courts for Telangana and Andhra Pradesh came into effect from 1st January, 2019.

24 In which of these States, High Courts were established in March, 2013?

(Chap 5, Class-VIII, New NCERT) (UPPSC Pre 2013)

1. Arunachal Pradesh
2. Meghalaya
3. Mizoram
4. Tripura

Codes

(a) 1 and 3 (b) 2 and 4 (c) 1, 2 and 3 (d) All of these

Ans. *(b)*

Exp. Options (2) and (4) are correct with reference to High Court. In March 2013, three new High Courts were established in Meghalaya, Manipur and Tripura. These High Courts were established by the Government of India by making amendments in the Constitution as well as North-Eastern Areas Act, 1971.

25 Consider the following statements about the High Courts. *(Chap 6, Class-XI, Old NCERT)*

1. It consists of a Chief Justice and such other judges as the President may from time to time deem it necessary to appoint.
2. The Chief Justice is appointed by the President in consultation with the Chief Justice of India and the Governor of that State.
3. In appointing other judges, the President besides consulting the Chief Justice of India and the Governor of that State, also consults the Chief Justice of the High Court.

How many of the statements given above is/are correct?

(a) Only one (b) Only two (c) All three (d) None of these

Ans. *(c)*

Exp. All three statements i.e., (1), (2) and (3) are correct about High Courts. High Courts of India are the principal civil courts of original jurisdiction in each state and Union Territory.

Article 217 of the Constitution states that the Judge of a High Court shall be appointed by the President in consultation with the Chief Justice of India (CJI) and the Governor of the State.

In the case of appointment of a judge other than the Chief Justice, the Chief Justice of the High Court is also consulted.

26 **Consider the following statements.**
(Chap 6, Class-XI, Old NCERT)

1. No person who has held an office as a permanent judge of a High Court can practice in any High Court.
2. Every Judge of a High Court, including the Chief Justice, holds office until he attains the age of sixty-five years.

Which of the statements given above is/are correct?

(a) Only 1
(b) Only 2
(c) Both 1 and 2
(d) Neither 1 nor 2

Ans. (d)

Exp. Neither statements (1) nor (2) are correct.

Person who has held an office as a permanent judge of a High Court can practice in a High Court other than the state where he was in office. For example, a permanent judge of Delhi High Court cannot practice in Delhi but can practice in Punjab and Haryana High Court. He/she can also practice in the Supreme Court.

Every judge of a High Court, including the Chief Justice, holds office until he attains the age of 62 years.

27 **Consider the following statements about the qualifications for becoming a judge of the High Court**
(Chap 6, Class-XI, Old NCERT)

1. a citizen of India.
2. should have held a judicial office at least for ten years.
3. has been an advocate of a High Court in any State for at least ten years.

Which of the statements given above is/are correct?

(a) Only 1
(b) Only 2
(c) 2 and 3
(d) All of these

Ans. (d)

Exp. All the statements are correct with reference to qualifications for becoming a judge of the High Court.

Qualifications to become a judge in High Court are

- a person must be a citizen of India.
- must have an LLB degree.
- He/she should have held a judicial office in India for ten years or he should have been an advocate of a High Court for ten years.

28 **Consider the following statements regarding the powers of High Court.** *(Chap 6, Class-XI, Old NCERT)*

1. A High Court has the right of superintendence over all other courts subordinate to it in judicial matters only.
2. It can make rules relating to the appointment, demotion, promotion and leave of absence for the officers of the district courts and other lower courts.
3. If a High Court feels that a case pending in a Subordinate Court, involves a substantial question of law, it may withdraw the case.

How many of the statements given above is/are not correct?

(a) Only one
(b) Only two
(c) All three
(d) None of these

Ans. (a)

Exp. Only one statement i.e., (1) is not correct regarding the powers of High Court as a High Court has the right of superintendence over all other courts subordinate to it in judicial as well as administrative matters.

The transfer, appointment, posting of junior judicial and administrative staff is done under the superintendence of state High Courts.

29 **Consider the following statements.**
(Chap 6, Class-XI, Old NCERT)
(IAS Pre 2007)

1. The mode of removal of a judge of a High Court in India is same as that of removal of a judge of the Supreme Court.
2. After retirement from the office, a permanent judge of a High Court cannot plead or act in any court or before any authority in India.

Which of the statements given above is/are correct?

(a) Only 1
(b) Only 2
(c) Both 1 and 2
(d) Neither 1 nor 2

Ans. (a)

Exp. Only satement (1) is correct as according to Article 217(1)(b), a judge of High Court may be removed from his office by the President in the same manner as provided in clause (4) of Article 124 for the removal of a judge of the Supreme Court.

Statement (2) is incorrect because as per Article 220, no person who, after the commencement of this Constitution, has held office as a permanent judges of a High Court, shall act or plead in any court or before any authority in India except the Supreme Court and the other High Courts.

Subordinate Courts

30 **Consider the following statements regarding the Subordinate Courts.** *(Chap 8, Class-IX & X, Old NCERT)*

1. The judges of the District Courts are appointed by the Governor in consultation with the Supreme Court.
2. A person eligible for appointment as a district judge should be either an advocate or a pleader of ten years standing.
3. The Union Public Service Commission conducts competitive examinations for the selection of candidates for appointment in the State Judicial Service.

How many of the statements given above is/are correct?

(a) Only one
(b) Only two
(c) All three
(d) None of these

Ans. (d)

Exp. None of the given statements i.e., (1), (2) and (3) are correct regarding Subordinate Courts. Appointments posting and promotion of district judges in any state shall be made by the Governor of the State in consultation with the High Court exercising jurisdiction in relation to such state.

A person is qualified to be a District Judge, if he has been practicing as an advocate or pleader for not less than 7 years. The State Public Service Commission or concerned High Court conducts competitive examinations for the selection of candidates for appointment in the State Judicial Service.

31 Consider the following statements.
(Chap 15, Module-3, NIOS) (IAS Pre 2004)

1. The highest Criminal Court of the district is the Court of District and Sessions Judge.
2. The District Judges are appointed by the Governor in consultation with the High Court.
3. A person to be eligible for appointment as a District Judge should be an advocate or a pleader of 7 years standing or more or an officer in judicial service of the Union or the State.
4. When the Session Judge awards death sentence, it must be confirmed by the High Court before it is carried out.

Which of the statements given above is/are correct?
(a) 1 and 2 (b) 2, 3 and 4 (c) 3 and 4 (d) 1, 2, 3 and 4
Ans. (*d*)

Exp. All the statements are correct.

The District Judge is the highest judicial authority in the district. He possesses original and appellate jurisdiction in both civil as well as criminal matters.

The appointment, posting and promotion of District Judges in a State are made by the Governor of the State in consultation with the concerned High Court.

A person to be eligible for appointment as a District Judge should be an advocate or a pleader of 7 years standing or more, or an officer in judicial service of the Union or the State.

When the Session Judge awards death sentence, it must be confirmed by the High Court before it is carried out.

The Sessions Judge has the power to impose any sentence including life imprisonment and capital punishment (death sentence).

32 According to the Constitution of India the term 'District Judge' shall not include
(Chap 6, Class-XI, Old NCERT) (IAS Pre 1996)

(a) Chief Presidency Magistrate
(b) Sessions Judge
(c) Tribunal Judge
(d) Chief Justice of a Small Cause Court
Ans. (*c*)

Exp. According to the Constitution of India, the term 'District Judge' shall not include Tribunal Judge.

As per Article 236 (a) of the Constitution 'District Judge' includes judge of a Civil Court, Additional District Judge, Joint District Judge, Assistant District Judge, Chief Judge of a Small Cause Court, Chief Presidency Magistrate, Additional Chief Presidency Magistrate, Sessions Judge, Additional Session Judge and Assistant Session Judge.

Judicial Review, Activism, PIL and Other Issues

33 Consider the following statements.
(Chap 12, Module-3, NIOS) (IAS Pre 2022)

1. Pursuant to the report of HN Sanyal Committee, the Contempt of Courts Act, 1971, was passed.
2. The Constitution of India empowers the Supreme Court and the High Court to Punish for contempt of themselves.
3. The Constitution of India defines civil contempt and criminal contempt.
4. In India, the Parliament is vested with the powers to make laws on contempt of Court.

Which of the statements given above is/are correct?
(a) 1 and 2 (b) 1, 2 and 4
(c) 3 and 4 (d) Only 3
Ans. (*b*)

Exp. Statements (1), (2) and (4) are correct as Contempt of Court Act, 1971, was passed on the recommendation of the HN Sanyal Committee. It is the power of the court to protect it own majesty and respect. The Constitution of India empowers Supreme Court and High Court to punish for contempt of themselves.

In India, the Parliament is vested with the power to make laws on contempt of court. However, Article 129 of the Constitution conferred on the Supreme Court the power to punish contempt of itself.

Statement (3) is incorrect because the Constitution of India does not define any type of contempt of court, neither civil nor criminal contempt. The Contempt of Courts Act of 1971 defines both civil and criminal contempt.

34 Consider the following statements.
(Chap 6, Class-XI, New NCERT)

1. The term judicial review is nowhere mentioned in the Constitution.
2. India has a written Constitution and the Supreme Court can strike down a law that goes against Fundamental Rights, implicitly gives the Supreme Court the power of judicial review.

Which of the statements given above is/are correct?
(a) Only 1
(b) Only 2
(c) Both 1 and 2
(d) Neither 1 nor 2
Ans. (*c*)

Exp. Both the statements (1) and (2) are correct.

Judicial review is not been mentioned in any part of the Constitution. However, it is a tool invented by the Judiciary in order to protect the Fundamental Rights as enshrined in Part III of our Constitution.

India has a written Constitution and it can strike down a law that violates Fundamental Rights. It implicitly gives the Supreme Court the power of judicial review.

35 Consider the following statements and select the correct answer from the codes given below. *(Chap 6, Class-XI, Old NCERT) (UPPSC Mains 2004)*

Statement-I The Public Interest Litigation permits public-minded citizens to reach the Court of Law.

Statement-II The public-minded people may seek justice for the person who is unable to reach the Court of Law for any reasons.

Codes

(a) Both Statement-I and Statement-II are correct and Statement-II is the correct explanation for Statement-I.
(b) Both Statement-I and Statement-II are correct and Statement-II is not the correct explanation for Statement-I.
(c) Statement-I is correct, but Statement-II is incorrect.
(d) Statement-I is incorrect, but Statement-II is correct.

Ans. (a)

Exp. Both Statement-I and Statement-II are correct and Statement-II is the correct explanation for Statement-I.

The Public Interest Litigation (PIL) permits public-minded citizens to reach the Court of Law.

Due to this permission, the public- minded people may seek justice for the person who is unable to reach the court of law for any reasons.

In India, any citizen can go to court for justice regarding the welfare of any other person, group or society through the Public Interest Litigation.

36 Consider the following statements regarding judicial activism. *(Chap 6, Class-XI, New NCERT)*

1. It has forced executive accountability.
2. It has also made an attempt to make the electoral system much more free and fair.
3. Judicial activism has blurred the line of distinction between the executive and legislature on the one hand and the judiciary on the other.
4. It has reduced the burden of the courts.

Which of the statements given above is/are not correct?

(a) Only 2 (b) Only 4 (c) 1, 3 and 4 (d) None of these

Ans. (b)

Exp. Only statement (4) is not correct regarding the judicial activism as it has increased the burden of judiciary though judicial activism has had manifold impact on the political system but it has negative impact as well.

37 Consider the following statements. *(Chap 6, Class-XI, New NCERT) (IAS Pre 2020)*

1. The Constitution of India defines its 'Basic structure' in terms of federalism, secularism, Fundamental Rights and democracy.
2. The Constitution of India provides for 'judicial review' through various articles to safeguard the liberties of citizen and to preserve the ideals on which the Constitution is based.

Which of the statements given above is/are correct?

(a) Only 1 (b) Only 2
(c) Both 1 and 2 (d) Neither 1 nor 2

Ans. (a)

Exp. Statement (1) is incorrect because the 'Basic Structure' has not been defined in the Constitution of India. This term was first time used by the Supreme Court in Kesavananda Bharati *Vs.* State of Kerala, 1973.

38 Consider the following options with reference to the issues of conflict between the Judiciary and Legislature. *(Chap 6, Class-XI, New NCERT)*

1. Appointment of judges.
2. Salaries and allowances of judges.
3. Scope of Parliament's power to amend the Constitution.

How many of the options given above is/are correct?

(a) Only one (b) Only two
(c) All three (d) None of these

Ans. (c)

Exp. All three options i.e., (1), (2) and (3) are correct in respect to the issues of conflict between Judiciary and Legislature.

The collegium system which appoints the judges is highly non-transparent and Legislature wants a say in judges appointments.

Salaries and allowances of judges are charged upon the Consolidated Fund of India after being passed by the Parliament. Judiciary has curtailed the Parliament's power to amend the Constitution by employing basic structure doctrine that's why there are issues of conflict.

39 Consider the following statements with respect to measures ensure the independence of Judiciary. *(Chap 6, Class-XI, New NCERT)*

1. The legislature is not involved in the process of appointment of judges.
2. Parliament cannot discuss the conduct of the judges under any circumstances.
3. The Constitution prescribes a very difficult procedure for removal of judges.
4. The Constitution provides that the salaries and allowances of the judges are not subjected to the approval of the legislature.

Which of the statements given above is/are correct?

(a) Only 3 (b) Only 2 (c) 1, 3 and 4 (d) 2, 3 and 4

Ans. (b)

Exp. Only statement (2) ensures the independence of Judiciary. As per Article 121 of the Constitution, the conduct of the judge of Supreme Court or High Court cannot be discussed in Parliament in the discharge of his duties.

It can be only discussed upon a motion for presenting an address to the President praying for their removal.

40 Which of the following ensures a fair trial by court? *(Chap 6, Class-VIII, New NCERT)*

1. Presenting a copy of the chargesheet and all other evidence.
2. Trial held in an open court.
3. Assumption of innocence until proven guilty.
4. Impartiality of Judge.

Codes

(a) 1, 2 and 4 (b) 2, 3 and 4 (c) 1, 2, 3 and 4 (d) 1 and 4

Ans. (c)

Exp. All the given options ensure a fair trial by court. A fair trial by Judiciary protects the Fundamental Rights to life and personal liberty provided under Article 21.

It upholds the principle of rule of law and procedure established by law.

A fair trial is possible in an open court where the accused is given the chance to defend his innocence by providing all the relevant material like copy of chargesheet and evidence against him by an impartial and unbiased judge.

41 With reference to India, consider the following statements. *(Class-XI, Old NCERT) (IAS Pre 2022)*

1. Government law officers and legal firms are recognised as advocates, but corporate lawyers and patent attorneys are excluded from recognition as advocates.
2. Bar Councils have the power to lay down the rules relating to legal education and recognition of law colleges.

Which of the statements given above is/are correct?

(a) Only 1
(b) Only 2
(c) Both 1 and 2
(d) Neither 1 nor 2

Ans. (c)

Exp. Both the statements i.e., (1) and (2) are correct with reference to India as according to Bar Council of India (Rule 49) an advocate shall not be a full time salaried employee of any person, government, firm, corporation or concern otherwise cease to practice as an advocate so long as he continues in such employment.

Bar Council have the Power to lay down the rules relating to legal education and recognition of law colleges. The Bar Council of India is a statutory body created by Parliament under the Advocates Act, 1961 to regulate and represent the Indian bar.

42 With reference to India, consider the following statements. *(Unit 9, Class-XII, Tamil Nadu Board)*

1. Judicial custody means an accused is in toe custody of the concerned magistrate and such accused is locked up in police station, not in jail.
2. During judicial custody, the police officer in charge of the case is not allowed to interrogate the suspect without the approval of the court.

Which of the statements given above is/are incorrect?

(a) Only 1
(b) Only 2
(c) Both 1 and 2
(d) Neither 1 nor 2

Ans. (a)

Exp. Statement (1) is incorrect because in Judicial custody, an accused is in the custody of the concerned Magistrate and lodged in jail.

While in the case of police custody, an accused is locked up in a police station.

Chapter 14

Federalism and Centre-State Relations

Federalism and Centre-State Relations

Federalism

Introduction
- A system in which powers are divided between the Centre and States
- An Institutional mechanism to accommodate two sets of polities
- One at the regional level and second one at the National level

Federalism in India
- Part XI and XII define power distribution
- First example of Federal Government (Government of India Act, 1935)
- Article 1 : India will be Union of States
- Article 2 : Admission or Establishment of new states

Federal Features of Indian Constitution
- **Division of Power** Seventh Schedule provide three lists
  - State List : Compries 61 subjects
  - Union List : Compries 100 subjects
  - Concurrent List : Compries 52 subjects
- **Written Constitution** Both the governments, Union and States is the Written Constitution
- **Rigidity of the Constitution** Constitution regarding the federal principle is rigid
- **Supremacy of the Constitution** Legislature, Executive and Judiciary get their power from the Constitution
- **Impartial Judiciary** Supreme Court has highest authority regarding the interpretation of the Constitution

Centre-State Relations

Legislative Relations
- Power to form new states
- Can alter the boundary of any state or even its name

Distribution of Powers
- Seventh Schedule has provide distribution of powers
- Distribution of powers heavily tilts in favour of the Union
- Concurrent List, more power with centre
- Centre can make laws on State List (exception)
- Executive powers of the centre are Superior to the Executive Power of the States
- Governor can reserved a bill for the consideration of the President

Financial Relations
- Central Government holds significant Financial powers and responsibilities
- Revenue generating items are under Central Government
- State rely on grants and financial assistance from the Centre
- President appoints Finance Commission, recommending grant allocation

Role of Finance Commission
- Recommends distribution of taxes between Union and States
- Allocate state's share and outlines principles for grants in-aid
- Suggests ways to add money to a State's Fund to help local Panchayats, following State Finance Commission's advice

Administrative Relations
- Governors appointed by President and are answerable for Discretionary Powers
- Sarkaria Commission (1983) recommended non-partisan Governor is appointments to address Centre-State issue
- Article 356 allow President's rule imposition if State Governance is disrupted
- Articles 33 and 34 empower Parliament to protect personnel during martial law
- All India Services personnel can be deputed by Union Government despite State Assignment
- Unified Judicial System in India, with Supreme Court as highest appellate for Union and State matters

Emergency Relations
- During emergency (Article 352), Parliament can legislate on State list matters
- Article 356 allows the President to take over state functions and High Court powers in Constitutional breakdown
- Article 360, Financial Emergency permits President to issue directions including salary reductions for Union and State Public Servants
- All money bill passed by the State Legislature

SOURCE *New NCERT Class X* (*Federalism*), *New NCERT Class X* (*Power-sharing*), *New NCERT Class XI* (*Federalism*), *Old NCERT Class XI* (*Indian Constitution : Preamble, Features and Indian Union*)

Federalism

1 Prof. KC Wheare in his work 'Federal Government' refers to the 'federal principle' without which no polity can be called 'federal'. Which one of the following is that principle? *(Chap 3, Class-XI, Old NCERT)*

(a) The field of government is divided between the Federal and State Governments
(b) Written Constitution
(c) Independent Judiciary
(d) All of the above

***Ans.* (a)**

Exp. Prof. KC Wheare in his work 'Federal Government' Feferred the field of government is divided between the federal and State Governments as 'federal principle'. He defined federalism as the method of dividing powers such that the federal and state governments are within a sphere of coordination and independence.

2 Given below are two statements, one is labelled as Assertion (A) and other as Reason (R). *(Unit 5, Class-XII, Tamil Nadu Board)*

Assertion (A) The primary objective of India's Federal design was to weave a nation out of its many diverse parts and protect national integration.

Reason (R) The accommodation of diversities has built a stronger, not weaker, Indian Nationhood.

Codes

(a) Both A and R are true and R is the correct explanation of A.
(b) Both A and R are true, but R is not the correct explanation of A.
(c) A is true, but R is false.
(d) A is false, but R is true.

***Ans.* (a)**

Exp. Both Assertion (A) and Reason (R) are true and Reason (R) is the correct explanation of Assertion (A). The primary objective of Indian Federal design was to weave a nation out of its many diverse parts and protect national integration. Therefore, the accommodation of diversities has resulted in strong Nationhood not a weaker one.

3 Consider the following statements about the holding-together federations. *(Chap 2, Class-X, New NCERT)*

1. In this system, a large country decides to divide its power between the constituent states and the national government.
2. India, Spain and Belgium are examples of this kind of 'holding-together' federations.
3. The Central Government tends to be more powerful vis-à-vis the states.
4. All units are given equal powers.

Which of the statements given above is/are not correct?

(a) Only 1 (b) Only 4 (c) 1, 3 and 4 (d) 1, 2 and 3

***Ans.* (b)**

Exp. Only statement (4) is not correct about holding-together federation. In a holding-together federation like India, a country decides to divide its power between the constituent states and the national government. In this kind of federation, the Central Government tends to be more powerful vis-à-vis the states.

4 Consider the following statements, with reference to the feature of India federalism. *(Unit 5, Class-XII, Tamil Nadu Board)*

1. Every State Government has powers of its own.
2. Courts have the power to interpret the Constitution and the powers of different levels of Government.
3. States are subordinate to the Central Government.
4. Sources of revenue for each level of Government are clearly specified.

Which of the statements given above is/are not a feature of India federalism?

(a) Both 1 and 2 (b) Both 3 and 4
(c) Only 3 (d) None of these

***Ans.* (c)**

Exp. Only statement (3) is not a feature of Indian federalism. There is the concept of federalism with unitary bias in India, with the clear division of power between the union and states i.e., none is subordinate to the other.

Both the Central and State Governments derive their power from the Constitution. State Governments are not agents of the Central Government nor do they draw their authority from them.

5 Consider the following statements with respect to federalism. *(Chap 2, Class-X, New NCERT)*

1. Federalism is a system of government in which the power is divided between a central authority and various constituent units of the country.
2. The Central Government can pass on orders to the provincial or the local government.
3. State Government has powers of its own for which it is not answerable to the Central Government.
4. Federalism as a principle of government has evolved differently in different situations.

How many of the statements given above is/are incorrect?

(a) Only one
(b) Only two
(c) All four
(d) None of the above

***Ans.* (a)**

Exp. Only one statement i.e., (2) is incorrect with respect to federalism as Central Government cannot pass any order to State Government in ordinary situation.

However, in extraordinary situation like emergency, Central Government can takeover state machinery and can pass appropriate order.

6 **Consider the following statements and choose the correct code.** *(Chap 3, Class-XI, Old NCERT) (UPPSC Pre 1995)*

Statement-I The Constitution of India provides for a federal system.

Statement-II It has created a very strong centre.

Codes

(a) Both Statement-I and Statement-II are corect and Statement-II is the correct explanation of Statement-I.
(b) Both Statement-I and Statement-II are correct and Statement-II is not the correct explanation for Statement-I.
(c) Statement-I is correct, but Statement-II is incorrect.
(d) Statement-I is incorrect, but Statement-II is correct.

Ans. (b)

Exp. Both Statement-I and Statement-II are correct and Statement-II is not the correct explanation for Statement-I.

The Constitution of India provides for a federal system of government in the country. The federal system was adopted due to two reasons–first, the large size of the country and second, its socio-cultural diversity.

But, at the same time, the division of power is in favour of the centre and makes it strong. Residuary powers have also been left with the centre. The Parliament can change the area, boundaries or name of the states by unilateral action.

7 **Which of the following is/are the key features of federalism?** *(Chap 7, Class-XI, New NCERT)*

1. Two or more tiers of government.
2. Each tier has its own jurisdiction.
3. Written Constitution
4. Independent Judiciary

Codes.

(a) 1, 2 and 3 (b) 2 and 4
(c) 1, 2 and 4 (d) All of these

Ans. (d)

Exp. All the given above are the key features of federalism.

In a federation, there are two or more tiers of government *viz*, Union, state or local level.

Centre and State has their own jurisdiction like mentioned in Schedule 7 *viz*. Union list, State list and Concurrent list.

Written Constitution is a *sine qua non* of a federation as it outlines rights and liabilities of respective tiers of government.

To prevent conflicts between the Centre and the State, there is an independent Judiciary to settle disputes.

8 **Consider the following statements with respect to the federal system.** *(Chap 2, Class-X, New NCERT)*

1. The only objective of federal system is to accommodate regional diversity.
2. An ideal federal system has both aspects-mutual trust and agreement to live together.

Which of the statements given above is/are correct?

(a) Only 1
(b) Only 2
(c) Both 1 and 2
(d) Neither 1 nor 2

Ans. (b)

Exp. Only statement (2) is correct with respect to the federal system as an ideal federal system require mutual trust and agreement to live together because of diversity of thoughts, beliefs, values, language, cuisine among others states coming together to form a federal union. Statement (1) is not correct because the federal system has dual objective; to safeguard and promote unity of country, as well as to accommodate regional diversity.

9 **Consider the following Assertion (A) and Reason (R) and choose the correct code.** *(Chap 2, Class-X, New NCERT)*

Assertion (A) The exact balance of power between the Central and the State Governments varies from one federation to another.

Reason (R) This balance depends mainly on the historical context in which the federation was formed.

Codes

(a) Both A and R are true and R is the correct explanation of A.
(b) Both A and R are true, but R is not the correct explanation of A.
(c) A is true, but R is false.
(d) A is false, but R is true.

Ans. (a)

Exp. Both Assertion (A) and Reason (R) are true and Reason (R) is the correct explanation of Assertion (A). Balance of power between Union and State Governments varies as can be seen in Indian and US federation.

In USA, state and Union are equally powerful whereas in India, Union is strong as compared to states. This is due to historical reasons as the states in USA, were independent before forming a Union whereas in India states were under British empire.

10 **Which of the following factors pushed Indian federation towards having a strong centre?**

1. Immense diversities *(Chap 7, Class-XI, New NCERT)*
2. Socio-economic problems
3. Unity and development

Codes

(a) 1, 2 and 3
(b) 2 and 3
(c) 1 and 2
(d) None of the above

Ans. (a)

Exp. Immense diversities, socio-economic problems and unity and development pushed Indian federation towards having a strong centre as there were many fissures in the society which could threaten the unity and integrity of Indian nation-state.

11 Consider the following statements with reference to the feature of Indian federalism.

(Chap 3, Class-XI, Old NCERT) (IAS Pre 2017)

1. There is an independent Judiciary in India.
2. Powers have been clearly divided between centre and the states.
3. The federating units have been given unequal representation in the Rajya Sabha.
4. It is the result of an agreement among the federating units.

Which of the statements given above is/are incorrect?

(a) Only 1 (b) 2 and 3 (c) Only 4 (d) 1, 3 and 4

Ans. *(c)*

Exp. Only statement (4) is not a feature of Indian federalism because it is not the result of an agreement among the federating units. Article 1 of our Constitution provides for India as a 'union of states'. It means that the Indian federation is not the result of an agreement by the states and also no state has the right to secede from the federation.

12 Which of the following are the factors that deviate from the generally accepted norms of federalism in India? *(Chap 3, Class-XI, Old NCERT)*

1. More items in the Union list.
2. Deployment of Central Reserve Police in states.
3. Governors of the states are appointed by President.
4. Dual citizenship.

Codes.

(a) 1 and 3 (b) 2 and 3 (c) 1, 2 and 4 (d) All are correct

Ans. *(c)*

Exp. Statements (1), (2) and (4) provide the factors that deviate from the generally accepted norms of federalism in India.

In India, the distribution of powers heavily tilts in favour of the Union. The Union list comprises the largest number of items. Thus, the Centre dominates in about two-third of the total number of subjects of the three lists together.

Though law and order is a state subject, the Centre deploys Central Reserve Police in states, whenever it deems necessary, without the concurrence of states.

Ordinarily in federation, dual citizenship prevails but in India there is no such provision as it provides for single citizenship.

13 Consider the following statements and choose the correct code. *(Chap 10, Class-XI, New NCERT)*

Statement-I Unlike the Constitutional symmetry of American federalism, Indian federalism has been constitutionally asymmetric.

Statement-II To meet the needs and requirements of some sub-units, it was always part of the original design to have a unique relationship with them or to give them special status.

Codes

(a) Both Statement-I and Statement-II are corect and Statement-II is the correct explanation of Statement-I.
(b) Both Statement-I and Statement-II are correct and Statement-II is not the correct explanation for Statement-I.
(c) Statement-I is correct, but Statement-II is incorrect.
(d) Statement-I is incorrect, but Statement-II is correct.

Ans. *(a)*

Exp. Both Statement-I and Statement-II are correct and Statement-II is the correct explanation for Statement-I.

In American federation, all the states have equal representation in the senate (Upper house) with 2 members each unlike Indian federation where representation in Rajya Sabha (Upper house) is in proportion to the population in states.

In India, there is too much diversity to have a symmetrical federalism without having special powers and relation with tribal and linguistic minorities and regions which is not the case in USA's federation.

Centre-State Relations

14 Who has the final power to resolve disputes between the Central Government and the States on legal matters about the division of power?

(Chap 2, Class-X, New NCERT)

(a) Supreme Court
(b) Central Government
(c) Inter-State Council
(d) President

Ans. *(a)*

Exp. Under Article 131, Supreme Court has the original jurisdiction and has the final power to resolve disputes between the Central Government and the States on legal matters about the division of power.

15 Consider the following pairs and choose the correct code. *(Chap 2, Class-X, New NCERT)*

1. Union List	–	Currency
2. State List	–	Police
3. Concurrent List	–	Education

How many of the pairs given above is/are correctly matched?

(a) Only one
(b) Only two
(c) All three
(d) None of the above

Ans. *(c)*

Exp. All three pairs i.e., (1), (2) and (3) are correctly matched.

The currency is in Union List (Article 246, List-1, Item no. 36) to maintain a uniform economic policy.

Police (including railway and village police) is in State List (Article 246, Item no. 2)

Education (Article 246, Item no. 25) is in Concurrent List.

16 Consider the following statements with respect to Coalition Government. *(Chap 1, Class-X, New NCERT)*

1. When no single party got a clear majority in the Lok Sabha, the major national parties had to enter into an alliance with many parties including several regional parties to form a Government at the Centre. This is known as Coalition Government.
2. Federal power sharing is not as much effective in today's scenario as it was in the early years after the Constitution came into force.
3. Coalition led to a new culture of power sharing and respect for the autonomy of State Governments.

Which of the statements given above is/are incorrect?

(a) Only 2 (b) Only 3 (c) Both 1 and 2 (d) Both 2 and 3

Ans. *(a)*

Exp. Only statement (2) is incorrect with respect to Coalition Government. Federal power sharing is more effective today than it was in the early years after the Constitution came into force. As no single party received a clear majority in the Lok Sabha, the major national parties were forced to establish an alliance with a variety of parties, including various regional parties, in order to form a Government at the federal level. This was termed as Coalition Government. This trend led to a new culture of power sharing and respect for the autonomy of State Governments.

17 With reference to the Indian Constitution, consider the following statements. *(Unit 5, Class-XII, Tamil Nadu Board)*

1. The Indian Constitution provides for the ratification of international treaties and conventions by Parliament.
2. The Indian Constitution does not provide for the ratification of international treaties and conventions by Parliament.
3. The Indian Constitution provides for the ratification of international treaties and conventions by Parliament under certain circumstances only.
4. The Indian Constitution provides for the ratification of international treaties by Parliament and not conventions.

Which one of the statements given above is/are true?

(a) Only 1 (b) Only 2
(c) Both 2 and 4 (d) Both 3 and 4

Ans. *(b)*

Exp. Only statement (2) is true regarding the Indian Constitution.

The Indian Constitution does not provide for the ratification of international treaties and conventions by Parliament.

Article 253 confers power on the Parliament to make any law for the whole or any part of the country to give effect to any international treaty, agreement, convention or decision.

18 Which of the statements is/are incorrect regarding administrative system of India? *(Chap 7, Class-XI, New NCERT)*

1. The administrative system of India is integrated.
2. All India Services belong to a particular state of India and officers chosen for these services serve in the administration of the States.
3. States can neither take disciplinary action nor can they remove IAS officers from service.

Select the correct answer using the codes given below.

(a) Only 2 (b) 1 and 3 (c) 1 and 2 (d) Only 3

Ans. *(a)*

Exp. Only statement (2) is incorrect regarding administration system of India because All India Services are common to the entire territory of India and officers chosen for these services serve in the administration of the states.

19 Consider the following statements regarding the centre's administrative directions to states. *(Chap 3, Class-XI, Old NCERT)*

1. The directions are binding on the states.
2. The Constitution provides adequate means for securing the compliance with the directions by the States.
3. Non-compliance can be treated as a failure of the constitutional machinery and entitle the President to impose, what in common parlance is called, President's rule in that State.

Which of the statements given above is/are incorrect?

(a) Only 1 (b) 1 and 2
(c) All of these (d) None of these

Ans. *(d)*

Exp. None of the given statement is incorrect regarding the centre's administrative direction to states.

Article 256 of the Indian Constitution deals with administrative relations between Centre and States.

It says the executive powers of the State are to be exercised in such a manner that it complies with the laws made by the Parliament or any other existing laws which are applicable in the State.

Under Article 356, if a State fails to comply with the directions issued by the Centre, then it is lawful for the President to hold that a situation has arisen wherein the State Government cannot be carried on according to the provisions of the Constitution.

20 Which of the following commissions appointed by the Central Government in 1983 to examine the issues relating to centre-state relations, recommended that appointments of Governors should be strictly non-partisan? *(Chap 7, Class-XI, New NCERT)*

(a) Malimath Commission (b) Sarkaria Commission
(c) Mandal Commission (d) Santhanam Committee

Ans. *(b)*

Exp. Sarkaria Commission appointed in 1983 and submitted its report in 1988. It recommended that the Governor should be from outside the state. He should be a non-political figure or retired from politics.
Also, he should not be a member of the ruling party. He should be appointed after effective consultations with the state Chief Minister and Vice-President and Speaker of the Lok Sabha should be consulted by the Prime Minister before his selection.

21 Given below are two statements, one is labelled as Assertion (A) and the other as Reason (R).
(Unit 5, Class-XII, Tamil Nadu Board)

Assertion (A) The Executive power of the state are exercised to ensure the compliance of the law of the Parliament and the laws applied in the state.

Reason (R) The Government of India can give necessary direction to the states by using its Executive Powers.

Codes
(a) Both A and R are true and R is the correct explanation of A.
(b) Both A and R are true, but R is not the correct explanation of A.
(c) A is true, but R is false.
(d) A is false, but R is true.

Ans. (a)
Exp. Both Assertion (A) and Reason (R) are true and Reason (R) is the correct explanation of Assertion (A).
Under Article 256, the Executive Power of every state shall be so exercised as to compliance with the laws made by the Parliament.
Under Article 257(1), the Executive Power of every state shall be exercised as not to impede or pre-judice the exercise of Executive Power of the union.

22 Which of the following pairs with respect to inter-state disputes is incorrectly matched?
(Chap 7, Class-XI, New NCERT)

	Dispute	States
(a)	Belgaum	Maharashtra and Karnataka
(b)	Cauvery	Karnataka and Andhra Pradesh
(c)	Chandigarh	Punjab and Haryana
(d)	Narmada	Gujarat and Madhya Pradesh

Ans. (b)
Exp. Pair (b) is incorrectly matched because Cauvery river water dispute is between Karnataka, Tamil Nadu, Puducherry and Kerala.
The final verdict of the Supreme Court came in 2018, where it declared Cauvery a national asset and largely upheld the water-sharing arrangements finalised by the Cauvery Water Dispute Tribunal (CWDT) and also reduced the allocation of water from Karnataka to Tamil Nadu.

Special Provisions for Certain States

23 Which of the following statements is not correct in respect of Inter-state river water disputes?
(Unit 5, Class-XII, Tamil Nadu Board)
(MPSC Pre 2012)

(a) Parliament, by law, can provide for adjudication of any dispute or complaint with respect to use, distribution or control of any water in any Inter-state river or river valley.
(b) Parliament by law, cannot restrict the jurisdiction of the Supreme Court as regards inter-state river or river valley water disputes.
(c) Parliament by law, can prohibit High Court and other lower courts from exercising jurisdiction on such Inter-state water disputes.
(d) In Maharashtra, Karnataka and Andhra Pradesh, Krishna river water distribution award has been pronounced under the provisions of Article 262 of the Constitution of India.

Ans. (b)
Exp. Statement (b) is not correct in respect of Inter-state river water disputes.
Article 262 provides that Parliament may by law provide that neither the Supreme Court nor any other court shall exercise jurisdiction in respect of any such dispute or complaint.

24 Which one of the following matters stands excluded from the jurisdiction of Inter-state Council in India?
(Class-XI, Old NCERT) (MPSC Pre 2020)

(a) Enquiring into and advice upon disputes which may have arisen between the states.
(b) Adjudication of any dispute with respect to the use, distribution or control of water of any Inter-state river.
(c) Investigation and discussion of subjects in which some or all of the states or the union and one or more states, have common interest.
(d) Making recommendation on any such subject and in particular, recommendations for the better co-ordination of policy and action with respect to the subject.

Ans. (b)
Exp. Adjudication of any dispute with respect to the use, distribution or control of water of any Inter-state river excluded from the Jurisdiction of Inter-State Council. To resolve water disputes and provide for the adjudication of any dispute related to water of the Inter-state river and river valleys, the Inter-State River Water Disputes (ISRWD) Act, 1956, was passed in the Parliament under Article 262 of Constitution of India.

25 Consider the following statements.
(Class-XI, Old NCERT)
(MPSC Pre 2017)

1. According to Article 262 of the Indian Constitution, the Parliament may by law provide for the adjudication of Inter-state river water dispute.
2. Article 262 empowers the President of India to set up an Inter-state river water dispute tribunal.

Which of the statements given above is/are incorrect?
(a) Both 1 and 2 (b) Only 1
(c) Only 2 (d) Neither 1 nor 2

Ans. (c)
Exp. Only statement (2) is incorrect as Article 262 empowers the Parliament to set-up an Inter-state river dispute tribunal not President.

Inter-state Water Dispute Act, 1956, in case, if a particular state or the states approach the Union Government for the Constitution of the tribunal, Central Government should try to resolve the matter by consultation among the aggrieved states.

In case, if it does not work, then it may constitute the tribunal. Under the same Act, Krishna river water distribution Award has been pronounced for the States of Maharashtra, Andhra Pradesh and Karnataka.

26 What criteria have been suggested by Sarkaria Commission when a person is to be appointed as the Governor of the State?
(Class-XI, Old NCERT) (MPSC Pre 2013)

1. He should be eminent in some walk of life.
2. He should be a person from outside the state.
3. He should be a person who has not taken part in politics generally and more particularly in the recent past.
4. He should be intimately connected with the local politics.

Select the correct answer using the codes given below.
(a) 1 and 2 (b) 1 and 3
(c) 1, 2 and 3 (d) All of these

Ans. (c)
Exp. Statements (1), (2) and (3) are correct. The criteria that have been suggested by Sarkaria Commission when a person is to be appointed as the Governor of the State are, he should be eminent in some walk of life, he should be a person from outside the state and he also should be a person who has not taken part in politics generally and more particularly in the recent past.

Statement (4) is not correct because the commission recommended that a person to serve as the Governor should be a detached figure with little record of participation in the local politics of the state.

27 Which of the following statements are correct regarding the legal relationship between the Central and State Government in India?
(Class-XI, Old NCERT) (MPSC Pre 2023)

1. The subject of transfer of property other than agricultural land is included in the Concurrent list.
2. The subject of wealth tax on property other than agricultural land is included in the Union list.
3. The subject of entertainment tax is included in the Concurrent list.
4. The subject of 'antiquities museum' is included in the State list.

Select the correct answer using the codes given below.
(a) 1, 2 and 3
(b) 2, 3 and 4
(c) 1, 2 and 4
(d) 1, 3 and 4

Ans. (c)
Exp. Statements (1), (2) and (4) are correct.

The transfer of property other than agricultural land is covered under the Concurrent list. The High Court of Kerala held that wealth-tax is specifically and in substance covered by entry 86 of the Union list of the Seventh Schedule to the Constitution of India.

Libraries, museums and other similar institutions controlled or financed by state, ancient and historical monuments and records other than those declared by under law made by Parliament to be of national importance is covered under the State list.

Statement (3) is not correct because the taxes and fees on entertainment, amusements, betting tax and gambling are levied by the State Government by virtue of the powers vested in it, under Article 246 (3) of Constitution.

Chapter 15

Emergency Provisions

Emergency Provisions

Constitutional Provisions

Introduction
- Adopted from Germany's Constitution
- Article 352 to 360 of Part XVIII
- At the time of emergency, federalism can turn into a unitary state

National Emergency (Article 352)
- President can declare a National Emergency if security is threatened by war, external aggression or armed rebellion

Process and Duration
- Proclamation must be laid before both Houses and approved within 30 days
- Approval requires absolute majority of total members and 2/3rd majority of present and voting members
- If Parliament approves, the proclamation stays in force for an additional six months

Suspension of Fundamental Rights
- Article 358 suspends six Fundamental Rights under Article 19
- Article 359 allows the President to suspend other Fundamental Rights (except Article 20 and 21)
- National Emergency has been imposed thrice so far

Effects of Proclam ation of Emergency (Article 353)
- Article 353, empowers union to extend Executive Power during emergency
- Parliament empowered to legislate on State List (Article 250)
- Tenure of Lok Sabha and State Legislative can be extend for one year

President's Rule/ State Emergency
- **Article 355** It shall be duty of the union to protect states from external aggression and internal disturbance
- **Article 356** President may pro claim emergency based on Governor's report or other reason
- **Article 365** If a State fails to comply with centre's direction, President may declare emergency

Process and Duration of Proclamation
- Proclamations must be approved by both Houses within two months

Financial Emergency
- Article 360
- President proclaim, if satisfied with a situation threatening India's financial stability or credit

Process and Duration
- Must be laid before each Houses, approval within two months
- If Lok Sabha dissolved, Rajya Sabha approval keeps it in force until one month after new Lok Sabha's first sitting

Effect of the Proclamation
- Union's executive authority includes directing states on specified financial property
- All Money Bill can be reserved for consideration after they have been passed by the State Legislature
- President can Issue direction for salary reduction, covering state personnel and judges

Punchhi Commission on Emergency Provisions

Punchhi Commission on Emergency Provisions
- Favours amending Article 356 and 365 for limited central rule in troubled areas
- Proposes localising emergency provisions to avoid misuse by the centre
- Suggests bringing specific area under Governor's rule, limiting duration to three months

Articles with the Provisions of Emergency

Article	Description
352	Proclamation of National Emergency
353	Effects of Proclamation of Emergency
354	Reduction of distribution of revenue between the Union and the State
355	Duty of the union to protect states against external aggression and internal disturbance
356	Provisions in case of failure of constitutional machinery in states
357	Exercise of Legislative Powers under proclamation issued
358	Suspension of provisions of Article 19 during emergency
359	Suspension of the enforcement of the right conferred by Part III
360	Provisions as to financial emergency

SOURCE **Old NCERT Class XI** *(Central Government)*, **New NCERT Class XII** *(The Crises of Democratic Order)*

1 **Consider the following statements and select the correct code.** *(Chap 6, Class-XII, Old NCERT)*

Statement-I Constitution of India is basically federal in nature.

Statement-II Article 352 has provisions to deal with the failure of Constitutional machinery in a state.

Codes

(a) Both Statement-I and Statement-II are correct and Statement-II is the correct explanation for Statement-I.

(b) Both Statement-I and Statement-II are correct and Statement-II is not the correct explanation for Statement-I.

(c) Statement-I is correct but Statement-II is incorrect.

(d) Statement-I is incorrect but Statement-II is correct.

Ans. *(c)*

Exp. Statement-I is correct but Statement-II is incorrect.

India is a Federal system, but with more tilt towards a unitary system of government. It is sometimes considered a Quasi-Federal system as it has features of both a federal and a unitary system. There is a government at two levels - Centre and State.

Under the Unitary features, the Centre is provided with emergency powers in Article 352. The provision of National Emergency has been made under Article 352 of the Constitution not in the context of failure of the Constitutional machinery of the state.

2 **Consider the following statements regarding the National Emergency.** *(Chap 5, Class-XI, Old NCERT)*

1. The decision of the Union Cabinet recommending a proclamation of emergency has to be given in writing to the President.
2. Every such proclamation of emergency must be laid before Lok Sabha only.
3. It shall remain in force till six months (from the day when such a resolution was passed by the Lok Sabha).
4. The resolution of the approval of each house should be passed by absolute majority of the total number of its members and by two-third majority of the members present and voting.

Which of the statements given above is/are not correct?

(a) Only 1 (b) Only 2
(c) 2 and 3 (d) 1, 3 and 4

Ans. *(b)*

Exp. Statement (2) is not correct regarding the National Emergency because every such proclamation of emergency must be laid before both the Houses of Parliament.

However, if such a proclamation has been issued at a time when Lok Sabha stands dissolved, it shall remain in force if approved by Rajya Sabha.

3 **Consider the following statements with reference to the effects of proclamation of emergency.** *(Chap 5, Class-XI, Old NCERT)*

1. The executive authority of the States becomes subordinate to the Union.
2. The legislative authority of the Parliament extends to the making of laws on the State List.
3. The operation of Article 19 relating to Right to Freedom remains suspended.
4. The Parliament is authorised to suspend by an order, the right to move any court of law for the enforcement of all the Fundamental Rights.

How many of the statements given below is/are not one of the effects of proclamation of emergency?

(a) Only one (b) Only two
(c) All four (d) None of these

Ans. *(a)*

Exp. Only one statement i.e., (4) is not correct with reference to the effect of proclamation of emergency. The 44th Amendment Act mandates that the President cannot suspend the right to move the court of law for the enforcement of Fundamental Rights guaranteed by Article 20 and 21.

However, Fundamental Rights under Article 19 can be suspended declared on the grounds of war or external aggression and not on the grounds of armed rebellion.

4 **Consider the following statements regarding the proclamation of emergency under Article 352.** *(Chap 6, Class-XII, Old NCERT) (Chap 9, Module-2, NIOS)*

1. It automatically comes to an end on the expiry of one month from its issue, unless it is approved by a resolution of the Lok Sabha before the expiry of that period.
2. The President is empowered to proclaim emergency only if the Council of Ministers recommends to him in writing that such a proclamation should be issued.

Which of the statements given above is/are correct?

(a) Only 1 (b) Only 2
(c) Both 1 and 2 (d) Neither 1 nor 2

Ans. *(d)*

Exp. Neither statements (1) nor (2) are correct about proclamation of emergency under Article 352. Proclamation of emergency under Article 352 is necessary to be approved within the period of one month by both the Houses of the Parliament by special majority i.e. two-third of the members present and voting, not only by Lok Sabha. After 44th Amendment in the Constitution, the emergency can be declared by the President under Article 352 only when the Cabinet (not Council of Ministers) gives such advice to the President in written format.

5 In which of the following cases President of India may declare the National Emergency?

(Chap 5, Class-XI, Old NCERT) (UPPSC Mains 2010)

1. External aggression
2. Internal disturbances
3. Armed rebellion
4. Communal clashes

Codes

(a) 1 and 2 (b) 2 and 3 (c) 3 and 4 (d) 1 and 3

Ans. (d)

Exp. In the cases of external aggression and armed rebellion, President of India may declare the National Emergency.

When the President feels that security of India or any part thereof is threatened or there is an imminent danger of such a threat by war or external aggression or by armed rebellion, he can proclaim an emergency under Article 352. The word 'Internal disturbance' has been replaced by the 'Armed rebellion' by 44th Constitutional Amendment Act, 1978. In communal clashes, there is no provision for declaration of National Emergency.

6 Consider the following statements regarding the steps taken during the National Emergency of 1975.

(Chap 6, Class-XII, New NCERT)

1. An Amendment was made declaring that elections of Prime Minister, President and Vice-President could not be challenged in the Court.
2. The 44th Amendment was also passed during the Emergency.
3. The duration of the Legislatures in the country was permanently extended from five to six years.

Which of the statements given above is/are not correct?

(a) Only 1 (b) Only 2
(c) All of these (d) None of these

Ans. (b)

Exp. Statement (2) is not correct regarding the steps taken during the National Emergency of 1975 because 44th Amendment was passed in 1978 after Janata Party Government came into power in 1977.

This Amendment aimed to undo several changes that had been made to the Constitution by the 42nd Amendment, 1976 during the Emergency. This Amendment repealed the right to property from the list of Fundamental Rights.

7 Consider the following statements with respect to failure of Constitutional machinery.

(Chap 6, Class-XI, New NCERT)

1. If the President feels satisfied that it is not possible to carry on the government of the State according to the provisions of the Constitution, the President can declare State Emergency.
2. Under such circumstances, the Union Government may assume all or any of the executive powers of the state.

Which of the statements given above is/are incorrect?

(a) Only 1 (b) Only 2
(c) Both 1 and 2 (d) Neither 1 nor 2

Ans. (b)

Exp. Statement (2) is incorrect with respect to failure of Constitutional machinery because the President acquires extraordinary powers when the President's rule is imposed in a state under Article 356. Under President's rule, the President can take up the functions of the State Government and powers vested in the Governor or any other executive authority in the state.

8 Consider the following statements regarding the effect of State Emergency/President Rule.

(Chap 5, Class-XI, Old NCERT)

1. The President may declare that the legislative authority of the State shall be exercised by or under the authority of Parliament.
2. The President may suspend operation of any provision of the Constitution relating to any authority in the State including that of a High Court.
3. Every such proclamation must be laid before each House of Parliament and receive approval of both the Houses within two months.
4. The Lok Sabha may pass the resolution approving its continuance for another six months.

How many of the statements given above is/are not correct?

(a) Only one (b) Only two (c) All four (d) None

Ans. (a)

Exp. Only one statement i.e., (2) is correct regarding the effect of State Emergency/President Rule because the President can take all other necessary steps including the suspension of the Constitutional provisions relating to any body or authority in the State. But, he cannot abrogate or diminish the powers of High Court as judiciary is independent and separate from executive.

9 Which of the following are not necessarily the consequences of the proclamation of the President's Rule in a State?

(Chap 5, Class-XI, Old NCERT)
(Uni 5, Class-XII, Tamil Nadu Board) (IAS Pre 2017)

1. Dissolution of the State Legislative Assembly.
2. Removal of the Council of Ministers in the State.
3. Dissolution of the local bodies.

Codes

(a) 1 and 2 (b) 1 and 3
(c) 2 and 3 (d) 1, 2 and 3

Ans. (b)

Exp. Statements (1) and (3) are not necessarily the consequences of the proclamation of the President's Rule in a State. According to Article 356 of the Indian Constitution, dissolution of the State Legislative Assembly and dissolution of the local bodies are not the valid consequences of the President's Rule in any State.

10 If the President of India exercises his power as provided under Article 356 of the Constitution in respect of a particular state, then
(Unit 5, Class-XII, Tamil Nadu Board)

(a) the Assembly of the State is automatically dissolved.
(b) the power of the Legislature of the State shall be exercisable by or under the authority of the Parliament.
(c) Article 19 is suspended in that State.
(d) the President can make laws relating to the State.

Ans. (b)

Exp. If the President of India exercises his power as provided under Article 356 of the Constitution in respect of a particular state, then the power of the Legislature of the State shall be exercisable by or under the authority of the Parliament.

11 Consider the following pairs.
(Chap 7, Class-XI, New NCERT)
(CGPSC Pre 2020)

	States		President's rule has been imposed till 2019.
1.	Manipur	–	10
2.	Uttar Pradesh	–	9
3.	Bihar	–	8
4.	Odisha	–	8

How many pairs given above is/are correct?

(a) Only one (b) Only two
(c) Only three (d) All four

Ans. (d)

Exp. All the pairs given above are correct.

Manipur President's rule has been imposed 10 times.

In Uttar Pradesh President's rule has been imposed 9 times.

In Bihar President's rule has been imposed 8 times.

In Odisha President's rule has been imposed 8 times.

12 Consider the following statements about vacancy in office of President. *(Chap 4, Class-XI, New NCERT)*

1. The Vice-President becomes President for the remainder term when the office of President falls vacant.
2. In case the office of Vice-President is also vacant, the Chief Justice of India takes charge as President of India.
3. The Chief Justice has certain limited powers when he acts as President of India.

How many statements given above is/are incorrect?

(a) Only one (b) Only two
(c) All three (d) None of these

Ans. (b)

Exp. Only two statements i.e., (1) and (3) are incorrect with reference to vacancy in the office of President.

When a vacancy occurs in the office of the President due to his resignation, removal, death or otherwise, the Vice-President acts as the President not till the remainder of the term but until a new President is elected. He can act as a President only for a maximum period of 6 months within which a new President has to the elected.

When any person, i.e., Vice-President, Chief Justice of India, or the senior most Judge of the Supreme Court is acting as the President or discharging the functions of the President, he enjoys all the powers and immunities of the Presient and is entitled to such emoluments, allowances and privileges as are determined by the Parliament.

13 Under which of the following circumstances, a proclamation of State Emergency can be extended beyond a period of one year? *(Chap 6, Class-XI, Old NCERT)*

1. A proclamation of National Emergency is in operation at the time of passing such a resolution.
2. The Election Commission certifies that on account of difficulties in holding general election to the Legislative Assembly of the State concerned, continuance of the proclamation (regarding failure of Constitutional machinery) is necessary.

Select the correct answer using the codes given below.

(a) Only 1
(b) Only 2
(c) Both 1 and 2
(d) Neither 1 nor 2

Ans. (c)

Exp. Both the statements (1) and (2) are correct regarding the extension of State Emergency beyond the period of one year.

Parliament is not allowed to pass any such resolution extending a proclamation beyond a period of one year unless a proclamation of Emergency (under Article 352) is in the operation at the time of passing such resolution and another condition is Election Commission must certify that the general elections to the Legislature Assembly of the concerned state cannot be held on account of difficulties.

14 Consider the following statements with respect to the Financial Emergency. *(Chap 5, Class-XI, Old NCERT)*

1. If the President is satisfied that a situation has arisen whereby the financial stability or credit of the whole of India is threatened, then only he proclaim a Financial Emergency.
2. Every such proclamation is laid before each House of the Parliament and receives approval of both the Houses within two months.

Which of the statementss given above is/are incorrect?

(a) Only 1 (b) Only 2
(c) Both 1 and 2 (d) Neither 1 nor 2

Ans. (d)

Exp. Neither statements (1) nor (2) are incorrect with respect to Financial Emergency.

If the President is satisfied that a situation has arisen whereby the financial stability or credit of India or any of its part is threatened, he may proclaim a Financial Emergency, under Article 360.

A proclamation declaring Financial Emergency must be approved by both the Houses of Parliament within two months from the date of its issue.

It includes the persons serving in connection with affairs of union including Judges of Supreme Court and High Courts.

15 Consider the following statements about the effects of the proclamation under Article 360.

(Chap 6, Class-XI, Old NCERT)

1. The executive authority of the Union shall extend to give directions to any State to observe such canons of financial propriety as may be specified in the directions.
2. It may also include a provision requiring all Money Bills to be reserved for the consideration of the President after the State Legislature passes them.
3. The President may issue directions for the reduction of salaries and allowances of all or any class of persons serving the State excluding the Judges of the Supreme Court and High Courts.

Which of the statements given above is/are not correct?

(a) Only 2 (b) Only 3 (c) 1, 2 and 3
(d) Both 2 and 3

Ans. (*b*)

Exp. Statement (3) is not correct about the effects of the proclamation under Article 360. As Article 360(4)(b) empowers the President may issue directions for the reduction of salaries and allowances of all persons serving the state.

16 Consider the following statements in respect of Financial Emergency under Article 360 of the Constitution of India.

(Chap 9, Module-2, NIOS) (UPPSC Pre 2007)

1. A proclamation of Financial Emergency issued shall cease to operate at the expiration of two months, unless before the expiration that period it has been approved by the resolution of both Houses of Parliament.
2. If proclamation of Financial Emergency is in operation, it is competent for the President of India to issue directions for the reduction of salaries and allowances of all of any class of persons and serving in connection with the affairs of the Union but excluding the Judges of the Supreme Court and the High Courts.

Which of the statements given above is/are incorrect?

(a) Only 1
(b) Only 2
(c) Both 1 and 2
(d) Neither 1 nor 2

Ans. (*b*)

Exp. Statement (2) is incorrect because during Financial Emergency, essential reduction can be made in the salary of the officers of the Union and the States, including the Supreme Court and High Court Judges.

It is not only competent for the President to issue such direction but the executive authority of center can also do so.

Chapter 16

Civil Services

Civil Services

Public Civil Services and It's Classification

Introduction

- Public Civil Services was started by the efforts Lord Warren Hastings and Lord Cornwallis's efforts
- Cornwallis, father of Civil Services
- Lord Cornwallis initiated Converted and Unconverted Civil Services, limiting Indian to lower post
- First Civil-Services exam held in London (1855)
- GoI Act, 1919, led to the formation of the Central Public Service Commission in 1928

Classification of Indian Civil Services

- **All India Services**
  - Common to both Centre and States
  - Trained and recruited by Central Government
  - Serve State Government
  - Service conditions governed by states
  - Serve Central Government on deputation
- **Central Services**
  - Class I (Group A) - IFS, IAS, Statistical Services, IRS, etc
  - Class-II (Group B)– CSS, GSI, ZSD, etc
  - Class-III (Group-C)– Post and Telegraph Service, Central Secretariat Clerical Service, etc
  - Class-IV (Group D)– Peons, Sweepers, etc
- **State Civil Services**
  - Administrator state subjects
  - Recruited through competitive exams similar to UPSC
  - Article 311 safeguards Civil Services members, no dismissal without inquiry and fair opportunity to be heard

Level of Administration

Central Administration

- **Article 77 (1)** Executive action in India's name by President
- **Article 77 (3)** President makes rule for government business

Bureauerats in Central Administration

- **Secretary** Administrative head of ministry
- Principle advisor to minister on policy and administration

Cabinet Secretary

- Heads the cabinet secretariat
- Holds top precedence among civil servants

Function of Central Secretariat

- Assist in policy making, framing legislation and supervising executive departments
- Prepare budget and control departmental expenditures

Constitutional Statutory Authorities Under Civil Services

- **UPSC** Assist in recruitment, promotion and discipline in the Central and All India Services

Appointment and Term of Office

- President appoints chairman and members on ministry advice
- Serve 6 years or until age 65, which ever is earlier

Removal/Resignation

- Resign by addressing the President
- Removal reasons include misbehaviour, insolvency, external employment or unfit due to health

Function of the Commission

- Conduct examination for Union Government Services
- Assesses candidate's suitability for appointments promotions, transfers

State Administration

- **Secretariat Department** Headed by Secretary (Generalist)
- **Executive Department** Headed by Director (Specialist)
- **Chief Secretary** Administrative Head of State Administration; Appointed by Chief Minister from senior secretaries, oversees cabinet secretariat, tenure based on experience, skill
- **Function of Chief Secretary** Ex-officio Cabinet Secretary; Attends all Cabinet and Sub-Committee meetings; Chief Minister's primary source of information and advice
- **State Public Service Commission**
  - Constitution mandates State Government to form public service commission for recruitment, promotion and discipline in state services
  - **Power and Functions** Conduct State Government Service exam; Commission reports annual work to the Governor
  - **Appointment and Tenure** Governor appoints chairman and other members
- Member serve 6 years or until 62 years, which ever is earlier

District Administration

- Executes government policies, addresses local issues and report to the State Government
- **Role and Function** Regulatory Functions, Developmental Functions

District Collector

- **Role and Functions** As a Collector leads the revenue department
- **As a District Magistrate** Supervise criminal administration, enforcement of criminal law

SOURCE **New NCERT Class X** *(Federalism)*, **Old NCERT Class XI** *(Features of Bureaucracy)*, **New NCERT Class XI** *(Executive)*, **Old NCERT Class XI** *(Public Administration : Working and Organisation)*, **Old NCERT Class XI** *(Public Administration in India)*, **Old NCERT Class XII** *(Regional Imbalances : Regionalism, Linguism and Separatism)*

Public Services in India

1 Consider the following statements regarding bureaucracy. *(Chap 9, Class-XI, Old NCERT)*

1. The political executive controls administration, the detailed working of which is left to the permanent officials of the government known as Bureaucracy.
2. It is a body of professional, full time officials employed to handle the civil affairs of a State in a political capacity.
3. It helps in implementing the policies which the political executive decides.
4. The term Civil Service was first used by the British and popularised by Sir Charles Trevelyan.

Which of the statements given above is/are incorrect?

(a) Only 3
(b) Only 2
(c) 1, 3 and 4
(d) 1, 2 and 3

Ans. *(b)*

Exp. Only statement (2) is incorrect regarding bureaucracy. Bureaucracy is a professional body where full time officials are appointed on merit base system through open recruitment to handle the civil affairs of a State in a non-political and impartial manner. It is a permanent executive as opposed to political executive.

2 Consider the following statements. *(Chap 4,Class-XII, New NCERT) (Chap 33, Module-2, NIOS) (MPSC Pre 2017)*

1. The Public Service Commissions are advisory bodies. It is open to the government to accept the recommendation or depart from it.
2. The government is under an obligation to explain the reasons why in any particular case the recommendation of the commission has been overridden.

Which of the statements given above is/are correct?

(a) Only 1
(b) Only 2
(c) Both 1 and 2
(d) Neither 1 nor 2

Ans. *(c)*

Exp. Both the statements (1) and (2) are correct.

The Public Service Commissions are advisory and recommendatory bodies. Its decisions are not mandatory.

The UPSC presents, annually, to the President a report on its performance. The President places this report before both the Houses of Parliament, along with a memorandum explaining the cases where the advice of the commission was not accepted and the reasons for such non-acceptance. All such cases of non-acceptance must be approved by the Appointment Committee of the Union Cabinet. An individual ministry or department has no power to reject the advice of the UPSC.

3 Consider the following statements. *(Chap 9, Class-XI, Old NCERT)*

1. The Constitution makers have provided for certain agencies for smooth functioning of executive.
2. In India, Public Service Commissions have been established under the authority of the Constitution.

Which of the statements given above is/are correct?

(a) Only 1 (b) Only 2
(c) Both 1 and 2 (d) Neither 1 nor 2

Ans. *(c)*

Exp. Both the statements (1) and (2) are correct.

In order that the executive functions of the government could be carried out without any fear or pressure, the Constitution makers have provided for setting up some constitutional authorities. These constitutional authorities have been constituted in the form of Public Service Commissions.

According to Article 315 of the Indian Constitution, there shall be a permanent Public Service Commission which will conduct exam to appoint candidates to different posts of Indian Civil Services under the Government of India.

4 Consider the following pairs. *(Chap 9, Class-XI, Old NCERT)*

Behavioural Characteristics		Meaning
1. Rationality	–	Strict rules
2. Impersonality	–	Decision on strict evidence
3. Rule Orientation	–	No irrational sentiments
4. Neutrality	–	Absence of bias

How many pairs given above is/are correct?

(a) Only one (b) Only two (c) Only three (d) All four

Ans. *(a)*

Exp. Only one pair i.e., (4) is correct as neutrality refers to political impartiality. It means not being biased in providing facts, feedback, opinions, etc.

pairs (1), (2) and (3) are not correct because rationality is identified as domination through knowledge, or that which allows things to be known and decisions made on strict evidence.

Impersonality can be defined as the inclination towards rules rather than the ties of kinship.

Rule Orientation refers to providing a rational and continuous basis for operations i.e., strict rules for any given procedure.

5 Consider the following statements about the Civil Services in India. *(Chap 9, Class-XI, Old NCERT)*

1. The concept of organised Civil Service originated with the Crown Rule.
2. The Indian Civil Service became a ruling class outside the main currents of Indian life and feelings.
3. The Indian Administrative Service was the continuation of the Indian Civil Service (ICS).

How many of the statements given above is/are incorrect?

(a) Only one (b) Only two
(c) All three (d) None of these

Ans. (a)

Exp. Only one statement i.e., (1) is incorrect about the Civil Services in India.

During the British Raj, Warren Hastings laid the foundation of Civil Service and Charles Cornwallis reformed, modernised and rationalised it.

Concept of organised Civil Service originated by Charles Cornwallis (also known as 'the Father of Civil Service in India'). Cornwallis introduced two divisions of the Indian Civil Service i.e., covenanted and uncovenanted. On the other hand, Government of India Act, 1858 transferred the function of East India Company to the British Crown, which was much later than the commencement of the Indian Civil Service.

6 Consider the following statements.
(Chap 9, Class-XI, Old NCERT)

1. Under the English Common Law, all civil servants of the country hold office during the pleasure of the Crown and are liable to be dismissed at any time.
2. A servant of the Crown can sue the Crown for his arrears and salary.

Which of the statements given above is/are correct?

(a) Only 1 (b) Only 2
(c) Both 1 and 2 (d) Neither 1 nor 2

Ans. (a)

Exp. Only statement (1) is correct as under the English Common Law, all civil servants of the country hold office during the pleasure of the Crown and are liable to be dismissed at any time. This was to maintain the superiority of the Crown and keep a check on bureaucracy.

Statement (2) is incorrect because, if a civil servant was dismissed from service, he cannot claim arrears of salary or damages for premature termination of his service. The doctrine of pleasure is based on the public policy.

7 Consider the following statements which do not form the part of safeguards for civil servants in India? *(Chap 9, Class-XI, Old NCERT)*

1. He/She has to be given a reasonable opportunity of being heard.
2. He/She can demand a declaration from the court regarding the dismissal or removal.
3. He/She has to be given a reasonable opportunity of making representation.
4. The concurrence of the Public Service Commission is essential before making any appointment.

Select the correct answer using the codes given below.

(a) 1 and 3 (b) Only 4
(c) 1, 2 and 4 (d) 2 and 4

Ans. (b)

Exp. Only statement (4) do not form the part of safeguard for civil servants in India. The Public Service Commission only recruits the civil servants by conducting an exam and interviews thereby forwarding the list to the home department of the government which then send appointments to successful candidates without any requirement of taking concurrence from the Public Service Commission.

8 Consider the following statements.
(Chap 9, Class-XI, Old NCERT)

1. The Constitution provides for the Indian Administrative Service and Indian Police Service as the All India Services.
2. The people of these services are controlled jointly by Central and State Governments.

Which of the statements given above is/are correct?

(a) Only 1 (b) Only 2
(c) Both 1 and 2 (d) Neither 1 nor 2

Ans. (c)

Exp. Both the statements (1) and (2) are correct.

Article 312 of our Constitution mentioned the Constitution of All India Services, such as, IAS and IPS. It states that these services shall be deemed to be created by Parliament. Apart from these services, it has also been mentioned to create All India Judicial Service.

The people of these services are jointly controlled by the Central and State Governments. The ultimate control lies with Central Government and the immediate control lies with State Government.

9 Which of the following provisions are concerned with independent working of UPSC?
(Chap 8, Class-XI, Old NCERT)

1. All the members including its Chairman will be appointed by the President of India for a fixed term.
2. No member after appointment can be removed easily.
3. The members of the commission are allowed to take further government employment except for the Chairman of UPSC.
4. The entire expenses of the commission including salaries of the members are charged from the Consolidated Fund of India.

Select the correct answer using the codes given below.

(a) Only 1 (b) 1 and 3
(c) 1, 2 and 3 (d) 1, 2 and 4

Ans. (d)

Exp. Statements (1), (2) and (4) are correct about the provisions that are concerned with independent working of UPSC.

The Chairman or a member of the UPSC can be removed from office by the President only in the manner and on the grounds mentioned in the Constitution. Therefore, they enjoy security of tenure.

The entire expenses including the salaries, allowances and pensions of the Chairman and members of the UPSC are charged from the Consolidated Fund of India.

Thus, they are not subject to vote in Parliament. Statement (3) is incorrect because a member of UPSC (on ceasing to hold office) is eligible for appointment as the Chairman of UPSC or a State Public Service Commission (SPSC), but not for any other employment in the Government of India or a State.

10 Consider the following statements about Union Public Service Commission of India.

(Chap 8, Class-XI, Old NCERT) (UKPSC Pre 2006)

1. It supervises the State Public Service Commission.
2. It is constitutionally separated from State Public Service Commission.
3. All its members are taken from State Public Service Commission.
4. It sends annual guidelines to State Public Service Commission.

Which of the statements given above is/are correct?

(a) Only 3 (b) Only 2 (c) 1, 3 and 4 (d) 2, 3 and 4

***Ans.* (b)**

Exp. Only statement (2) is correct about Union Public Service Commission of India. It shall be the duty of the Union Public Service Commission (UPSC) to conduct examinations for appointments to the services of the Union government. As per Constitution, the Union Public Service Commission and the Public Service Commission of States are free from each other for their work.

Statements (1), (3) and (4) are incorrect because it does not supervise the State Public Service Commission. The Constitution provides that, as nearly as may be one-half of the members of UPSC (not State Public Service Commission) must be persons who have held office for at least ten years under the Government of India. UPSC does not send annual guidelines to State Public Service Commission.

11 Consider the following pairs.

(Chap 33, Optional Module-2, NIOS)

1.	Indian Service of Engineers	–	1907
2.	Indian Medical Service	–	1906
3.	Indian Education Service	–	1897

How many pairs given above is/are correct?

(a) Only one (b) Only two
(c) Only three (d) None of these

***Ans.* (d)**

Exp. None of the pair given above is correct.

In 1892, the Indian Service of Engineers (irrigation, roads and building branches) was created.

In 1897, the Indian Medical Service was constituted.

The Indian Educational Service was created in 1906.

The Indian Agricultural Services are said to have been started in 1907 by Lord Minto II.

12 Consider the following statements with respect to the Public Service Commission. *(Chap 4, Class-XI, New NCERT)*

(Unit 6, Class-XII, Tamil Nadu Board)

1. The Public Service Commission established in 1926, became the Federal Public Service Commission (FPSC) in 1937.
2. FPSC was replaced by the Union Public Service Commission in 1950 as a constitutional body.

Which of the statements given above is/are correct?

(a) Only 1
(b) Only 2
(c) Both 1 and 2
(d) Neither 1 nor 2

***Ans.* (c)**

Exp. Both the statements (1) and (2) are correct with respect to Public Service Commission.

The Public Service Commission was established in 1926. It became Federal Service Commission in 1937, after passing of Government of India Act, 1935.

The Federal Public Service Commission became the Union Public Service Commission after Independence. It was given a constitutional status on 26th January, 1950.

13 Consider the following statements.

(Chap 8, Class-XI, Old NCERT) (MPSC Pre 2014)

1. A member of State Public Service Commission holds office for a term of 6 years from the date he/she enters upon his/her office or until he/she attains the age of 62 years.
2. If a member on the retirement is appointed as the Chairman of the State PSC, he gets an additional term of 6 years, irrespective of his age.

Which of the statements given above is/are correct?

(a) Only 1 (b) Only 2
(c) Neither 1 nor 2 (d) 1 and 2

***Ans.* (a)**

Exp. Statement (1) is correct as the Chairman and members of the State Public Service Commission holds office for a term of 6 years or until they attain the age of 62 years, whichever is earlier.

Statement (2) is incorrect because when a member of a SPSC cease to hold office he/she is eligible for appointment as the Chairman or a member of the UPSC or as the Chairman of that SPSC or any other SPSC, but not for any other employment under the Government of India or a State.

14 Consider the following statements.

(Chap 33, Optional Module-2, NIOS)

1. Articles from 308 to 314 in Part XIV of the Constitution contain provisions with regard to Central Services and State Services.
2. Article 311 provides safeguards of civil servants with regard to tenure of office.

Select the correct answer using the codes given below.

(a) Only 1 (b) Only 2
(c) Both 1 and 2 (d) Neither 1 nor 2

Ans. (c)

Exp. Both the statements (1) and (2) are correct. Articles from 308 to 314 Part XIV of the Indian Constitution contain provisions with regard to All India Services, Central Services and State Services.

Article 311 provides constitutional protection to civil servants. It assures a measure of security of tenure to civil servants. To provide certain safeguards against arbitrary dismissed or removal of a civil servant or reduction to a lower rank.

15 In which of the following matters the State Public Service Commission is not consulted?

(Chap 8, Class-XII, Old NCERT)

(a) On the method of recruitment of Civil Services.
(b) On the principles to be followed in making appointments to Civil Services.
(c) On the principles of the followed in making promotions in Civil Services and transfers from one service to another.
(d) On making transfers of Civil Servants.

Ans. (c)

Exp. On making transfers of Civil Servants, the State Public Service Commission is not consulted. Executive takes final call on transfer of Civil Servants.

Some of the matters on which State Public Service Commission is consulted are as follows:

- All matters relating to methods of recruitment to Civil Services and for Civil Posts.
- The principles to be followed in making appointments to Civil Services and Posts.
- The principle to be followed in making promotions and transfers from one Service to another.

16 Consider the following statements.

(Chap 8, Class-XI, Old NCERT)

1. The post of the Secretary of the Executive Council, later on, when India became independent, began to be called the Cabinet Secretary.
2. The Cabinet Secretary is usually the seniormost civil servant of the country and the official precedence gives him the first place among the civil servants.

Which of the statements given above is/are correct?

(a) Only 1
(b) Only 2
(c) Both 1 and 2
(d) Neither 1 nor 2

Ans. (c)

Exp. Both the statements (1) and (2) are correct.

The precursor to the Cabinet, the Executive Council of the Viceroy, used to have a Secretariat, was headed by the Private Secretary of the Viceroy.

This post of Secretary of the Executive Council became the Cabinet Secretary, when India became independent. The Cabinet Secretary is the top-most executive official and seniormost civil servant of the Government of India.

17 Consider the following statements with respect to the District Collector. *(Chap 8, Class-XI, Old NCERT)*

1. The District Collector is the head of the revenue department of the district.
2. He also exercises powers of a First Class Magistrate.
3. He is the Chief Protocol Officer of the district.

Which of the statements given above is/are incorrect?

(a) 1 and 3 (b) 2 and 3
(c) Only 2 (d) Only 3

Ans. (c)

Exp. Only statement (2) is incorrect with respect to District Collector, as previously he used to exercise powers of a First Class Magistrate but now, after the separation of executive from judiciary, he no longer exercises the judicial functions. It is now performed by Additional District Magistrate or Judicial Officer.

A District Magistrate (also known as District Collector or Deputy Commissioner) is an officer who is in-charge of a district, the basic unit of administration.

Chapter 17

Official Language

Official Language

History of Official Language

Introduction

- Official language gets special status in a country, state, or jurisdiction, designated by its Government
- **Official Language Bill, 1963**
    - Permits indefinite English use for official purposes
    - Review of acceptance of Hindi as official language in 1975
- **Three language formula**
    - For national integration, schools teach regional language, English and either Hindi (in non-Hindi areas) or Hindi, English and another regional language (in Hindi areas)
- **Amendment to Official Language Bill, 1967**
    - English remains official language untill non-Hindi states agree, through State Legislature resolution, to switch to Hindi

Official language Commission

- **Article 344** Parliament's commission and Committee on official language
- **Commission Duty** is to Recommend to President
    - Progressive use of Hindi for Union's official purposes
    - Restrictions on English language use for Union's official purpose

Languages with Official States in India

- **Part XVII (Article 343)** (1) Official language will be Hindi in Devanagari Script
- Indian Parliament conducts business in Hindi or English only
- States can legislate their official languages at the state/territory level
- Constitution recognises 22 regional languages

Official Language of the Union and Important Articles

Official Language of the Union

- Official language of the union is Hindi in Devanagari Script
- Official Languages Act allows continued use of English alongside Hindi even after 1965

Important Articles Related to Languages

- **Article 29** Right to preserve distinct language, script, culture
- **Article 30** Affirm's minorities right, based on religion or language
- **Article 120** Chairman or Speaker shall use Hindi or English to address Houses
- **Article 210** Requires State Legislature to conduct business in the official language, Hindi or English
- **Article 344** Parliament's official language committee
- **Article 345** Grants states the authority to choose their official language
- **Article 346** Allows Hindi, with English for official purpose and parliamentary proceedings
- **Article 347** Empowers the President to direct States on official language matters
- **Article 348** Language used in Supreme Court, High Court, proceedings of authorities
- **Article 349** Requires the President to consider parliamentary language committee recommendations for language related Bills or Amendments
- **Article 350** Language for representations for grievance redressal
- **Article 350 (A)** Mother tongue at primary level
- **Article 350 (B)** Special officer of linguistic minorities
- **Article 351** Offers directives for Hindi development

Eighth Schedule Related to Languages

- Eighth Schedule in Article 344(1) and 351, promotes Hindi and 22 languages
- Originally, 14 languages in the Constitution; Sindhi added in 1967; Konkani, Manipuri and Nepali added in 1992; Bodo, Dogri, Maithili and Santhali in 2004

List of Languages in Eighth Schedule

Language	Percent of Speakers (%)
Assamese	1.26
Bengali	8.30
Gujarati	4.58
Hindi	43.63
Kannada	3.61
Kashmiri	0.56
Konkani	0.19
Malayalam	2.88
Manipuri	0.15
Marathi	6.86
Nepali	0.24
Oriya	3.10
Punjabi	2.74
Sanskrit	0.03
Sindhi	0.61
Tamil	5.70
Telugu	6.70
Urdu	4.19
Bodo	0.12
Santhali	0.61
Maithili	1.12
Dogri	0.21

SOURCE *Old NCERT, Class-XII, Chap-14, New NCERT, Class-X, Chap-2.*

Official Languages

1 Which of the following statements is incorrect regarding the official languages?

(Chap 14, Class-XII, Old NCERT)

(a) The Constitution declared Hindi to be the Official Language.
(b) It also provided for the continued use of English for all official purposes till the time the Government desires.
(c) It provided that the legislature of a State by law might adopt any one or more of the languages in use in the State for official purposes.
(d) None of the above

Ans. (d)

Exp. None of the given statement is incorrect regarding the official languages. Article 343 of the Indian Constitution stated that the official language of the Union is Hindi in Devanagari script instead of English.

Later, the Official Languages Act, 1963, allowed for the continuation of English alongside Hindi in the Indian Government indefinitely until legislation decides to change it.

2 The number of official languages recognised under Eighth Schedule of the Indian Constitution is

(Chap 2, Class-X, New NCERT) (UPPSC Pre 2010)

(a) 22 (b) 20 (c) 18 (d) 17

Ans. (a)

Exp. The number of official languages recognised under Eighth Schedule of the Indian Constitution is 22. These languages have been referred to as Scheduled Languages and given recognition, status and official encouragement.

3 Arrange the following Scheduled languages in decreasing order of their use as mother tongue in India and choose the correct code.

(Chap 2, Class-X, New NCERT)

1. Marathi
2. Bengali
3. Tamil
4. Telugu

Codes

(a) 2, 1, 4, 3 (b) 1, 2, 3, 4 (c) 4, 3, 2, 1 (d) 1, 4, 3, 2

Ans. (a)

Exp. The correct sequence of the given scheduled languages in decreasing order of their use as mother language is Bengali > Marathi > Telugu > Tamil.

Bengali is spoken by 8.3% of total population while Marathi, Telugu and Tamil are spoken by 6.86%, 6.70% and 5.70% of the population respectively.

4 Consider the following statements.

(Chap 14, Class-XII, Old NCERT)

1. The Commission on Official Languages formed in 1955, recommended replacing English with Hindi as the official language.
2. Hindi is the most spoken language in India.

Which of the statements given above is/are correct?

(a) Only 1
(b) Only 2
(c) Both 1 and 2
(d) Neither 1 nor 2

Ans. (c)

Exp. Both the statements (1) and (2) are correct.
The Commission on Official Languages was formed in 1955. It recommended replacing English with Hindi as the official language. Official Language Commission is an Indian commission, constituted by President of India in pursuance to the provisions stated in Article 344 of Indian Constitution.

Hindi is spoken by 43% of Indian population which is highest in India. Hence, it is the most spoken language.

5 Under which Article of the Constitution a Speaker allows any member to speak in Parliament in his/her mother language? *(Chap 24, Module-2, NIOS)*

(a) Article 19(1)
(b) Article 343(1)
(c) Article 120(1)
(d) Article 210(1)

Ans. (c)

Exp. Under Article 120(1) of the Indian Constitution a Speaker allows any member to speak in Parliament in his/her mother language.

6 Under which one of the following Constitutional Amendment Acts, four languages were added to the languages under the Eighth Schedule of the Constitution, thereby raising their number to 22?

(Chap 14, Class-XII, Old NCERT) (IAS Pre 2007)

(a) 90th Constitutional (Amendment) Act
(b) 91st Constitutional (Amendment) Act
(c) 92nd Constitutional (Amendment) Act
(d) 93rd Constitutional (Amendment) Act

Ans. (c)

Exp. Under the Constitution (92nd Amendment) Act 2003, four languages were added to the languages under the Eighth Schedule of the Constitution thereby raising the number to 22. The four languages were Bodo, Dogri, Maithili and Santhali which were commenced on 7th January, 2004.

7 Consider the following statements about the languages mentioned in the Constitution of India.

(Chap 14, Class-XII, Old NCERT)

1. State can compel the linguistic minorities to choose their mother tongue as a medium of instruction in primary schools.
2. 'Angika' is now included in the Eighth Schedule of the Constitution.
3. Hindi is the National language of India.
4. Bodo is a recognised language in the Eighth Schedule of the Constitution.

Which of the statements given above is/are correct?

(a) Only 3
(b) Only 4
(c) 1 and 4
(d) 1, 2 and 3

Ans. (c)

Exp. Statements (1) and (4) are correct about the languages mentioned in the Constitution of India.

Every state and every local authority within the state to provide adequate facilities for instruction in the mother tongue at the primary stage of education.

Bodo was recognised as an official language under the Eighth Schedule by 92nd Amendment Act of 2003. The language is widely spoken in Assam and Bodoland Territorial region.

Statement (2) and (3) are not correct because Angika is not listed in the Eighth Schedule of the Constitution. It has the status of second state language.

There is no national language in India. Article 343 (1) states that "The official language of the Union shall be Hindi in Devanagari Script".

8 Which three languages have been added to the Eighth Schedule of the Constitution by 71st Amendment? ***(Chap 24, Module-4, NIOS)***

(a) Sindhi, Manipuri and Konkani
(b) Konkani, Kashmiri and Nepali
(c) Nepali, Konkani and Manipuri
(d) Nepali, Konkani and Assamese

Ans. (c)

Exp. Nepali, Konkani and Manipuri were added in the Eighth Schedule of the Constitution by the 71st Amendment Act of 1992. Nepali is the official language in the state of Sikkim and the Gorkhaland Territorial region of West Bengal. Other states where the language is widely spoken include Arunachal Pradesh, Manipur, Assam and Uttarakhand.

Konkani is the official state language of Goa along with native speakers mainly throughout the Central West coast of India. It belongs to the Indo-Aryan group of languages. Manipuri is the official state language of North-Eastern State of Manipur. It belongs to the Tibeto-Burman language family.

9 Which one of the following is correct about the languages mentioned in the Constitution of India? ***(Chap 14, Class-XII, Old NCERT)***

(a) State can compel the linguistic minorities to choose their mother tongue as a medium of instruction in primary schools.
(b) 'Angika' is now included in the Eighth Schedule of the Constitution.
(c) Hindi is National language of India.
(d) Bodo is a recognissed language in the Eighth Schedule of the Constitution.

***Ans.* (d)**

Exp. Statement (d) is correct about the languages mentioned in the Constitution of India.

Bodo was recognised as an official language under the Eighth Schedule by 92nd Amendment Act of 2003. The language is widely spoken in Assam and Bodoland Territorial region. The official script of is Devanagari Bodo. The language has three scripts, other two Bodo are Assamese and second being Roman.

There is no national language in India. Article 343 (1) states that "The official language of the Union shall be Hindi in Devanagari Script".

10 Which of the following languages was added in the Eighth Schedule of the Constitution in 2003? ***(Chap 14, Class-XII, Old NCERT)***

(a) Konkani
(b) Sindhi
(c) Manipuri
(d) Santhali

***Ans.* (d)**

Exp. Santhali was added in the Eighth Schedule of the Constitution in 2003. It was commenced on 7th January, 2004. Alongwith this, Bodo, Dogri and Maithili were also added. Sindhi was added by 21st CAA, 1967 while Konkani and Manipuri were added by 71st CAA, 1992. The Santhali is written in Ol Chiki script created by Raghunath Murmu. He is also known as the Father of Santhali Language. Santhali along with Bangla, Bhojpuri, Maithili, Angika and Magahi have been accorded the second language status in Jharkhand. There is an ongoing demand to adopt Santhali as the Official Language of the Tribal State.

Chapter 18

Special Provisions for Marginalised Sections

Special Provisions for Marginalised Sections

Scheduled Castes and Scheduled Tribes

Scheduled Castes
- Specifies in the Constitution under Article 341 remain marginalised and socio-economically poor

Socio-Economic Conditions of SCs
- Oppressed and exploited
- Mostly illiterate
- Economically depended on upper caste

Scheduled Tribes
- Specifies in the Article 342
- The native associated with forests
- Population over 8% (Census 2011)
- 500 + Aadivasi groups

Socio-Economic Conditions of STs
- Remote forest dwellers, lack of modern socio-economic access, deprived of land and autonomy
- Poor, largely illiterate, engage in agriculture; Unique identity and culture

Minorities
- **National Commission on Minorities**
  - Established in 1983 under National Commission for Minorities Act, 1992.
  - Nominated by Central Government
  - Tenure -3 years
- **Functions** Evaluate minority development progress under union and states
- **Power of the Commission** Possess civil court powers for summoning and enforcing attendance of any person in India and examining him on oath

Children
- **National Commission for Protection of Child Rights**
  - Statutory body
  - Established in 2005
- **Composition** Chairperson and six other members; two women appointed by Central Government
- **Functions** Review and assess safeguards under current laws for child rights protection

Measures, Safeguards and Special Schemes

Constitutional Provisions
- Constitution protects SCs, ensuring specific or general citizens rights

Reservation and Affirmative Action
- Reserves seats in education and employment based on their population

Fundamental Rights Provisions
- Article 17 abolishes untouchability
- Article 15 (1) bars discrimination
- Article 14 deals with equality before law and protection of law

National Commission for SCs
- Established in 2004 under Article 338 (2)
- Comprises Chairperson, Vice-Chairperson and three members
- Appointed by President

Other Backward Classes
- Article 340 empowers Government to appoint OBC Commission
- **Other Backward Classes Commissions** Constitution does not specify backward class group
- **Kaka Kalekar Commission**
  - Constituted in 1953
  - First Backward Classes Commission
  - Identified 2399 castes
- **Mandal Commission** Formed in 1979, Leadership BP Mandal
- 3743 castes identified as OBCs
- **National Commission for Backward Classes**
  - 102nd CAA, 2018
  - Introduced two new Articles 338 (B) and 342 (A), 342(A)

Constitution for Welfare of Woman and National

106th Constitutional Amendment Act
- Reservations 1/3rd of all seats for women in Lok Sabha State Legislative Assemblies and Legislative Assembly of National Capital Territory of Delhi

Fundamental Provision
- Article 14 confers equality
- Article 15 prohibits any discrimination
- Article 16 freedom of speech and expression

Legal Provisions for Women Protection
- Special Marriage Act, 1954
- Hindu Marriage Act, 1955
- Dowry Prohibition Act, 1961, etc

National Commission for Women
- Enacted in 1960; Came into existance on 31st January, 1992

Appointment
- Appointed by Central Government
- Atleast one member from SC and one from ST

Power of the Commission
- Possesses powers of a civil court
- Can surrounded enforce attendance of any person in India

Functions of the Commission
- Safeguard and promotes women's rights; Review legislation
- Take remedial actions to safeguard women's interests

National Policy for the Empowerment of Women, 2001
- Formed in 2001
- Create positive economic and social environment for women's full development
- Ensure equal status of Human Rights for women in political, economic, social cultural, etc

SOURCE **New NCERT Class VIII** *(Understanding Marginalisation)*, **New NCERT Class VIII** *(Confronting Marginalisation)*, **Old NCERT Class VIII** *(Untouchability, Welfare of Scheduled Castes and Scheduled Tribes)*, **New NCERT Class XII** *(Recent Development in Indian Politics)*, **Old NCERT Class XII** *(Development of Weaker Sections : Scheduled Castes, Scheduled Tribes and Other Backward Classes, Inequality : Social and Economic)*

Scheduled Castes

1 Which of the following forms the part of vulnerable groups? *(Chap 10, Class-XII, Old NCERT)*

1. Scheduled Castes 2. Scheduled Tribes
3. Minorities 4. Women
5. Disabled

Codes

(a) 1, 2, 3 and 5 (b) 1, 2, 3, 4 and 5
(c) 2, 3 and 4 (d) 1, 2, 3 and 4

Ans. (b)

Exp. All the given options forms the part of vulnerable groups. Vulnerable section refers to those people whose stakes in developmental activities are less while they are disproportionately represented at lower level of health, education and other indicators.

The examples of vulnerable group are Scheduled Tribes, Scheduled Castes, Minorities, Women, Disabled and Children.

2 Consider the following statements. *(Chap 10, Class-XII, Old NCERT)*

1. Scheduled Castes are people belonging to those castes/races which have been specified in Article 342 of the Constitution.
2. In traditional terms, they are the people who were considered outcastes, categorised as untouchables.

Which of the statements given above is/are correct?

(a) Only 1 (b) Only 2
(c) Both 1 and 2 (d) Neither 1 nor 2

Ans. (b)

Exp. Only statement (2) is correct as in traditional terms, Scheduled Castes are people who were considered outcastes and categorised as 'untouchables'. They were oppressed and exploited by those who belonged to the so called higher castes.

Statement (1) is incorrect because Scheduled Castes are people belonging to those castes/races which have been or may in future be specified in a list in accordance with Article 341 of the Constitution. Article 342 states about the status of Scheduled Tribes.

3 Consider the following statements which initiatives are taken to protect the interest of Scheduled Castes as per the Constitution. *(Chap 7, Class-VIII, Old NCERT)*

1. No child belonging to the Scheduled Caste can be denied admission to a school or any other institution maintained by the State.
2. No person belonging to the Scheduled Caste can be prevented from entering shops, restaurants, hotels or temples.
3. They cannot be denied the use of public wells and tanks.

Which of the statements given above is/are correct?

(a) Only 1 (b) 2 and 3 (c) 1 and 3 (d) All of these

Ans. (d)

Exp. All the statements are correct with respect to the initiatives taken to protect the interests of Scheduled Castes as per the Constitution.

Article 15 of the Indian Constitution forbids discrimination on grounds of religion, race, caste, sex, place or birth. According to this, no Scheduled Castes' children can be denied admission in state maintained school.

Also, according to Article 15(2)(a) and (b), no person belonging to the Scheduled Caste can be prevented from entering shops, restaurants, hotels, temples and cannot be denied the use of public wells and tanks.

4 Consider the following statements. *(Chap 10, Class-XII, Old NCERT)*

1. The Untouchability (Offences) Act was passed in 1955.
2. It was renamed as Protection of Civil Rights Act.

Which of the statements given above is/are correct?

(a) Only 1 (b) Only 2
(c) Both 1 and 2 (d) Neither 1 nor 2

Ans. (c)

Exp. Both the statements (1) and (2) are correct. The Untouchability (Offences) Act was passed in 1955. It was passed to abolish the untouchability in any form.

It was renamed as 'Protection of Civil Rights Act' in 1976. This bill further advocated harsh penalties for individuals who continue to practice untouchability.

Scheduled Tribes

5 Consider the following statements. *(Chap 8, Class-VIII, New NCERT)*

1. Article 342 of our Constitution provides for Scheduled Tribes.
2. There is single definition of Scheduled Tribes in our Constitution.
3. One of the principal feature of the tribal population has been its ecological, economic and social isolation.
4. Scheduled Tribes are weaker sections in terms of castes.

Which of the statements given above is/are correct?

(a) 1 and 2 (b) 2 and 3
(c) 1 and 3 (d) 1, 2, 3 and 4

Ans. (c)

Exp. Statements (1) and (3) are correct as Article 342 of our Constitution provides for Scheduled Tribes. As per this article, the President may with respect to any state or Union Territory, specify the tribes or tribal communities.

Historically, one of the principal features of the tribal population has been its ecological, economic and social isolation.

Statements (2) and (4) are incorrect because there is no single definition of Scheduled Tribes in our Constitution as it is difficult to define the tribal people of India in terms of any single set of formal criteria.

Scheduled Tribes are weaker sections not in terms of castes. They are weak because they are the people living in remote areas without any access to modern socio-economic inputs.

6 Consider the following statements.

(Chap 10, Class-XII, Old NCERT)

1. There is provision for reservation of seats for Scheduled Tribes in Lok Sabha and State Assemblies.
2. There is provision of setting up of Tribal Advisory Council (TAC) in each state of India.

Which of the statements given above is/are correct?

(a) Only 1 (b) Only 2 (c) Both 1 and 2 (d) Neither 1 nor 2

Ans. *(c)*

Exp. Both the statements (1) and (2) are correct. There is provision for reservation of seats for Scheduled Tribes in Lok Sabha and State Assemblies. At present, 47 seats in Lok Sabha have been reserved for Scheduled Tribes.

There is provision for setting up of Tribal Advisory Council (TAC) in each state with scheduled area. There is also a provision for separate departments in states for welfare of Scheduled Tribes. There is also a provision for appointment of a special officer at the centre to promote their welfare and safeguard their interests.

7 Consider the following statements.

(Chap 8, Class-VIII, New NCERT)

1. The Central Government passed the Scheduled Tribes and Other Traditional Forest Dwellers (Recognition of Forest Rights) Act, 2006.
2. This Act recognises their right to homestead, cultivable and grazing land and to non-timber forest produce.

Which of the statements given above is/are correct?

(a) Only 1 (b) Only 2 (c) Both 1 and 2 (d) Neither 1 nor 2

Ans. *(c)*

Exp. Both the statements (1) and (2) are correct. Scheduled Tribes and Other Traditional Forest Dwellers (Recognition of Forest Rights) Act, 2006 has been passed by Central government to recognise and vest the forest rights and occupation of forest land in traditional forest dwellers, Scheduled Tribes who have been residing in such forests for generations.

This Act also recognises their right to cultivable and grazing land as well as to the other minor forest produce.

8 The specifications required for a community to be declared as a Scheduled Tribe are

(Chap 8, Class-VIII, New NCERT)
(BPSC Pre 2023)

1. indications of primitive traits.
2. distinctive culture.
3. shyness of contact with the community at large.
4. backwardness and geographical isolation.

Which of the statements given above is/are correct?

(a) 1 and 2 (b) 2, 3 and 4 (c) 1, 3 and 4 (d) All of these

Ans. *(d)*

Exp. The criteria presently followed for specification of a community as a Scheduled Tribe are indication of primitive traits, distinctive culture, geographical isolation, shyness of contact with the community at large and backwardness. This criterion is not spelt out in the Constitution but has become well established.

The criteria for declaration of Scheduled Tribes is not defined in Constitution. The term Scheduled Tribes is defined in the Constitution of India under Article 366(25) as such tribes or tribal communities or parts of groups within such tribes or tribal communities as are deemed under Article 342 to be Scheduled Tribes.

9 Consider the following statements.

(Chap 10, Class-XII, Old NCERT) (IAS Pre 2019)

1. As per recent amendment to the Indian Forest Act, 1927, forest dwellers have the right to fell the bamboos grown on forest areas.
2. As per the Scheduled Tribes and Other Traditional Forest Dwellers (Recognition of Forest Rights) Act, 2006, bamboo is a minor forest produce.
3. The Scheduled Tribes and Other Traditional Forest Dwellers (Recognition of Forest Rights) Act, 2006 allows ownership of minor forest produce to forest dwellers.

Which of the statements given above is/are correct?

(a) 1 and 2 (b) 2 and 3 (c) Only 3 (d) 1, 2 and 3

Ans. *(b)*

Exp. Statements (2) and (3) are correct. According to the Scheduled Tribes and Other Traditional Forest Dwellers (Recognition of Forest Rights) Act, 2006, bamboo is a minor forest produce. Apart from bamboo, herbs are also considered as minor forest produce. The Scheduled Tribes and Other Traditional Forest Dwellers (Recognition of Forest Rights) Act, 2006 allows forest dwellers to own minor forest produce.

Statement (1) is incorrect because an ordinance was issued in December 2017 to amend the Indian Forest Act, 1927, according to which no permit would be required for harvesting and transporting bamboo in non-forest areas.

10 Which of the following is/are the steps taken to abolish manual scave ·ng in India?

(Chap 8, Class-VIII, New NCERT)

1. In 1993, the government passed the Employment of Manual Scavengers and Construction of Dry Latrines (Prohibition) Act.
2. It prohibits the employment of manual scavengers as well as the construction of dry latrines.

3. The Prohibition of Employment of Manual Scavengers and their Rehabilitation Act came into force on 6th December, 2013.

Select the correct answer using the codes given below.

(a) 1, 2 and 3
(b) 2 and 3
(c) 1 and 2
(d) None of these

Ans. (a)

Exp. All the given statements (1), (2) and (3) are the steps taken to abolish manual scavenging in India.

Employment of Manual Scavengers and Construction of Dry Latrines (Prohibition) Act,1993 was passed to provide for the prohibition of employment of manual scavengers as well as construction or continuance of dry latrines and for the regulation of construction and maintenance of water-seal latrines.

The Prohibition of Employment as Manual Scavengers and their Rehabilitation Bill Act, 2013 (came into effect on 6th December, 2013) prohibits the employment of manual scavengers, the manual cleaning of sewers and septic tanks without protective equipment, and the construction of insanitary latrines. Both the Acts seek to abolish manual scavenging.

11 **Under the Scheduled Caste and Scheduled Tribes (Prevention of Atrocities) Act, 1989, Whoever, not being a member of a Scheduled (Caste or Scheduled Tribe, causes physical harm or mental agony of member of a Scheduled Caste or a Scheduled Tribe on the allegation of practicing witch craft or being a witch shall be punishable.**

(Chap 10, Class-XII, Old NCERT)

(a) with imprisonment for a term which shall not be less than six months, but which may extend to five years and with fine.
(b) with imprisonment for a term which shall not be less than six months and with fine.
(c) with imprisonment for a term which shall be one year and with fine.
(d) with imprisonment for term which shall be five years and with fine.

Ans. (a)

Exp. Statement (a) is correct as with the imprisonment for a term which shall not be less than six months, but which may extend to 5 years with fine will be give if someone who is not a member of SCs and STs community, causes physical harm or mental agony to a member of SCs and STs community.

12 **Consider the following features.**

(Chap 8, Class-VIII, New NCERT)

1. This Act contains a list of few crimes against the Scheduled Castes and Scheduled Tribes.
2. It lists actions that dispossess dalits and adivasis of their meagre resources or force them into performing slave labour.
3. It lists modes of humiliation that are both physically horrific and morally reprehensible.

How many of the above is not one of features of the Scheduled Castes and the Scheduled Tribes (Prevention of Atrocities) Act 1989?

(a) Only one (b) Only two (c) All three (d) None of these

Ans. (a)

Exp. Feature (1) is not one of feature of the Scheduled Castes and Scheduled Tribes (Prevention of Atrocities) Act, 1989. This Act was framed to protect the Scheduled Castes and Scheduled Tribes from the ill-treatment and humiliation by the people of higher castes.

This Act contains a long list of morally reprehensible crimes, some of which are physically horrible even to contemplate.

13 **Consider the following statements.**

(Chap 10, Class-XII, Old NCERT)

1. Offences, under Scheduled Castes and Scheduled Tribes (Prevention of Atrocities) Act, are committed by a person who is not a member of Scheduled Caste or Scheduled Tribe.
2. 'Exclusive Special Court' established under Section 14(1) of the Scheduled Castes and Scheduled Tribes (Prevention of Atrocities) Act is defined under Section 2(d).
3. 'Victim' is defined under Section 2(ec) of the Scheduled Castes and Scheduled Tribes (Prevention of Atrocities) Act.
4. 'Dependent' is defined under Section 2(bb) of the Scheduled Castes and Scheduled Tribes (Prevention of Atrocities) Act.

Which of the statements given above is/are incorrect?

(a) Only 1 (b) Only 2 (c) 1, 2 and 4 (d) 2 and 3

Ans. (b)

Exp. Only statement (2) is incorrect because 'Special Court and Exclusive Special Court' is mentioned under Section 14(1) of the Scheduled Castes and Scheduled Tribes Act and it is defined under it.

It is mentioned under Section 14(1) that 'for purpose of providing speedy trial, the State Government shall, with the concurrence of the Chief Justice of the High Court, by notification in the official Gazette, establish an Exclusive Special Court for one or more districts'.

14 **Consider the following statements.**

(Chap 10, Class-XII, Old NCERT)

1. The word 'Backward Class' means a group of people having general characteristics of backwardness.
2. The Indian Constitution specifies which groups constitute backward classes.

Which of the statements given above is/are correct?

(a) Only 1
(b) Only 2
(c) Both 1 and 2
(d) Neither 1 nor 2

Ans. (a)

Exp. Only statement (1) is correct as 'Backward Class' means a group of people having general characteristics of backwardness. A class is considered to be backward if its members are economically and educationally less privileged as compared to other classes in that society. Statement (2) is incorrect because the Constitution does not specify which groups constitute backward classes.

15 Consider the following statements about the Mandal Commission. *(Chap 9, Class-XII, New NCERT)*

1. This Commission was officially known as the First Backward Classes Commission.
2. The Commission gave its recommendations in 1980.
3. It recommended reserving 27% of seats in educational institutions and government jobs for the OBCs.
4. The National Front government implemented the recommendations of the Mandal Commission.

Which of the statements given above is/are not correct?

(a) Only 3 (b) Only 1 (c) 1, 3 and 4 (d) 2 and 4

Ans. (b)

Exp. Only statement (1) is not correct because Mandal Commission was officially known as the Socially and Educationally Backward Classes Commission (SEBC). It was formed in 1979 to identify the socially and educationally backward classes of India.

16 If a particular area is brought under the Fifth Schedule of the Constitution of India, which one of the following statements best reflects the consequence of it? *(Chap 7, Class-VIII, Old NCERT) (IAS Pre 2022)*

(a) This would prevent the transfer of land of tribal people to non-trible people.
(b) This would create a local self-governing body in that area.
(c) This would convert that area into a Union Territory.
(d) The State having such areas would be declared as Special Category State.

Ans. (a)

Exp. If a particular area is brought under the Fifth Schedule of the Constitution of India, this would prevent the transfer of land of tribal people to non-tribal people. The Fifth Schedule of the Constitution deals with the administration and control of Scheduled Areas as well as of Schedule Tribes residing in any states other than the States of Assam, Meghalaya, Tripura and Mizoram.

If a particular area is brought under the Fifth Schedule, it means that all land in Scheduled Area is presumed to have been Adivasi land; hence, not only should no land now pass into the hands of non-Adivasis, but any land presently owned by non-tribal should, if being transferred, come back to the hands of Scheduled Tribes.

17 Consider the following Assertion (A) and Reason (R) and choose the correct code. *(Chap 10, Class-XII, Old NCERT)*

Assertion (A) The concept of creamy layer makes it clear that caste alone is no longer a sufficient condition for OBCs.

Reason (R) Economic condition should be applied along with the already existing reservation criterion.

Codes

(a) Both A and R are true and R is the correct explanation of A.
(b) Both A and R are true, but R is not the correct explanation of A.
(c) A is true, but R is false.
(d) A is false, but R is true.

Ans. (a)

Exp. Both Assertion (A) and Reason (R) are true and Reason (R) is the correct explanation of Assertion (A).

The creamy layer is a category of Other Backward Classes (OBCs) for reservation in government jobs.

The term 'creamy layer' refers to some members of backward class who are highly progressed socially, economically and educationally.

So, the concept of creamy layer makes it clear that caste alone is not a sufficient condition for availing reservation and economic condition should be applied along with existing reservation criterion.

18 With reference to Scheduled Areas in India, consider the following statements. *(Chap 11, Class-XII, Old NCERT) (IAS Pre 2023)*

1. Within a State, the notification of an area as Scheduled Area takes place through an Order of the President.
2. The largest administrative unit forming the Scheduled Area is the District and the lowest is the cluster of villages in the Block.
3. The Chief Ministers of the concerned states are required to submit annual reports to the Union Home Ministery on the administration of scheduled areas in the states.

How many of the statements given above is/are correct?

(a) Only one
(b) Only two
(c) All three
(d) None of the above

Ans. (b)

Exp. Only two statements i.e., (1) and (2) are correct.

In the Article 244(1) of the Constitution, expression Scheduled Areas means such areas as the President may by order declare to be Scheduled Areas.

Criteria for declaring any area as a 'Scheduled Area under the Fifth Schedule' are

Preponderance of tribal polulation
Compactness and reasonable size of the area
A viable administrative entity such as a district, block or taluk.
Statement (3) is not correct because the Governor of each State having Scheduled Areas therein shall annually, or whenever so required by the President, make a report to the President regarding the administration of the Scheduled Areas in that State and the excutive power of the Union shall extend to the giving of directions to the State as to the administration of the said areas.

19 Consider the following statements.
(Chap 11, Class-XII, Old NCERT)

1. The Government of India in 1953 established the Central Social Welfare Board.
2. It promoted welfare and development services for women only.

Which of the statements given above is/are incorrect?
(a) Only 1 (b) Only 2
(c) Both 1 and 2 (d) Neither 1 nor 2

Ans. (b)

Exp. Only statement (2) is incorrect because the Central Social Welfare Board was established in 1953 to carry out welfare activities for promoting voluntarism, providing technical and financial assistance to the voluntary organisations for the general welfare of family, women and children.

20 Consider the following statements.
(Chap 11, Class-XII, Old NCERT)

1. There is provision for reservation of seats for women in Panchayati Raj Institutions.
2. There is provision for reservation of 35% seats for women in State Legislative Assemblies.

Which of the statements given above is/are correct?
(a) Only 1 (b) Only 2
(c) Both 1 and 2 (d) Neither 1 nor 2

Ans. (a)

Exp. Only statement (1) is correct as 73rd and 74th Constitutional Amendments provide for 33% reservation of seats for women in Panchayati Raj Institutions, Municipalities and Municipal Corporations.
Statement (2) is incorrect because there is no provision for the reservation of seats for women in State Legislative Assemblies and Parliament.

21 Consider the following Acts which are related to special provisions for women.
(Chap 11, Class-XII, Old NCERT)

1. Dowry Prohibition Act, 1961
2. Equal Remuneration Act, 1976
3. Child Marriage (Restraint) Act, 1978

How many of the provisions given above is/are related to women?
(a) Only one (b) Only two
(c) All three (d) None of these

Ans. (c)

Exp. All the given Acts are related to special provisions for women.
Dowry Prohibition Act, 1961 intended to prevent the giving or receiving of a dowry.
Equal Remuneration Act, 1976 provide for the payment of equal remuneration to men and women workers and for the prevention of discrimination, on the grounds of sex, against women in the matter of employment. The Child Marriage Restraint Act, 1929, was amended in 1978, where the lawful age of marriage of girls was increased from 15 to 18 years and boys from 18 to 21 years.

Chapter 19

Local Self Government

Local Self Government

Local Institutions

Decentralisation and People's Participation

- Participation of people in planning has been increases
- National Development Council facilitates coordination between Union and States
- Evolution of Local Self Government in India

Evolution of Local Self Government in India

- Third-tier Government in India
- Panchayats in Rural Areas and Municipalities in Urban Areas
- Lord Ripon-Father of Local-self Government
- Ripon Resolution passed in 1882
- Montague-Chelmsford Reform-1919

Panchayati Raj System

- **Various Committees**
- **Balwant Rai Mehta Committee**
  - Formed in 1957; Recommended Democratic Decentralisation known as Panchayati Raj
  - Proposed three-tier system
  - Gram Panchayat, Panchayat Samiti and Zila Parishad
- **Ashok Mehta Committee**
  - Constituted in 1977
  - Recommends two-tier system
  - Zila Parishad at District Level and Mandal Panchayat for Village
- **CM Singhvi Committee**
  - Appointed by Rajiv Gandhi Government in 1986
  - Recommends PRI constitutionality
  - Proposed Nyaya Panchayat

Rural Local Government Institutions

Gram Sabha

- Village's Miniature Legislature
- Gram Sabha's Powers are determined by State Legislature
- Elected by all Adult Village Members

Power and Function of Gram Sabha

- Elects Gram Panchayat
- Approves annual budget of Panchayat
- Directly elect Sarpanch

Gram Panchayats

- Elected Executive Body by Gram Sabha for Village Administration
- Head Sarpanch

Functions of Gram Panchayat

- Maintain Roads, Footpaths and Water Supply
- Supervise Development Projects in the Village
- Promote Cottage Industries in rural areas

Panchayat Samiti

- Middle Level in Panchayat System
- At Block Level
- Members : Sarpanch of Gram Panchayats in a Block
- Headed by Block Development Officer

Composition of Panchayat Samiti

- Pradhan and Panch from village
- Panchayats elect block Samiti representatives
- Block Samiti members elect Chairperson and Vice-Chairperson

Urban Local Government Institutions

- Modern Urban Government System's Foundation was laid by British Government
- Lord Mayo's 1870 Resolution aimed at Strengthening Municipal Institutions and Increasing Indian Participation

74th Constitutional Amendment Act, 1992

- Established Statutory Provisions for Urban local Self-Governing Institutions
- **Compulsory Provisions** Establish Nagar Panchayats, Municipal Councils and Municipal Cooperation; Reserved Seats in Urban local bodies for SC/ST

Types of Urban local bodies

- **Municipality**
  - Size depends on Local Body Populations
  - Cities have Municipalities or Municipal Committees
  - Reserved Seats for SC, ST and women

Composition of Municipality

- Each Municipality elects one Vice-Chairperson to act as Chairperson in their absence
- Permanent Officials Executive Officer, Secretary, Health Officer, etc
- **Municipal Council**
- Population 1 Lakh Crore or more

Composition of Municipal Council

- Elected representatives for five years
- Member elect a Chairperson from among themselves

SOURCE **New NCERT Class VI** *(Panchayati Raj)* **New NCERT Class VI** *(Rural Administration)*, **New NCERT Class VI** *(Urban Administration)*, **Old NCERT Class IX & X** *(Our Local Government)*, **New NCERT Class X** *(Federalism)*, **New NCERT Class XI** *(Local Government)*, **Old/New NCERT Class XI** *(Federalism)*, **Old NCERT Class XII** *(Multi-Level Planning and Role of District Development Agencies)*

Panchayati Raj System

1 **Consider the following statements.**

(Chap 8, Class-XI, New NCERT)

1. After India achieved independence in 1947, a number of provinces enacted a new Village Panchayat Act.
2. The MP Village Panchayat Act of 1947 was regarded as model Act for all states.

Which of the statements given above is/are correct?

(a) Only 1 (b) Only 2
(c) Both 1 and 2 (d) Neither 1 nor 2

Ans. (a)

Exp. Only statement (1) is correct as after India achieved independence in 1947, a number of provinces enacted a new Village Panchayat Act that tried to develop Village Panchayats as unit of self-government.

Statement (2) is incorrect because the UP Village Panchayat Act of 1947 was regarded as a model Act by conference of the local self-government ministers of the states.

2 **Consider the following statements in respect of Ashok Mehta Committee on Panchayati Raj System in India.** *(Chap 16, Module-3, NIOS) (IAS Pre 2022)*

This committee recommended.

1. Replacement of the then three-tier system by a two-tier system.
2. Setting up of peace committees at each district level to resolve non-secular issues.
3. Supremacy of elected bodies through devolution of powers.
4. Non-participation of political in Panchayati elections.

Which of the statements given above is/are correct?

(a) 1 and 2 (b) 3 and 4 (c) 2 and 4 (d) 1 and 3

Ans. (d)

Exp. Statements (1) and (3) are correct in respect of Ashok Mehta Committee on Panchayati Raj System in India as in December, 1977 the Janata Government appointed a committee on Panchayati Raj institutions under the Chairmanship of Ashok Mehta. It submitted its report in August, 1978 and made 132 recommendations to revive and strengthen the declining system in the country. Its main recommendation were the three-tier system of Panchayati Raj should be replaced by the two-tier system.

Supremacy of elected local bodies through devolution of power. Devolution is a form of decentralisation which seeks to create independent level of authority of government with functions and responsibilities.

Statements (2) and (4) are incorrect because committee recommended official participation of political party in Panchayat election and there is no mention about peace committee in recommendation.

3 **Consider the following statements.**

(Chap 8, Class-XI, New NCERT)

1. The subject of local government has been assigned to the states as per the Constitution.
2. It was mentioned in the Directive Principles as one of the policy directives to all governments in the country.

Which of the statements given above is/are correct?

(a) Only 1 (b) Only 2 (c) Both 1 and 2 (d) Neither 1 nor 2

Ans. (c)

Exp. Both the statements (1) and (2) are correct. Local government has been mentioned in Schedule 7 under the State List (List II) over which state has executive and legislative powers. Also, Article 40 of Directive Principles mention that the State shall take steps to organise Village Panchayats as units of self-government.

4 **Consider the following statements with respect to the Balwant Rai Mehta Committee.**

(Chap 9, Class-XII, Old NCERT)

1. It was appointed in 1957 to make a report on the problems of development at the rural level.
2. It recommended a two tier structure of Panchayati Raj Institutions with elected panchayats at village and district level.

Which of the statements given above is/are correct?

(a) Only 1 (b) Only 2
(c) Both 1 and 2 (d) Neither 1 nor 2

Ans. (d)

Exp. Neither statement (1) nor (2) is correct with respect to the Balwant Rai Mehta Committee. This committee was originally appointed by the Government of India on 16th January, 1957.

Its main aim was to examine the working of the Community Development Programme and the National Extension Service and to suggest measures for their better working. It also recommended establishment of a three-tier Panchayati Raj System with elected panchayats at village level and indirectly elected members at district level.

5 **Consider the following statements with reference to the recommendations of the Ashok Mehta Committee.**

(Chap 7, Class-XI, Old NCERT)

1. Creation of a three-tier system of Panchayati Raj.
2. The Mandal Panchayat was formed for a number of villages having a population of 15,000 to 20,000.
3. Zila Parishad to be made responsible for planning at the district level.
4. Open participation of political parties in the elections to the Panchayati Raj.

How many of the statements is/are not mentioned in the recommendations of the Ashok Mehta Committee?

(a) Only one (b) Only two (c) Only three (d) All four

Ans. (a)

Exp. Only one statement i.e., (1) was not mentioned in the recommendations of the Ashok Mehta Committee. Ashok Mehta Committee's main recommendations were that the three-tier system of Panchayati Raj should be replaced by the two-tier system. It proposed Constitution of Zila Parishad at the district level and below it, the Mandal Panchayat consisting of a group of villages covering a population of 15000 to 20000.

Creation of three-tier system of Panchayati Raj was mentioned in Balwant Rai Mehta Committee.

6 **Which of the following statements is incorrect regarding the local governments in independent India?**

(Chap 8, Class-XI, New NCERT)

(a) The Community Development Programme was launched on 2nd October, 1952 to promote people's participation in local development in a range of activities.
(b) In 1989, the LM Singhvi Committee recommended constitutional recognition for the local government bodies.
(c) PK Thungon Committee recommended to provide for periodic elections to local government institutions and enlistment of appropriate functions to them, along with funds.
(d) All of the above

Ans. (b)

Exp. Statement (b) is incorrect regarding the local governments in independent India because the LM Singhvi Committee recommended that the Panchayati Raj Systems should be constitutionally recognised in 1986 (not in 1989). It also recommended Constitutional provisions to recognise free and fair elections for the Panchayati Raj Systems.

7 **Which of the following committee/commissions recommended for the creation of Nyaya Panchayat?**

(Chap 7, Class-XI, Old NCERT) (UKPSC Pre 2016)

(a) Balwant Rai Mehta Committee
(b) Ashok Mehta Committee
(c) GVK Rao Committee
(d) Sarkaria Commission

Ans. (b)

Exp. Ashok Mehta Committee recommended for the creation of Nyaya Panchayat. It was set-up in 1977 by Janta Government. It submitted its report in 1978. The committee recommended that Nyaya Panchayat should be kept as a separate body. It also recommended that Nyaya Panchayat would be presided over by a qualified judge.

Rural Local Government Institution

8 **Consider the following statements regarding the evolution of local-self government.**

(Chap 8, Class-XI, New NCERT)

1. The 73rd and 74th Constitutional Amendments were passed by the Parliament in 1993.
2. The 73rd Amendment was about urban local governments.
3. The 74th Amendment made the provisions relating to rural local government.

How many of the statements given above is/are correct?

(a) Only one (b) Only two (c) All three (d) None of these

Ans. (d)

Exp. None of the given statement is correct.

The 73rd and 74th Constitutional Amendment was passed by the Parliament in 1992. 73rd Constitutional Amendment was about rural government which is popularly known as Panchayati Raj Institutions or PRIs. On the other hand, 74th Constitutional Amendment made the provision relating to urban local government known as Nagarpalikas. The 73rd and 74th Constitutional Amendments came into force in 1993.

9 **Which of the following is not one of the voluntary provisions of the 73rd Constitutional Amendment Act, 1992?** *(Chap 7, Class-XI, Old NCERT)*

(a) Giving voting rights to members of the Central and State Legislatures.
(b) Providing reservation for Backward Classes.
(c) The Panchayati Raj Institutions should be given financial powers in relation to taxes, levy fees etc.
(d) Organisation of Gram Sabha.

Ans. (d)

Exp. Organisation of Gram Sabha is not one of the voluntary provisions of the 73rd Constitutional Amendment Act, 1992. Mandatory provisions incorporated by the 73rd Amendment which include three tiers of Panchayats, direct election to seats at all three tiers of Panchayats and indirect elections to offices of Chairpersons of Block and District Panchayats, reservations in seats and offices for the SCs, STs and women.

10 **Given below are two statements, one is labelled as Assertion (A) and the other as Reason (R).**

(Chap 12, Class-XI, Tamil Nadu Board) (UPPSC Pre 2022)

Assertion (A) The 73rd Amendment of the Constitution is considered to be a watershed in the history of local self-government in India.

Reason (R) The 73rd Constitution Amendment conferred the much coveted Constitutional status on Panchayats.

Codes

(a) Both A and R are true and R is the correct explanation of A.
(b) Both A and R are true, but R is not the correct explanation of A.
(c) A is true, but R is false.
(d) A is false, but R is true.

Ans. (a)

Exp. Both Assertion (A) and Reason (R) are true and Reason (R) is the correct explanation of Assertion (A).

The Constitution (73rd Amendment) Act was passed in 1992 and it came into effect on 24th April, 1993.

The Act empowered State Governments to take the necessary steps that would lead to the formalisation of the Gram Panchayat and help them operate as units of self-governance. This Act made the Panchayati Raj Institutions in the country constitutional bodies. Under Article 243 B, it has become compulsory for every state to establish panchayats in their territories.

11 Consider the following statements.
(Chap 5, Class-VI, New NCERT)

1. It is a key factor in making the Gram Panchayat play its role and be responsible.
2. It is the place where all plans for the work of the Gram Panchayat are placed before the people.
3. It prevents the Panchayat from doing wrong things like misusing money or favouring certain people.
4. It plays an important role in keeping an eye on the elected representatives and in making them responsible to the persons who elected them.

The above characteristics refer to which of the following?
(a) Sarpanch
(b) Gram Sabha
(c) Panchayat Secretary
(d) Village Development Officer

Ans. (b)

Exp. The given statements mention the above are characteristics of Gram Sabha. The term Gram Sabha is defined in the Constitution of India under Article 243(A). Gram Sabha is the primary, permanent and the largest body of the Panchayati Raj System. The decisions taken by the Gram Sabha cannot be repeated by any other body.

12 Consider the following statements regarding the Gram Sabha. *(Chap 5, Class-VI, New NCERT)*

1. The Gram Sabha is a meeting of all adults who live in the area covered by a Panchayat.
2. Anyone who is 18 years old or more and who has the right to vote is a member of the Gram Sabha.
3. The Secretary is responsible for calling the meeting of the Gram Sabha.

Which of the statements given above is/are correct?
(a) Only 1 (b) 1 and 2
(c) Only 3 (d) All of these

Ans. (d)

Exp. All the above given statements are correct regarding Gram Sabha as persons, who are above 18 years of age and living in the village and whose names are included in the electoral rolls for the Panchayat at the village level are members of the Gram Sabha. The Panchayat Secretary after obtaining approval of the Sarpanch organises Gram Sabha.

13 The Constitution 73rd Amendment Act, 1992 which aims at promoting the Panchayati Raj institutions in the country, provides for which of the following?
(Unit 12, Class-XI, Tamil Nadu Board)
(IAS Pre 2011)

1. Constitution of District Planning Committees.
2. State Election Commissions to conduct all Panchayat elections.
3. Establishment of State Finance Commissions.

Select the correct answer using the codes given below.
(a) Only 1
(b) 1 and 2
(c) 2 and 3
(d) 1, 2 and 3

Ans. (c)

Exp. Statements (2) and (3) are correct about 73rd Amendment Act.
73rd Constitutional Amendment Act, 1992 which aims at promoting the Panchayati Raj institutions in the country provides for establishment of Independent Election Commission in each state for superintendence, direction and control of the electoral rolls of all Panchayat Elections under Article 243 (K).
It also provides for the establishment of a finance commission by the Governor of a state to determine the principles on the basis of which adequate financial resources would be ensured for Panchayats and Municipalities under Article 243 (1).
Statement (1) is incorrect because the 74th Amendment Act provides for a District Planning Committee to consolidate the plans prepared by Panchayats and Municipalities under Article 243Z(D).

14 Consider the following statements regarding Nyaya Panchayat. *(Chap 3, Class-IX & X, Old NCERT)*

1. They function in all the states.
2. Their members are drawn by a combination of election and nomination.
3. They decide small civil and criminal cases.
4. They also have the power to impose fines on the offenders.

Which of the statements given above is/are incorrect?
(a) Only 1
(b) 1 and 2
(c) 1, 2 and 4
(d) None of the above

Ans. (a)

Exp. Statement (1) is incorrect regarding Nyaya Panchayat because they are village courts where disputes between villagers are settled. They are not functioning in all the states as all the states have not notified their formation due to various administrative and political reasons.

15 **Which of the following statements is incorrect regarding the three-tier structure of Panchayati Raj?** *(Chap 5, Class-VI, New NCERT)*

(a) In rural areas, the Gram Panchayat is the second-tier (level) of democratic government.
(b) The Panchayat Samiti has many Gram Panchayats under it.
(c) With the help of Panchayat Samitis, Zila Parishad regulates the money distribution among all the Gram Panchayats.
(d) None of the above

Ans. (a)

Exp. Statement (a) is incorrect because in rural areas, the Gram Panchayat is the first-tier (level) of democratic government as Gram Panchayat is a basic village-governing institute in Indian villages. It is a democratic structure at the grass-roots level in India. It is a political institute, acting as cabinet of the village.

16 **Consider the following statements.** *(Chap 3, Class-IX & X, Old NCERT)*

1. Village Development Officer heads the Panchayat Samiti.
2. Sarpanch, MPs and MLAs from that block and representatives of SCs, STs and Women generally form the part of Panchayat Samiti.

Which of the statements given above is/are incorrect?

(a) Only 1 (b) Only 2
(c) Both 1 and 2 (d) Neither 1 nor 2

Ans. (a)

Exp. Only statement (1) is incorrect because Panchayat Samiti is not headed by Village Development Officer (VDO). It is headed by a Chairman and Deputy Chairman. In some states, it is known as Block Pramukh.

Panchayat Samiti is an intermediate level body in Panchayati Raj Institution. The Samiti is elected for five years. Panchayat Samiti is composed of the following

- Block Development Officer
- Sarpanch
- Members of State Legislative Assemblies belonging to that area
- Member of Parliament belonging to that area
- Representative of Scheduled Castes and Tribes and women
- Elected members of Panchayat block (tehsil) on the Zila Parishad

17 **Consider the following statements regarding the Zila Parishad.** *(Chap 3, Class-IX & X, Old NCERT)*

1. This is the Panchayat at the district level.
2. It usually consists of the Chairpersons of the Panchayat Samities of that district.
3. It also includes MPs, MLAs and MLCs from the district.
4. Its President is the District Collector.

Which of the statements given above is/are incorrect?

(a) Only 1
(b) 1 and 2
(c) 1, 2 and 3
(d) Only 4

Ans. (d)

Exp. Only statement (4) is incorrect because District Collector is not the President of Zila Parishad.

Zila Parishad is headed by Adhyaksha or President, who is elected from among the directly elected members.

Zila Parishad is the upper body in three-tier of Panchayati Raj System, situated in district level. The Chairman of Panchayat Samiti is its ex-officio member. MP and MLA's belonging to the district are also its member.

The role of Zila Parishad is to provide essential services and facilitate rural development.

18 **Consider the following statements regarding elections of the Panchayati Raj.** *(Chap 8, Class-XI, New NCERT)*

1. All the three levels of Panchayati Raj Institutions are elected directly by the people.
2. The term of each Panchayat body is five years.
3. If the State Government dissolves the Panchayat before the end of its five year term, fresh elections must be held within three months of such dissolution.

How many of the statements given above is/are incorrect?

(a) Only one (b) Only two
(c) All three (d) None of these

Ans. (a)

Exp. Only one statement i.e., (3) is incorrect because if the State Government dissolves the Panchayat before the end of its five year term, fresh elections must be held within six months of such dissolution.

A Panchayat reconstituted after premature dissolution shall continue only for the remainder period. But, if the remainder period is less than six months it shall not be necessary to hold elections.

19 **Consider the following statements.** *(Chap 8, Class-XI, New NCERT)*

1. One-third of the positions in all Panchayat institutions are reserved for women in the general category only.
2. Reservations for Scheduled Castes, Scheduled Tribes and Other Backward Classes (OBCs) are also provided for all the three levels, in proportion to their population.

Which of the statements given above is/are correct?

(a) Only 1
(b) Only 2
(c) Both 1 and 2
(d) Neither 1 nor 2

Ans. (d)

Exp. Neither statement (1) nor (2) is correct because not less than one-third of the total number of seats to be filled by direct elections in every panchayat shall be reserved for women (Including the number of seats reserved for women belonging to SCs and STs).

Also Article 243D provides that seats are to be reserved for Scheduled Castes and Scheduled Tribes only. The reservation shall be in proportion to their population.

20 The 73rd Constitutional Amendment Act, 1992 refers to the *(Class-XI, Old NCERT)* *(IAS Pre 2000)*

(a) generation of gainful employment for the unemployed and the under-employed men and women in the rural area.

(b) generation of employment for the capable adults who are in need and desirous of works during the lean agricultural season.

(c) laying the foundation of strong and vibrant Panchayati Raj Institutions in the country. .

(d) guarantee of the right to life, liberty and security of person equality before the law and equal protection without discrimination.

Ans. (c)

Exp. The 73rd Constitutional Amendment Act, 1992 refers to laying the foundation of vibrant and strong Panchayati Raj Institutions in the country. 73rd Amendment Act was passed in 1992 and it took effect on 24th April, 1993. The primary goal of the Act was democratic decentralisation of power and resources from the centre to locally elected authorities in order to encourage public involvement in governance.

21 Which of the following subjects are listed in the 11th Schedule? *(Chap 8, Class-XI, New NCERT)*

1. Poverty alleviation programme
2. Education, including primary and secondary schools
3. Technical training and vocational education
4. Adult and non-formal education
5. Libraries

Select the correct answer using the codes given below.

(a) 1, 2 and 5 (b) 1, 3 and 4
(c) 1, 2, 3 and 5 (d) 1, 2, 3, 4 and 5

Ans. (d)

Exp. All the given subjects are listed in the 11th Schedule. The State Legislatures are needed to enact laws to endow powers and authority to the Panchayats to enable them functions of local government.

The 11th Schedule enshrines the distribution of powers between the State Legislature and the Panchayats by providing a list of 29 subjects. Some of them are as follows

poverty alleviation programme
education, including primary and secondary schools
technical training and vocational education
adult and non-formal education
libraries

22 Which of the following is not one of the sources for funds of Panchayat? *(Chap 5, Class-VI, New NCERT)*

(a) Collection of taxes on houses, market places.

(b) Government scheme funds received through various departments of the government.

(c) Donations for community works.

(d) Tax on agricultural income.

Ans. (d)

Exp. Tax on agricultural income is not one of the sources for funds of Panchayat. The Gram Panchayat receives revenue from the taxes imposed by the Village Panchayats.

Some of the taxes that are imposed by the Village Panchayats are the taxes on land and houses, toll tax, customs duty, license fees on transport and communication, etc.

23 Consider the following statements with respect to the State Finance Commission. *(Chap 8, Class-XI, New NCERT)*

1. It is required to appoint a State Finance Commission once in five years.
2. This Commission would examine the financial position of the local governments in the state.
3. It would also review the distribution of revenues between the state and local governments on the one hand and between rural and urban local governments on the other.
4. This innovation ensures that allocation of funds to the rural local governments remains a political matter.

Which of the statements given above is/are incorrect?

(a) Only 3
(b) 1 and 2
(c) 1, 3 and 4
(d) Only 4

Ans. (d)

Exp. Only statement (4) is incorrect with respect to the State Finance Commission (SFC).

It is an institution created by 73rd and 74th constitutional amendment.

Under Article 243 I, the Governor of state is required to constitute a Finance Commission for every five year to review financial position of Panchayats.

Thats why State Finance Commission (SFCs) support allocation of funds to the rural government remains constitutional matter not political matter.

24 **Which of the following are the functions of State Election Commission?** *(Chap 7, Class-XI, New NCERT)* *(RAS/RTS Pre 2013)*

1. Prepares the electoral rolls for Panchayats and Municipalities elections in the state.
2. Conducts elections for Panchayats and Municipalities of the state.
3. Conducts elections for other bodies in addition to Panchayats and Municipalities in accordance with the directions given by the Governor.
4. Prepares the electoral rolls and conducts elections as assigned by the Election Commission of India.

Select the correct answer using the codes given below.

(a) 1 and 2 (b) 3 and 4 (c) 1, 2 and 4 (d) Only 4

Ans. (c)

Exp. Statements (1), (2) and (4) are the functions of State Election Commission. 73rd and 74th Constitutional Amendment Act, 1992 provides for State Election Commission. As per this Act, the State Government is required to appoint a State Election Commissioner, who would be responsible for conducting elections to the Panchayats and Municipalities.

It conducts, supervise, direct and control the elections of Panchayats and Muncipalities. The State Election Commissioner is appointed by the Governor and cannot be removed from his office except in the manner and on the grounds similar to that of a judge of a High Court.

Urban Local Government Institution

25 **Match the following lists correctly and choose the correct code.** *(Chap 3, Class-IX & X, Old NCERT)*

List I (Name of Local Body)	List II (Tribe)
A. Municipal Corporation	1. Larger Urban Area
B. Municipal Council	2. Smaller Urban Area
C. Nagar Panchayat	3. Transitional Area

Codes

	A	B	C		A	B	C
(a)	1	2	3	(b)	3	1	2
(c)	2	1	3	(d)	1	3	2

Ans. (b)

Exp. The correct matching is A-3, B-1, C-2.

Municipal Corporation is established in a transitional area with a population of more than one million. It is created for the administration of big cities like Delhi, Mumbai, Kolkata. It is headed by Mayor.

Municipal Council also known as Municipality, they are established for large urban areas i.e., cities or towns having population of 1,00,000 or more. The Council is headed by a President.

Nagar Panchayat is established in a urban settlement i.e., smaller urban areas that has the population between 12,000 to 40,000.

26 **Which of the following is not a criteria for an area to be called an urban area?** *(Chap 8, Class-XI, New NCERT)* *(Chap 16, Module-3, NIOS)*

(a) A minimum population of 5,000.
(b) At least 75% of male working population engaged in non-agricultural occupations.
(c) A density of population of atleast 400 persons per sq. km.
(d) Literacy rate of at least 60%.

Ans. (d)

Exp. Option (d) is not the criteria for an area to be called urban area. According to the Census of India 2011, following are the criteria for an area to be called an urban area

- Minimum population of 5,000, at least 75% of the male main working population engaged in non-agricultural pursuits.
- A density of population of atleast 400 persons per sq. km.

27 **Consider the following statements with reference to the compulsory provisions of 74th Amendment Act.** *(Chap 7, Class-XI, Old NCERT)*

1. Constitution of Nagar Panchayats, Municipal Councils and Municipal Corporations.
2. Reservation of seats in urban local bodies for Scheduled Castes/Scheduled Tribes in proportion to their population.
3. Reservation of seats for women up to one-third seats.
4. Giving voting rights to members of the Union and State Legislatures in these bodies.

Which of the statements given above is/are not correct?

(a) Only 2 (b) 1 and 2 (c) Only 4 (d) 3 and 4

Ans. (c)

Exp. Only statement (4) is not correct because it is not one of the compulsory provisions of 74th Amendment Act.

Giving voting power to MPs and MLAs in meetings of municipalities is upon the discretion of State Legislature and not a compulsory provision. Only elected members of municipalities can vote in meeting.

Compulsory provisions are those which cannot be ditached from composition and functioning of municipalities. For ex-Reservation of seats for Scheduled Castes and Scheduled Tribes, one-third reservation of seats for women, Constitution of Nagar Panchayats, etc.

28 **Consider the following statements.** *(Chap 7, Class-XI, Old NCERT)*

1. There should be wards committee, consisting of one or more wards, within the territorial area of a municipal body having a population of three lakhs or more.
2. The Legislature of a State may, by law, make provision with respect to the composition and the territorial area of a wards committee and the manner in which the seats in a wards committee should be filled.

Which of the statements given above is/are correct?

(a) Only 1 (b) Only 2
(c) Both 1 and 2 (d) Neither 1 nor 2

Ans. (c)

Exp. Both the statements (1) and (2) are correct as Article 243(S) provides for the composition and function of wards committee. It states that they shall be constituted, consisting of one or more wards, within the territorial area of a municipality having a population of three lakhs or more.

Wards give community members the opportunity to express their needs, their opinions on issues that affect their lives and to have them heard at the municipal level via the ward councillor.

29 Consider the following statements about the Municipal Corporations. *(Chap 7, Class-VI, New NCERT)*

1. The city is divided into different wards and ward councillors get elected.
2. While the councillor's committees and the councillors decide on various issues, the Commissioner and the administrative staff implement these.
3. The Commissioner, the administrative staff and councillors are elected by the ward members.

Which of the statements given above is/are incorrect?

(a) Only 2 (b) Both 1 and 2
(c) Only 3 (d) Both 2 and 3

Ans. (c)

Exp. Only statement (3) is incorrect about Municipal Corporations because the Commissioner is appointed by the State Government from the Indian Administrative Services (IAS) or State Civil Services.

Administrative staff is selected and appointed by State Service Commission or other recruiting agency. Councillor is only elected by the ward members who are elected by people through direct elections of municipality.

30 Consider the following statements. *(Chap 8, Class-XI, Old NCERT)*

1. 12th Schedule of our Constitution contains the powers, authority and responsibilities of municipalities.
2. This Schedule was added by 73rd Constitutional Amendment.

Which of the statements given above is/are correct?

(a) Only 1
(b) Only 2
(c) Both 1 and 2
(d) Neither 1 nor 2

Ans. (a)

Exp. Only statement (1) is correct as 12th Schedule of the Indian Constitution contains the powers, authorities and responsibilities of municipalities. This Schedule has 18 items.

Statement (2) is not correct because this Schedule was not added by 73rd Constitutional Amendment Act but in 74th Constitutional Amendment Act, 1992.

31 Which of the following recommended that there should be a District Planning Committee consisting of the representatives of the Zila Parishad, Municipal Bodies in the district? *(Chap 9, Class-XII, Old NCERT)*

(a) Balwant Rai Mehta Committee
(b) Administrative Reforms Commission
(c) Santhanam Committee
(d) Ashok Mehta Committee

Ans. (b)

Exp. Administrative Reforms Commission recommended the formation of a District Planning Committee (DPC). It was created as per Article 243ZD of the Constitution, for planning at the district level and below.

DPC in each district should consolidate the plans prepared by the Panchayats and the Municipalities. This committee prepares of the draft development plan for the district.

32 Consider the following statements. *(Chap 9, Class-XII, Old NCERT)*

1. The 74th Amendment, makes provision for the Constitution of a Planning Committee at the district level to consolidate plans prepared by the Panchayats and Municipalities.
2. The District Magistrate has been empowered to make provisions with respect to the composition of the District Planning Committee.

Which of the statements given above is/are incorrect?

(a) Only 1 (b) Only 2
(c) Both 1 and 2 (d) Neither 1 nor 2

Ans. (b)

Exp. Only statement (2) is incorrect because District Planning Committee (DPC) is the committee created as per Article 243ZD of the Constitution of India at the district level. District Magistrate is not empowered to make provisions with respect to the composition of such committees. The State Legislature has been empowered to make provisions with respect to the composition of District Planning Committees.

33 In India, a Metropolitan Planning Committee *(Chap 7, Class-XI, Old NCERT) (IAS Pre 2011)*

1. is constituted under the provisions of the Constitution of India.
2. prepares the draft development plans for the metropolitan areas.
3. has the sole responsibility for implementing government sponsored schemes in the metropolitan areas.

Which of the statements given above is/are correct?

(a) 1 and 2 (b) Only 2 (c) 1 and 3 (d) 1, 2 and 3

Ans. (a)

Exp. Statements (1) and (2) are correct as according to Article 243-ZE, a Metropolitan Planning Committee has been constituted.

Every metropolitan area should have a Metropolitan Planning Committee to prepare a draft development plan for the Metropolitan areas as a whole.

The Legislature of a State may by law, make provision with respect to composition of the metropolitan committees. Every Metropolitan Planning Committee should prepare the draft development plan. It should regard the plans prepared by the Municipal bodies and the Panchayats in Metropolitan areas.

Statement (3) is incorrect beause it has limited responsibility for implementing government sponsored schemes in Metropolitan areas.

34 Match List I with List II and select the correct answer from the codes given below the lists.

(Class-XI, Old NCERT) (UPSC Pre 2022)

List I (Committees)	List II (Year of Appointments)
A. Balwant Rai Mehta Committee	1. 1957
B. Ashok Mehta Committee	2. 1977
C. LM Singhvi Committee	3. 1986
D. PK Thungon Committee	4. 1988

Codes

	A	B	C	D		A	B	C	D
(a)	3	4	2	1	(b)	1	2	3	4
(c)	2	3	1	4	(d)	4	1	2	3

Ans. (b)

Exp. The correct matching is A-1, B-2, C-3, D-4.

Balwant Rai Mehta Committee submitted its report on 24th November, 1957 and recommended the establishment of the scheme of 'democratic decentralisation' which finally came to be known as Panchayati Raj.

In December 1977, the Janata Government appointed a committee named-**Ashok Mehta Committee** under the Chairmanship of Ashok Mehta.

The main recommendations of the Committee were : the three-tier system of Panchayati Raj should be replaced by the two-tier system.

LM Singhvi Committee is a committee on the revitalisation of the Panchayati Raj institution for democracy and development. It was appointed by the Rajiv Gandhi government in 1986.

In 1988, the **PK Thungon Committee** recommended constitutional recognition for the local government bodies.

35 In the areas covered under the Panchayat (Extension to the Scheduled Areas) Act, 1996, what is the role/power of Gram Sabha?

(Class-XI, Old NCERT) (IAS Pre 2012)

1. Gram Sabha has the power to stop transfer of land in Scheduled Areas.
2. Gram Sabha has the ownership of minor forest produce.
3. Recommendation of Gram Sabha is required for granting prospecting license or mining lease for any mineral in the Scheduled Areas.

Which of the statements given above is/are correct?

(a) Only 1
(b) 1 and 2
(c) 2 and 3
(d) 1, 2 and 3

Ans. (b)

Exp. Statements (1) and (2) are correct regarding the role of Gram Sabha in the areas covered under the Panchayat (Extension to the Scheduled Areas) Act, 1996.

According to the PESA Act 1996, PESA is a law enacted by the Government of India to cover the 'Scheduled Areas', which are not covered in the 73rd Amendment. It has the power to prevent the land allienation. The Gram Sabha in the Act was entrusted with wide-ranging power starting from the consultation on land acquisition to that of ownership over minor forest produces and leasing of minor minerals.

Statement (3) is incorrect because the recommendation of Gram Sabha or Panchayat at the appropriate level shall be mandatory for grant of prospecting licence or mining lease for minor minerals in the Scheduled Areas.

Chapter 20

Election and Party System in India

Election and Party System in India

Election and Election Commission of India

Election
- Political contest for Public Support
- Voting, Universal Adult Franchise
- Article 326 deals with Election
- Person aged 18 or above has the Right to Vote
- **Condition for Disqualification of Voter** Unsound Mind; Punished for Election related Offences; Non-citizen of India
- **Election Process** Secret ballot and announces election dates
- **Nomination** Candidates file nominations to election offices post selection

Election Commission of India
- Constitutional body
- Oversees free and fair election
- Established on 26th January, 1950
- **Appointment and Term of Office**
  - Appointed by President
  - Service cannot be changed after appointment
- **Removal and Resignation of Members of EC** (Election Commission)
  - Chief Election Commissioner (CEC), removal like Supreme Court Judges
  - Other ECs, removal requires CEC recommendation
- **Power and Function**
  - Supervise direct and control electoral roll preparation
  - Conduct Parliament, State Assemblies, President and Vice-President elections
  - Examine candidate's election expenses

Electoral System and Election Laws

The Electoral System
- **Plurality System** (First Past the Post)
  - Divides country into single-member constituencies
  - Voters choose one candidate
  - Candidate with most votes, even if less them half, wins
- **Majority System**
  - **Second Ballot System** Utilises single choice voting like first past the post system, Requires on overall majority for a candidate to win the first ballot
  - **Alternative Voting System** Preferential voting, winning candidate needs atleast 50% of overall votes

The Election Laws
- **Representation of People's Act, 1950**
  - Establishes election machinery at the state, district and constituency levels
  - Addresses preparation and revision of electoral rolls
- **Representation of People's Act, 1951**
  - Legal Sanction for election conduct
  - Ensure peace, order during elections, ensure fairness civil services neutrality
- **Election symbols** (Reservation and Allotment Order, 1968)
  - Allotment of symbols
  - Settlement of dispute between political parties

Anti-defection Law
- 52nd Constitutional Amendment Act, 1985
- Disqualifies MP and MLAs for defection

Electoral Reform and Political Parties

Electoral Reform
- Aims to enhance the representation of public desire in election results
- Election Commission powers were strengthened

Electoral Reforms by Election Commission
- Model code of conduct
- Candidates must submit affidavits disclosing criminal records
- EVM introduced to prevent rigging
- **Model Code of Conduct**
  - Comes into immediate effect after election announcement
  - EC guidelines for parties and candidates post-poll announcement
- **Features**
  - Prohibits activities causing tension between different regions, castes, communities, etc
  - Forbids the use of places of worship for election propaganda

Characteristics of Political Parties
- Exercise government power through winning political office
- **Functions of Political Parties**
  - Unify, simplify and stabilises political processes
  - Raise awareness through campaigns about potential outcomes of particular policies

Political Parties in India
- **National Party**
  - $\geq$ 6% of total votes in previous general election in atleast 4 states
  - Major National party, INC, BJP, CPI(MS, BSP, NPP, AAP)
- **Criteria for Being Re-organised State Party**
  - Secure 6% of valid votes and win atleast 2 seats in State Legislative Assembly
  - Secure 6% of valid vote in an election and also wins atleast 1 seat in the Lok Sabha from the same state win minimum 3% of total seats or three seats in Legislative Assembly

SOURCE New NCERT Class IX **(Electoral Politics)**, Old NCERT Class IX & X **(Election, Political Parties)**, New NCERT Class X **(Political Parties, Popular Struggles and Movements)**, New NCERT Class XI **(Election and Representation)**, Old NCERT Class XII **(Adult Franchise and Electoral Participation, Election Commission and Election Procedure, Election Reforms, Political Parties and Party Systems, National and State Parties, Interest Groups and Pressure Groups)**, New NCERT Class XII **(Era of One-party Dominance, Challenges to and Restoration of the Congress System)**

Elections and Electoral System

1 Consider the following statements regarding elections. *(Chap 3, Class-IX, New NCERT)*

1. The list of those who are eligible to vote is officially called the Electoral Roll and is commonly known as the Voters' List.
2. Universal Adult Franchise means that no one should be denied the right to vote under any circumstance.
3. Every person who wishes to contest an election has to fill a 'nomination form' and give some money as 'security deposit'.

How many of the statements given above is/are not correct?

(a) Only one (b) Only two (c) All three (d) None of these

Ans. (a)

Exp. Only one statement i.e., (2) is not correct regarding elections. Universal Adult Franchise means that all the citizens who are 18 years and above, have the Right to Vote irrespective of their caste, religion, education and economic condition. This is to ensure the principle of equality and non-discrimination.

2 Consider the following statements regarding the demerits of electoral competition. *(Chap 3, Class-IX, New NCERT)*

1. It creates a sense of disunity and 'factionalism' in every locality.
2. It allows sensible long-term policies to be formulated.
3. Parties and candidates often use dirty tricks to win elections.

Which of the statements given above is/are not correct?

(a) 1 and 3 (b) Only 2 (c) 2 and 3 (d) Only 3

Ans. (b)

Exp. Only statement (2) is not correct regarding the demerits of electoral competition as it does not lead to the formulation of sensible long-term policies. It is because political parties in power and opposition try to appropriate the voters by populist measures resulting in short-term and parochial policy framework.

3 Consider the following statements. *(Chap 3, Class-XII, Old NCERT)* *(Chap 11, Module-3, NIOS) (IAS Pre 2004, 2020)*

1. According to the Constitution of India, any person who is eligible to vote can be made a minister in a state for six months, if he is not a member of the Legislature of that state.
2. According to the Representation of the People Act, 1951, any person who has been found guilty of a criminal offence and sentenced to imprisonment for a term of five years, becomes permanently disqualified from contesting an election; even though he has been released from prison.

Which of the statements given above is/are correct?

(a) Only 1
(b) Only 2
(c) Both 1 and 2
(d) Neither 1 nor 2

Ans. (d)

Exp. Neither statements (1) nor (2) are correct. According to the Constitution of India, the age of 25 years has been fixed for the member of the State Legislative Assembly and 30 years for the member of the Legislative Council and it is necessary to have a name in the voter list of the State Legislative Assembly. Any person having the qualification of Vidhan Sabha or Legislative Council can be made a minister without taking membership, but it is necessary to take membership within 6 months. While according to the Representation of the People Act, 1951 person stoods disqualified from contesting polls under the election law. If his conviction in a criminal case, in which a Jail term of two or more years has been awarded. The person is disqualified for the period of imprisonment and a further six years but not permanently.

4 Consider the following statements. *(Chap 3, Class-XI, Old NCERT)*

Statement-I Reservation of 33% seats for women in Parliament and State Legislatures does not require constitutional amendment.

Statement-II Political parties contesting elections can allot 33% of the seats they are contesting for women without any constitutional amendment.

Codes

(a) Both Statement-I and Statement-II are correct and Statement-II is the correct explanation for Statement-I.
(b) Both Statement-I and Statement-II are correct and Statement-II is not the correct explanation of Statement-I.
(c) Statement-I is correct, but Statement-II is incorrect.
(d) Statement-I is incorrect, but Statement-II is correct.

Ans. (d)

Exp. Statement-I is incorrect, but Statement-II is correct. Reservation of 33% of seats for women in Parliament and State Legislatures required constitutional amendment. Reservation requires amendment to the Constitution by a special majority requires two-thirds of the member present and voting and supported by more than 50% of the total strength of the house (As per Article 368) Lok Sabha and Rajya Sabha both passed the Women Reservation Bill 2023 (Nari Shakti Vandan Adhiniyam, 2023) by 128th Constitutional Amendment.

Political parties can allot 33% of the seats they are contesting for women without any constitutional amendment. Although there is a provision of reservation for Scheduled Castes and Tribes in the Parliament and State Legislatures (Assemblies) in the Indian Constitution.

5 Consider the following Assertion (A) and Reason (R) and choose and correct code.

(Chap 3, Class-IX, New NCERT)

Assertion (A) Our Constitution requires that each constituency should have a roughly equal population living within it.

Reason (R) One of the features of a democratic election is that every vote should have equal value.

Codes

(a) Both A and R are true and R is the correct explanation of A.
(b) Both A and R are true, but R is not the correct explanation of A.
(c) A is true, but R is false.
(d) A is false, but R is true.

Ans. (a)

Exp. Both Assertion (A) and Reason (R) are true and Reason (R) is the correct explanation of Assertion (A).

Each state is divided into territorial constituencies in such a manner that the ratio between the population of each constituency and the number of seats allotted to it remains same throughout the state. Due to this, every vote gains same quantifiable value throughout the country.

6 Consider the following statements.

(Chap 3, Class-IX, New NCERT)

1. In a Schedule Castes (SC) reserved constituency, only someone who belongs to the Scheduled Castes can vote and stand for election.
2. The reserved seats for SC do not take away the legitimate share of any other social group as number is in proportion to their share in the total population.

Which of the statements given above is/are incorrect?

(a) Only 1 (b) Only 2
(c) Both 1 and 2 (d) Neither 1 nor 2

Ans. (a)

Exp. Only statement (1) is incorrect because in a reserved constituency, only a member of reserved community can stand for election as a candidate but every eligible adult member of the constituency irrespective of caste, race and community can vote in the election. There is no provision of separate electorate in India.

7 Which of the following is/are not one of the characteristics of First Past the Post System?

(Chap 3, Class-XI, New NCERT)(Chap 18, Module-4, NIOS)

(a) It is also called the Singularity System.
(b) The candidate who secures the highest number of votes in that constituency is declared elected.
(c) The entire country is divided into various constituencies and each constituency elects one representative.
(d) None of the above

Ans. (a)

Exp. Statement (a) is not considered as the characteristics of First Past the Post System. This is a plurality voting system where candidate with the highest votes among all candidates is declared winner. It means that the candidate with the maximum number of votes among all candidates is the winner.

8 Consider the following statements with respect to the Proportional Representation (PR) System.

(Chap 3, Class-XI, New NCERT)

1. In this system, a party gets the same proportion of seats as its proportion of votes.
2. Each party fills its quota of seats by picking those many of its nominees from a preference list that has been declared before the elections.

Which of the statements given above is/are correct?

(a) Only 1 (b) Only 2
(c) Both 1 and 2 (d) Neither 1 nor 2

Ans. (c)

Exp. Both the statements (1) and (2) are correct as Proportional Representation (PR) System awards seats in legislative bodies to political parties in proportion to their strength in the electorate. If party A gets 35% of the votes, it gets 35% of the legislative seats; if party B gets 15% of the vote, it gets 15% of the seats.

Each party fills its quota of seats by picking those many of its nominees from a preference list that has been declared before the elections.

9 Consider the following statements.

(Chap 3, Class-XI, Old NCERT) (IAS Pre 2021)

1. In India, there is no law restricting the candidates from contesting in one Lok Sabha election from three constituencies.
2. In 1991, Lok Sabha Election, Shri Devi Lal contested from three Lok Sabha constituencies.
3. As per the existing rules, if a candidate contests in one Lok Sabha election from many constituencies, his/her party should bear the cost of by-elections to the constituencies vacated by him/her in the event of him/her winning in all the constituencies.

Which of the statements given above is/are correct?

(a) Only 1 (b) Only 2
(c) 1 and 3 (d) 2 and 3

Ans. (b)

Exp. Only statement (2) is correct as in 1991, Lok Sabha Election, Shri Devi Lal contested from three Lok Sabha constituencies.

Statements (1) and (3) are incorrect because in 1996, the Representation of the People Act, 1951, was amended which restricted the number of seats one candidate could contest in one election to two constituencies. And whenever they have won more than one, the candidates have retained only one, forcing by polls in the rest.

There is no such provision that if a candidate contests in one Lok Sabha elections from many constituencies, then his/her party should bear the cost of bye-elections to the constituencies vacated by him/her in the event of him/her winning in all the constituencies.

10 Consider the following Assertion (A) and Reason (R) and choose the correct code.

(Chap 2, Class-IX, Old NCERT) (UP Lower Sub Mains 2013)

Assertion (A) The system of Proportional Representation may solve the problem of minority representation to some extent.

Reason (R) The system of Proportional Representation enables due representation to all types of groups based on ethnicity, gender, interests, and ideologies.

Codes

(a) Both A and R are true and R is the correct explanation of A.
(b) Both A and R are true, but R is not the correct explanation of A.
(c) A is true, but R is false.
(d) A is false, but R is true.

Ans. (a)

Exp. Both Assertion (A) and Reason (R) are true and Reason (R) is the correct explanation of Assertion (A).

The system of Proportional Representation may solve the problem of minority representation to some extent.

It is based on the principle that parties should be represented in an assembly or Parliament in direct proportion to their overall electoral strength, their percentage of seats equalling their percentage of votes. It is claimed that under Proportional Representation System any party or interest group would secure representation in proportion to the support, it has among the electors.

Election Commission and Other Officials

11 Consider the following statements.

(Chap 2, Class-XII, New NCERT) (Chap 18, Module-4, NIOS)

1. The Election Commission of India was set up on 25th January, 1950.
2. TN Seshan became the first Chief Election Commissioner.

Which of the statements given above is/are incorrect?

(a) Only 1 (b) Only 2
(c) Both 1 and 2 (d) Neither 1 nor 2

Ans. (b)

Exp. Only statement (2) is incorrect because Sukumar Sen was an Indian Civil Servant who became the first Chief Election Commissioner of India, serving from 21st March, 1950 to 19th December, 1958.

TN Sheshan was the 10th Chief Election Commissioner of India (1990-1996) and was well known for his electoral reforms.

12 Consider the following statements.

(Chap 3, Class-XI, Old NCERT)
(IAS Pre 2017)

1. The Election Commission of India is a five-member body.
2. The Union Home Ministry, for both general elections and bye-elections, decides the election schedule.
3. The Election Commission resolves disputes related to the split/merger of recognised political parties.

Which of the statements given above is/are correct?

(a) and 2 (b) 2 and 3
(c) Only 2 (d) Only 3

Ans. (d)

Exp. Only statement (3) is correct as the Election Commission gives recognition to political parties. He also allots election symbols to them. It acts as a court for settlement of disputes in the matter of granting recognition to political parties and giving election symbols.

Statements (1) and (2) are incorrect because the Election Commission works as a multi-member body consisting of three Election Commissioners. The Chief Election Commissioner and two other Election Commissioners have equal powers and authority as President. In case of difference of opinion, decisions are taken on the basis of majority. It sets the election years for both general elections and bye elections.

13 Consider the following statements regarding Election Commission of India.

(Chap 3, Class-XI, Old NCERT)

1. The Election Commission of India is a five member body.
2. The Election Commission decides the election schedule for the conduct of both general elections and bye-elections.
3. The Election Commission resolves the disputes relating to splits/mergers of recognised political parties.
4. The Election Commission of India provides election symbols for newly registered parties.

Which of the statements given above is/are not correct?

(a) 1 and 3 (b) 2 and 4
(c) Only 1 (d) 1, 2 and 3

Ans. (c)

Exp. Only statement (1) is not correct because the Election Commission is a three member body which include one Chief Election Commissioner and two Election Commissioners. Since its inception in 1950 and till 15th October, 1989, the Election Commission functioned as a single member body consisting of the Chief Election Commissioner. On 16th October, 1989, the President appointed two more Election Commissions.

14 Consider the following statements about the Central Election Commission. *(Chap 2, Class-XII, Old NCERT)*

1. Till 1989, the Election Commission was a single member body and it remained multi-member since 1993.
2. The Chief Election Commissioner (CEC) presides over the Election Commission, and has similar powers than the other Election Commissioners.
3. The Chief Election Commissioner (CEC) and other commissioners are appointed for a six year term or continue till the age of 65, whichever is earlier.
4. The CEC can be removed before the expiry of the term, by the President, if both Houses of Parliament make such a recommendation with a special majority, on grounds of proved misbehaviour or incapacity.

Which of the statements given above is/are not correct?

(a) 1 and 3 (b) Only 1
(c) 2 and 4 (d) 1, 2 and 4

Ans. (b)

Exp. Only statement (1) is not correct about the Central Election commission.

Since, 1950 to 15th October, 1989 Election Commission functioned as single member body. On 16th October, 1989, President appointed two more Election Commissioners.

However, two post of Election Commissioners were abolished in January 1990. Again in October 1993, the President appointed two more members and since then, it is a three member body. A three member commission has been in operation, since then and the decisions by the commission are made by a majority of vote.

15 The powers of the Election Commission include which of the following? *(Chap 3, Class-XII, Old NCERT)*

1. Election Commission takes decisions on every aspect of conduct and control of elections from the announcement of elections to the declaration of results.
2. It implements the Code of Conduct and punishes any candidate or party that violates it.
3. During the election period, the EC can order the government to dismiss some government officials.
4. When on election duty, government officers work under the control of the Election Commission and not the government.

Codes

(a) 1, 2 and 3 (b) 1, 2, 3 and 4
(c) 1, 3 and 4 (d) 1, 2 and 4

Ans. (d)

Exp. Statements (1), (2) and (4) are included in the powers of Election Commission.

The powers of the Election Commission can be Administrative, Advisory and Quasi-Judicial. It empowers Election Commission of India (ECI) to take decisions with respect to conduct of elections. It also enforce the 'Model Code of Conduct' for election campaigns and ensures its implementation. It also has the power to appoint officers as election observers and expenditure observers from different departments of the Civil Services.

Statement (3) is not included in the powers of Election Commissioner as he is not empowered to dismiss government officials.

16 Consider the following statements with reference to India. *(Chap 8, Class-XI, Old NCERT) (IAS Pre 2002)*

1. The Chief Election Commissioner and other election commissioners enjoy equal powers but receive unequal salaries.
2. The Chief Election Commissioner is entitled to the same salary as is provided to a judge of the Supreme Court.
3. The Chief Election Commissioner shall not be removed from his office except in like manner and on like grounds as a judge of the Supreme Court.
4. The term of office of the Election Commissioner is five years from the date he assumes his office or till the day he attains the age of 62 years, whichever is earlier.

Which of the statements given above are correct?

(a) 1 and 2 (b) 2 and 3 (c) 1 and 4 (d) 2 and 4

Ans. (b)

Exp. Statements (2) and (3) are correct as the Chief Election Commissioner is entitled to the same salary as is provided to Judge of the Supreme Court.

The Chief Election Commissioner cannot be removed from his office except in like manner and on the like grounds as a Judge of Supreme Court.

Statements (1) and (4) are incorrect because the powers, salaries and allowances of Chief Election Commissioner and other Election Commissioners are equal.

The term of office of the Election Commissioner is six years from the date he assumes his office or till the day he attains the age of 65 years, whichever is earlier.

17 With reference to the Chief Election Commissioner, consider the following statements. *(Chap 3, Class-XI, Old NCERT)*

1. The Chief Election Commissioner of the Election Commission of India is paid a salary equal to the salary of the judge of the Supreme Court.
2. The term of Chief Election Commissioner of India shall be for a period of six years from the date of assuming office or till the age of 65 years whichever comes first.
3. An Election Commissioner may at any time by writing under his hand addressed to the Chief Election Commissioner, resign his office.

Which of the statements given above is/are correct?

(a) 1 and 2 (b) 1 and 3
(c) 1, 2 and 3 (d) Only 3

Ans. (a)

Exp. Statements (1) and (2) are correct as the Chief Election Commissioner and the two other Election Commissioner have equal powers and receive equal salaries, allowances and other perquisites, which are similar to those of a judge of the Supreme Court.

The term of Chief Election Commissioner of the Election Commission of India shall be for a period of six years from the date of assuming office or till the age of 65 years, whichever comes first.

The Chief Election Commissioner is provided with the security of tenure. He can be removed by the President on the basis of a resolution passed to that effect by the both the Houses of Parliament with the special majority, either on the ground of proved misbehaviour or incapacity.

Statement (3) is incorrect as the Chief Election Commissioner or an Election Commissioner may, at any time, by writing under his hand addressed to the President resign from his office.

18 Consider the following statements with respect to the State Election Commissioner.

(Chap 7, Class-XI, Old NCERT)

1. The State Election Commissioner is appointed by the Governor and cannot be removed from his office except in the like manner and on the like grounds as a judge of a High Court.
2. The State Election Commissioner conducts the election to rural local bodies only.

Which of the statements given above is/are correct?

(a) Only 1
(b) Only 2
(c) Both 1 and 2
(d) Neither 1 nor 2

Ans. (a)

Exp. Only statement (1) is correct as Article 243K(2) states that the tenure and appointment of State Election Commissioner will be directed as per the law made by the State Legislature.

However, State Election Commissioner shall not be removed from his/her office except in like manner and on the like grounds as a judge of a High Court.

Statement (2) is incorrect because the State Election Commissioner conducts the elections to rural as well as urban local bodies in the state.

19 Consider the following statements.

(Unit 2, Class-XI, Tamil Nadu Board)

Statement-I The State Election Commission is a Constitutional Authority.

Statement-II Elections to rural local bodies are overseen by the Election Commission of India.

Codes

(a) Both Statement-I and Statement-II are correct and Statement-II is the correct explanation for Statement-I.
(b) Both Statement-I and Statement-II are correct and Sstatement-II is not the correct explanation for Statement-I
(c) Statement-I is correct, but Statement-II is incorrect.
(d) Statement-I is incorrect, but Statement-II is correct.

Ans. (c)

Exp. Statement-I is correct, but Statement-II is incorrect.
The State Election Commission is a Constitutional Authority. The State Election Commission is constituted under the provisions of Article 243 (K) and 243 (ZA) of the Constitution of India.

The State Election Commission has been given the responsibility of superintendence, direction and control to conduct all elections to Panchayati Raj Institutions (PRI) and Municipal bodies in the state.

Election to rural local bodies are not overseen by the Election Commission of India, but it controlled and overseen by the State Election Commission.

20 Consider the following statements regarding the Returning Officer (RO). *(Chap 2, Class-XII, Old NCERT)*

1. He is nominated by the Election Commission in consultation with the State Government concerned.
2. He can be nominated as RO for a single constituency only.
3. He supervises the election work in every constituency.
4. The Assistant ROs generally do not do the scrutiny of nomination papers.

How many of the statements given above is/are incorrect?

(a) Only one (b) Only two (c) All four (d) None of these

Ans. (a)

Exp. Only one statement i.e., (2) is incorrect because a Returning Officer (RO) is responsible for overseeing the election in a constituency or sometimes in two constituencies, as directed by the Election Commission (EC).

The EC appoints the Returning Officer and Assistant Returning Officer for a constituency in consultation with the government of the State or Union Territory.

21 Consider the following statements.

(Chap 2, Class-XII, Old NCERT)

1. The 42nd Constitution Amendment (1976) had put a ban on any further delimitation of constituencies till 1996.
2. 91st Amendment of the Constitution extended this freeze of seats in Lok Sabha and Legislative Assemblies till 2025.

Which of the statements given above is/are correct?

(a) Only 1 (b) Only 2
(c) Both 1 and 2 (d) Neither 1 nor 2

Ans. (d)

Exp. Neither statements (1) nor (2) are correct.

The 42nd Constitutional Amendment (1976) had put a ban on any further delimitation of constituencies till 2001 and the total number of seats has remained the same till then. This was done to check the growth of the population. 84th Amendment of the Constitution passed in 2001, has extended this freeze of seats till 2026. The year 2026 has been chosen because the population planners have projected that by the year 2026, the population of India would stabilise and the country would hope to have zero growth rate of population thereafter.

22 Consider the following statements, with reference to the commencement of the election process in India.

(Chap 2, Class-XI, Old NCERT) (IAS Pre 1995)

1. The recommendation for election is made by the Government and the notification for election is issued by the Election Commission.
2. The recommendation for election is made by the Election Commission and the notification for election is issued by the Home Ministry at the centre and home departments in the states.
3. The recommendation for election is made by the Election Commission and the notification for election is issued by the President and Governors of the State concerned.
4. Both the exercise of making a recommendation for election and that of issuing a notification in respect of it are done by the Election Commission.

Which of the statements given above is/are correct?

(a) 1, 2 and 4 (b) Only 3 (c) Both 2 and 3 (d) All of these

Ans. (b)

Exp. Only statement (3) is correct in respect of the commencement of the election process in India. Under Section 15 of the Representation of People, the recommendation for election is made by the Election Commission and the notification for election is issued by the President and Governors of the State concerned.

Statements (1), (2) and (4) are incorrect because in India, the Government does not make the recommendation for Election, the Election Commission does.

The notification for election is not issued by the Home Ministery or State Home Departments, but by President and Governors. While the Election Commission indeed recommends the election, it does not issue the notification. The notification is issued by the President and Governors.

23 Which of the following is/are not the functions of the Election Commission of India?

(Chap 2, Class-XII, New NCERT)
(Unit 2, Class-XI, Tamil Nadu Board) (IAS Pre 1994)

1. To conduct elections for the post of Speaker and Deputy Speaker of Lok Sabha and the Chairperson of Rajya Sabha.
2. To conduct elections for the municipality and municipal corporations.
3. To make a decision on all the doubts and disputes arising from the election.

Select the correct answer using the codes given below.

(a) 1 and 2 (b) 1 and 3
(c) 2 and 3 (d) None of these

Ans. (d)

Exp. None of the given statements are functions of the Election Commission of India.

The election of post of Speaker and Deputy Speaker of Lok Sabha is done internally by the members of the house.

Whereas the Chairperson of Rajya Sabha is the Vice-President of India who gets elected indirectly, by an electoral college consisting of members of both Houses of Parliament.

The election of Municipality and Municipal Corporation is conducted by the State Election Commission. Supreme Court makes decisions on all doubts and disputes arising from the election not Election Commission.

Electoral Reforms

24 Consider the following statements.

(Chap 2, Class-XII, Old NCERT)
(Chap 3, Class-XI, New NCERT)

1. The Representation of the People's Act, 1950 deals with the actual conduct of elections.
2. The Representation of the People's Act, 1951 deals with the preparation of electoral rolls.

Which of the statements given above is/are correct?

(a) Only 1 (b) Only 2
(c) Both 1 and 2 (d) Neither 1 nor 2

Ans. (d)

Exp. Neither statements (1) nor (2) are correct as Representation of the People's Act (RPA), 1950 lays down procedures for delimitation of constituencies, qualification of voters and preparation of electoral rolls among other such things.

The Representation of the People's Act (RPA), 1951 regulates the actual conduct of elections and by-elections.

25 With reference to Anti-Defection Law in India, consider the following statements.

(Chap 3, Class-XII, Old NCERT) (IAS Pre 2022)

1. The law specifies that a nominated legislator cannot join any political party within six months of being appointed to the House.
2. The law does not provide any time-frame within which the presiding officer has to decide a defection case.

Which of the statements given above is/are correct?

(a) Only 1 (b) Only 2
(c) 1 and 2 (d) Neither 1 nor 2

Ans. (b)

Exp. Only statement (2) is correct as the law does not specify a time period for the Presiding Officer to decide on a disqualification plea under the Tenth Schedule.

Statement (1) is incorrect because a nominated member of a House shall be disqualified for being a member of the House if he joins any political party after the expiry of six months from the date on which he takes his seat. Thus he/she is free to join any political party within six months and would not be disqualified for the same.

26 **With reference to the Anti-Defection Bill, consider the following statements.** *(Chap 3, Class-XII, Old NCERT)*

1. An MP or an MLA will be disqualified if he has voluntarily given up the membership of the party to which he belonged.
2. In the event of a member's absence from voting in the House on a particular issue, an MP or MLA will be disqualified.
3. A member shall not be disqualified if there is a merger of political parties.
4. The Speaker of the Lok Sabha will not be disqualified if he becomes a member of another political party later on.

Which of the statements given above is/are not true?

(a) Only 3 (b) Only 4 (c) 1, 3 and 4 (d) Both 2 and 3

Ans. (b)

Exp. Only statement (4) is not true about the Anti-Defection Bill. A person who has been elected to the office of the Speaker or the Deputy Speaker of the House of the People or the Deputy Chairman of the Council of States or the Chairman or the Deputy Chairman of the Legislative Council of a State or the Speaker or the Deputy Speaker of the Legislative Assembly of a State, shall not be disqualified .

(a) if he, by reason of his election to such office, voluntarily gives up the membership of the political party to which he belonged immediately before such election and does not, so long as he continues to hold such office thereafter, rejoin that political party or become a member of another political party; or

(b) if he, having given up by reason of his election to such office his membership of the political party to which he belonged immediately before such election, rejoins such political party after he ceases to hold such office.

27 **Consider the following statements about the amendments to the elections law by the Representation of People's (Amendment) Act 1996.** *(Chap 3, Class-XII, Old NCERT) (IAS Pre 1999)*

1. Any conviction for the offence of insulting the Indian National Flag or the Constitution of India shall entail disqualification for contesting elections to Parliament and State Legislatures for six years from the date of conviction.
2. There is an increase in the security deposit which a candidate has to make to contest the election to Lok Sabha.
3. A candidate now cannot contest election from more than one Parliamentary constituency.
4. No election will now be countermanded on the death of a contesting candidate.

Which of the statements given above are correct?

(a) 2 and 3 (b) 1, 2 and 4
(c) 1 and 3 (d) 1, 2, 3 and 4

Ans. (b)

Exp. Statements (1), (2) and (4) are correct about the amendments to the elections law by the Representation of People's (Amendment) Act 1996.

In 1996, some important changes were made in the Representation of People's Act. These include

- Person convicted for insulting the National flag, the National Anthem or the Constitution of India stands debarred from contesting elections for six years from the date of such convictions as in the case of other offences.
- To check the multiplicity of non-serious candidates, the amount of security deposit has been increased.
- Previously, the election in the constituency was countermanded on the death of the candidate, now the election would not be countermanded rather a new candidate of the respective party will have to contest on his place.

Statement (3) is incorrect because a candidate can now contest election from more than two Parliamentary Constituencies.

28 **Consider the following statements.** *(Chap 3, Class-XII, Old NCERT)*

1. Party system in India is unregulated and undefined.
2. Anti-defection has been inserted into Eighth Schedule of the Constitution.
3. Indian National Congress was a dominant party upto 1977.

Which of the statements given above is/are correct?

(a) 1 and 2 (b) 2 and 3
(c) 1 and 3 (d) 1, 2 and 3

Ans. (c)

Exp. Statements (1) and (3) are correct.

Various provisions of the Constitution provided opportunities for parties to be established, develop and function as in any representative democracy. Thus, party system in India is undefined and unregulated except for their registration by the Election Commission and under the provisions of Anti-defection Law.

Indian National Congress was a dominant party since 1977. The first non-Congress party government was formed in 1977 and since then Congress Party has not remained the dominant party.

Statement (2) is not correct because Anti-defection Law has been inserted by 52nd Amendment Act, 1985, in the Tenth Schedule of the Constitution.

29 Consider the following Assertion (A) and Reason (R) and choose the correct code.

(Chap 3, Class-IX, New NCERT) (UPPSC Pre 2017)

Assertion (A) Model Code of Conduct is to be followed by political parties as soon as election is announced.

Reason (R) Model Code of Conduct was enacted by Parliament.

Codes

(a) Both A and R are true and R is the correct explanation of A.
(b) Both A and R are true, but R is not the correct explanation of A.
(c) A is true, but R is false.
(d) A is false, but R is true.

Ans. (c)

Exp. Assertion (A) is true, but Reason (R) is false. Model Code of Conduct is a set of guidelines for the guidance of political parties and candidates during the election. It comes into force as soon as Election Commission announces the schedule of election.

Model Code of Conduct is enacted by Election Commission of India and not by the Parliament.

30 According to the Model Code of Conduct for election campaigns, any party or candidate is prohibited to do which of the following?

(Chap 3, Class-IX, New NCERT)

1. Use any place of worship for election propaganda.
2. Use government vehicles, aircrafts and officials for elections.
3. Ministers shall not lay foundation stones of any projects, take any big policy decisions or make any promises of providing public facilities.

Which of the statements given above are correct?

(a) 1 and 3 (b) 2 and 3 (c) 1, 2 and 3 (d) 1 and 2

Ans. (c)

Exp. All the given statements (1), (2) and (3) are correct. The Model Code of Conduct for guidance of political parties and candidates is a set of norms which has been evolved with the consensus of political parties who have consented to abide by the principles embodied in the said code and also bind them to respect and observe it in its letter and spirit.

31 Consider the following statements.

(Chap 3, Class-XI, New NCERT)

1. One of the main plank of movement launched by Jayaprakash Narayan was electoral reform.
2. Jayaprakash Narayan set up a committee under Tarapore for electoral reforms.

Which of the statements given above is/are correct?

(a) Only 1 (b) Only 2
(c) Both 1 and 2 (d) Neither 1 nor 2

Ans. (a)

Exp. Only statement (1) is correct as in 1974, Jayaprakash Narayan had launched a movement, known as, 'Total revolution'. One of the main planks of this movement was electoral reform.

Statement (2) is incorrect because on behalf of the citizens for democracy, Jayaprakash Narayan set up a committee under the Chairmanship of VM Tarkunda, a former judge of Bombay High Court, for electoral reform. This committee after holding discussions with representatives of a number of organisations in February, 1975 produced a comprehensive set of recommendations.

32 Which of the following forms part of the electoral reforms in India? *(Chap 3, Class-XII, Old NCERT)*

1. Introduction of Postal Ballot.
2. By-elections within 6 months.
3. Intermediate as minimum educational qualification for candidates.

Select the correct answer using the codes given below.

(a) 1 and 2 (b) 1 and 3
(c) Only 2 (d) 2 and 3

Ans. (a)

Exp. Statements (1) and (2) are forms part of the electoral reforms in India.

Electoral reforms were introduced by introduction of Postal Ballot giving opportunity to vulnerable people by elections within 6 months, so that no one remain unrepresented.

Statement (3) is not form the part of electoral reforms as there is no minimum qualification for contesting election.

Party System and Political Parties

33 Consider the following statements regarding the political parties. *(Chap 6, Class-X, New NCERT)*

1. A party that secures at least 6% of the total votes in an election to the Legislative Assembly of a state and wins at least two seats is recognised as a state party.
2. A party that secures at least 6% of the total votes in Lok Sabha elections or Assembly elections in four States and wins at least four seats in the Lok Sabha is recognised as a national party.
3. Recognised parties are given a unique symbol, which only the official candidates of that party can use.
4. Only state and national parties in the country have to register with the Election Commission.

Which of the statements given above is/are incorrect?

(a) 1, 3 and 4 (b) Only 4
(c) 2 and 3 (d) 1, 2 and 4

Ans. (b)

Exp. Statement (4) is incorrect about the registration of political parties in India.

The registration of all political parties is governed by the provisions of the Representation of the People's Act 1951. Political parties seeking registration has to submit an application to the commission within a period of 30 days. This is done as per guidelines prescribed by the Election Commission (EC), in exercise of the powers conferred by the Article 324 of the Constitution and Section 29(A) of the Representation of the People's Act 1951 (RP Act 1951).

34 Consider the following statements. *(Chap 6, Class-X, Old NCERT)*

Statement-I Political parties have to follow the model code of conduct as soon as the election is announced.

Statement-II The Model code of conduct was enacted by the Parliament.

Codes

(a) Both Statement-I and Statement-II are correct and Statement-II is the correct explanation for Statement-I.
(b) Both Statement-I and Statements-II are correct and Statement-II is not the correct explanation for Statement-I.
(c) Statement-I is correct, but Statement-II is incorrect.
(d) Statement-I is incorrect, but Statement-II is correct

Ans. (c)

Exp. Statement-I is correct, but Statement-II is incorrect.

Political parties have to follow the model code of conduct as soon as the election is announced.

The Model code of conduct is a set of guidelines issued by the Election Commission for the regulation of political parties and their candidates before elections and to ensure free and fair elections. It remains in force from the date of announcement of election till the date of declaration of result.

The Model code of conduct is a set of guidelines which is issued by Election Commission.

35 Consider the following statements regarding political parties in India. *(Chap 6, Class-XII, Old NCERT)*

1. A party gets recognition as a National Party if it gets recognition as a State Party in atleast five states.
2. A party should win a minimum 8% of the total valid votes polled in the state to get recognised as a State Party.

Which of the statements given above is/are correct?

(a) Only 1 (b) Only 2
(c) Both 1 and 2 (d) Neither 1 nor 2

Ans. (d)

Exp. Neither statements (1) nor (2) are correct about political parties in India.

A party gets recognition as a National Party if it gets recognition as a State Party in atleast four seats in Lok Sabha general election.

A party should secure atleast 6% of the valid votes in an Assembly or a Lok Sabha general election to get recognised as a State Party.

36 Match the following lists correctly and choose the correct code. *(Chap 2, Class-XII, New NCERT)* *(UPRO/ARO Mains 2017)*

List-I (Political parties)	List-II (Year)
A. Indian National Congress	1. 1951
B. Bharatiya Jana Sangh	2. 1972
C. Communist Party of India	3. 1885
D. AIADMK	4. 1925

Codes

	A	B	C	D
(a)	3	1	4	2
(b)	2	3	4	1
(c)	4	3	2	1
(d)	2	1	4	3

Ans. (a)

Exp. The correct matching is A-3, B-1, C-4, D-2.

Indian National Congress was formed in 1885. It dominated the National and State politics till 1977.

Bharatiya Jana Sangh was formed in 1951. Shyama Prasad Mukherjee was its founder President.

Communist Party of India was formed on 26th December 1925. In 1964, it was splitted due to regional variations. The left faction of the party became Communist Party of India (Marxist).

AIADMK (All India Anna Dravida Munetra Kazhgam) was formed in 1972. At present, it is a State Party which is active in Tamil Nadu and Puducherry.

37 Consider the following pairs, with reference to the National Party of India and their years of establishment. *(Chap 6, Class-X, Old NCERT) (BPSC Pre 2023)*

	National Party of India	Year of Establishment
1.	Communist Party of India (Marxist) CPI-M	1964
2.	Communist Party of India (CPI)	1926
3.	Bahujan Samaj Party (BSP)	1984
4.	All India Trinamool Congress (AITC)	1998

How many of the pairs given above is/are incorrect?

(a) Only 1 (b) Only 2
(c) All four (d) None of these

Ans. (a)

Exp. Only one pair i.e., (2) is incorrect because the Communist Party of India was formed on 26th December, 1925, at the first party conference in Kanpur. Its founders included MN Roy, his wife Evelyn Trent, Abani Mukherji and MPT Acharya. SV Ghate was the first General Secretary of CPI.

38 Match the following lists correctly and choose the correct code. *(Chap 2, Class-XII, New NCERT)*

List-I (Leaders)	List-II (Associated Party)
A. KM Munshi	1. Praja Socialist Party
B. Shyama Prasad Mukherjee	2. Swatantra Party
C. AK Gopalan	3. Bharatiya Jana Sangh
D. Ashoka Mehta	4. Communist Party of India

Codes

	A	B	C	D		A	B	C	D
(a)	3	2	4	1	(b)	2	3	4	1
(c)	1	3	2	4	(d)	2	1	3	4

Ans. *(b)*

Exp. The correct matching is A- 2, B-3, C-4, D-1.

KM Munshi was a part of Indian National Congress before independence of India. After independence, he joined Swatantra Party.

Shyama Prasad Mukherjee with the help of the Rashtriya Swayamsevak Sangh, founded the Bharatiya Jana Sangh in 1951.

Ayillyath Kuttiari Gopalan, popularly known as AK Gopalan or AKG, was an Indian communist politician. He was one of 16 Communist Party of India's members elected to the first Lok Sabha in 1952.

Ashoka Mehta was a founder member of Socialist Party and in September 1952, the Kisan Mazdoor Praja Party and the Socialist Party was merged to form the Praja Socialist Party (PSP).

39 Arrange the formation of the following political parties in correct chronological order. *(Chap 5, Class-XII, Old NCERT)*

1. Communist Party of India
2. Bharatiya Janata Party
3. Communist Party of India-Marxist (CPI-M)
4. Nationalist Congress Party (NCP)

Codes

(a) 1, 2, 3 and 4 (b) 2, 3, 1 and 4
(c) 1, 3, 2 and 4 (d) 3, 2, 1 and 4

Ans. *(c)*

Exp. The correct chronological order of the formation of given political parties is (1), (3), (2) and (4).

Communist Party of India was formed in 1925; Communist Party of India-Marxist (CPI-M) was formed in 1965; Bharatiya Janata Party was formed in 1980 and Nationalist Congress Party was formed in 1999.

40 Which of the following will lead to political party reforms? *(Chap 6, Class-X, New NCERT)*

1. Promoting Defection.
2. Candidates giving details of his property and criminal cases.
3. Candidates filing their income tax returns.
4. Law to regulate the internal affairs of political parties.
5. State funding of elections.

Codes

(a) 1, 2 and 5 (b) 1, 3 and 4
(c) 1, 2, 3 and 5 (d) 2, 3, 4 and 5

Ans. *(d)*

Exp. Options (2), (3), (4) and (5) will lead to political party reforms.

Political party reforms may result, if there is transparency and accountability by political party which can be achieved by filing of income tax returns, internal democracy through a party Constitution, transparency in terms of property and income sources along with any criminal cases pending or conviction, a law should be made to regulate the internal affairs of political parties and there should be state funding of elections.

Option (1) is not correct because promoting defection will undermine the internal democracy of party system in India and hence, anti-defection and not defection will lead to political party reforms.

41 The merger of a political party with another political party in India is recognised in which of the following conditions? *(Chap 5, Class-XII, Old NCERT)*

(a) When not less than one-third members of the Legislature party have agreed to such merger.
(b) When not less than half members of the Legislature party have agreed to such merger.
(c) When not less than two-third members of the Legislature party have agreed to such merger.
(d) When not less than three-fourth members of the Legislature party have agreed to such merger.

Ans. *(d)*

Exp. The merger of a political party with another political party in India is recognised when not less than two-third members of the Legislature party have agreed to such merger.

Usually a merger leads to defection under Tenth Schedule of the Indian Constitution. But there are certain exception under the law.

The law allows a party to merge with another party when not less than 2/3rd members of the Legislative party have agreed to such merger.

In such scenario, neither the members who decide to merge will face disqualification.

42 Consider the following statements regarding political parties in India. *(Chap 5, Class-XII, Old NCERT)*

1. A party gets recognition as a National Party if it gets recognition as a State Party in atleast five states.
2. A party should win a minimum 8% of the total valid votes polled in the state to get recognised as a State Party.

Which of the above statements is/are correct?

(a) Only 1 (b) Only 2

(c) Both 1 and 2 (d) Neither 1 nor 2

Ans. (d)

Exp. Neither 1 nor is correct.

As per the ECI's Political parties and Election Symbols, 2019 handbook, a political party would be considered a national party if.

It is 'recognised' in four or more states; or If its candidates have secured at least 6% of total valid votes in at least 4 states (in latest Lok Sabha or Assembly elections) and the party has at least 4 MPs in the last Lok Sabha polls.

If it has won at least 2% of the total seats in the LS from at least 3 states.

Pressure Groups and Interest Groups

43 Consider the following statements. *(Chap 5, Class-X, New NCERT)*

1. Pressure groups are organisations that attempt to influence government policies.
2. Like political parties, pressure groups also aim to directly control or share political power.
3. Pressure groups are formed when people with common occupation, interest, aspirations or opinions come together in order to achieve a common objective.

How many of the statements given above is/are incorrect?

(a) Only one (b) Only two

(c) All three (d) None of these

Ans. (a)

Exp. Only one statement i.e., (2) is incorrect because the pressure groups are different from the political parties, as they neither contest elections nor try to capture political power.

They are concerned with specific programmes and issues, and their activities are confined to the protection and promotion of the interests of their members by influencing the government policies.

44 Consider the following statements with respect to sectional interest groups. *(Chap 5, Class-X, New NCERT)*

1. Usually interest groups seek to promote the interests of a particular section or a group of society.
2. Trade unions, business associations and professional bodies are some examples of interest groups.
3. Their principal concern is the betterment and well-being of society in general.

Which of the statements given above is/are incorrect?

(a) Both 2 and 3 (b) Only 3

(c) 1, 2 and 3 (d) Both 1 and 2

Ans. (b)

Exp. Statement (3) is incorrect with respect to the sectional interest groups as they seek to promote the interests of a particular section or a group of society.

For example, trade unions, business associations and professional (lawyers, doctors, teachers, etc.) bodies, truck union, labour union, etc.

45 Consider the following statements with respect to the Pressure groups and movements exert influence on politics. *(Chap 7, Class-XII, Old NCERT)*

1. They try to gain public support and sympathy for their goals and their activities by carrying out information, campaigns, organising meetings, filing petitions, etc.
2. They often organise protest activity like strikes or disrupting government programmes.
3. Some persons from pressure groups or movement groups may participate in official bodies and committees that offer advice to the government.

How many of the statements given above is/are correct?

(a) Only one

(b) Only two

(c) All three

(d) None of the above

Ans. (c)

Exp. All three statements i.e., (1), (2) and (3) are the ways to exert influence on politics by pressure groups and movements.

Pressure groups are organised on the basis of common interests. They are concerned with influencing the decision making by putting pressure from outside. These groups do not aspire to form the government nor to fight elections. These groups adopt various techniques like electioneering, lobbying, propagandising etc. to exert influence on politics.

Chapter 21

Special Provisions for Some States and Regional Aspirations

Special Provisions for Some States and Regional Aspirations

Special Provisions for North-East India

Nagaland
- Article 371 A
- **Exempted Matters** Religious and social practices of the Nagas, their customary law, civil and criminal justice
- **Special Provision for Tuensang District** Minister for Tuensang affairs in State Council of Minister appointed from Tuensang district, Governor has discretionary power for final devisions on all Tuensang district matters

Assam
- Article 371-B empowers the President to create a committee in Assam consisting of members elected from the Tribal areas of the State
- The committee is a part of the Assam Legislative Assembly
- **Assam Movement Regional Aspiration of People**
- Assam Movement 1979-1985, **Concern** Suspected illegal Bengali Muslim settlers from Bangladesh
- **Initiator** All Assam Students Union (AASU), 1979
- **Objective** Anti-Foreigner movement, against Bengali domination
- **Assam Treaty** Accord in 1985, Rajiv Gandhi Government's negotiated with AASU leader, Agreement focused on identifying and deporting foreigners who migrated to Assam

Manipur
- Article 371-C
- President can create a Committee in Manipur Legislative Assembly for members of hilly areas
- Governor submits an annual report to the President on administration of hilly areas

Mizoram
- Article 371-G; Acts of Parliament on specific matters not applicable unless State Legislative Assembly decides
- Mizoram Legislative Assembly must have a minimum of 40 members

Sikkim
- Article 371-F 36th Constitutional Amendment Act of 1975
- Sikkim Legislative Assembly consists atleast 30 members

Arunachal Pradesh
- Article 371-H; Governor has special responsibility for law and order Arunachal Pradesh Legislative Assembly to have minimum 30 members

Special Provisions for other States

Maharashtra and Gujarat
- Article 371; President authorised to grant special responsibilities to Governors

Karnataka
- Article 371-J; President can assign special responsibilities to the Governor for Hyderabad-Karnataka regions
- Governor ensures equitable funds allocation for developmental expenditure in the region

Goa
- Article 371-I
- Goa Legislative Assembly to have minimum 30 members

Andhra Pradesh and Telangana
- Article 371 (D) and 371 (E)
- Article 371 (D) outlines special provisions, granting the President authority for equitable opportunities in public employment and education
- Article 371 (E) empowers Parliament to establish a Central University in Andhra Pradesh

Punjab Treaty
- In July, 1985 Rajiv Gandhi and Harchand Singh Longowal agree on the Punjab Accord
- Transfer of Chandigarh to Punjab
- Appointment of a Commission to resolve the Punjab-Haryana border disputes

Operation Blue Star
- Operation Blue Star in 1984 aimed to eliminate militants, causing damage to the temple

Condition after the Re-organisation of Punjab
- Re-organisation of Punjab : Akalis in power in 1976 and 1977 through Coalition Government
- Religious leaders raised concerns about autonomous Sikh identity

Regional Aspirations in Punjab
- 1980 saw significant changes in Punjab
- Social composition changed due to partition and the creation of Haryana and Himachal Pradesh
- Punjab became a Punjabi Speaking State in 1966

SOURCE ***New NCERT Class XI, Chap-10** (The Philosophy of the Constitution), **New NCERT Class VII, Chap-10** (Federalism) **New NCERT Class X, Chap-2***

Special Provisions for Certain States

1 Which of the following pairs is not matched correctly? *(Chap 10, Class-XI, New NCERT)*

State		Special provisions
(a) Manipur	–	371 D
(b) Mizoram	–	371 G
(c) Goa	–	371 I
(d) Nagaland	–	371 A

Ans. (a)

Exp. Pair (a) is not matched correctly.

Under Article 371 (C) President is authorised to provide for the creation of a committee of the Manipur Legislative Assembly consisting of the members elected from the hilly areas of the state.

2 By introducing which of the following articles, the Indian Constitution anticipates the very important concept of asymmetric federalism? *(Chap 10, Class-XI, New NCERT)*

(a) Article 356 (b) Article 352
(c) Article 371 (d) Article 372

Ans. (c)

Exp. Article 371 of the Indian Constitution anticipates the very important concept of asymmetric federalism as it included special provision with respect to 11 states. It provides for special treatment of regions which are tribal and backward economically, geographically remote and thus require special treatment.

3 Which among the following are reasons for states be governed by special provisions? *(Chap 7, Class-XI, New NCERT)*

(a) It helps in forging greater unity among the other regions of the country.
(b) It helps states which are at disadvantage due to unavoidable historical reasons like hilly Terrain and infrastructure.
(c) Both a and b
(d) Neither a nor b

Ans. (c)

Exp. Both the statements (a) and (b) are reasons for states be governed by special provision. Some states should be governed by special provisions because it helps in forging greater unity among the other regions of the country. It also helps states which are at disadvantage due to unavoidable historical reasons like hilly terrain and infrastructure, etc.

4 The most unusual element of India's federal set-up is that numerous states receive varied treatment. In the light of this statements, consider the following statements. *(Chap 2, Class-X, New NCERT)*

1. The Indian Constitution establishes a power division that applies to all Indian states.
2. Due to their unique social and historical conditions, certain states have particular provisions in the Constitution.

Which of the statements given above is/are incorrect?

(a) Only 1
(b) Only 2
(c) Both 1 and 2
(d) Neither 1 nor 2

Ans. (d)

Exp. Neither statements (1) nor (2) are incorrect.

The Indian Constitution establishes a power division that applies to all Indian states. Due to their unique social and historical conditions, certain states have particular provisions in the Constitution.

5 Consider the following statements. *(Chap 10, Class-XI, New NCERT)*

1. Under Article 371 (B), the privilege of special status was accorded to the North-Eastern State of Nagaland.
2. It not only confers validity on pre-existing laws within Nagaland, but also protects local identity through restrictions on immigration.

Which of the statements given above is/are correct?

(a) Only 1
(b) Only 2
(c) Both 1 and 2
(4) Neither 1 nor 2

Ans. (b)

Exp. Statement (2) is correct as Article 371(A) not only provides special provisions with respect to Nagaland and confers validity on pre-existing laws within Nagaland, but also protects local identity through restrictions on immigration. The Governor has special powers regarding maintaining law and order and tribal identity in the state of Nagaland.

Statement (1) is incorrect because the privilege of special status was accorded to the North-Eastern state of Nagaland comes under Article 371 (A).

6 Which region of the country conferred special status under Article 371 (J) of the Constitution of India? *(Chap 10, Class-XI, New NCERT) (UPSC Pre 2020)*

(a) Nagaland
(b) Hyderabad and Karnataka
(c) Maharashtra and Gujarat
(d) Ladakh

Ans. (b)

Exp. Hyderabad and Karnataka region was conferred special status under Article 371 (J) of the Indian Constitution. It empowers the Governor of Karnataka to take the step for development of Hyderabad and Karnataka region. The Article 371 (J) was inserted into Part 21 of the Indian Constitution by 98th Amendment Act, 2012.

A proportion of seats in educational institutions and State Government jobs in Hyderabad and Karnataka can be reserved for individuals from that region.

7 **Choose the correct matches.**

(Chap 7, Class-XI, New NCERT)

1. Article 371	–	Provision with respect to the states of Maharashtra and Gujarat
2. Article 371(A)	–	Provision with respect to the state of Nagaland
3. Article 371(D)	–	Provision with respect to the state of Andhra Pradesh
4. Article 371(H)	–	Provision with respect to the state of Tamil Nadu

Which of the pairs given above is/are correctly matched?

(a) 2 and 4 (b) 2, 3 and 4
(c) 1 and 4 (d) 1, 2 and 3

Ans. *(d)*

Exp. Pairs (1), (2) and (3) are correctly matched as Article 371 of the Indian Constitution deals with special provision with respect to the states of Maharashtra and Gujarat. Article 371(A) deals with special provisions with respect to the state of Nagaland and Article 371(D) deals with special provision with respect to the State of Andhra Pradesh.

Pair (4) is incorrectly matched because Article 371(H) deals with special provisions with respect to the state of Arunachal Pradesh not with Tamil Nadu.

8 **Consider the following statements.**

(Chap 10, Class-XI, New NCERT) (IAS Pre 2005)

1. Articles 371 (A) to 371 (J) were inserted in the Constitution of India to meet regional demands of Nagaland, Assam, Manipur, Andhra Pradesh, Sikkim, Mizoram, Arunachal Pradesh and Goa.
2. Constitution of India and the United States of America envisage a dual policy (the Union and the States) but a single citizenship.
3. A naturalised citizen of the India can never be deprived of his citizenship.

Which of the statements given above is/are correct?

(a) 1, 2 and 3 (b) 1 and 3
(c) Only 3 (d) Only 1

Ans. *(d)*

Exp. Only statement (1) is correct as Article 371 (A) to 371 (J) has special provisions with respect to different states of Nagaland, Assam, Manipur, Andhra Pradesh, Sikkim, Mizoram, Arunachal Pradesh, Goa and Karnataka.

Statements (2) and (3) are incorrect because Constitution of India provides for single citizenship and there is no separate citizenship for states. In countries like USA, each person is not only a citizen of USA, but also a citizen of the particular state to which he belongs. Thus, enjoying dual sets of rights. Deprivation is a compulsory termination of Indian citizenship if the citizen has within 5 years after registration or naturalisation, been imprisoned in any country for 5 years.

Union Territories and Scheduled and Tribal Area

9 **Consider the following statements with respect to the Union Territories.** *(Chap 7, Class-X, Old NCERT)*

1. They are not given the status of full-fledged states because they usually have small territories and populations.
2. The administration of the Union Territories is run under the direct supervision of the Central Government.
3. The Chief Executive of a Union Territory is appointed by the Union Government.

How many of the statements given above is/are not correct?

(a) Only one (b) Only two (c) All three (d) None of these

Ans. *(a)*

Exp. Only one statement i.e., (1) is not correct with respect to the Union Territories (UTs) because they are not given the status of full-fledged states because they are the federal territories, administered by the Union Government of India.

In Union Territories, the Central Government appoints the Lieutenant Governor, who is the administrator and the representative of the President of India.

10 **Consider the following statements.**

(Chap 7, Class-XI, New NCERT)

1. Jammu and Kashmir Reorganisation Bill, 2019 abrogated the special status of Jammu and Kashmir.
2. Jammu and Kashmir and Ladakh both have legislative assemblies.

Which of the statements given above is/are correct?

(a) Only 1 (b) Only 2 (c) Both 1 and 2 (d) Neither 1 nor 2

Ans. *(a)*

Exp. Statement (1) is correct as Jammu and Kashmir Reorganisation Bill, 2019 abrogated the special status of Jammu and Kashmir by scrapping most of the part of Article 370. Under Article 370, Jammu and Kashmir was given special status. It was given autonomy and most of the rules framed by Government of India, were not applicable in Jammu and Kashmir.

After the passage of Jammu and Kashmir Reorganisation Bill, 2019, it got the status of Union Territories. Hence, all the rules and laws are now applicable in Jammu-Kashmir and Ladakh.

Statement (2) is incorrect because only Jammu and Kashmir has Legislative Assembly and not Ladakh.

11 **Consider the following statements.**

(Chap 7, Class-XI, New NCERT)

1. Our Constitution has special provisions for some states given their peculiar social and historical circumstances.
2. Most of the special provisions pertain to the North-Eastern states like Assam, Nagaland, etc.

3. The provisions for special status have been mentioned in Article 375 of our Constitution.

Which of the statements given above is/are correct?

(a) 1 and 2 (b) 2 and 3 (c) 1, 2 and 3 (d) 1 and 3

Ans. (a)

Exp. Statements (1) and (2) are correct.

Our Constitution is largely due to a sizeable indigenous tribal population with a distinct history and culture, which is preserved till date.

Most of the special provisions pertain to North-Eastern states, such as Assam, Nagaland, Arunachal Pradesh, Mizoram, etc. Special provisions also exist for hilly states like Himachal Pradesh and some other states like Andhra Pradesh, Goa, Gujarat, Maharashtra, Sikkim and Telangana.

Statement (3) is incorrect because the provisions for special status have been mentioned in Article 371 of our Constitution.

12 Which of the following statements is/are incorrect? *(Chap 7, Class-XI, New NCERT)*

1. The carving out of Haryana from the erstwhile state of Punjab led to dispute over the capital city Chandigarh.
2. Chandigarh is capital of both states, Punjab and Haryana.
3. In 1985, Rajiv Gandhi Government, reached to an understanding with the leaders, and it was decided that Chandigarh will be handed over to Haryana.

Select the correct answer using the codes given below.

(a) Only 1 (b) 1 and 3
(c) Only 3 (d) 1, 2 and 3

Ans. (c)

Exp. Only statement (3) is incorrect because in 1985, the then Prime Minister Rajiv Gandhi reached to an understanding with the leaders of Punjab. According to this understanding, Chandigarh was to be handed over to Punjab, but this has not happened yet.

13 The following states were created after 1960. Arrange them in ascending chronological order of the formation. *(Chap 7, Class-XI, New NCERT) (UPPSC Pre 2010)*

1. Haryana
2. Sikkim
3. Nagaland
4. Meghalaya

Codes

(a) 1, 2, 3, 4 (b) 2, 3, 4, 1 (c) 3, 1, 4, 2 (d) 2, 4, 1, 3

Ans. (c)

Exp. The correct chronological order of the given states in ascending order of the formation is 3, 1, 4, 2.

Nagaland was formed in 1963.

Haryana was formed in 1966 by separating from Punjab.

Meghalaya was formed in 1972, carving out from Assam.

Sikkim was formed in 1975.

14 Consider the following statements. *(Chap 7, Class-XI, New NCERT) (IAS Pre 2000)*

1. Goa got statehood in the year 1987.
2. Diu is an island in the Gulf of Khambhat.
3. Daman and Diu was separated from Goa by the 56th Amendment of Indian Constitution.
4. Dadra and Nagar Haveli was under French Colonial Rule till the year 1964.

Which of the statements given above is/are incorrect?

(a) Only 1 (b) 1, 2 and 3 (c) Only 4 (d) 2, 3 and 4

Ans. (c)

Exp. Only statement (4) is incorrect because the Territory of Dadra and Nagar Haveli was under the control of Portuguese till the year 1954. It was freed by pro-India forces in Dadra and Nagar Haveli. In the year 1961, it was annexed by India through virtue of the '10th Amendment of the Constitution of India'.

15 Consider the following pairs with reference in terms of power of President to make regulation for certain Union Territories under Article 240 of Indian Constitution. *(Chap 7, Class-XI, New NCERT)*

1. 240 (1) (c) - Puducherry
2. 240 (1) (d) - Daman and Diu
3. 240 (1) (b) - Lakshadweep
4. 240 (1) (a) - Andaman and Nicobar islands

How many of the pairs given above is/are incorrectly matched?

(a) Only one (b) Only two
(c) All four (d) None of these

Ans. (a)

Exp. Only one pair i.e., (2) is not correctly matched because in terms of power of President to make regulation for certain Union Territories under Article 240 of the Indian Constitution.

Under Article 240(1) (c), the President has the power to make regulations for peace, progress and good governance of Dadra and Nagar Haveli.

16 Match List-I with List-II and select the correct answer from the codes given below the lists. *(Chap 7, Class-X, Old NCERT)*

List-I (Union Territories)	List-II (Years of Creation)
A. Lakshadweep	1. 1961
B. Daman and Diu	2. 1966
C. Chandigarh	3. 1962
D. Dadra and Nagar Haveli	4. 1956

Codes

	A	B	C	D
(a)	1	2	3	4
(b)	4	3	2	1
(c)	4	2	3	1
(d)	1	3	2	4

Ans. (b)

Exp. The correct matching is A-4, B-3, C-2, D-1.

On 1st November, 1956, during the reorganisation of Indian states, the **Lakshadweep** islands were separated from Malabar district and organised into a separate Union Territory.

Daman and Diu became part of India on 19th December, 1961 and was made a Union Territory in 1962.

Under Section (4) of the Punjab Reorganisation Act, 1966, the Central Government made **Chandigarh** a Union Territory on 1st November, 1966. In 1961, **Dadra and Nagar Haveli** became part of India and was annexed by 10th Amendment of the Indian Constitution.

17 If a particular area was brought under the Fifth Schedule of the Constitution of India, which one of the following statements best reflects the consequence of it?

(Chap 7, Class-XI, New NCERT) (IAS Pre 2022)

1. This would prevent the transfer of land of tribal people to non-tribal people
2. This would create a local self-governing body in that area.
3. This would convert that area into a Union Territory.
4. The state having such areas would be declared a Special Category State.

Select the correct answer using the codes given below.

(a) Only 1
(b) Only 2
(c) Both 1 and 2
(d) None of the above

Ans. (a)

Exp. Only statement (1) reflects the consequence of the Fifth Schedule of the Constitution of India.

The Fifth Schedule of the Constitution of India deals with the administration and management of Scheduled Areas and Scheduled Tribes. This would prevent the transfer of land of tribal people to non-tribal people.

Statements (2), (3) and (4) are incorrect because according to Article 244 (1) of the Constitution of India (which is under Fifth Schedule of Constitution), the Tribes Advisory Council (TAC) shall be established in each state having Scheduled Areas. Tribal Advisory Council is an advisory body, not a governing body.

Bringing any particular area under the Fifth Schedule of the Constitution does not convert the area into an Union Territory.

Bringing any particular area under the Fifth Schedule of the Constitution does not get declared as a Special Category State.

18 The following question consists of two statements, namely, Assertion (A) and Reason (R).

(Chap 8, Class-XI, NCERT)

Assertion (A) The Balwant Rai Mehta Committee laid the foundation for the three-tier Panchayati Raj system in India.

Reason (R) The Ashok Mehta Committee proposed a two-tier Panchayati Raj system with Zila Parishad and Mandal Panchayats.

For selecting the correct answer,use the following code

(a) Both Assertion A and Reason R are the true and Reason R is a correct explanation of Assertion A.
(b) Both Assertion A and Reason R are the true but Reason R is not a correct explanation of Assertion A.
(c) Assertion A is true and Reason R is false.
(d) Assertion A is false and Reason R is true.

Ans. (b)

Exp. Assertion correctly states that the Balwant Rai Mehta Committee recommended the three-tier Panchayati Raj system, which is the foundation of the system in India. Their recommendation for a three-tier structure-Gram Panchayat (village level), Panchayat Samiti (block level) and Zila Parishad (district level) - became the foundation of the system we see today. Ashok Mehta Committee proposed a two-tier panchayati raj system with Zila parishad and Mandal Panchayat. However, their proposal wasn't implemented, and India continues to follow the three-tier Panchayati Raj system established based on the Balwant Rai Mehta Committee's recommendations.

19 **Statement (1)** Zila Parishad actually makes developmental plans at the district level.

Statement (2) With the help of Panchayat Samitis, Zila Parishad also regulates the money distribution among all the Gram Panchayats.

(Chap 5, Class-VI, NCERT)

Which of the statement given above is/are correct?

(a) Only 1
(b) Only 2
(c) Both 1 and 2
(d) Neither 1 nor 2

Ans. (b)

Exp. Both the statement are correct. The Zila Parishad is tasked with carrying out social justice and development programmes under the eleventh schedule of the Indian Constitution.

With the assistance of Panchayat Samiti, Zila Parishad develops district-level development plans and controls how money is distributed across all of the gram panchayats.

Chapter 22

Constitutional and Non-Constitutional Bodies

Constitutional and Non-Constitutional Bodies

Constitutional Bodies

Established by Constitution of India

Finance Commission

- Deals with financial relation between Centre and States
- Article 280 – First commission formed in 1951
- Advise President on fiscal distribution between Union and States

Composition, Appointment and Qualifications

- Chairman and four other members
- Appointed by President – Parliament determines qualification

Tenure

- Five years – Pleasure of the President

Power and Functions

- Recommends to the President on
  1. distribution of tax between states centre
  2. allocation of the share from proceeds among states

Comptroller and Auditor General (CAG)

- Article 148
- Empowered to audit all reciepts and expenditure of the Government of India and States, including autonomous bodies
- Serves as the head of the Indian audit and accounts department

Appointment and Term

- Appointed by President
- Takes Oath or affirmation before President
- Term-6 years or until age 65
- Can resign by addressing letter to President

Remuneration and Allowances

- All expenses charged upon the consolidated fund of India

Removal from office

- Same as Judge of Supreme Court

Duties and Power

- Article 149
- Audit reports on centre's account submitted to President (Article 151)

Attorney General of India

- Article 76 – Highest law officer of the country

Qualifications

- Citizen of India, Judge of High Court for-five years, advocate of High Court for ten years

Term, Resignation and Allowances

- Tenure not fixed; Hold office during the pleasure of the President
- Can resign office any time by addressing letter to President
- Salary determined by President

Non-Constitutional Bodies

Created by Act, not mentioned in Constitution

Planning Commission

- Formulated Five Year Plans – Established in 15th March, 1950

NITI Aayog

- Established in 2015
- Policy think-tank for the Government of India

National Development Council

- Recommended in the First-Five Year Plan draft for a national character
- It is crucial for symbolising India's federal planning approach
- Chaired by Prime Minister
- Reviews approach papers and drafts for Five Year Plans

National Human Rights Commission

- Established in 1993 by Protection of Human Rights Act
- Amended in 2006
- Acts as a watchdog for life, liberty, equality and dignity rights

State Human Rights Commission

- Established by Protection of Human Rights Act, 1993
- Investigates Human Rights violation in subjects listed in State list and Concurrent list
- Multi-member body; Chairperson : Retired Chief Justice of a High Court
- Governor appoints chairperson and members

Central Bureau of Investigation (CBI)

- Premier investigating police agency in India
- Superintendence of CBI for offences under Prevention of Corruption Act, 1988

Lokpal and Lokayuktas

- Anti-corruption body
- Established by Lokpal and Lokayukt a Act, 2013
- Moderates creation of Lokpal for Union and Lokayukt a for States

Central Information Commission

- Established under Right to Information Act, 2005
- Under Ministry of Personnel

SOURCE **New NCERT Class IX** *(Democratic Rights)*, **Old NCERT Class XI** *(Indian Administration : Organisation and Working)*, **Old NCERT Class XII** *(Development of Weaker Sections: Scheduled Castes, Scheduled Tribes and Other Backward Classes)*, **Old NCERT Class XII** *(Socio-Economic Development and Planning in India)*, **Old NCERT Class XII** *(Development of Weaker Sections: Women)*

Constitutional Bodies

1 Consider the following statements regarding the Finance Commission. *(Chap 8, Class-XI, Old NCERT)* *(Unit 5, Class-XII, Tamil Nadu Board)*

1. The Constitution provides for a Finance Commission consisting of a Chairman and four other members.
2. The Chairman is a retired High Court judge.
3. Every member of the Commission holds office for such a period as is specified in the order of the President.
4. They are eligible for re-appointment.

Which of the statements given above is/are not correct?

(a) Only 2 (b) Only 3
(c) 1, 3 and 4 (d) Both 3 and 4

Ans. (a)

Exp. Statement (2) is not correct regarding the Finance Commission because the Chairman of a Finance Commission is selected from people with experience of public affairs. Article 280(2) empowers Parliament to make laws with respect to qualifications of Chairman and members of Finance Commission.

2 With reference to the Finance Commission of India, consider the following statements. *(Chap 8, Class-XI, Old NCERT)* *(Unit 5, Class-XII, Tamil Nadu Board) (IAS Pre 2011)*

1. It encourages the inflow of foreign capital for infrastructure development.
2. It facilitates the proper distribution of finances among the public sector undertakings.
3. It ensures transparency in financial administration.

How many of the statements given above is/are correct?

(a) Only one
(b) Only two
(c) All three
(d) None of the above

Ans. (d)

Exp. None of the given statements are correct regarding Finance Commission. Article 280 of our Constitution provides for Finance Commission.

The Finance Commission is required to make recommendations to the President of India in following cases

- Distribution of receipts of taxes between Union and States.
- Grants-in-aid, under Article 275 to the states.
- The measures needed to augment the Consolidated Fund of the state to supplement the resources of the Panchayats and the Municipalities, on the basis of recommendation made by the State Finance Commission.

3 Consider the following. *(Chap 8, Class-XI, Old NCERT) (IAS Pre 2023)*

1. Demographic Performance
2. Forest and Ecology
3. Governance Reforms
4. Stable Government
5. Tax and Fiscal Efforts

For the horizontal tax devolution, the Fifteenth Finance Commission used how many of the above as criteria other than population, area and income distance?

(a) Only two (b) Only three
(c) Only four (d) All five

Ans. (b)

Exp. Only three statements i.e., (1), (2) and (5) are correct with reference to criteria used by Finance Commission for Horizontal tax devolution.

Demographic performance refers to the assessment of population-related factors such as population growth rate, demographic composition and demographic changes over time. The Commission used 2011 population data for its recommendations. States with a lower fertility ratio will be scored higher on this criterion. The 15th Finance Commission suggested 12.5% weightage to the Demographic performance.

Forest and ecology refer to the assessment of environmental factors, including the preservation and conservation of forests, biodiversity and ecological balance. This criterion has been determined by calculating the proportion of dense forest within each state relative to the total dense forest across all states. The 15th Finance Commission suggested 10% weightage to the Forest and Ecology.

Tax and fiscal efforts involve the assessment of a state's efforts in tax collection and fiscal management. This criterion has been employed to incentivise states with better efficiency in tax collection.

4 With reference to the Finance Commission of India, consider the following statements. *(Chap 8, Class-XI, Old NCERT)* *(BPSC Pre 2021)*

1. The Finance Commission is a statutory body.
2. The Finance Commission was setup under Article 280 of the Constitution.
3. The recommendations made by the Finance Commission are only advisory in nature.
4. The first Finance Commission was setup in 1950.

Which of the statements given above are correct?

(a) 1 and 4 (b) 3 and 4
(c) 2 and 3 (d) 2 and 4

Ans. (c)

Exp. Statements (2) and (3) are correct. The first Finance Commission of India was established in 1951 under Article 280 of the Constitution of India.

The recommendations made by the Finance Commission are advisory and hence not binding on the government.

Statements (1) and (4) are incorrect because Finance Commission is a constitutional body and not a statutory body. It is mentioned in Article 280 of Indian Constitution. It derives its powers and authorities from the Indian Constitution.

5 Consider the following statements. *(Chap 8, Class-XI, Old NCERT) (IAS Pre 2022)*

1. Attorney-General of India and Solicitor General of India are the only officers of the Government who are allowed to participate in the meetings of the Parliament of India.
2. According to the Constitution of India, the Attorney-General of India submits his resignation when the Government which appointed him resigns.

Which of the statements given above is/are correct?

(a) Only 1 (b) Only 2
(c) Both 1 and 2 (d) Neither 1 nor 2

Ans. (d)

Exp. Neither statements (1) nor (2) are correct. The Attorney-General of India is appointed by the President of India under Article 76 of the Constitution and holds office during the pleasure of the President. In the performance of his duties, he has the right to audience in all Courts in India as well as the right to take part in the proceedings of Parliament without the right to vote. Solicitor General of India has no such privilege.

As per Article 76, the Attorney-General shall hold office during the pleasure of the President and shall receive such remuneration as the President may determine Conduct of Government Business. There is no mention in the Indian Constitution of the need for him to submit his resignation when the Government which appointed him resigns.

6 Consider the following statements regarding the Attorney-General of India. *(Chap 8, Class-XI, Old NCERT)*

1. The President appoints a person who is qualified to be appointed as a judge of the Supreme Court, as the Attorney-General of India.
2. It is the duty of the Attorney-General to give advice to the Government of India upon such legal matters as referred or assigned to him by the Government of India.
3. He also discharges the functions conferred upon him by or under the Constitution.

How many of the statements given above is/are not correct?

(a) Only one
(b) Only two
(c) All three
(d) None of the above

Ans. (a)

Exp. Only one statement i.e., (2) is not correct regarding the Attorney-General of India as Article 76(2) states that it is the duty of the Attorney-General to give advice to the Government of India upon such legal matters as referred or assigned to him by the President of India. He also perform other legal duties from time-to-time as referred or assigned by the President.

7 Consider the following statements with respect to the Attorney-General of India. *(Chap 8, Class-XI, Old NCERT)*

1. Attorney-General of India is a part of Indian Judiciary.
2. Attorney-General of India is appointed by President on the advice of Chief Justice of India.
3. The term of office of Attorney-General of India is not fixed by the Constitution.
4. Attorney-General of India has right to take part in the proceedings of both Houses of Parliament.

Which of the statements given above is/are correct?

(a) 1, 2 and 4 (b) 2 and 3 (c) 1 and 3 (d) 3 and 4

Ans. (d)

Exp. Statements (3) and (4) are correct about Attorney-General of India. The term of the office of the Attorney-General of India is not fixed by the Constitution. He has the right to take part in the proceedings of both Houses of Parliament.

Statements (1) and (2) are incorrect because the Attorney-General of India is a part of the Union Executive. The Attorney-General of India is appointed by the President on the advice of the Prime Minister and not the Chief Justice of India.

8 Consider the following statements with respect to the Advocate-General. *(Chap 8, Class-XI, Old NCERT)*

1. The Constitution provides for the office of an Advocate-General who is appointed by the Governor.
2. He holds office during the pleasure of the Government.
3. The only qualification laid down is that he should be qualified to be a judge of a Supreme Court.
4. He is also the Public Prosecutor in all cases coming up before the High Court in exercise of its Original Civil Jurisdiction.

Which of the statements given above is/are incorrect?

(a) 1, 2 and 4 (b) 2 and 4 (c) 1, 2 and 3 (d) 2, 3 and 4

Ans. (d)

Exp. Statements (2), (3) and (4) are incorrect with respect to the Advocate-General because the Advocate-General shall hold office during the pleasure of the Governor. To be an Advocate-General of the State, the person must be qualified to become a judge of a High Court.

Advocate-General is not the Public Prosecutor in all cases coming to the High Courts in exercise of its Original Criminal Jurisdiction.

9 Consider the following statements about the Comptroller and Auditor-General of India (CAG).
(Chap 8, Class-XI, Old NCERT)

1. The reports of the Comptroller and Auditor-General of India relating to the accounts of the Union are submitted to the Parliament.
2. He can be removed from office in the like manner and on the like grounds as a Judge of the Supreme Court.
3. He is eligible for appointment in any office under the Government of India or under the Government of any State.
4. The administrative expenses of the office of the Comptroller and Auditor-General of India, including salaries, allowances and pensions are made out of the Consolidated Fund of India.

Which of the statements given above is/are correct?
(a) Only 3 (b) Only 2
(c) Both 1 and 4 (d) None of these

***Ans.** (b)*

Exp. Only statement (2) is correct about the CAG as he can be removed only on an address from both the Houses of Parliament on the ground of proved misbehaviour or incapacity. This is similar to the removal process of Judges of the Supreme Court.

Statements (1), (3) and (4) are incorrect because the reports of the Comptroller and Auditor-General of India relating to accounts of the Union are submitted to the President.

CAG is not eligible for further office, either under the Government of India or any of the state, after he ceases to hold his office.

The salaries, allowances and pensions of persons serving in the office are charged on the Consolidated Fund of India.

10 Consider the following statements with respect to the CAG. *(Chap 3, Class-XI, Old NCERT)*

1. The Comptroller and Auditor-General of India has power to audit only expenditures of Government of India.
2. The accounts of the Union and of the States are kept in such forms as the President prescribes on the advice of the Comptroller and Auditor-General of India.

Which of the statements given above is/are incorrect?
(a) Only 1 (b) Only 2 (c) Both 1 and 2 (d) Neither 1 nor 2

***Ans.** (a)*

Exp. Statement (1) is incorrect with respect to the CAG, as under Article 148, CAG is empowered to audit all receipts and expenditure of the Government of India and the State Governments, including those of autonomous bodies and corporations substantially financed by the Government.

11 Consider the following statements about the Comptroller and Auditor-General of India.
(Chap 3, Class-XI, Old NCERT) (UPPSC RI 2014)

1. He is appointed by the President.
2. His salary is equal to that of the Judge of Supreme Court.
3. He is disqualified for any further Government office after retirement.
4. He can be removed by the President.

How many of the statements given above is/are not correct?
(a) Only one
(b) Only two
(c) All four
(d) None of the above

***Ans.** (a)*

Exp. Only one statement i.e., (4) is not correct about the Comptroller and Auditor-General of India as the Constitution of India provides for the appointment of a Comptroller and Auditor-General of India by the President. Though, he is appointed by the President but he is not removed by him. He can be removed from the office in the like manner and on the like grounds as a judge of the Supreme Court.

12 Which of the following statements is/are incorrect?
(Chap 10, Class-XII, Old NCERT)

1. The 66th Amendment of the Constitution substituted the Special Officer post by the National Commission for Scheduled Castes and Scheduled Tribes.
2. The Commission shall consist of a Chairperson, a Vice-Chairperson and five other members appointed by the President.

Codes
(a) Only 1
(b) Only 2
(c) Both 1 and 2
(d) Neither 1 nor 2

***Ans.** (c)*

Exp. Both the statements (1) and (2) are incorrect.
In 1990, by 65th Constitutional Amendment, the Special Officer's post was substituted by the National Commission for Scheduled Castes and Scheduled Tribes, under Article 338. Again, 89th Constitutional Amendment Act, 2003 bifurcated this Commission into two separate bodies. The separate bodies were named as National Commission for Scheduled Castes (under Article 338) and National Commission for Scheduled Tribes (under Article 338A).

These Commissions consist of a Chairperson, a Vice-Chairperson and three other members. They are appointed by the President by a warrant under his hand and seal.

13 **Consider the following organisations/bodies in India.** *(Chap 7, Class-XI, Old NCERT) (IAS Pre 2023)*

1. The National Commission for Backward Classes
2. The National Human Rights Commission
3. The National Law Commission
4. The National Consumer Disputes Redressal Commission

How many of the organisations given above is/are constitutional bodies?

(a) Only one
(b) Only two
(c) Only three
(d) All four

Ans. (a)

Exp. Only one organisation given above i.e., National Commission for Backward Classes is a constitutional body. It was initially constituted by the Central Government by the National Commission for Backward Classes Act, 1993. The present Commission (8th) has been accorded Constitutional Status and constituted through 'The Constitution (One Hundred and Second Amendment) Act, 2018' Act, whereby Article 338(B) has been inserted, forming a Commission for the socially and educationally backward classes to be known as National Commission for Backward Classes.

14 **Which of the following are Constitutional authorities?** *(Chap 7, Class-XI, Old NCERT) (UPPSC Pre 2012)*

1. State Election Commission
2. State Finance Commission
3. District Panchayat
4. State Electoral Officer

Select the correct answer using the codes given below.

(a) 1 and 2
(b) 1, 2 and 3
(c) 2, 3 and 4
(d) 1, 2, 3 and 4

Ans. (b)

Exp. State Election Commission, State Finance Commission and District Panchayat are the Constitutional authorities. State Electoral Officer is not a Constitutional authority.

The 73rd Constitutional Amendment provides for State Election Commission, State Finance Commission and District Panchayat, under Panchayati Raj Institutions.

The State Election Commission is constituted for conducting elections in the Panchayati Raj bodies. It also conducts elections to the Urban Local Self-Governing bodies. The State Finance Commission is constituted with reference to financial affairs of the Local Urban Self-Governing bodies as well as Panchayati Raj bodies.

Article 243(B) of our Constitution provides for Constitution of Panchayats at village, intermediate and district level.

Non-Constitutional Bodies

15 **Consider the following statements with respect to National Commission for Women.** *(Chap 10, Class-XII, Old NCERT)*

1. It is a Constitutional body under Article 338(B).
2. Its mandated activities only include review of legislation and interventions in specific individual complaints of atrocities.

Which of the statements given above is/are correct?

(a) Only 1 (b) Only 2
(c) Both 1 and 2 (d) Neither 1 nor 2

Ans. (d)

Exp. Neither statements (1) nor (2) are correct with respect to National Commission for Women (NCW).

NCW is the statutory body (not constitutional body) of the Government of India. It is concerned with advising the government on all policy matters affecting women. The objective of the NCW is to represent the rights of women in India and to provide a voice for their issues and concerns.

Its mandated activities include review of legislations, interventions in specific individual complaints of atrocities and remedial action to safeguard the interest of women were appropriate and feasible.

16 **Consider the following statements with reference to the National Human Rights Commission (NHRC).** *(Chap 5, Class-IX, New NCERT)*

Statement-I The National Human Rights Commission (NHRC) is to be headed by a person who has been a former Chief Justice of India.

Statement-II The Chairperson of NHRC holds office for a term of five years or till he attains the age of 70 years, whichever is earlier.

Codes

(a) Both Statement-I and Statement-II are correct and Statement-II is the correct explanation for Statement-I.
(b) Both Statement-I and Statement-II are correct and Statement-II is not the correct explanation for Statement-I.
(c) Statement-I is correct but Statement-II is incorrect.
(d) Both Statement-I and Statement-II are incorrect.

Ans. (c)

Exp. Statement-I is correct but statement-II is incorrect because according to the Protection of Human Rights Act, 1993, the Chairperson of the NHRC is a person who has been a Chief Justice of the Supreme Court. The Protection of Human Rights (Amendment), 2019 amends this to provide that a person who has been Chief Justice of the Supreme Court or a Judge of the Supreme Court will be the Chairperson of the NHRC.

The Chairperson of NHRC holds office for a term of three years or till he attains the age of 70 years, whichever is earlier.

17 Consider the following statements above the minorities in India. *(Chap 25, Module-4, NIOS) (IAS Pre 2001)*

1. The Government of India has notified five communities namely, Muslims, Sikhs, Christians, Buddhists and Zoroastrians as minorities.
2. The National Commission for Minorities was given statutory status in 1993.
3. The smallest religious minority in India are the Zoroastrians.
4. The Constitution of India recognises and protects religious and linguistic minorities.

How many of the statements given above is/are correct?

(a) Only one
(b) Only two
(c) All four
(d) None of these

Ans. (b)

Exp. Only two statements i.e., (3) and (4) are correct. The smallest religious minority in India are the Zoroastrians and the Constitution of India recognises and protects religious and linguistic minorities.

Statements (1) and (2) are incorrect because Muslims, Sikhs, Christians, Buddhists, Jains and Zoroastrians (Parsis) have been notified as minority communities under Section 2 (c) of the National Commission for Minorities Act, 1992.

18 Consider the following statements. *(Chap 25, Module-4, NIOS)*

Statement-I The definition of term 'minority' is not given in the Constitution of India.

Statement-II Minority Commission is not a constitutional body.

Codes

(a) Both Statement-I and Statement-II are correct and Statement-II is the correct explanation for Statement-I.
(b) Both Statement-I and Statement-II are correct and Statement-II is not the correct explanation for Statement-I.
(c) Statement-I is correct but Statement-II is incorrect.
(d) Statement-I is incorrect but Statement-II is correct.

Ans. (b)

Exp. Both Statement-I and Statement-II are correct and Statement-II is not the correct explanation for Statement-I.

The term 'Minority' is not defined in the Indian Constitution. However, the Constitution recognises religious and linguistic minorities. Linguistic and religious minorities are covered by the expression 'minority' under Article 30 of the Indian Constitution. The National Commission for Minorities (NCM) is a statutory body set up by the Parliament of India by passing the National Commission for Minorities Act of 1992. The first statutory National Commission was set up on 17th May, 1993.

Chapter 23

Constitutional Amendments

Constitutional Amendments

Meaning and Types

Meaning of Constitutional Amendment

- Inspired by South African Constitution
- Process is a combination of rigid and flexible
- Procedure outlined in Article 368
- Part XX outlines distinctive features of the Constitutional Amendment process
- Certain provisions forming the Basic Structure of the Constitution cannot be amended (Keshvanand Bharati Case, 1973)

Types of Constitutional Amendments

- **By Simple Majority**
    - A majority of more than 50% of the total members present and voting
    - No special procedure needed; no distinction from ordinary law
    - Amendments outside Article 368 scope with simple majority
- **By Special Majority**
    - A majority of 2/3rd of the members present and voting supported by more than 50% of the total strength
    - Fundamental Rights; DPSP
    - Other categories not needing state consent
- **Special Majority and State Consent**
    - Election of the President and its manner; Executive power of Union and States
    - Supreme Court and High Courts
    - Any Seventh Schedule list

Nature and Procedure

Nature of Amendments

- Some amendments are technical or administrative, involving classification and minor modification
- 44th CAA, 1978 classified that in a Parliamentary Government President would normally abide the advice of Council of Ministers
- Later amendment to Article 74 (1) emphasised that President shall act in accordance with the advice of Council of Minister

Controversial Amendments

- 38th, 39th and 42nd CAA, were highly controversial, made during emergency
- 42nd amendment was extensive, attempting to override the Supreme court's ruling in the Keshvanand Bharati Case
- Extended Lok Sabha term from five to six years and introduced Fundamental Duties
- The 43rd and 44th amendments, introduced by the new Government in 1977, repealed most changes from the controversial amendments

Amendment Through Political Consensus

- Political consensus driven amendments reflect alignment with societal aspirations
- Post 1984, key changes include Anti defection (52nd, 91st), 61st amendment lowering voting age, and 73/74th amendments for decentralisation

Basic Structure of the Constitution and Constitutional Amendments

- Basic structure theory from Keshvanand Bharati (1973) impacts Constitution
- Set limits on Parliament's power to amend the Constitution stating no amendment can violate basic structure

Review of the Constitution

- Late nineties, efforts to review Constitution
- Commission appointed by Government
- Basic structure doctrine's significance in Constitutional practice highlighted
- Supreme Court divisions limit reservations to 50% in job and education
- Judiciary's informal amendment through interpretations on Right to Education (RTE), Life, Liberty and Managing Minority

Procedure for Amendment

- Initiated only in Parliament, not State Legislature
- Introduced by Minister or private member
- No prior notice to President needed
- Special majority require
- No joint sitting provision
- If bill amends federal provisions, State Legislature must ratify by simple majority
- President cannot withold or return bill

SOURCE **New NCERT Class XI** *(Constitution a Living Document)*

1 Consider the following statements regarding the amendability of the Constitution.

(Chap 9, Class-XI, New NCERT)

1. A Constitution that can be very easily changed or modified is often called flexible.
2. Constitutions, which are very difficult to amend, are described as rigid.
3. The Indian Constitution is an example of a rigid Constitution.

Which of the statements given above is/are incorrect?

(a) Only 3 (b) Only 2 (c) Both 1 and 2 (d) None of these

Ans. *(a)*

Exp. Only statement (3) is incorrect regarding the amendability of the Constitution because the Constitution of India is a combination of rigidity and flexibility, some of the provisions in Constitution can be amended by simple majority and other important provision require special majority of both the House of Parliament and of the amendment related to any matter concerning states, then consent of half of the total states is also required to amend such provisions of Constitution.

2 Consider the following statements.

(Chap 9, Class-XI, New NCERT) (IAS Pre 2013)

1. An amendment to the Constitution of India can be initiated by introduction of a Bill in the Lok Sabha only.
2. If such an amendment seeks to make changes in the federal character of the Constitution, the amendment also requires to be ratified by the Legislatures of all the States of India.

Which of the statements given above is/are correct?

(a) Only 1 (b) Only 2 (c) Both 1 and 2 (d) Neither 1 nor 2

Ans. *(d)*

Exp. None of the statements are correct. Article 368 in Part XX of the Constitution deals with the powers of Parliament to amend the Constitution and its procedure. Amendment can be initiated only by the introduction of a bill for the purpose in either House of the Parliament.

If the bill seeks to amend the federal provisions of the Constitution, it must also be ratified by the Legislatures of half of the states by a simple majority.

3 Consider the following statements.

(Chap 9, Class-XI, New NCERT)

Statement-I Under Article 368 , the Parliament can amend any part of the Constitution.

Statement-II The Parliament is the Supreme Legislative body elected by the people of India.

Codes

(a) Both Statement-I and Statement-II are correct and Statement-II is the correct explanation for Statement-I.

(b) Both Statement-I and Statement-II are correct and Statement-II is not the correct explanation for Statement-I.

(c) Statement-I is correct, but Statement-II is incorrect.

(d) Statement-I is incorrect, but Statement-II is correct.

Ans. *(a)*

Exp. Both Statement-I and Statement-II are correct and Statement-II is the correct explanation for Statement-I. Parliament under Article 368 can amend any part of the Constitution including the Fundamental Rights, but without affecting the 'basic structure' of the Constitution. Article 368 in Part XX of the Constitution of India provides for two types of amendments. i.e., by a special majority of Parliament, by a special majority of the Parliament with the ratification by half of the total states.

Parliament is India's Supreme Legislative Body. The Indian Parliament is made up of the President and two Houses i.e., Rajya Sabha (Council of States) and Lok Sabha (House of the People) which are democratically elected. Hence, any amendment passed by the representatives elected by people is considered to be according to the will of people.

4 Consider the following statements.

(Chap 9, Class-XI, New NCERT)

1. The amendment procedure is provided in the Constitution of India, under Article 368.
2. There were 98 Amendments to the Constitution of India till 2012.
3. Prior permission of the President is required for introducing the Amendment Bill.

Which of the statements given above is/are correct?

(a) Only 1 (b) 2 and 3 (c) 1 and 2 (d) Only 3

Ans. *(c)*

Exp. Statements (1) and (2) are correct as the amendment procedure is provided in the Constitution of India, under Article 368.

There were 98 Amendments to the Constitution of India till 2012. There are 127 Amendments as of 2023.

Statement (3) is incorrect because prior permission of the President is not required for introducing the Amendment Bill.

5 In India, which one of the following Constitutional Amendments was widely believed to be enacted to overcome the judicial interpretations of Fundamental Rights.

(Chap 9 , Class-XI, New NCERT) (IAS Pre 2023)

(a) 1st Amendment (b) 42nd Amendment
(c) 44th Amendment (d) 86th Amendment

Ans. *(a)*

Exp. In India, 1st Constitutional Amendments was widely believed to be enacted to overcome the judicial interpretations of the Fundamental Rights. The First Amendment Act made a number of important changes to the Constitution, including, it empowered the state to make special provisions for the advancement of socially and economically backward classes. It provided for the saving of laws providing for the acquisition of estates, etc. It added the Ninth Schedule of estates, etc. It added the Ninth Schedule to the Constitution, which protects certain laws from judicial review.

6 According to the Indian Constitution, the Constitutional Amendment of the following statements require consent of atleast half of the State Legislatures. *(Chap 9, Class-XI, New NCERT)*

1. Federal provision of the Constitution.
2. Right of the Supreme Court.
3. The process of Constitutional Amendment.
4. Formation of new states or transformations in the borders and names of the states.

Codes

(a) 1, 2 and 3
(b) 1, 2 and 4
(c) 1, 3 and 4
(d) 2, 3 and 4

Ans. *(a)*

Exp. Statements (1), (2) and (3) require consent of atleast half of the State Legislature.

When an Amendment aims to modify an article related to distribution of powers between the States and the Central Government, or articles related to representation, it is necessary that the States must be consulted and give consent. In other words, it requires special majority of the Parliament and consent of half of the State Legislatures.

Statement (4) is incorrect as the formation of new states or transformations in the borders and names of the state is done by simple majority.

7 Consider the following statements. *(Chap 9, Class-XI, New NCERT) (IAS Pre 2022)*

1. A Bill amending the Constitution requires a prior recommendation of the President of India.
2. When a Constitution Amendment Bill is presented to the President of India, it is obligatory for the President of India to give his/her assent.
3. A Constitution Amendment Bill must be passed by both the Lok Sabha and the Rajya Sabha by a special majority and there is not provision for joint sitting.

Which of the statements given above are correct?

(a) 1 and 2
(b) 2 and 3
(c) 1 and 3
(d) 1, 2 and 3

Ans. *(b)*

Exp. Statements (2) and (3) are correct.

The 24th Amendment of the Indian Constitution amended Article 368 to provide expressly that Parliament has the power to amend any provision of the Constitution. The amendment further made it obligatory for the President to give his assent when a Constitution Amendment Bill was presented to him.

Article 368 of the Indian Constitution requires that the Constitutuion of India can be amended by both Houses of Parliament by a 2/3 majority (special majority). In case of disagreement between both Houses, there is no provision to summon a joint session of Parliament. The reasoning behind this is so as not let the running government's majority in Lok Sabha undermine the Rajya Sabha in a joint sitting.

Statement (1) is incorrect because Constitution Amendment Bill can be introduced either by a minister or by a private member and does not require prior permission from the President.

8 Consider the following pairs. *(Chap 9, Class-XI, New NCERT)*

	Amendment		Provision
1.	15th Amendment	–	Retirement age of High Court Judges
2.	54th Amendment	–	Salaries of Judges of High Court and the Supreme Court
3.	52nd Amendment	–	Minimum age for voting

How many pair(s) given above is/are correct?

(a) Only one
(b) Only two
(c) All three
(d) None of the above

Ans. *(b)*

Exp. Two pairs i.e., (1) and (2) are correct.

15th Amendment Act, 1963 increased the retirement age of High Court Judges from 60 to 62 years.

54th Amendment Act, 1986 enhanced the salaries of the Judges of the High Courts and Supreme Court of India.

52nd Amendment Act, 1985 introduced anti-defection provisions in the 10th Schedule which provided disqualification on grounds of defection.

9 Match the following lists correctly and choose the correct code. *(Chap 9, Class-XI, New NCERT) (Chap 16, Module-3, NIOS) (UPPSC Pre 2017)*

List-I (Amendment)	List-II (Provision)
A. 42nd Amendment	1. Curtailment of the Power of judicial review.
B. 38th Amendment	2. Abolition of Right to Property as a Fundamental Right.
C. 44th Amendment	3. Addition of the word 'Secular' in the Preamble.

Codes

	A	B	C
(a)	1	2	3
(b)	3	2	1
(c)	3	1	2
(d)	2	1	3

Ans. *(c)*

Exp. The correct matching is A-3, B-1, C-2.

42nd Amendment Act It added the word 'Secular' to our Preamble. Besides it, this Amendment also added the words 'Socialist' and 'Integrity' to the Preamble.

38th Amendment Act It curtailed the power of judicial review by barring the court to review the proclamation of emergency.

44th Constitutional Amendment Act It abolished the Right to Property as a Fundamental Right.

10 Which of the following is/are unmatched in the context of Constitutional Amendment Procedure?
(Chap 9, Class-XI, New NCERT)

1. Extension of Executive Powers of Centre and State
2. Supreme and High Court
3. Election of President
4. Qualification of President
5. Condition of the Office of the President
6. Tenure of President
7. Distribution of Legislative Power in Centre and State
8. States representation in Parliament

Codes
(a) 1, 2, 3 (b) 2, 3, 4
(c) 3, 4, 5 (d) 4, 5, 6

Ans. (d)
Exp. Statements (4), (5) and (6) are unmatched in the context of Constitutional Amendment Procedure. Qualification of President, Condition of the Office of the President and Tenure of President do not cover Constitutional Amendment Procedure under Article 368. But Extension of Executive Powers of Centre and State, Supreme and High Court, Election of President and Distribution of Legislative Power in Centre and State cover Constitutional Amendment.

11 Consider the following statements regarding the 42nd Amendment to the Constitution of India.
(Chap 16, Module-3, NIOS) (BPSC Pre 2023)

1. It added three words to the Preamble-'Socialist', 'Secular' and 'Integrity'.
2. It added eight Fundamental Duties to the Constitution.
3. It added new Directive Principles, i.e., Article 39(A), Article 43(A) and Article 47.
4. It granted power to the President, in consultation with the Election Commission, to disqualify members of the State Legislatures.

Which of the statements given above are incorrect?
(a) 1 and 2 (b) 3 and 4 (c) 2 and 3 (d) 1 and 4

Ans. (c)
Exp. Statements (2) and (3) are incorrect because the 42nd Amendment Act, 1976 added 10 Fundamental Duties to the Indian Constitution. The 42nd Amendment added new Directive Principles, *viz.* Article 39(A), Article 43(A) and Article 48(A).

The 42nd Amendment Act, 1976, introduced significant changes to the Indian Constitution, including the addition of the terms 'Socialist' 'Secular' and 'Integrity' to the Preamble.

12 **Assertion (A)** The requirement of a special majority for amending the Constitution ensures a deliberate and well-considered process.

Reason (R) Special majority for constitutional amendments necessitates significant support from both the total strength of the House as well as those participating in the voting, preventing arbitrary changes. *(Chap 9, Class-XI, New NCERT)*

Codes
(a) Both Assertion (A) and Reason (R) are the true and Reason (R) is a correct explanation of Assertion (A).
(b) Both Assertion (A) and Reason (R) are true but Reason (R) is not a correct explanation of Assertion (A).
(c) Assertion (A) is true and Reason (R) is false.
(d) Assertion (A) is false and Reason (R) is true.

Ans. (a)
Exp. Both Assertion (A) and Reason (R) are the true and Reason (R) is a correct explanation of Assertion (A). The special majority requirement for constitutional amendments mandates substantial support from both the total strength of the House (at least half) and those participating in the voting (two-thirds).

This ensures that constitutional amendments are not made hastily or arbitrarily but are the result of careful consideration and broad consensus among the members of the legislature.

13 How does the basic structure doctrine impact the amending power of the Parliament?
(Chap 1, Class-XII, Tamil Nadu Board)

(a) It empowers Parliament to make any amendments deemed necessary to meet the changing needs of society.
(b) It restricts Parliament from amending certain core principles and features of the Constitution.
(c) It grants Parliament unlimited authority to amend any part of the Constitution without restrictions.
(d) It requires the consent of the President before any amendment related to the basic structure can be passed by Parliament.

Ans. (b)
Exp. The basic structure doctrine, established by the Supreme Court of India, places limitations on the amending power of Parliament by prohibiting amendments that would alter or destroy the essential features of the Constitution. While Parliament retains the authority to amend the Constitution, it cannot do so in a manner that violates the basic structure. This ensures the preservation of the foundational principles and values of the Constitution, safeguarding its integrity and stability.

Chapter 24

Political Theories and Ideologies

Political Theories and Ideologies

Introduction
- Philosophical Study of Government, exploring nature, scope and legitimacy of public agents, institutions and their relationships
- It encompasses liberty, justice, property rights, law and the

Law
- Generally accepted rules governing human society for order and balanced development
- Conditions : Rule for behaviour or regularities in nature and society
- Austin, Holland, Barker, etc

Sources of Law
- Natural law
- Other sources of law (Constitution, Statutes, Conventions, Treaties, etc)

Types of Law
- Private law : Include family law, property law
- Public law : Right of citizen and the state

Liberty

Types of Liberty
- Political liberty : maintain atmosphere
- Economic liberty : provide basic things
- Moral liberty : pursuit the universal object

Equality

Types of Equality
- Political Equality
- Civil Equality or Equality Before Law
- Economic Equality

Justice

Dichotomies in the Concept of Justice
- Legal and Moral Justice
- General Order and Individual Interests
- Conservative and Social Justice

Concept of Justice
- Numerical concept of Justice
- Geometrical concept of Justice

Rights

Kinds of Right
- Political Rights
- Economic Rights
- Cultural Rights
- Human Rights

Classification of Human Rights
- First Generation Human Rights
- Second Generation Human Rigths
- Third Generation Human Rights

Citizenship
- Full and equal membership – Equal Rights

Nationalism
- Emerged as compelling of political creeds

Characteristics of Nation
- Shared Beliefs
- Shared History
- Territory
- Shared Political Ideals
- National Self Determination

Peace
- Elimination violence
- Pacifism
- Contemporary challenges for peace

Secularism
- Secular State
- Indian Model of Secularism
- Model of Secularism
- Western Model of Secularism

Dharma
- Derived from Sanskrit word root 'dhr', means to adopt, to support or to sustain

Liberalism

Phase in Evolution of Liberalism
- Phase one – Phase two – Phase three

Concept of Welfare State
- Roosevelt Idea of Liberty and State
- Keynesian Idea of liberalism
- Empirical Liberalism

Socialism

Features of Socialism by Karl Marx
- Egalitarion Society
- Satisfaction of Basic Needs
- Common Ownership
- Ideal of Service

Types of Socialism
- Chartists
- Democratic Socialists
- Fabian Socialist
- Syndicalism
- Guild Socialism

Marxism

Tenets of Marxism
- Dialectial Materialism
- Historical Materialism
- Class Struggle
- Critique of Capitalism
- Emergence of Classless Society

Limitation of Marxism
- Ethnocentrism
- Simplistic Understanding
- Naive Anti = Statism

Gandhism
- Critique of Western Civilisation
- View on Democracy
- Freedom and the State
- Freedom and Economic Organisation
- Methods of conflict resolution
- Difference between Satyagraha and Passive Resistance

SOURCE **New NCERT Class VI** *(What is Government?)*, **New NCERT Class VIII** *(Understanding Secularism)*, **New NCERT Class IX** *(What is Democracy? Why Democracy?)*, **New NCERT Class XI** *(Political Theory : An Introduction, Freedom, Equality, Social Justice, Nationalism, Secularism, Peace, Development)*, **Old NCERT Class XII** *(Law, Liberty, Equality, Justice, Human Rights, Dharma, Liberalism, Socialism, Marxism, Facism, Gandhism, Humanism)*

1 Consider the following statements regarding the types of government. *(Chap 3, Class-VI, New NCERT)*

1. In a democracy, the government has to explain its actions and defend its decisions to the people.
2. Like a democracy, monarchs do have to explain their actions or defend the decisions they take.
3. In representative democracies, people do not participate directly but, instead, choose their representatives through an election process.

Which of the statements given above is/are not correct?

(a) Only 2 (b) Only 3
(c) Both 1 and 2 (d) 1, 2 and 3

Ans. *(a)*

Exp. Only statement (2) is not correct regarding the types of government because in a monarchy or dictatorship, the power of decision-making is in the hands of a dictator or monarch (king or queen) who is not answerable to the people on the other hand, in a democracy, government is answerable to the people.

2 Consider the following statements regarding the features of democracy. *(Chap 1, Class-IX, New NCERT)*

1. In a democracy, the final decision- making power must rest with those elected by the people.
2. A democracy must be based on a free and fair election where those currently in power have a fair chance of winning.
3. In a democracy, each adult citizen must have one vote and each vote must have one value.
4. A democratic government rules within limits set by Constitutional law and citizens' rights.

How many of the statements given above is/are not one of the features of democracy?

(a) Only one (b) Only two
(c) All four (d) None of these

Ans. *(a)*

Exp. Only one statement i.e., (2) is not one of the features of democracy. In a democracy, a free and fair election is conducted and not only, those in power but also for opposition who has a fair chance of coming into power by winning an election.

In a democracy, people vote in elections and directly or indirectly choose the Prime Minister, President and other leaders of the country.

3 Which of the following statements is/are correct with respect to secularism?

(Chap 2, Class-VIII, New NCERT) (Chap 15, Module-3, NIOS)

1. In USA, the separation between state and religion means that neither the state nor religion can interfere in the affairs of one another.
2. In Indian secularism, though the state is not strictly separate from religion, it does maintain a principled distance vis-à-vis religion.

Select the correct answer using the codes given below.

(a) Only 1 (b) Only 2
(c) Both 1 and 2 (d) Neither 1 nor 2

Ans. *(c)*

Exp. Both the statements (1) and (2) are correct with respect to secularism.

Secularism in USA and India are of different kinds. USA practices negative conception of secularism and India follows positive conception of secularism. In USA, there is a strict separation between the state and religion. State does not fund religious activities nor does church endorse any particular political ideology.

In India, there is principled distance type of secularism where the state is close to all the religions equally. There is no strict separation of religion and state.

4 Which of the following is incorrect regarding Western Model of Secularism?

(Chap 8, Class-XI, New NCERT)
(Unit 9, Class-XI, Tamil Nadu Board)

1. No policy of the state can have an exclusively religious rationale.
2. No religious classification can be the basis of any public policy.
3. The state will not intervene in the affairs of religion and, in the same manner, religion will not interfere in the affairs of the state.
4. There is greater scope for community-based rights or minority rights.

Select the correct answer using the codes given below.

(a) 2 and 3 (b) Only 4
(c) 1 and 4 (d) None of these

Ans. *(b)*

Exp. Only statement (4) is incorrect regarding Western Model of Secularism as in Western Model of Secularism, there is strict separation of religion and state. Therefore, minority rights are not recognised as they are recognised in Indian Constitution.

In Western Model of Secularism, community based rights and minority rights are not protected by the state and thus, there is less scope of their protection in West.

5 Which of the following are the characteristics of the Indian Model of Secularism?

(Chap 8, Class-XI, New NCERT) (Chap 15, Module-3, NIOS)

1. Inter-religious equality
2. Inter-religious tolerance
3. Religious freedom of minority communities
4. State-supported religious reform

Select the correct answer using the codes given below.

(a) 1, 2 and 4 (b) 1, 3 and 4
(c) 1, 2 and 3 (d) 1, 2, 3 and 4

Ans. *(d)*

Exp. All the given statements are the characteristics of the Indian Model of Secularism. Articles 25-28 of the Indian Constitution provides Right to Freedom of Religion. Inter-religious equality means that state should be impartial towards all religions.

Inter-religious tolerance provides for fraternity and brotherhood among different religions as mentioned in the Preamble.

Religious freedom of minority communities is provided as a Fundamental Right to profess, practice and propagation of religion.

State is empowered to bring in religious reform which is contrary to public safety and health.

6 Consider the following Assertion (A) and Reason (R) and choose and correct code. *(Chap 3, Class-XII, Old NCERT) (Unit 9, Class-XI, Tamil Nadu Board)*

Assertion (A) The concept of equality invokes the idea that all human beings have equal worth regardless of their colour, gender, race, or nationality.

Reason (R) Equality maintains that human beings deserve equal consideration and respect because of their common humanity.

Codes

(a) Both A and R are true and R is the correct explanation of A.
(b) Both A and R are true, but R is not the correct explanation of A.
(c) A is true, but R is false.
(d) A is false, but R is true.

Ans. (a)

Exp. Both Assertion (A) and Reason (R) are true and Reason (R) is the correct explanation of Assertion (A). Right to Equality is provided as a Fundamental Right (from Article 14-18) of the Indian Constitution.

Equality provides that everyone is equal irrespective of race, religion, caste and sex among others. All human beings have equal worth. Equality among human beings is due to the varying nature of human beings which is to protect common humanity.

7 Which of the following statements is incorrect regarding inequality? *(Chap 3, Class-XI, New NCERT)*

1. Natural inequalities are those that emerge between people as a result of their different capabilities and talents.
2. Socially produced inequalities emerge as a consequence of inequalities of opportunity or the exploitation of some groups in a society by others.
3. Inequalities which are short-lived are more dangerous for a society.
4. Ensuring public control over essential resources and forms of property are important to tackle inequality.

Select the correct answer using the codes given below.

(a) 1 and 2 (b) Only 3
(c) 3 and 4 (d) None of these

Ans. (b)

Exp. Only statement (3) is incorrect because inequalities which are short-lived i.e., have a shorter period, are less dangerous for a society. Inequalities which are entrenched, i.e., which remain relatively untouched over generations, are more dangerous for a society. Over time such inequalities can give rise to resentment and violence.

8 One common agreement between Gandhism and Marxism is *(Chap 16, Class-XII, Old NCERT) (IAS Pre 2020)*

(a) the final goal of a stateless society
(b) class struggle
(c) abolition of private property
(d) economic determinism

Ans. (a)

Exp. One common agreement between Gandhism and Marxism is the concept of a stateless society. A stateless society refers to a society that lacks formal institutions of government.

According to Gandhi, the state is a social order free from political bindings and consisting of self-governing individuals.

Karl Marx has also predicted that the proletariats will take control of the state and production, destroy all class differences and class antagonisms which finally results into withering away of the state.

9 "A Just society is that society in which an ascending sense of reverence and descending sense of contempt is dissolved into the creation of a compassionate society." Who gave this statement? *(Chap 4, Class-XI, New NCERT)*

(a) Mahatma Gandhi
(b) Jawaharlal Nehru
(c) C Rajagopalachari
(d) BR Ambedkar

Ans. (d)

Exp. The above statement was given by BR Ambedkar. He was a stalwart of the Social Justice in India. Through the statement, Ambedkar emphasised that his justice is based on moral values and self-respect. According to BR Ambedkar, a just society is a society which is moving towards equality and distancing from exploitation.

10 Other than the Fundamental Rights, which of the following parts of the Constitution of India reflect/reflects the principles and provisions of the Universal Declaration of Human Rights (1948)? *(Chap 5, Class-XI, New NCERT) (IAS Pre 2020)*

1. Preamble
2. Directive Principles of State Policy
3. Fundamental Duties

Select the correct answer using the codes given below.

(a) 1 and 2 (b) Only 2 (c) 1 and 3 (d) 1, 2 and 3

Ans. (d)

Exp. Apart from the Fundamental Rights, Preamble, Directive Principles of State Policy and Fundamental Duties reflect the principles and provisions of the Universal Declaration of Human Rights (UDHR), 1948.

On 10th December, 1948, the General Assembly of the United Nations adopted and proclaimed the Universal Declarations of Human Rights. According to the charter of UDHR, recognition of the inherent dignity and equal and inalienable rights of all the members of the human family is the foundation of freedom, justice and peace in the world.

11 Consider the following statements with respect to development and participation.
(Chap 10, Class-XI, New NCERT)

1. To ensure participation in development of local, decision-making bodies are allowed to take decisions about development projects in the local area.
2. Task of democracies include negotiating the competing demands of different sections of a population as well as achieving a balance between the claims of the present and future.
3. The 'top-down' model tends to view people as objects of development.

How many of the statements given above is/are incorrect?

(a) Only one (b) Only two
(c) All three (d) None of these

Ans. (d)

Exp. None of the given statement is incorrect with respect to development and participation. The 'top down' approach is where richer individuals and larger companies are the driving force behind economic growth. The wealth created by them will naturally trickle down and benefit everyone. People are viewed as objects of development.

Local area participation takes place by involving people at bottom of developmental pyramid.

12 Consider the following statements.
(Chap 6, Class-XI, New NCERT)

1. Citizenship is defined as full and equal membership of a political community.
2. In South Africa, the black African population had to undertake a long struggle for equal citizenship.

Which of the statements given above is/are correct?

(a) Only 1 (b) Only 2
(c) Both 1 and 2 (d) Neither 1 nor 2

Ans. (c)

Exp. Both the statements (1) and (2) are correct. Citizenship has been defined as full and equal membership of a political community. The precise nature of the right granted to citizens may vary from state to state. But, in most democratic countries today, they would include some political rights, civil rights and socio-economic rights.

In South Africa, the black African population had to undertake a long term struggle against the ruling white minority for equal citizenship.

This continued until the early 1990s. Struggle to achieve full citizenship and equal rights continues even now in many parts of the world.

13 Which of the following statements is/are correct?
(Chap 1, Class-XII, Old NCERT)

1. Private law refers to those rights, goods and services which would be secured to the individual depending on the existence of the state.
2. Municipal law deals with the relationship between the individuals and their organisations within a state.

Select the correct answer using the codes given below.

(a) Only 1 (b) Only 2
(c) Both 1 and 2 (d) Neither 1 nor 2

Ans. (b)

Exp. Only statement (2) is correct as Municipal law is the national, domestic or internal law of a sovereign state defined in opposition to international law.

Municipal law includes many levels of law not only national law but also state, provincial, territorial, regional, or local law.

Common examples of Municipal laws are zoning ordinances; permits and occupational licenses; expropriation laws and police power.

Statement (1) is incorrect because private law is a branch of the law that deals with the relations between individuals or institutions rather than relations between them and the state.

14 With reference to nationalism, consider the following statements.
(Chap 1, Class-XII, Old NCERT)

1. Nationalism has emerged as one of the most compelling of political creeds in shaping history.
2. Nationalism led to unification of a number of small kingdoms into large nation states, in 19th century Europe.
3. Nationalism also contributed in breaking up of large empires.

Which of the statements given above are correct?

(a) 1 and 2 (b) 2 and 3 (c) 1 and 3 (d) 1, 2 and 3

Ans. (d)

Exp. All the given statements are correct regarding nationalism as it has emerged as one of the most compelling political creeds which has helped to shape history.

It has contributed to drawing and redrawing of boundaries of states and empires.

In 19th century Europe, it led to unification of small kingdoms into large nations states. The present day German and Italian states were formed through such process of unification and consolidation.

Nationalism also helped in breaking up of large empires e.g. Austro-Hungarian and Russian empires in the early 20th century in Europe as well as the break up of the British, French, Dutch and Portuguese empires in Asia and Africa.

15 **"Patriotism cannot be our final spiritual shelter, my refuge is humanity. I will not allow patriotism to triumph over humanity as long as I live." Who said it?** *(Chap 7, Class-XI, New NCERT)*

(a) Mahatma Gandhi (b) Rabindranath Tagore
(c) Jawaharlal Nehru (d) Subhash Chandra Bose

Ans. (b)

Exp. Rabindranath Tagore said, "Patriotism cannot be our final spiritual shelter, my refuge is humanity. I will not buy glass for the price of diamonds and I will never allow patriotism to triumph over humanity as long as I live". A critique of what he called 'Patriotism' is a persistent theme in his writing. He was very critical of the narrow expressions of nationalism that he found at work in parts of Independence Movement.

16 **Which of the following two dimensions give the most appropriate meaning of the term 'Freedom'?**

1. Liberty and fewer laws. *(Chap 2, Class-XI, New NCERT)*
2. Absence of constraints and opportunity to develop potential.
3. Fewer laws in force and opportunity to develop potential.

Select the correct answer using the codes given below.

(a) Only 1 (b) Both 2 and 3 (c) Only 2 (d) 1, 2 and 3

Ans. (c)

Exp. Absence of constraints and opportunity to develop potential, give the most appropriate meaning of the term 'Freedom'. Something is 'free' if it can change easily and is not constrained in its present state.

A person has the freedom to do things that will not, in theory or in practice, be prevented by other forces. Freedom is the state of being allowed to do what you want to do, without encroaching into others freedom.

17 **Which of the following statements is/are correct with respect to negative liberty?** *(Chap 12, Class-XII, Old NCERT)*

1. Negative liberty seeks to define and defend an area in which the individual would be inviolable.
2. This is the minimum area only in which external authority can interfere.
3. The existence of the 'minimum area of non-interference' is the recognition that human nature and human dignity need an area where the person can act unobstructed by others.

Select the correct answer using the codes given below.

(a) Only 1 (b) 1 and 3 (c) Only 2 (d) None of these

Ans. (b)

Exp. Statements (1) and (3) are correct with respect to negative liberty.

Negative liberty is freedom from interference by other people. Negative liberty is primarily concerned with freedom from external restraint on one's actions.

Rights considered negative rights may include civil and political rights such as freedom of speech, life, private property and freedom from violent crime, freedom of religion, Habeas Corpus, a fair trial and freedom from slavery.

18 **Which of the following statements is/are incorrect regarding positive liberty?** *(Chap 2, Class-XI, New NCERT)*

1. The person must not be constrained by poverty or unemployment.
2. They must have adequate material resources to pursue their wants and needs.
3. Positive liberty is not enhanced by participation.

Codes

(a) Only 1
(b) 1 and 2
(c) Only 3
(d) None of the above

Ans. (c)

Exp. Statement (3) is incorrect because positive liberty is enhanced by the ability of citizens to participate in government and have their voices, interests, and concerns recognised and acted upon.

19 **Which of the following statements is/are correct?** *(Chap 2, Class-XII, Old NCERT)*

1. Marxist thought, rejecting both positive and negative views of liberty, states that there can be no freedom in a capitalist system.
2. In order to be free, Marxist maintains there must be a rational control of productive forces in society by the state.

Select the correct answer using the codes given below.

(a) Only 1 (b) Only 2
(c) Both 1 and 2 (d) Neither 1 nor 2

Ans. (c)

Exp. Both the statements (1) and (2) are correct as Marxists believe that there can be no freedom in a capitalist state because they viewed capitalism as immoral.

It is a system in which workers were exploited by capitalists, who unjustly extracted surplus value for their own gain. Marx believed that freedom can only be achieved by controlling the means of production of resources such as labour, instruments and raw material.

20 **Consider the following statements.**

(Chap 3, Class-XI, New NCERT)

1. Socialism refers to a set of political ideas that emerged as a response to the inequalities present in, and reproduced by the industrial capitalist economy.
2. The main concern of Socialism is how to minimise existing inequality and distribute resources justly.

Which of the statements given above is/are correct?

(a) Only 1 (b) Only 2
(c) Both 1 and 2 (d) Neither 1 nor 2

Ans. (c)
Exp. Both the statements (1) and (2) are correct.
Socialism is an economic and political system where the community or state owns the general means of production like land, labour, capital etc.
This is different from capitalism, where the means of production are privately owned.
The aim of public ownership is to ensure that production is responsive to the needs and desires of the general population and that goods and services are distributed equitably.

21 **Consider the following statements regarding the Feminism.** *(Chap 3, Class-XI, New NCERT)*

1. It is a political doctrine of equal right for men and women.
2. Feminists believe that many inequalities in society between men and women are natural.
3. According to feminists, inequality between men and women in society is the result of 'Patriarchy'.

Which of the statements given above is/are incorrect?

(a) Only 1 (b) 1 and 3
(c) 2 and 3 (d) Only 2

Ans. (d)
Exp. Statement (2) is incorrect regarding the Feminism because according to Feminists, inequality between men and women in society is the result of patriarchy.
Patriarchy is based on the assumption that men and women are different by nature and that this difference justifies the unequal positions in the society.

22 **Consider the following statements with reference to the characteristics of Socialism.**

(Chap 13, Class-XII, Old NCERT)

1. An egalitarian society
2. Satisfaction of basic needs
3. Ideal service
4. Private ownership of vital instruments of production

How many of the statements given above is/are not correct?

(a) Only one (b) Only two
(c) All four (d) None of these

Ans. (a)
Exp. Only one statement i.e., (4) is not correct. Private ownership of vital instruments of production is not one of the characteristics of socialism. In capitalism, it is believed to be beneficial for private ownership of vital instruments, so that efficiency and effectiveness of resources is maximised. Socialism talks about withering away of private property and common ownership of means of production.

23 **Which of the following is/are correct with respect to tenets of Marxism?** *(Chap 14, Class-XII, Old NCERT)*

1. Dialectical materialism
2. Class struggle
3. Emergence of class-based society
4. Critique of capitalism

Select the correct answer using the codes given below.

(a) 1, 2 and 3 (b) 2, 3 and 4
(c) 1, 2 and 4 (d) 1, 2, 3 and 4

Ans. (c)
Exp. Options (1), (2) and (4) are correct with respect to tenets of Marxism.
The basic tenets of Marxism are Dialectical materialism, historical materialism, the theory of surplus value, class struggle, revolution, dictatorship of the proletariat and communism (the critique of capitalism).
However, the concept of class-based society was not a creation of Marxism. In ancient Greece, Aristotle divided society into slaves and free men.

24 **Consider the following Assertion (A) and Reason (R) and choose and correct code.**

(Chap 4, Class-XII, Old NCERT)

Assertion (A) Marx declared "from each according to his ability, to each according to his needs".
Reason (R) The burden should be distributed according to our capacity while benefits be distributed according to our needs.

Codes

(a) Both A and R are true and R is the correct explanation of A.
(b) Both A and R are true, but R is not the correct explanation of A.
(c) A is true, but R is false.
(d) A is false, but R is true.

Ans. (a)
Exp. Both Assertion (A) and Reason (R) are true and Reason (R) is the correct explanation of Assertion (A).
"From each according to his ability, to each according to his needs" is a slogan popularised by Karl Marx in his 1875 Critique of the Gotha Programme.
The principle refers to free access to and distribution of goods, capital and services.
The term simply means that each worker in a socialist society receives compensation and benefits according to the quantity and value of the labour which he or she contributed.

Chapter 25

India's Foreign Policy, Neighbouring Countries and National Symbols

India's Foreign Policy, Neighbouring Countries and National Symbols

Foreign Policy of India

- **Introduction**
  - For international peace, security and peaceful coexistence
  - Article 51 lays down some DPSP
- **Influential Factors of India's Foreign Policy**
  - **Internal Determinants**
    - History and Culture
    - Geographical Factors
    - National Philosophy and Identity
    - Demands of Economic Development
    - Political Structure of India
    - External International Determinants
- **Fundamental Doctrine of India's Foreign Policy**
  - **Freedom in Policy Making**
    - Independent Foreign Policy since, 1947
    - Ministry of External Affairs overseas foreign affairs
  - **Promotion of International Peace and Security**
    - Emphasis on peaceful relations with neighbours
    - Non-interventionist policy in domestic affairs
  - **Support for United Nations**
    - Indian philosophy embraces 'Vasudhaiva Kutumbakam', signifying the world as one family
  - **Anti-Colonialism, Anti-Imperialism and Anti-Racialism**
    - India sees colonialism and imperialism as a violation of the Fundamental Human Rights of colonial people and a constant source of global conflict

India and its Neightbouring Countries

- **India-China Relations**
  - China has a relationship with India dating back more then 2000 years
  - **India-China Disputes**
    - In 1950, China took over control of Tibet
    - Border Dispute : By LAC
- **India-Pakistan Relation**
  - Four wars between India and Pakistan (1948, 1965, 1971, 1999)
  - **Conflicts between India and Pakistan**
    - Kashmir Crisis, Indus water Treaty, War of 1965 and Tashkent Agreement, Shimla Agreement, Gujarat Doctrine
- **India-Nepal Relations**
  - Nepal is India's closest neighbour, sharing a 1850 km border with 20 districts and 5 Indian States
  - **India-Nepal Treaty of Peace and Friendship (1950)**
    - Grants Nepalese citizens equal benefits as Indians in India under the treaty
    - Provides advantages for Nepalese citizens in Facilities and Opportunities
- **India-Bangladesh Relations**
  - Shared past, common Heritage, cultural
  - India was the first country to recognise Bangladesh Independent and establish diplomatic relations
- **India-Sri Lanka Relations**
  - Both nations have a rich history of intellectual cultural, religious and linguistic interactions

National Symbols

- **National Flag**
  - Every country has its national symbols
  - Design based on the Pingali Venkayya's
  - On 22nd July, 1947 Constituent Assembly adopted it as free India National flag
  - Width of the flag to its length is 2 : 3
- **National Emblem**
  - Adopted from Sarnath Lion Capital of Ashoka
  - Four lion symbolise Power, Courage, Pride and Confidence
- **National Tree**
  - Banyan (Ficus benghale nsis)
  - Referred as Kalpavriksha
- **National/Flower**
  - Lotus (Nelumbo nucifera)
  - Symbol of purity and fecundity
- **National Fruit**
  - Mango; Mangifera indica is widely cultivated fruit
- **National Bird**
  - Peacock (Pavo cristatus); colourful bird
  - Also called 'Sun bird' or Sarp Bhuj

SOURCE *Old NCERT Class VII (Our National Symbols), Old NCERT Class VIII (National Integration), Old NCERT Class XII (The Cold War Era), Old NCERT Class XII (Alternative Centres of Power), Old NCERT Class XII (Foreign Policy of India: Determinants and Basic Principles), Old NCERT Class XII (India and Her Neighbours: Nepal, Sri Lanka, China, Bangladesh and Pakistan)*

Foreign Policy/Non-Aligned Movement

1 Consider the following with reference to the objectives of India's Foreign Policy. *(Chap 16, Class-XII, Old NCERT)*

1. Maintenance of freedom in policy formulation.
2. Cooperation with World Bank Organisations.
3. Disarmament.
4. Opposition to colonialism, racism and imperialism.

How many of the above is not one of the objective of India's Foreign Policy?

(a) Only one (b) Only two (c) All four (d) None of these

Ans. *(a)*

Exp. Only one statement i.e., (2) is not correct because Cooperation with the World Bank Organisations is not one of the objectives of India's Foreign Policy. It is because India is an independent and sovereign nation working to enhance its own national interest on the basis of its historical and moral principles of anti-racialism, anti-colonialism and anti-imperialism.

2 Consider the following statements regarding Non-Aligned Movement. *(Chap 1, Class-XII, New NCERT)*

1. The roots of NAM went back to the friendship between Yugoslavia's Josip Broz Tito, India's Jawaharlal Nehru and Egypt's leader Gilani.
2. The first Non-Aligned Summit was held in Bandung in 1961.
3. The policy of staying away from alliances was based on isolationism or neutrality.

How many of the statements given above is/are correct?

(a) Only one (b) Only two
(c) All three (d) None of these

Ans. *(d)*

Exp. None of the given statements are correct regarding Non- Aligned Movement. The Non-Aligned Movement (NAM) is a term used for an international organisation that does not want to officially align itself with, or against, any major power bloc. The Non-Aligned Movement (NAM) originated in the 1950s. The roots of NAM went back to the friendship of Indian Prime Minister Jawaharlal Nehru, Yugoslav President Josip Broz Tito, Egyptian President Gamal Abdel Nasser, Ghanaian President Kwame Nkrumah and Indonesian President Sukarno. The policy of staying away from alliances was based on the individuality and sovereignty of nations.

3 Consider the following statements, with reference to the Panchsheel Agreement. *(Chap 26, Module-6, NIOS)*

1. It was signed on 31st January, 1958 between India and China.
2. It was signed between the Prime Minister of India Pt. Jawaharlal Nehru and China's first Prime Minister Chou-En-lai.
3. It was a thought provoking step taken to repair the economic and political relations between India and China.

How many of the statements given above is/are correct?

(a) Only one (b) Only two
(c) All three (d) None of these

Ans. *(b)*

Exp. Only two statements i.e., (2) and (3) are correct regarding the Panchsheel Agreement. The Agreement was signed between the Prime Minister of India Pt. Jawaharlal Nehru and China's first Prime Minister Chou-En-lai. The Panchsheel Agreement was a thought provoking step taken to repair the economic and political relations between India and China. China has taken the wrong advantage of it and stabbed India in the back many times.

Statement (1) is incorrect because the Panchsheel Agreement was signed on 29th April, 1954 between India and China.

4 Consider the following statements with respect to India's Nuclear Policy. *(Chap 4, Class-XII, New NCERT)*

1. India will keep the nuclear weapons as deterrence and will not be the first to use it.
2. India is committed towards global disarmament and non-proliferation.

Which of the statements given above is/are correct?

(a) Only 1 (b) Only 2
(c) Both 1 and 2 (d) Neither 1 nor 2

Ans. *(c)*

Exp. Both the statements (1) and (2) are correct with respect to India's Nuclear Policy.

India's Nuclear Policy is a 'No First Use' posture which says nuclear weapons to be used only in retaliation against a nuclear attack on Indian territory or on Indian forces anywhere. India will be building and maintaining a credible minimum deterrent. India is committed towards goal of a nuclear weapon-free world, through global, verifiable and non-discriminatory disarmament.

5 With reference to 'Look East Policy' of India, consider the following statements. *(Chap 20, Class-XII, Old NCERT) (IAS Pre 2011)*

1. India wants to establish itself as an important regional player in the East Asian affairs.
2. India wants to plug the vacuum created by the terminations of the cold war.
3. India wants to restore the historical and cultural ties with its neighbours in South-East and East India.

Which of the statements given above is/are correct?

(a) Only 1 (b) 1 and 3 (c) Only 3 (d) 1, 2 and 3

Ans. *(d)*

Exp. All the given statements (1), (2) and (3) are correct with reference to 'Look East Policy' of India.

'Look East Policy' was launched in 1992 to give a strategic push to India's engagement with the South-East Asian region to bolster its standing as a regional power and a counter weight to strategic influence of China.

It order to recover from the loss of strategic partner USSR (Now Russia) and of the Cold War in 1991, India sought to build up a relationship with the USA and allies of the USA in South-East Asia.

It is a diplomatic initiative to promote economic strategic and cultural relations with Asia-Pacific region at different level.

6 Consider the following statements, with reference to the Indo-Sri Lanka Agreement.

(Chap 5, Class-XII, New NCERT)

1. Formation of a new state by merging the Eastern and Northern Provinces
2. Establishment of the North-Eastern Council
3. Complete independence
4. Integrity of Sri Lanka

Which one of these was not covered under the Indo-Sri Lanka Agreement?

(a) Only 1 (b) 2 and 3 (c) Only 3 (d) 2, 3 and 4

Ans. *(c)*

Exp. India-Sri Lanka accord does not include complete independence. The agreement between India and Sri Lanka was signed in the year 1987, between Indian Prime Minister Rajiv Gandhi and Sri Lankan President J.R. Jayewardene under the terms of the agreement Sri Lanka agreed to a devolution of power to the provinces.

7 Which is the correct chronological order of the following? *(Chap 18, Class-XII, Old NCERT) (UPPSC Mains 2002)*

1. Shimla Agreement
2. Indo-Soviet Treaty
3. Farakka Accord
4. Tashkent Agreement

Select the correct answer using the codes given below.

(a) 4, 2, 1, 3 (b) 3, 2, 1, 4 (c) 2, 3, 4, 1 (d) 1, 2, 3, 4

Ans. *(a)*

Exp. The correct chronological order is 4, 2, 1, 3 sd Tashkent Agreement–Indo-Soviet Treaty–Shimla Agreement– Farakka Accord.

Tashkent Agreement was signed between India and Pakistan, after the end of the war, in a meeting held at Tashkent (then Soviet Union) from 3rd to 10th January, 1966. It was a peace process.

In August 1971, a treaty of friendship and cooperation known as Indo-Soviet Treaty was signed between India and the erstwhile USSR. It was the first political treaty concluded by India with one of its superpowers.

Shimla Agreement was signed between India and Pakistan on 2nd July, 1972.

The Farakka Accord was signed between India and Bangladesh in 1975, which was related to Farakka Barrage constructed in India to augment water supply in the river Hooghly.

8 With reference to the United Nations General Assembly, consider the following statements.

(Chap 6, Class-XII, New NCERT)(IAS Pre 2022)

1. The UN General Assembly can grant observer status to the non-member states.
2. Inter-governmental organisations can seek observer status in the UN General Assembly.
3. Permanent observers in the UN General Assembly can maintain missions at the UN headquarters.

Which of the statements given above are correct?

(a) 1 and 2 (b) 2 and 3 (c) 1 and 3 (d) 1, 2 and 3

Ans. *(d)*

Exp. Statements (1), (2) and (3) are correct with reference to the United Nations General Assembly. The United Nations General Assembly may grant non-member states, international organisations and other entities permanent observer status, whose activities cover matters of interest to the assembly. Permanent Observers may participate in the sessions and workings of the General Assembly and maintain missions at the UN headquarters. The General Assembly is the main deliberative, policymaking and representative organ of the UN. All 193 member states of the UN are represented in the General Assembly making it the only UN body with universal representation.

9 With reference to the 'United Nations Credentials Committee', consider the following statements.

(Chap 6, Class-XII, New NCERT) (IAS Pre 2022)

1. It is a committee set-up by the UN Security Council and works under its supervision.
2. It traditionally meets in March, June and September every year.
3. It assesses the credentials of all UN members before submitting a report to the General Assembly for approval.

Which of the statements given above is/are correct?

(a) Only 3 (b) 1 and 3 (c) 2 and 3 (d) 1 and 2

Ans. *(a)*

Exp. Only statement (3) is correct with reference to the 'United Nations Credentials Committee'.

The Committee reports to the Assembly on the credentials of representatives. The Committee is mandated to examine the credentials of representatives of Member States and to report to the General Assembly thereon.

The credentials of representatives and the names of members of the delegation of each member state are submitted to the Secretary-General and are issued either by the Head of the State or Government or by the Minister for Foreign Affairs .

Statements (1) and (2) are incorrect because the United Nations Credentials Committee is a standing committee of the United Nations General Assembly that is responsible for examining the credentials of representatives of UN member states.

National Symbols

10 Consider the following statements in respect of the National Flag of India according to the Flag Code of India, 2022. *(Chap 12, Class-VIII, Old NCERT) (IAS Pre 2023)*

Statement-I One of the standard sizes the National Flag of India is 600 mm × 400 mm.

Statement-II The ratio of the length to the height (width) of the Flag shall be 3:2.

Which one of the following is correct in respect of the above statements?

(a) Both Statement-I and Statement-II are correct and Statement-II is the correct explanation for Statement-I.
(b) Both Statement-I and Statement-II are correct and Statement-II is not the correct explanation for Statement-I.
(c) Statement-I is correct, but Statement-II is incorrect.
(d) Statement-I is incorrect, but Statement-II is correct.

***Ans.** (d)*

Exp. Statement-I is incorrect, but Statement-II is correct.

As per the Flag Code of India 2002, the National Flag cannot be in the dimension of 600 mm × 400 mm.

The National Flag shall be rectangular in shape and the ratio of the length to the height (width) of the Flag shall be 3 : 2.

The use, display and hoisting of the National Flag in the country is guided by an overarching set of instructions called the 'Flag Code of India 2002'. The code brings together all laws, conventions, practices and instructions for the display of the National Flag.

11 Which of the following is/are the National symbols of India? *(Chap 13, Class-VII, Old NCERT)*

1. Tri-colour Flag
2. Vande Mataram
3. Jana Gana Mana
4. Ashok Chakra

Codes

(a) 1 and 2 (b) 1, 2 and 3
(c) 1, 3 and 4 (d) 2 and 4

***Ans.** (c)*

Exp. Among the given options, Tri-colour Flag, Jana Gana Mana and Ashok Chakra are the National symbols of India. Jana Gana Mana (National Anthem) was written by Rabindranath Tagore.

Ashok Chakra has been taken from Lion Capital of Ashoka and it consists of 24 Spokes. It is included in the middle of the National Flag of India.

Vande Mataram is the National Song and not a National Symbol.

12 Consider the following statements. *(Chap 13, Class-VII, Old NCERT)*

1. National Flag and National Anthem are inter-related.
2. National Song was written by Rabindranath Tagore.

Which of the statements given above is/are correct?

(a) Only 1 (b) Only 2
(c) Both 1 and 2 (d) Neither 1 nor 2

***Ans.** (a)*

Exp. Only statement (1) is correct. National Anthem and National Flag are inter-related. It is because National Anthem is sung after the hoisting of the Flag. National Flag is the symbol of independence, unity and equality, whereas National Anthem adores our motherland.

Statement (2) is incorrect because National Song was written by Bankim Chandra Chatterjee. It has been taken from his Novel 'AnandaMath' on the other hand, National Anthem was composed by Rabindranath Tagore. It is sung in 52 seconds.

13 Which of the following statements is/are correct regarding National Panchang? *(Chap 24, Module-4, NIOS) (UPPSC Pre 2019)*

1. Indian National Calendar is based on Vikram Samvat.
2. The National Calendar has been adopted with effect from 26th January, 1950.

Select the correct answer using the codes given below.

(a) Only 1 (b) Only 2
(c) Both 1 and 2 (d) Neither 1 nor 2

***Ans.** (d)*

Exp. Neither statement (1) nor (2) is correct regarding National Calendar (Panchang) because the National Calendar of India (calendar for the whole country along with the Gregorian calendar) is based on the Shaka Samvat.

The National Calendar was adopted for official use on 22nd March, 1957. According to this, the first month is Chaitra and the last month is Falgun. Its first month usually begins on 22nd March in a normal year and on 21st March in a leap year.

NCERT MCQ

Practice Set (1-3)

Indian Polity & Governance

Scan the QR Code given below to get the PDF of these Practice Sets.

Notes

Notes

Notes